MW01034014

"*Theatre Work* is a fascinating, at times difficult, exploration into some of the deep flaws in the current American Theatre, yet it offers hope and pathways to help remedy those flaws."

Beowulf Boritt, *Tony-Winning Set Designer and author of* Transforming Space Over Time

"*Theatre Work* provokes crucial questions about the future of American theatre and the people who make it. At a moment when the field is at a crossroads, Robin and Cotton provide a valuable set of considerations for moving forward with equity and care for a sustainable future."

Jessica Brater, *Associate Professor of Theatre at Montclair State University and Coordinator of the BA and MA in Theatre Studies and graduate certificate in Theatre of Diversity, Inclusion, and Social Change*

"Natalie and Brídín's book is an essential primer on the history of theater production. It then goes further to provide thoughtful insights as to how we got where we are, and foster valuable thinking about how we can conceptualize new labor and produce models for the future of the theater industry. I would recommend this book to anyone who cares about how theater sustains itself."

Jenny Gersten, *Interim Artistic Director of the Williamstown Theatre Festival, VP and Producer of Musical Theater at New York City Center, and commercial producer*

"*Theatre Work* succeeds in both illuminating populations left in the dark, and offering a hand to those looking to join the cause toward equity in the workplace. It's a sharp criticism of unsustainable business practices failing workers while simultaneously providing avenues for progressive, safe, and essential restructuring in the theater industry."

Z Infante, *Multidisciplinary artist focused on amplifying the voices of underrepresented and at-risk youth through the arts*

"This book gives a detailed overview of how we have gotten to a place of pay inequity in the arts especially within theatre. The authors take great care and understanding to lay it out clearly and then follow through with actionable ways it could be remedied."

Katie Irish, *Costume Designer and co-chair of Local USA 829's Pay Equity Task Force*

"Natalie and Brídín have taken considerable and incredibly thoughtful, conscious efforts to highlight the conditions and composition of today's production labor force while contextualizing it in theater industry history, rooting it in decades of systemic inequity, bias, and racism. For those of us trying to influence change in the industry, it both validates how challenging pay equity work can be (AND WHY, given the deep deep normalizing of exclusion and working for passion not payment) yet also how important and necessary and urgent it is to work rigorously to dismantle the inequitable systems and industry assumptions of how things should be because "that's how it's always been/that's show business." We are so fortunate to have this research and data all in one place! And a forward by artEquity's Carmen Morgan?! Yes, please!"

Danielle King, *Producer & Director of Organizational Culture, Williamstown Theatre Festival*

"This book is a must read for anyone in theater or anyone interested in getting into theater. Natalie and Brídín have done incredible research into everything from the history of the designer's union to the value or not of university education. You will want to have your highlighters near with this wonderful resource. This book made me think about all behavior including my own."

Allen Lee Hughes, *Lighting Designer/Educator*

"*Theatre Work* is an accessible and timely intervention that zeroes in on the white-supremacist structures governing the labor and compensation of production workers in contemporary American theatre. Building on the work of activists and advocates including the We See You, White American Theater collective, Cotton and Robin consolidate existing studies with their own industry surveys and interviews to make transparent the practices that limit and prevent equitable labor practices. From the impact of networks on recruitment to accessibility and safety issues, they expertly interrogate the areas of theatre production where inequity is most entrenched. With great hope, Cotton and Robin offer strategies for incremental change as well as grand, disruptive imaginings that might change the conversations and structures of American theatre today."

Laura MacDonald, *Assistant Professor, Residential College in the Arts and Humanities, Michigan State University*

"*Theatre Work* explores the complicated dynamics of production and design work and workers in the United States with a nuanced, deep, and empathic lens. The book centers theatre production and design professionals as workers within the labor movement. The authors offer intriguing provocations and questions that the entire United States theatre community needs to explore further together."

Porsche McGovern, *author of the series "Who Designs in LORT Theatres by Pronoun" for Howlround Theatre Commons*

"This book is an essential piece of the puzzle that is fixing the professional theater landscape. It is required reading for anyone in a decision-making role in the arts. Although the book examines a specific period of time and group of organizations, the principles are widely applicable to all businesses that seek to balance art and commerce."

Valerie Novakoff Britten, *Founder of the Broadway Women's Fund and Interim Executive Director of Open Stage Project*

"This is a meaningful read for all theatre makers and patrons, and for those of us practitioners who are not production workers, this should be a must read – so we can better understand the experiences, frustrations, hopes, desires, and dreams of our colleagues in production. This galvanizing work by Brídín and Natalie not only illustrates how unsustainable practices have been born and preserved, but also how we can and must strive towards a fairer industry, if we join together. Onwards and upwards!"

Tatiana Wechsler, *NYC-based actor, singer/songwriter, and creative*

Theatre Work: Reimagining the Labor of Theatrical Production

Theatre Work: Reimagining the Labor of Theatrical Production investigates both the history and current realities of life and work in professional theatrical production in the United States and explores labor practices that are equitable, accessible, and sustainable.

In this book, Brídín Clements Cotton and Natalie Robin investigate the question of artmaking, specifically theatrical production, as work. When the art is the work, how do employers navigate the balance between creative freedom and these equitable, accessible, and sustainable personnel processes? Do theatrical production operations value the worker? Through data analyses, worker narratives, and analogues to the evolving gig economy, *Theatre Work* questions everything about theatrical production work – including our shared history, ways of operating, and assumptions about how theatre is made – and considers what might happen if the American Theatre was reborn in an entirely new form.

Written for members of the theatrical production workplace, leaders of theatrical institutions and productions, labor organizers, and industry union leaders, *Theatre Work: Reimagining the Labor of Theatrical Production* speaks to the ways that employers and workers can reimagine how we work.

Brídín Clements Cotton (she/her) is an arts manager, educator, and maker. Currently an arts instructor for stage and project management at NYU Abu Dhabi, she has held a variety of management and teaching roles at arts organizations and educational institutions. Her approach to facilitating collaboration is driven by belief in the potential for theatre as a space for human connection and interest in how gatherings can create collective meaning.

Natalie Robin (she/her) is a lighting designer, labor organizer, and educator. She is the full-time organizer for United Scenic Artists, Local 829, IATSE, of which she is a proud and longtime member. Previously she taught at several institutions of higher education. She believes everyone should have the protections of a union and is committed to deconstructing the traditional capitalist, hierarchical, ego-driven collaborative structures in theatremaking.

Theatre Work

Reimagining the Labor of Theatrical Production

Brídín Clements Cotton and Natalie Robin

NEW YORK AND LONDON

Designed cover image: Noah Mease

First published 2024
by Routledge
605 Third Avenue, New York, NY 10158

and by Routledge
4 Park Square, Milton Park, Abingdon, Oxon, OX14 4RN

Routledge is an imprint of the Taylor & Francis Group, an informa business

ISBN: 978-1-032-36135-2 (hbk)
ISBN: 978-1-032-36134-5 (pbk)
ISBN: 978-1-003-33039-4 (ebk)

DOI: 10.4324/9781003330394

Typeset in Times New Roman
by codeMantra

Contents

Credits

Data Analyst:	Wayne Carino
Bibliographer:	Christie Debelius
Illustrator:	Noah Mease
Foreword Author:	Carmen Morgan
Research Assistant:	Delaney Teehan

Foreword

Carmen Morgan

When Leslie Ishii, Artistic Director at Perseverance Theater, realized that by including Tlingít protocols, a traditional Alaskan Native ancestral practice, at the opening of the season meant that the premiere of Vera Starbard's Devilfish production would not start on time, she did not remove the protocols, instead, the entire cast and production relaxed the curtain time and honored the Tlingít ancestors. And every night, the play started after the spirit moved. *There is another way.*

My parents came to the US in the late 1960s as part of a wave of migration from Costa Rica. The rapidly changing and arbitrary immigration policies allowed my mother at twenty three to be "sponsored" by the family she worked for as a maid. This luck of policy allowed her to successfully apply for, and receive, a green card that anchored my family's safe and legal passage into the US.

After her position as a maid, my mother worked in a sweatshop for several years. Not a metaphorical sweatshop, but a windowless, materially sound sweatshop, where migrant workers, mostly women, did piecework, making five cents for every shirt or skirt they sewed.

On a few occasions when I was in middle school, I remember going with my mother to her workplace. What was most vivid during those visits was the buzzing of the sewing machines and the rows and rows of women; Mexican, El Salvadorian, Guatemalan, Costa Rican, all women of color sitting behind machines sewing. Los Angeles' garment industry, sweatshop industry, then and now, was made up of almost exclusively women of color.

Decades later, when I began working with theatres to address issues of equity and racism, I was introduced to some of the largest production and costume departments in the US and saw other rows of women sewing, this time they were almost entirely white.

Women of color who made up the sewing base of an entire garment industry, were not sewing in the American theatre. At the time, in 2008, I was new to the arts sector and just beginning to apply community organizing strategies to arts organizations - an ideology and practice that would ultimately lead to the launching of artEquity. But back then, looking into these rooms of mostly white women holding down labor that I had previously seen only being performed by black and brown women, was stark. I remember thinking to myself, *Wow, this can't be a coincidence. There are no coincidences when it comes to racial disparities.* I knew there must be clear barriers keeping women of color away from sewing for theatre companies. The production jobs in theatre were low wage, yes, but they offered far better conditions than the sweatshops in the garment industry.

I raised this observation in a training over a decade ago. I raised it again with Production Departments across the country, in conversations with Artistic Directors, at national conferences, at United States Institute for Theatre Technology (USITT). I suggested there were structural barriers that kept tradespeople of color (electricians, carpenters, sewers) out of the field. I was told repeatedly that the skills needed in making or moving sets, or sewing costumes, were not transferable, but rather unique, highly professionalized, and theatre-specific. In some instances, even a background in Shakespeare was desired.

This was the widely shared narrative and racist discourse used at the time to explain the endemic patterns of white supremacy and structural racism in theatre production. Fifteen years after those initial observations, co-authors Brídín Clements Cotton and Natalie Robin lay bare the racist history of "for whites only" policies and overt segregationist union practices that successfully maintained the mostly white production departments of an entire industry. Yes, it wasn't a coincidence.

Theatre Work: Reimagining the Labor of Theatrical Production connects this shameful past to our current moment by providing a different narrative, one that reveals a hostile, intentionally racist theatre ecology. In its pages, we are challenged to take note, understand the historical implications, and more importantly, wrestle with the fact that another way is needed, is coming, and may already be here.

At a time when most white women are unclear about their social capital and strategic role, Brídín and Natalie explain their agency, privilege, and challenges with being conduits of this message. It is not a perfect exercise, but the authors contribute a body of valuable research to an important and pressing conversation – one that will transcend theatre.

We are reminded by this book that if there is anything we have learned after the seismic upheaval of an industry that was already struggling, it is that *there is another way*. In this moment when our best solutions have yet to be created, we've needed a reference book of this kind, one that uses a social justice lens and antiracist theory (adrienne maree brown, Kimberlé Crenshaw, bell hooks, Kenneth Jones and Tema Okun,) to center those individuals and stories not often told. If theatre is to withstand, thrive, and level up, it must do so with a new understanding, one that this book makes very clear; we must "disrupt the systems in which arts organizations and productions operate." We will no doubt need another volume, and another, and another.

– Carmen Morgan

Carmen Morgan is a national activist, leading conversations on equity, inclusion, and racial justice issues in the arts. She is the founding executive director of artEquity, a national organization that provides tools, resources, and training at the intersections of art and activism. She has provided training, leadership development, and organizational planning for staff, executives, boards, faculty, and students for over 100 organizations. She is the 2020 Actors' Equity Paul Robeson recipient and a YBCA 100 honoree. As faculty at Yale's David Geffen School of Drama, she addresses issues of identity, equity, and inclusion in the arts.

Carmen's work is rooted in popular education, community organizing, and a commitment to social justice. She remains dedicated to community building and activism, and has worked on social justice issues in the non-profit sector for over 25 years.

Preface

Natalie is a Philadelphia-based lighting designer, labor organizer, and educator.

Brídín is a UAE-based performing arts manager and educator.

Natalie is a cisgender queer white woman.

Brídín is a cisgender white woman who is part of an opposite-sex marriage.

Natalie went to an excellent public school district, graduated from her high school class as Valedictorian and attended an Ivy League university, intending to go into Neuroscience research. Her performing arts background began in dance, grew into theatre in middle and high school and really solidified into a focus on design in college.

Brídín went through the public school system and had access to private music lessons and art classes throughout her youth. When she was eight, her older sister was in the ensemble of a community theatre production, which got Brídín hooked; as soon as she reached the nine-year-old age requirement, she began volunteering backstage. She discovered stage management as a middle schooler and by high school, was running a theatre company in a church basement.

Natalie freelanced as a lighting designer in NYC beginning in 2001 and completed one of the top MFA design programs in the country.

Brídín moved out-of-state for university and, with partial scholarship, attended a prestigious – and exorbitantly expensive – institution. She later continued her education as a part-time master's student, receiving tuition remission as a full-time employee of the university.

Natalie and Brídín met in 2011, and spent four winters together in NYC's Lower East Side managing contemporary performance festival American Realness (and eating the very best Grand Street doughnuts and dumplings).

When we began writing this book, Natalie was the Program Director of Theater Design & Technology in the Ira Brind School of Theater Arts at the University of the Arts in Philadelphia. Brídín was Department Administrator for NYU Tisch School of the Arts' Undergraduate Film & Television Department and an adjunct faculty member at NYU Tisch Drama.

While writing the book, Natalie attended the NYS AFL-CIO/Cornell Workers' Institute Union Leadership Institute; and Brídín completed her graduate studies, receiving an MPA in Public & Nonprofit Management Policy from NYU's Robert F. Wagner Graduate School of Public Service.

In 2022, Brídín moved to the United Arab Emirates to join NYU Abu Dhabi as Arts Instructor of Project & Stage Management.

In 2023, Natalie left UArts to become the full-time labor organizer for United Scenic Artists / IATSE Local USA 829.

In our work together and our individual practices, we have participated in many of the inequitable systems the book critiques. We have been in the privileged position of being able to take unpaid or underpaid work; we have benefited from affinity bias, receiving opportunities because people in power find us relatable; we have gotten gigs through who we know; we have been the in positions of power perpetuating problematic staffing, scheduling, and budgeting practices.

Interrogating many of these practices, we came to the point where it felt like we couldn't continue discussing a single issue within a silo, and rather, needed to follow the thread weaving them together.

We both recognize that many norms of white supremacist culture have been prevalent in spaces where we have worked, and that we have each often perpetuated these norms. We have felt and encouraged a culture of urgency and perfectionism, participated in approaches that value quantity over quality, facilitated power hoarding, have at times exercised a belief in there being a single "right" way, and have supported the definition of progress being more.

This book was in large part made possible by our privileged relationships with predominantly white institutions. Natalie received both a creative leave and funding support from University of the Arts. Brídín received publication support and professional development support from NYU Abu Dhabi.

We have used our funding to pay the researchers, interviewees and readers of this book. However, we have not had the resources to pay people at a reasonable hourly wage for their contributions, and there are people who contributed in various ways who were not compensated.

We recognize our privilege as two educated white women with access to many resources that make this sort of project possible. Throughout the process of developing this book, we have continued to question our relationships with power, privilege, and prejudice. We are both constantly examining our own approach to theatremaking. In our individual practices and as educators, we aim to deconstruct the traditional capitalist, hierarchical, ego-driven collaborative structure that is foundational to theatre making in the US.

We aim to amplify voices of underrepresented workers in the book. We try to do this by digging deep into historical research and bringing these stories to the forefront, by surveying and speaking with people who have been and continue to be slighted by the practices in our field, and by lifting up the advocacy that has and continues to be done. We strive to be cognizant of the difference between speaking for someone and amplifying their voice. Our inspirations for radical change stands on the shoulders of those organizing in various movement spaces and specifically the work of adrienne marie brown and the Emergent Strategies framework.

At times, the research here is discouraging and can feel hopeless.

The American Theatre is failing the workers, but it is worth fixing.

We are hopeful optimists.

Section One

HOW WE GOT HERE

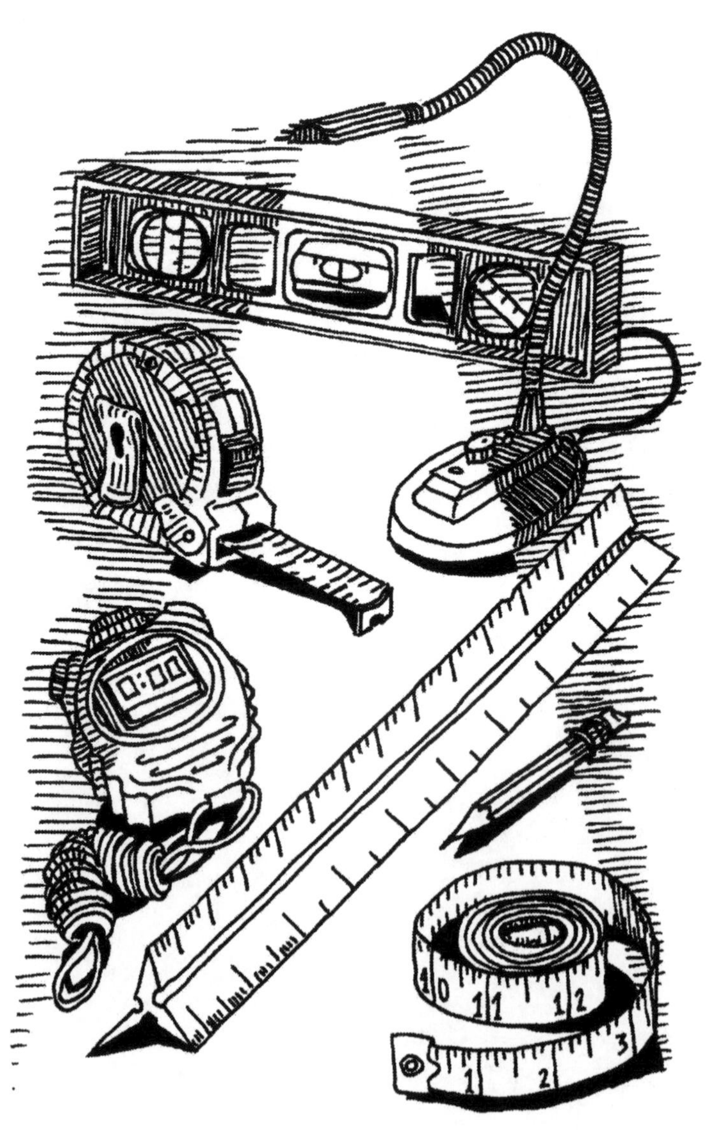
0:00
10 11 12
1 2 3

1

SCOPE

Costume Designer. Electrician. A1. Assistant Stage Manager. Technical Director. Board Operator. Lighting Designer. Scenic Painter. Prop Supervisor. The list goes on and on. It takes a village to put on a show. And that village works very hard under extreme conditions. Inequitable and unsafe working conditions are pervasive. Lack of management transparency and biased hiring practices limit opportunities across the field. Inherent assumptions about workers' identities lead to inequitable pay and support systems. As an industry, professional theatrical design and production is built on the old adage that "the show must go on." But at what cost?

Looking specifically at designers, assistant designers, artisans, technicians, and stagehands in the United States, it's clear that the sacrifices are huge. Actors, managers, and directors are also impacted by these practices, but their positions of power, and the working structures which privilege the performers, mean that the burden of these conditions on production workers is often less visible. Traditional labor practices in theatrical production have a disproportionate impact on BIPOC workers; LGBTQIAA+, women, trans* and non-binary workers; workers with disabilities or neurodivergences; caregiving workers; and others who do not benefit from the privileges of white, able-bodied, neurotypical, cis-gendered men without primary caregiving responsibilities.

DOI: 10.4324/9781003330394-2

This book examines a series of existing conditions in theatrical production operations, and the systems which put them into place, to both identify what isn't working right now and to imagine what might work. An examination of the field requires looking at workplaces in small professional theatres across the country, the League of Resident Theaters (LORT), commercial productions, and the highly regulated Broadway theatres. Anywhere that theatre production workers are being paid for their work contributes to the overall ecosystem of the field. This research focuses on these professional theatre environments and, explicitly, on those workers involved in technical production, not performance or working in offices. This cohort includes designers, technicians, fabricators, and managers. It does not include actors, directors, choreographers, dramaturgs, or administrative staff. Though academic and volunteer or community spaces aren't included, the research may certainly be applicable. We acknowledge that not all theatremaking should be considered professional or held to the same workplace standards. As in the garage band who plays a few gigs together a year, some groups of theatre collectives gather for the joy of the making, the challenges of the seemingly impossible task, rather than for the rewards of a livelihood, health insurance, and retirement savings. Sometimes theatre is a hobby. That work has great value. And is not the focus of this book.

The world of theatrical production very clearly parallels other gig-based fields – restaurant work, the building trades and other industries which depend on short term labor. The work can be dangerous. The hours are long. The availability of work to make enough is precarious. Workers need to understand collaboration and work across disciplines to coordinate different players, departments, and, in some cases, labor unions. The struggles for theatrical production workers should resonate for those in these adjacent fields. And we can learn from each other about how to improve working conditions for everyone.

Workers often enter theatrical production professionally because they fell in love with it in high school or college. Academic theatre programs are often refuges for artistic "weirdos" who don't fit into other cliques. The work is demanding but rewarding. It challenges people to work their hardest to make the best possible art. Production work appeals to many workers interested in energetic, fast-paced and artistic environments. These environments often continue to appeal to workers who thrive under self-direction, who may think and work in ways unsuitable for office environments, who like to focus their creativity into tangible results outside of a corporate structure. For many, satisfying collaborations, exciting moments of artistic synergy, and the smiles on the audience members' faces are enough to keep them coming to work every day. Few days at work are the same; each production may require different skills and new ways of problem solving. For those without familial obligations, the non-traditional hours – late nights and working weekends – can be appealing. There is a lot of autonomy in the work, and creativity and outside-of-the-box thinking are highly valued. The intensity of the work environment often creates strong feelings of community in an ever rotating group of workers, leading to strong relationships between individuals which extend beyond the workplace. Many workers first experience this feeling of a "theatre family" in high school or early community theatre experiences and are drawn to an environment where they feel welcomed and accepted. And though the pay is often low, it's higher and typically more consistent than in many comparable fields like restaurant work, non-union construction, or music.

Beginning with the history of representation in the field and then looking at more recent events which have shaped the theatrical production industry, we will examine the structures which have become integral to how the labor system works now. Citing a variety of studies and extensive work done by predecessors working in and outside of theatre, we will look at how the performing arts industry in the US is built on a foundation of white supremacy, patriarchy, and ableism. Building on this existing work, our research centers the first-person accounts of workers' experiences.

Through these accounts, we examine the framework of how theatrical producers and managers think about production operations when they are staffing, budgeting, and scheduling a production. In the production workplace, the performers' safety and time is prioritized. Production workers are almost always at the losing end of this negotiation, being expected to arrive earlier, leave later, and often be paid less than their onstage counterparts. These extensive hours, made worse by the potential inaccessibility of cheap and fast transportation, makes the field particularly challenging for caregivers. How can opening up both hiring practices and scheduling structures to include those most impacted by intentionally exclusive practices create more equitable conditions for all?

As in many other fields, there are many protocols in place in production to protect workers' physical safety. But sometimes those fail. And sometimes they don't take into account all of the potential dangers and harms. Safety protocols are particularly prevalent in unionized workplaces, but what about those theatre environments that are non-union or only partially organized? And how do freelance production workers know where to report safety hazards they notice on the job? Traditionally, physical safety is prioritized over mental or emotional safety. Falling off of a ladder can change a worker's life, but so can working in an environment ripe with microaggressions and overt harassment. This book also asks: what is a safe production environment? Who has access to safety information? What kinds of safety are valued? Who is responsible for protecting production workers' safety?

Everything works until it doesn't.

So many of the working practices in theatrical production were ignored or dismissed before the Pause created by the COVID-19 pandemic. As the professional theatre industry shut down across the country, workers stopped working and started talking. Workers across the industry came together to share experiences, listen, and finally acknowledge the harm that had been, and was continuing to be, done. This time of reflection revealed many of the inequities and inequitable practices which have long plagued the industry. It also revealed many possible ideas for change and recovery. In the time since March 2020, there has been an increase in production union activity and demands from members. Letters requesting actions to make massive industry-wide changes have been written, circulated, and responded to. Workers have formed advocacy coalitions and working groups to share and create resources. Events and agencies have been launched to connect under-represented workers with opportunities. Workers have been more empowered to turn down or walk away from productions and careers that prove to have problematic labor practices. Some of these changes have already come into effect, some are in process, and some are just over the horizon. Some have caused new questions to emerge. Others seem to have been forgotten or put aside as shows have resumed and the focus has returned to selling tickets. And while many have returned to production work, many have and continue to leave it. Recent studies suggest that around 30% of theatrical production workers have questioned whether or not to leave the field since the start of the COVID-19 pandemic.

Some of the challenges facing theatrical production and design are unique and some are not. Historical hiring practices have long been dependent on unpaid or underpaid labor and the assumption that abuses will be tolerated "for the art." The representation of those hired and the value placed on academic credentials from a select group of mostly private institutions reflect the systemic racism and marginalization found in higher education and perpetuated by the racial wealth gap, a huge interference to representation in the field. In contrast to similar fields like performance and even the building trades, the theatrical production industry offers fewer worker protections. Most production work is temporary and contract-based, which renders commonly accepted workplace practices irrelevant. Workers who speak up aren't necessarily protected from retaliation. And there is a pervasive idea that there is always someone waiting in the wings to do the work faster, cheaper, and potentially less safely. Even within these same institutions, full-time staff are often afforded protections that just aren't available to production workers. How can the production industry become sustainable, accessible, and equitable under these conditions? Whose responsibility is it to make these changes?

When workers' needs aren't being met, or when those unmet needs unreasonably affect some workers over others, the system has to change at its core. This isn't the action of a small group of producers; this isn't the result of a mismanaged workplace or two or a badly negotiated contract. These challenges are systemic and overarching, manifesting in theatrical workplaces from small professional theatres to Broadway and every place in between.

But there is undeniably hope. Across the industry, thought leaders are experimenting with ways to address any number of these problems. One Broadway show provided childcare to its all-parent design team. LORT theatres are hiring firms to expand their job searches. However, many of these solutions are not sustainable on a large scale. The labor movement is strong in the arts; new leadership in several unions, including the United Scenic Artists and Actors Equity Association, has prioritized questions of representation and access. But across the field, the majority of workers still don't benefit from union representation. Coming back from the Pause allows for a different approach. Now is the moment to change the industry. Now is the moment to fix what is broken. But the work of making these changes is not only that of the workers themselves. Through industry-wide research, case studies, and comparative analysis, we have seen models for sustainable, accessible, and equitable labor practices, but many are too small, too individual and too incomplete. We are not setting out to solve all the problems but rather to propose that it can be different. Labor leaders and unions; general, company, and production managers; artistic directors and producers; board members; department heads; theatre educators; stage managers; and production workers themselves will be instrumental in the work to come. Coalition building, collaboration, and questioning of the norms will lead us to a better place.

This book will provide some framing for these questions and issues, zoom into the nitty-gritty of production workers' day to day lives, and then imagine systemic changes. These systemic changes need to be supported by cultural changes at every level. We invite readers to read the book in any order. We wrote it out of order but conceptualized it in sequence. Different chapters or sections will resonate with different people and some of it won't make sense out of context. This book will use data to contextualize and support our understanding of the workers' varied identities and experiences in theatrical production. We recognize the ways in which data has been manipulated by colonization and that the dependence on data reflects a white supremacist value around "hard facts" and the supremacy of the written word. Acknowledging that, we invite the reader to engage with the data as it makes sense: let it wash over you or dig into the details and case studies provided; skip the graphs and focus on the words or refer to the graphs and charts repeatedly. We have attempted to share our data in a variety of ways in order to connect with people's different ways of receiving information. And we know that funders and institutional leaders, specifically, rely on hard data to institute change, and we hope that our data can assist in that work.

Throughout this book we will use a variety of vocabulary in our investigation and critique. We have specifically chosen to use the word *worker* to describe those who work in production. We are aiming to intentionally collapse the false class divide between those who are considered artists – designers, assistant designers, etc. – those who are considered managers but who are subject to the same broken systems, and those who complete the technical and, at times, menial tasks of executing the artistic ideas. We use *labor* (with a lowercase L) to refer to the work being done, and *Labor* (with an uppercase L) to refer to the Labor Movement. In keeping with much current antiracist practice, we will capitalize *Black* as a racial descriptor, except when it has been lowercase in a written quotation, and we will keep *white* lowercase. And we accept and use the definition of *white supremacy* used by the San Francisco Challenging White Supremacy workshop:

> White supremacy is an historically based, institutionally perpetuated system of exploitation and oppression of continents, nations and peoples of color by white peoples and nations of the European continent, for the purpose of maintaining and defending a system of wealth, power and privilege.[1]

As defined by the National Association of Colleges and Employers:

> the term "equity" refers to fairness and justice and is distinguished from equality: Whereas equality means providing the same to all, equity means recognizing that we do not all start from the same place and must acknowledge and make adjustments to imbalances.[2]

Workplace equity is the concept of providing fair opportunities for all of your employees based on their individual needs. We accept this definition of *equity*.

We invite you to go on a journey with us.

NOTES

1 "White Supremacy," Challenging White Supremacy Workshop. https://www.cwsworkshop.org/pdfs/WIWS/Defn_White_Supremacy.PDF.

2 "Equity," National Association of Colleges and Employers. https://www.naceweb.org/about-us/equity-definition/.

THEATE

2

THE PAST

Demographic surveys consistently show the American theatre production workforce to be predominantly white (far more than the national workforce average), and certain fields within production to be overwhelmingly male dominated. How did we get here? American theatrical production is built on a basis of white supremacist capitalist patriarchal values. Before digging into an investigation of current labor practices in production, we look at our past, tracing the historical exclusion of workers with certain identities and some of the worker-driven movements that have attempted to rectify this.

Throughout the history of production labor in the United States, BIPOC (Black, Indigenous and People of Color) workers have been intentionally excluded from, and thus underrepresented in, work opportunities and professional development. Like in the rest of American labor, white supremacy and racism have a stronghold on hiring and labor practices in the American theatre. Even through intentional exclusion and underrepresentation, there have been BIPOC theatre production workers. In her journal article "Black Backstage Workers, 1900–1969," lighting designer and educator Kathy Anne Perkins notes that

> there is a paucity of in-depth information on black designers, stagehands, dressers, stage managers, and various producers and directors in the twentieth-century

DOI: 10.4324/9781003330394-3

> American theatre, even though these black artists and craftspeople have always played a major role in the development of American theatre.[1]

In this chapter, we trace the representation – and exclusion – of BIPOC workers throughout our shared history with the in-depth information that does exist. We then shift to looking at gender representation and the sexism that has also been prevalent in the field.

A note: much of this chapter focuses on union representation; this is not to message that all production workers have the representation or support of a union, but that there are more historical records from unions than from non-union work. It's truly impossible to know the details of production labor in unorganized sectors. Historically, and in the present day, most theatre production workers fall under the jurisdiction of one or more locals of the International Alliance of Theatrical Stage Employees (though as mentioned previously, this doesn't mean that the majority of workers are actually union members).

Founded in 1893 to establish fair wages and working conditions for its members, the International Alliance of Theatrical Stage Employees, Moving Picture Technicians, Artists and Allied Crafts of the United States, Its Territories and Canada (IATSE) was restricted to white workers only.[2] According to Perkins:

> Doll Thomas, one of the first Black people to join IATSE in Washington, D.C., [explained in an interview,] 'the constitution and bylaws of the IA, up until the twenties, stated in a nice way instead of blatant language – no Negroes. This organization is for white males only.'[3]

In order to bypass the IATSE's constitutional racism, the first Black local, Local 224-A, was organized in Washington, DC in 1918:

> Whites established Black auxiliary or "A" locals to prevent Blacks and Whites from working together, and receiving the same benefits. This "A" local, like the ones to come, was governed by the white or parent local, to which dues were paid. After this group received union status, it encouraged Black stagehands around the country to do the same, and "A" locals eventually emerged in such cities as Philadelphia, St. Louis, Norfolk, New Orleans, Chicago, and so forth. Washington, D.C.'s local was, however, to remain the largest and one of the strongest of the Black locals.[4]

In the early 1930s as the Great Depression spread, Black workers found themselves competing with unskilled laborers for manual jobs. In New York City, most skilled theatrical production work was under the jurisdiction of IATSE Local One. Only a few theatres, located in Harlem, employed Black stagehands. In 1935, the Roosevelt administration established the

Works Progress Administration (WPA), a government relief program that included the Federal Theatre Project, which offered theatre work according to skills and experience to many, including Black workers. In addition to Yiddish, Italian, Spanish, French, and German "units," the program established sixteen "Negro Units."[5] The creation of the WPA allowed some Black workers to break through the racial barriers. Perry Watkins, for example, was the first Black man allowed to join United Scenic Artists.[6] However, when Watkins attempted to work outside of the Federal Theater Project, he encountered resistance from his own union.

In tandem with Watkins's success, a select group of New York

> Black stagehands, such as Henry Kinnard, who [worked] at NBC, were allowed to form an auxiliary in the stagehand's union. Although they paid full dues, they were forced to remain an auxiliary until 1955. Nevertheless, this was a vital step, since it allowed Black stagehands to work 'downtown' for the first time, to gain experience, to be allowed to do a variety of plays, not just musicals.[7]

With the closing of the Federal Theater Project in 1939, the situation for Black workers became more urgent. Black production workers found themselves with union status as members of this auxiliary Local No. 1-A, but with few places to work. Some worked at the Apollo in Harlem or in the various movie houses.[8] In 1955, two executive members of Local No. 1-A complained to the New York State Division of Human Rights, which was headed by Commissioner Elmer A. Carter, a former FTP officer. They filed verified complaints against IATSE Local One, that the members of Local No. 1-A were, because of their race and color, deprived of the work opportunities and benefits accorded to the members of Local One. The Investigating Commissioner found probable cause in these complaints; Local No. 1-A was dissolved; and the members of Local No. 1-A were unanimously approved for membership in Local One, with full and equal rights, benefits, and privileges. "On June 25, 1955, thirty 1-A members. Of this group twenty-four were Blacks, three Puerto Ricans, and three whites."[9] The merging of Local No. 1-A with Local One followed a similar merger in Chicago in the Twenties, followed years later by the last locals to merge in Washington, DC in 1981.[10]

Prior to the 1955 merger of Local No. 1-A with Local One, there had been no Black stagehands on Broadway. Black workers had worked below 110th Street in certain non-union, legitimate Off-Broadway houses. Richard Brown, for example, worked at the Henry Street Settlement from 1927 to about 1955 as a technical director and as a lighting and set designer, which were rare positions for Black workers to hold at this time.[11] The first Broadway production that employed black stagehands was *Jamaica* (1957), which starred Lena Horne. Horne and the Coordinating Council of Negro Performers were mainly responsible for the stagehands' presence.[12]

In spite of the merger of the locals, which should have provided more access to work for the Black stagehands, by 1960, the New York State Division of Human Rights (NYSDHR) began receiving complaints from Black workers attempting to gain membership into Local One who alleged that the union was discriminating against them because of race. In the late 1960s, the NYSDHR conducted hearings on employment patterns, policies, and practices in the theatre and motion-picture industries. The investigation showed that, during the 1967–68 Broadway season, which consisted of 22 productions, 381 stagehands were employed, of whom two were Black. It was revealed that between 1955 and 1960, 300 white workers had joined Local One, and no new Black workers or Puerto Rican workers had received membership. By 1968, the local had 1,400 workers, of which 20 were Black and six were Puerto Rican. No Black or Puerto Rican workers were in the 24 apprenticeship workshop jobs, as of 1969. The Commissioner directed Local One to come up with concrete plans for increasing minority membership within its ranks. The State Division and Local One established conditions whereby minority membership might be increased. These conditions included publicly announcing the date, time, and place for the union exam, adding more minorities to the waiting list, and the union office informing the State Division of all new openings in the apprenticeship workshop. Even then, it was evident to union leaders that providing clear, accessible information on union membership was a step to breaking down the barriers that had kept BIPOC workers out.[13] The impact of these changes is not clear; it was not until the 2021 Quadrennial Convention that the IATSE membership passed a resolution to conduct a member census.

In 1897, United Scenic Artists (USA 829) was founded as the United Scenic Artists Association. After a long history as an independent local and a member of the International Union of Painters and Allied Trades, in 1999, the local, which had grown to include Scenic, Costume, Lighting, and Sound Designers for live performance, Mural and Diorama Artists, and designers working in many aspects of film production,[14] joined the IATSE as Local USA 829. United Scenic Artists would go on to include Projection Designers for live performance as well.

Documentation of the USA members' identities from the early 1900s is very limited, but union records suggest who was creating scenery in America at this time. Records indicate that the union was predominantly male. USA members were likely older than their colleagues in other painting and theatre unions, with the youngest artists being in their late twenties or early thirties. Many of the workers were immigrants, some speaking so little English that they had a family member or union officer serve as translator in their interview;[15] "most names found in union records and minutes reflect European origin, with the highest percentage of surnames indicating Germanic or Italian origin, though English, Spanish, and Asian names appear occasionally."[16] USA 829 placed strict limitations on the inclusion of foreign artists after World War I (at a time of increased immigration and xenophobia), requiring all union applicants to have completed one year of residency. This rule was only in place for eighteen months, but there continued to be fines for members working with foreign scenic artists or for not reporting their presence in studios.[17]

Records also indicate that the union included at least one non-white member in this era: "The minutes from 1920, however, state that W.B. Williams had difficulties obtaining a job 'due to his color.' The union conducted an investigation, with most of the members testifying that Williams was unworthy of an 'artist' rating. Williams was then permitted to accept positions at a lower scale, until he was able to find work at 'artist' scale."[18]

In 1938, Perry Watkins was offered his first Broadway design gig on the production of *Mamba's Daughters* starring Ethel Waters.[19] However, when he submitted the signed contract to the union office, USA officers refused to accept it. "They declared that, since Watkins was officially only a class B scenic artist, he was not qualified to work as a designer on Broadway. Watkins' lawyer appeared before the union board and presented his client's case as one of racial discrimination."[20] USA officers claimed that Watkins had been denied the contract not because of his race, but rather because he had not taken the designers' exam, despite having been given the opportunity. The officers ended up giving Watkins a one-time permit for the show, with the caveat that he would not be permitted to design another show until he passed the exam.[21] Watkins remained USA's only Black member for several more years, eventually being elevated to full membership, working as a designer, and later becoming an officer of the union.[22]

Following the Civil Rights era, there was a burst of activity in the labor movement specifically around supporting workers from marginalized groups. In 1972, the Coalition of Black Trade Unionists formed. In 1973, the Labor Council for Latin American Advancement was founded. And, in 1974, the Coalition for Labor Union Women was founded.[23] The growth in union strength was halted with Reagan's defeat of the 1981 air traffic controllers' strike, ushering in twelve years of Republican leadership and anti-labor legislation in Washington and beyond.

As the labor movement continued to diversify, the desire for representation spread throughout the theatrical production workforce. But racial parity was slow. In 1998, the 34 members of the stage crew of the Apollo Theater approached Local One to request representation.[24] Together, Local One and the predominantly Black workforce protested against the Apollo Theater management with a voluntary recognition strike, demanding decent wages, health-care benefits, and a pension plan.[25, 26]

> The lines, which are set up 24 hours a day, drew support from several other IATSE locals in the city. At first, strikers said, the pickets tended to divide into groups of Black and white strikers. One striker explained that some of the Black

workers decided to organize a barbecue for everyone, which helped break this down.[27]

Ultimately, Local One succeeded in being recognized as the union for the Apollo workers and negotiated a contract which provided their basic needs.[28]

Theatrical production labor continues to be less racially and ethnically diverse than the overall American workforce. In September 2021, the United States Institute for Theatre Technology, Inc. (USITT) and SMU DataArts released the results from their Entertainment Design & Technology Workforce Demographic Study. The study collected data from individuals who work within the technical theatre industry. Of participating theatre organizations, People of Color accounted for 13% of the staff, compared to 40% POC in the national workforce.[29] (Specifically, 2% of respondents selected "Hispanic/Latino(a)" while represented in the national population at 18%; 2% selected "Black" compared to 12% of the population; and 2% selected "Asian" compared to 6% of the population.[30]) The study continued to explain that "younger respondents tend to be more racially diverse, with 17% of the 15–34 age group identifying as a person of color or multi-racial, compared to 14% of those in the 35–49 age group and 7% of those 65 and older."[31]

In the summer of 2020, United Scenic Artists also conducted a voluntary census of its current membership. Forty-four point seven (44.7%) percent of the membership participated in the census which showed that members self-identified in the following ways: 0.4% Indigenous; 0.6% Middle Eastern / North African; 1.9% Black; 2.7% Asian; 3.6% Latin/ Latinx; and 34.2% White. It is important to note that in this USA census, although 2,185 members participated, percentages were calculated against the full membership of 5,230. In the racial demographics, each category is presented separately, allowing a single multi-racial member to be presented in the above statistics multiple times.[32] Like the USITT/SMU study, the USA census shows a distinct difference between representation in the field of theatre production and that of the general population. It is clear that the history of racist hiring and employment practices has contributed to this lack of representation.

It's also not surprising that the workforce is predominantly white, since the industry's leaders are as well. As of 2021, "Broadway comprises 41 theaters. All of them are owned and managed by white people. The artistic directors of Broadway's four non-profit theaters are white, as are those of the major Off Broadway companies that transfer their shows uptown."[33] Similarly, the Broadway League's governing board at the same time was 90% white. When the people who hold the most power are of the dominant group, it's no wonder that the power doesn't trickle down.

In addition to upholding racist hiring and employment practices, theatre production practices are built on values now commonly associated with White Supremacy, most notably urgency, perfectionism, worship of the written word, power hoarding, and progress is bigger/more. As Tema Okun writes in "White Supremacy Culture," "The characteristics… are damaging because they are used as norms and standards without being pro-actively named or chosen by the group. They are damaging because they promote white supremacy thinking."[34] In their writing and public speaking, stage managers Narda E. Alcorn and Lisa Porter frequently discuss how theatrical stage management practices in the US have historically upheld white supremacy culture within the production process:

> Characteristics like binary thinking, a sense of urgency, and individualism are identified as white supremacist traits and are often embedded in a stage manager's work. Responsibilities that include tracking time, enforcing rules and policies, and recording and reporting information make the stage manager especially susceptible to upholding systems of oppression.[35]

These characteristics are foundational to how theatre has been produced and taught, and to how success has been defined. Dr. Nicole Caridad Ralston describes the "covert & overt beast" of white supremacy and anti-blackness, sharing a pyramid of examples of overt white supremacy (generally considered unacceptable), and covert white supremacy (socially acceptable).[36] Many of the covert tactics she lays out – the bootstrap theory, hiring discrimination, color blindness, Eurocentric curriculum, prioritizing white voices as experts, meritocracy myth (to name only a handful)[37] – are endemic to the theatre industry.

Ableism is a byproduct of white supremacy. In the 2020 United Scenic Artists census, only 2.3% of the members identified as having a disability. There have always been innumerable hindrances for those with disabilities to be hired and successful in theatrical production, because there have always been innumerable assumptions about what workers need to be able to do to be successful. And the success of the production has been prioritized over what might make the work and workplaces more accessible.

The American theatre also sits on a strong foundation of patriarchy and heteronormative values. Sociologist Sylvia Walby defines patriarchy as "a system of social structures, and practices in which men dominate, oppress, and exploit women."[38] She frames capitalism and patriarchy as dual systems but suggests that there is likely to be tension between patriarchy and capitalism over the exploitation of women's labor. Like white supremacy, patriarchy is the system in which theatre is made, not necessarily the belief system of all of its makers. As Dr. bell hooks explained to feminist Gloria Steinem, "Patriarchy has no gender, and I think we have to remember people's allegiance to patriarchy isn't static. People can start out in feminism and end up in patriarchy." She added later, "Women have more economic power than ever, and yet we remain wedded to patriarchy in ways that are so unclear."[39] Here it is also important to remember that "women" can be replaced with "those with marginalized genders." In a society where cisgender and maleness is the "norm," everything outside that norm is subject to oppression. It is also important to note that caregiver bias is tied to the foundation of patriarchy.

Women are underrepresented in many parts of the professional theatre industry. The underrepresentation of those with marginalized genders in the professional American theatre has been documented in a variety of ways over the years. Specifically, a number of studies in the late twentieth and early twenty-first centuries look at the representation of female directors and playwrights being hired or produced at the Off-Off-Broadway, Off-Broadway, and regional theatres. In the late 1970s, the group Action for Women in Theatre studied US theatres from 1969 to 1975 and found that the number of female playwrights and directors working in regional and Off-Broadway theatres was at merely seven percent of total productions.[40] Twenty years later, in 1998, a study on women directors and playwrights commissioned by the New York State Council on the Arts (NYSCA) found that at Off-Off-Broadway theatres with total operating budgets of less than $500,000, the participation of women increased: productions by women playwrights were at around 30%, and director participation rose to over 40% of the total productions.[41] Thus, it was not a lack of women directors and playwrights but a lack of access to the most notable and high-paying jobs. In 2002, NYSCA published a follow-up report on its three-year research initiative assessing the status of women in theatre. The study showed that progress with regard to women's participation in the theatre has been both inconsistent and slow. In the 1994–95 season, nineteen years after the Action for Women in Theatre study, female playwright representation was at 17% and women directors at 19% for Off-Broadway and regional theatres.[42] Most of the research around gender representation upholds a binary of male and female, which may confuse the issue at times.

In 2008, playwrights Julia Jordan, Sarah Schulman, and Anna Zigler organized a town-hall-style meeting at New Dramatists in New York City of almost 150 women playwrights and prominent theatre leaders to discuss the still-inequitable production opportunities Off-Broadway.[43] Schulman noted that, at the time, only ten out of the 50 plays being produced by major Off-Broadway theatre companies were penned by women playwrights, and there were no women playwrights represented on Broadway.[44] Six years later, in 2014, Pulitzer Prize-winning Black playwright Lynn Nottage wrote in the *New York Times* about the continued lack of representation of women playwrights on Broadway and at the Tony Awards.

Nottage cited that not a single new Broadway play that season was written by a woman or person of color, and of the 47 book writers/composers and lyricists represented on Broadway, only six were women. Nottage went on to say, "The fact remains that Tony voters, like myself, are being asked to reward a community that has continually denied us access to the stage."[45] She went on to suggest that the Tony Awards should establish categories for best new play and musical Off-Broadway, sending a powerful message that the best new writing is not the domain of white men alone, but that Broadway is not supporting that other writing.

The commercial theatre has always been slow in its representation. In 2016, the Broadway production of *Waitress* made history with its all-female creator team. It was the first musical on Broadway to have women in all four of its most prominent creator roles – book writer, music composer/lyricist, director, and choreographer. Two other Broadway musicals since 1975 have had all-female creator teams – the 1978 production of Elizabeth Swados' *Runaways* and the 1984 production of *Quilters* led by Molly Newman and Barbara Damashek – but those were primarily created by a solo or pair of creators, rather than by teams of women.[46]

This isn't solely an American theatre problem. In 2012, the *Guardian* collaborated with theatre director Elizabeth Freestone to document women's representation in theatre in the United Kingdom. The research looked at female representation in a variety of areas from actors employed to the number of playwrights commissioned, as well as boards of directors, chief executives, and creative teams. They found that women were still badly underrepresented, with a persistent 2:1 male-to-female ratio. Looking at the creative teams, including directors, designers, and composers, they found that only 23% of the total theatremakers employed were women and that sound design was particularly male dominated.[47]

Is all this data and commentary about women playwrights, directors, and choreographers relevant when thinking specifically about production workers? There is more available data regarding these more forward-facing positions. Studies looking at gender parity in these areas have been conducted for over 40 years, and still an all-female creator team is newsworthy – so one can imagine what this means for the types of positions that don't get as much press and therefore societal pressure. The available data around theatre production workers and gender paints a similar, potentially even more stark, picture.

The unions share in the responsibility of creating a male-dominated industry. In 2009, President Barack Obama signed the Lilly Ledbetter Fair Pay Act, which restored the rights of working women to sue over pay discrimination,[48] but it wasn't until 2015 that IATSE president Matthew D. Loeb established a Women's Committee, demonstrating that the union "recognizes the voices of the many diverse women in IATSE."[49] Stagehand locals were slow to diversify their membership in terms of gender. IATSE Local 4, the Stagecraft local in Brooklyn, NY, didn't accept its first female member, Karen Sunderlin, until 1997.[50] In the early years after its founding, United Scenic Artists did not accept Scenic Artists other than "older males of European descent" without controversy.[51] Though there are potentially contradictory claims of who was the first female member of USA, the earliest record is more than 20 years after the creation of the union. According to Don Stowell's "Unionization of the Stage Designer-Male and Female" and Philip Andrew Alexander's "Staging Business," Mabel Buell was the first female member welcomed into the union in 1917.[52] According to Victoria Nidweski's "Through the Stage Door, a Spotlight on 'Backstage' Work: Women Designers and Stagehands in Theatrical Production," in 1926, Aline Bernstein was the first female designer to join USA.[53] The distinction seems to be that Buell was a scenic artist, not a designer, in which case Bernstein may have been the first designer. Regardless of the details, women had to wait to be accepted by the male gatekeepers. In discussing the 1919 application of Brenda Smith,

> Some members argued that the profession was too strenuous for a woman. Others felt that 'the influence of woman' would be beneficial to the union. It was determined that Smith had sufficient experience and she was voted in as an artist. It seems that employers were more skeptical of her abilities, as union records indicate that she had difficulty securing a position and asked to be re-rated as an assistant.[54]

United Scenic Artists would eventually become one of the more progressive of the IATSE locals in gender representation: "As of 1940 the membership numbers of USA 829 had doubled compared to 1933. Howard Bay is [*sic*] the first Designer to be elected President in 1940–1946. And Lighting Designer Peggy Clark, the first woman elected President in 1968."[55] The local would go on to have both a female president for 24 years and a female president and a female National Business Agent for twelve years. Scenic Artist Beverly Miller was elected as president in 1996, having served as a Business Representative in Motion Pictures. In 2010, Costume Designer Cecilia Friederichs joined her in leadership as the elected National Business Agent from her position as Business Representative for Live Performance. These two women led the local until they both retired from office in 2020.

Gender parity and support has been a recurring theme in USA negotiations. Costume Design has long been a feminized role, seen to be filled mostly by women since sewing was traditionally seen as domesticated or "women's work." In considering the foundation of patriarchy, we must focus on how costume design has been slighted in comparison to the other theatrical design fields: "Fashion design [and subsequently costume design] is seen as a female pursuit."[56] In the late 1940s, United Scenic Artists renewed talks with the League of New York Theatres to negotiate raising the minimum design fee for scenic designers. For costume designers, on the other hand, the focus was on payment guarantees and work rules.[57] Unsurprisingly, "union costume designers were still struggling to be accepted as professionals."[58] Payment was often a problem, and several costume designers turned to USA when they did not receive full payment from producers. To ensure full payment, USA added a clause to the costume designers' standard contract in 1946 that required producers to supply full advance payment, a stipulation that had already been a standard feature of the scenic designers' contract since 1941.[59] As Alexander explains, these USA negotiations with producers in the late 1940s "highlight the different struggles of union scenic designers and costume designers. Although producers objected to scenic design fees, they typically hired union scenic designers; union costume designers, however, were not as regularly employed by producers."[60] In 1955, USA raised scenic design rates by almost 40% and costume design rates by almost 20%.[61] Costume design rates today still reflect a discrepancy in support, both material and labor.

In the USA 2020 member census, using the same calculations where though 2,185 members participated, percentages were calculated against the full membership of 5,230; when asked about their gender identity, members identified:

- 0.4% Nonbinary/Third-Gender;
- 19.7% male; 21.2% female;
- 0.2% chose to self-describe;
- 0.4% of the membership identified as transgender.[62]

This addresses the vast range of gender identities. However, contrary to what stereotypes might exist:

- 27.9% of the membership identified as heterosexual or straight;
- 0.6% identified as queer;
- 2.3% as bisexual;
- 6.8% as gay or lesbian;
- 0.5% choosing to self-describe.[63]

Looking beyond union representation shows some additional depth to the gender representation issue. Since 2014, lighting designer and labor advocate Porsche McGovern has been examining who designs and directs in League of Resident Theatres (LORT) theatres by gender identity. These studies have been published by HowlRound, a free and open platform for theatremakers. The most recent study, published in 2020, includes data from seven seasons: the 2012–13 season up through the 2018–19 season.

For clarity in comparing the data, the first four phases of the study were "by gender" and the two most recent phases have been "by pronoun."

Over the seven years of the study, McGovern found that of the 15,311 total LORT design positions, 68.9% were filled by "he" designers, 31.0% were filled by "she" designers, 0.1% were filled by "they" designers, and fewer than 0.1% were filled by "she/they" designers. Of the 2,451 LORT designers included in the survey, 63.1% were "he" designers, 36.7% were "she" designers, 0.2% were "they" designers, and fewer than 0.1% were "she/they" designers.[64] Across the board, in all of the design disciplines except for costume design, there were significantly more "he" designers hired than "she" or "they" designers.

When "looking at yearly percentages of design team breakdowns, 2018–19 shows significant increases in the number of teams with more than one 'she designer.'"[65] In her analysis of the data, McGovern points out that

> when we look at yearly percentages of who designs by discipline, there's a clear pattern as well: as the years have passed, there has been a larger percentage of 'she designers.' This pattern is due to a greater number of theatres hiring more 'she designers,' not because there were fewer 'she designers' capable in 2012–13 than in 2018–19.[66]

The gender demographics of those working in traditional Broadway production roles has also been documented. Most recently, using the gender binary framework, Broadway By The Numbers documented the male/female ratios of who was working on Broadway in the 2019 season.[67] Like in McGovern's studies, men outnumbered women in all design roles except costumes, most extremely in sound design, where 87% of sound designers were men and 13% women.[68] These statistics reflect an even greater discrepancy than McGovern's studies, in which:

> over the seven seasons studied, he designers filling sound design positions decreased 9.2 percentage points, and she designers filling sound design positions increased 9.1 percentage points. Over the four seasons represented, they designers decreased 0.2 percentage points. He designers went from 89.9% in the 2012–13 season to 80.7% in the 2018–19 season.[69]

Looking at managers and technical production worker demographics, the same rules seem to apply: the traditionally female gendered departments – wardrobe and hair and makeup – are overwhelmingly occupied by women and the more traditionally male-gendered roles – carpenters, audio technicians, electricians and the like – are overwhelmingly held by men. In 2019, 94% of carpenters were men and 6% women; 92% of sound personnel were men and 8% women; 35% of wardrobe personnel were men and 65% women; and 34% of hair and makeup personnel were men and 66% women. Management was the most evenly representative with 53% of stage managers identifying as men and 47% as women.[70]

This stands in contrast to the assumption stage managers are predominantly women. Some attribute this to the traits that people associate with stage management – organization, nurturement, patience – many of which are also attributes associated with mothering. Data on stage management also shows the prevalence of the gender wage gap. In 2021, Actor's Equity Association, the union that represents actors and stage managers, reported that the average weekly salary for male stage managers was $1,156.97, whereas the average for female stage managers was $1,006.06, and for stage managers who identify as non-binary or third gender, the average weekly salary was $804.55.[71]

Interestingly, representation Off-Broadway and Off-Off-Broadway, where fees are consistently lower, has been more equitable. In 2012, Judith Binus began to collect production credits for major Off-Broadway theatre companies "with an interest in using the data in conversations with theatre artistic directors and staff members to consider ways to promote hiring parity in Off-Broadway theatres."[72] In 2013, Martha Wade Steketee joined the data collection effort. Steketee and Binus wrote six Women Count reports between 2014 and 2022 which sought to assess these questions of gender parity in theatre hiring decisions since 2014. The goal of the report series is to change the conversation from anecdotes to advocacy on behalf of women playwrights, performers, and off-stage theatre workers.[73] In 2022, the sixth edition in the Women Count series was published: "The Women Count VI Report: Women and Non-Binary Hires Off-Broadway 2019/20 and 2021/22."[74] In these two seasons:

- Set designer credits for women or non-binary designers grew from 38% in 2019–20 to 45% in 2021–22;
- Lighting designers among study productions were increasingly female, with no non-binary designers in the two study years, increasing from 38% of lighting credits for women in 2019–20 to 58% of lighting credits for women in 2021/22;
- Consistent, however, with the other demographic studies, costume designers were primarily female and non-binary, growing from 71% in 2019–20 to 80% in 2021/22;
- Sound designers were 28% female or nonbinary in 2019/20 and 2021–22;
- Projection and video designer credits were 47% female in 2019–20 and 2021–22. Female projection and video designer credits (there were no non-binary designers in this area for the two report seasons) continue their rise to parity;
- Production stage managers were just over 60% female or non-binary in 2019–20 and 2021–22, representing a decrease in non-male stage manager credits from prior seasons. Stage managers and assistant stage managers hovered around 70% female or non-binary, 72% in 2019–20 and 67% in 2021–22, reflecting national trends.[75]

In 2018, Millikin University researchers conducted a study that similarly illustrates the challenging workplace cultures that female-identifying workers experience in technical theatre. Drawing on almost 600 responses from female-identifying theatre design and production practitioners, the study found that this group faces two significant obstacles in theatrical design and production industry careers: lack of support for working parents and negative workplace environments. Over 40% of the respondents reported leaving the industry, citing various types of discrimination and negative workplace environments, and a lack of support for parenting and family obligations. Of the 589 respondents, 533 had experienced a negative workplace environment, gender-based harassment, and pay gaps.[76]

The Millikin study also sought to confirm if women were leaving the industry at a faster rate than men, and for what reasons. The top four reasons cited for leaving the industry were: change of career (25%); lack of promotion opportunities (18%); negative workplace environment (18%); and family obligations (18%). Almost half of the respondents who said they were a parent or guardian have left the industry, citing many logistical struggles. Of the respondents who are parents, only 21% said their theatre company or union offered them paid maternity leave.[77] In her 2020 reflections on the data and how we move forward, McGovern noted that while it is important to focus on the hiring of designers to increase diversity, it is also important to support designers once they've been hired: how practices like ten-out-of-twelves drive people out of the industry and how the lack of clear pathways to report abuse of all kinds particularly hurts freelance theatre artists.[78] All of these challenges disproportionately affect caregivers who are, inside of a patriarchal system, disproportionately women.

In her research about demarginalizing the intersection of race and sex, scholar Kimberlé Crenshaw coined the term intersectionality.[79] Specifically examining the marginalization of Black women, Crenshaw asserts:

> Black women are regarded either as too much like women or Blacks and the compounded nature of their experiences is absorbed into the collective experience of the group or thought of as too different, in which case Black women's Blackness or femaleness sometimes has placed their needs and perspectives at the margin of the feminist and Black liberationist agendas.[80]

Crenshaw posits that the "adoption of a single-issue framework for discrimination not only marginalizes Black women within the very movements that claim them as part of their constituency but it also makes the illusive goal of ending racism and patriarchy even more difficult to attain." [81]

In a recent interview, Crenshaw reflected on how the idea of intersectionality has morphed in the 30 years since she coined the term:

> It's not identity politics on steroids. It is not a mechanism to turn white men into the new pariahs. It's basically a lens, a prism, for seeing the way in which various forms of inequality often operate together and exacerbate each other. We tend to talk about race inequality as separate from inequality based on gender, class, sexuality or immigrant status. What's often missing is how some people are subject to all of these, and the experience is not just the sum of its parts.[82]

In this book, we investigate how people with various identities encounter barriers to accessing careers in theatrical production and workplace discrimination, and we acknowledge that the marginalization is compounded for individuals with multiple historically excluded identities. Workers in the theatre have fought against these historical exclusions. Particularly in recent years, a number of individuals and organizations have spoken up, begun initiatives and taken action to make the changes the industry needs. As director Rachel Chavkin said in her Tony acceptance speech for the direction of *Hadestown*:

> There are so many women who are ready to go. There are so many artists of color who are ready to go. And we need to see that racial diversity and gender diversity reflected in our critical establishment, too. This is not a pipeline issue. It is a failure of imagination by a field whose job is to imagine the way the world could be.[83]

NOTES

1 Kathy Anne Perkins, "Black Backstage Workers, 1900–1969," *Black American Literature Forum* 16, no. 4 (1982): 160, https://doi.org/10.2307/2904226.
2 Perkins, 160–63.
3 Perkins, 160.
4 Perkins, 161.
5 Lorraine Brown, "A Story Yet to Be Told: The Federal Theatre Research Project," *The Black Scholar* 10, no. 10 (1979): 70, https://doi.org/10.1080/00064246.1979.11412728.
6 Brown, 75.
7 Brown, 75.
8 Perkins, 161.
9 Perkins, 162.
10 Perkins, 162.
11 Perkins, 160–63.
12 Perkins, 160–63.
13 Perkins, 160–63.
14 "History," IATSE Local USA 829. https://www.usa829.org/About-Our-Union/History.
15 Philip Andrew Alexander, "Staging Business: A History of the United Scenic Artists, 1895–1995" (PhD diss., City University of New York, 1999), 35.
16 Alexander, "Staging Business," 34–35.

17 Alexander, 53.
18 Alexander, 36.
19 Perkins, 161.
20 Alexander, 103.
21 Alexander, 104.
22 Alexander,104.
23 "Our Labor History Timeline," AFL-CIO. https://aflcio.org/about-us/history.
24 "Apollo Theater Stagehands Join IATSE," IATSE. https://www.legacy.iatse.net/history/apollo-theater-stagehands-join-iatse.
25 IATSE, "Apollo Theater Stagehands."
26 Brian Taylor and Al Duncan, "Stage Workers Strike for Benefits at Theater in Harlem," *The Militant*, September 14, 1998, https://themilitant.com/1998/6232/6232_16.html.
27 Taylor and Duncan.
28 IATSE, "Apollo Theater Stagehands."
29 United States Institute for Theatre Technology, "Entertainment Design and Technology Workforce Demographics Study Results" (United States Institute for Theatre Technology, September 2021), 4, https://www.usitt.org/sites/default/files/2021–09/USITT%20WDS%20Final%200921.pdf.
30 United States Institute for Theatre Technology, 4.
31 United States Institute for Theatre Technology, 4.
32 "We Will Do Better: United Scenic Artists, Local USA 829, IATSE, Releases Membership Demographic Data," IATSE Local USA 829, September 8, 2022, https://www.usa829.org/News-Detail/ArticleID/1148.
33 Lee Seymour, "'We're Not Going Back': Inside Broadway's Racial Reckoning," *Forbes*, April 28, 2021, https://www.forbes.com/sites/leeseymour/2021/04/28/were-not-going-back-inside-broadways-racial-reckoning/?sh=6650a52da60c.
34 Tema Okun, "White Supremacy Culture," White Supremacy Culture. https://www.whitesupremacyculture.info.
35 Narda E. Alcorn and Lisa Porter, "We Commit to Anti-Racist Stage Management Education," HowlRound Theatre Commons, July 28, 2020, https://howlround.com/we-commit-anti-racist-stage-management-education.
36 Nicole Caridad Ralston, "White Supremacy & Anti-Blackness: A Covert & Overt Beast," Beloved Community, accessed April 17, 2023, https://www.wearebeloved.org/blog/2020/5/29/white-supremacy-amp-anti-blackness-a-covert-amp-overt-beast.
37 Ralston.
38 Sylvia Walby, "Theorising Patriarchy," *Sociology* 23, no. 2 (May 1989): 214, https://doi.org/10.1177/0038038589023002004.
39 "Teaching to Transgress: bell hooks Returns to The New School," New School News, October 7, 2014, https://blogs.newschool.edu/news/2014/10/bellhooksteachingtotransgress/.
40 Jenny Lyn Bader, "A Brief History of the Gender Parity Movement in Theatre," *Women in Theatre Journal Online*, March 18, 2017, https://witonline.org/2017/03/18/on-the-gender-parity-movement-jenny-lyn-bader/.
41 Susan Jonas and Suzanne Bennett, "Report on the Status of Women: A Limited Engagement?" (Berkeley, CA: Women Arts, January 2022), https://www.womenarts.org/nysca-report-2002/.

42 Jonas and Bennett.
43 "Women Playwrights Organize in NYC," International Centre for Women Playwrights, accessed April 17, 2023, https://www.womenplaywrights.org/jordan.
44 Adam Hetrick, "Women Playwrights, Citing Inequitable Production Opportunities, Hold Meeting Oct. 27," *Playbill*, October 27, 2008, https://playbill.com/article/women-playwrights-citing-inequitable-production-opportunities-hold-meeting-oct-27-com-154666.
45 Lynn Nottage, "Women are Missing from Tonys and Broadway," *New York Times*, June 6, 2014, https://www.nytimes.com/roomfordebate/2014/06/06/can-tony-award-voting-be-improved/women-are-missing-from-tonys-and-broadway.
46 Joanna Kao, "'Waitress' is Making Broadway History with its All-Female Creative Team," *FiveThirtyEight,* March 25, 2016, https://fivethirtyeight.com/features/waitress-is-making-broadway-history-with-its-all-female-creative-team/#:~:text=The%20creative%20team%20for%20the,charge%20of%20a%20Broadway%20show.
47 "Women in Theatre: How the '2:1 problem' Breaks Down," Datablog, *The Guardian*, https://www.theguardian.com/news/datablog/2012/dec/10/women-in-theatre-research-full-results.
48 AFL-CIO.
49 "IATSE Women's Committee," IATSE, accessed April 17, 2023, https://www.legacy.iatse.net/history/iatse-womens-committee.
50 IATSE Local 4 (@iatse_local4), "Today @iatse_local4 celebrates #internationalwomansday by celebrating our very first sister and lead #electrician over @sesamestreet Sister Karen Sunderlin," Instagram Photo, March 8, 2023, https://www.instagram.com/iatse_local4/?hl=en.
51 Alexander, 35.
52 Don Stewell, "Unionization of the Stage Designer-Male and Female," *Theatre Design & Technology: Journal of the United States Institute for Theatre Technology*, no. 38, (Oct 1974): 6–9, 36–37. https://www.nxtbook.com/nxtbooks/hickmanbrady/tdt_1974Oct/index.php?startid=7; Alexander, 35–36.
53 Victoria Nidweski, "Through the Stage Door, a Spotlight on 'Backstage' Work: Women Designers and Stagehands in Theatrical Production" (master's thesis, Sarah Lawrence College, 2021), 57, https://digitalcommons.slc.edu/womenshistory_etd/57.
54 Alexander, 35–36.
55 IATSE Local USA 829, "History of the United Scenic Artists, Local USA 829, IATSE," *Vimeo*, February 24, 2023, https://vimeo.com/802026723?share=copy.
56 Anna Wyckoff, "Pay Equity – We Can Do It," Costume Designers Guild, February 10, 2020, https://www.costumedesignersguild.com/press_news/pay-equity-we-can-do-it/.
57 Alexander, 131–32.
58 Alexander, 131.
59 Alexander, 131–32.
60 Alexander, 132–33.
61 Alexander, 138–39.
62 IATSE Local USA 829, "We Will Do Better."
63 IATSE Local USA 829, "We Will Do Better."

64 Porsche McGovern, "Who Designs and Directs in LORT Theatres by Pronoun," *HowlRound Theatre Commons*, December 22, 2020, https://howlround.com/who-designs-and-directs-lort-theatres-pronoun-2020.
65 McGovern.
66 McGovern.
67 Sean Patrick Henry, "Broadway by the Numbers 2019," ProductionPro, April 9, 2019, https://production.pro/broadway-by-the-numbers.
68 Henry.
69 McGovern.
70 Henry.
71 Danee Conley, "Progress During an Atypical Year: Hiring Bias and Wage Gaps in Theatre in 2021" (New York, NY: Actors' Equity Association, 2021), 20, https://cdn.actorsequity.org/docs/HiringBiasWageGaps2021.pdf.
72 Martha Wade Steketee with Judith Binus, "Women Count Women Hired Off-Broadway," League of Professional Theatre Women, https://archive.theatrewomen.org/women-count/.
73 Steketee and Binus, "Women Count."
74 Martha Wade Steketee and Judith Binus, "Women Count VI: Women and Non-Binary Hires Off-Broadway 2019/20," Women Count Report Series (New York, NY: League of Professional Theatre Women, May 2022), https://msteketee.files.wordpress.com/2022/05/wc-vi-report-may-2022-1.pdf.
75 Steketee and Binus, 1.
76 Caitlyn Garrity, "Building a Better Workplace; Women+ Increasingly Abandon Technical Theatre over Lack Of Parity and Equity," *Theatre Design & Technology*, Summer 2019, 26, https://www.nxtbook.com/nxtbooks/hickman-brady/tdt_2019summer_public/index.php#/p/22.
77 Garrity, 26.
78 McGovern.
79 Kimberlé Crenshaw, "Demarginalizing the Intersection of Race and Sex: A Black Feminist Critique of Antidiscrimination Doctrine, Feminist Theory and Antiracist Politics," *University of Chicago Legal Forum*, no. 1 (1989): 139–67, https://doi.org/10.4324/9780429499142-5.
80 Crenshaw, 150.
81 Crenshaw, 152.
82 Katy Steinmetz, "She Coined the Term 'Intersectionality' Over 30 Years Ago. Here's What It Means to Her Today," *Time*, February 20, 2020, https://time.com/5786710/kimberle-crenshaw-intersectionality/.
83 Nancy Coleman, "'Hadestown' Director Rachel Chavkin: Diversity 'Is Not a Pipeline Issue,'" *New York Times*, June 9, 2019, https://www.nytimes.com/2019/06/09/theater/hadestown-rachel-chavkin-tony-awards.html.

BLACK
LIVES
MATTER.

3

THE PAUSE

On March 12, 2020, Broadway shows in New York City suspended performances by order of Governor Andrew Cuomo. Performances were expected to resume the week of April 13. As we know now, that was an overly optimistic plan. The COVID-19 pandemic was here to stay. Theatres all over the country, and world, ceased performances. Tours shut down. Everyone went home. And waited. It was the first time in modern memory that theatre across the country and the world stopped. And in stopping, put thousands of people out of work.

Before universal masking mandates and accessible testing, before vaccines and adequate risk assessment, the only way to keep people safe was to keep them at home. It became immediately obvious that the entertainment fields would be more impacted than other industries:

> By their very nature, many of the constituent parts of the creative economy necessitate the congregation of large groups of unrelated people, often in close proximity. Whether the venue is a small local bar, a large outdoor concert venue, or an art museum, many of the protective actions implemented in adherence to the U.S. Center for Disease Control and Prevention (CDC) guidance on social distancing forced the closure of businesses and facilities that directly support artistic endeavors.[1]

DOI: 10.4324/9781003330394-4

Theatres, with their closely seated audience members and intimate backstage spaces, afford the exact opposite of social distancing opportunities.

In June 2020, the Broadway League announced that all productions would remain closed through at least January 3, 2021,[2] a timeline they would revisit again and again until Broadway reopened in summer 2021. After 16 months, in June 2021, Bruce Springsteen opened his Broadway concert. Not long after, Broadway shows resumed with the opening of *Pass Over* on August 22 and the reopening of *Hadestown* and *Waitress* soon after.[3] There was a long awaited sigh of relief:

> After a year and a half of so much uncertainty and tragedy, Broadway's reopening amid the ongoing pandemic is seen as a major win for one of New York's biggest businesses. Yet, many in the industry say that theatre's journey back to 'normal' may actually take a few years – if what was once normal ever returns.[4]

The big question remained for most workers: Is normal what we want to return to?

The global COVID-19 pandemic affected everyone differently. For theatre production workers, it was a full stop to their high pressure and hectic lives, offering a prolonged period of self-reflection. Prior to this moment, most workers had been working too hard and too much to assess their quality of life or imagine working differently. The Pause also revealed some of the financial insecurities and realities faced by all workers, and production workers in particular. Thanks to the unusual ability of independent contractors and freelancers to receive unemployment benefits and the additional $600 a week granted by the Pandemic Unemployment Assistance (PUA) program, many production workers made more money during their pause in employment than they had been making before.

Once it was clear that the shutdown wasn't going to be brief, organizations and productions started making longer term plans. The overall financial impacts were as yet unknown, but it was clear that ticket sales would be greatly impacted for all theatres. In September 2020, Rosie Brownlow-Calkin, researcher and educator, sent a survey to hundreds of managing and financial directors of Actor's Equity-affiliated theatres across the country to find out the impact of the Pause on their company's financial health. She received 60 responses from companies in 27 states and Washington, DC, with operating budgets ranging from under $200,000 a year to nearly $90 million.[5] To save funds, producing organizations instituted layoffs, furloughs, and pay cuts during the shutdown:

> While some companies have actually seen their coffers swell in the past six months, almost a third of the 60 companies surveyed will be forced to consider closure some time in 2021 if restrictions on gatherings persist, without additional government support.[...] Almost as many theatres surveyed think they'll need to close next year as think they will not need to consider closing at all.[6]

Due to the governmental recognition of the impact of the pandemic on the arts:

> In 2020, state arts agencies (SAAs) and regional arts organizations (RAOs) played a crucial role in distributing state and federal relief funding and in providing financial and technical assistance for arts organizations and artists seeking to adapt rapidly to a post-pandemic environment.[7]

In December 2020, Congress passed the Save Our Stages Act – a $15-billion bill to provide emergency funding for venues focused on live performances as well as movie theatres – as part of the $900-billion Coronavirus Response and Relief Supplemental Appropriations Act.[8] Due to government support such as this bill, some arts organizations were able to secure recovery assistance to help sustain their operations. "For example, as of July 2020, 173,243 loans totaling $13.7 billion were issued to arts organizations through the Small Business Administration Paycheck Protection Program. Of those, nonprofit arts organizations received 9,917 loans worth $1.8 billion."[9] Though the Save Our Stages Act provided much needed support, it wasn't enough: "Equity [Actor's Equity Association] has said that the relief bill doesn't go far enough in helping unemployed artists. The $900 billion is a step down from the $3 trillion that was originally proposed by the House of Representatives in May."[10] By continuing to receive donations and government support, but not actually producing live theatre, some organizations' income outweighed their costs. But this windfall did not necessarily find its way to the workers.

Some of this institutional support made its way to production workers during the initial lockdown and the subsequent extended theatre pause. David J. McGraw and Meg Friedman's January 2021 Return to the Stage study found that, overall, "Employer communication has been fragmented. Respondents who have heard from previous employers have felt (largely) good about it."[11] The group of respondents who had heard from employers included 88 of 319 designers, 296 of 729 technical and project management staff, and 289 or 658 technicians.[12]

To examine how the pandemic impacted production labor specifically, we need to also zoom out and examine how the pandemic impacted the American labor market more generally. In September 2020, the *Washington Post* called the COVID recession "the most unequal in modern U.S. history."[13] Despite the narratives around essential workers, pandemic job losses hit low wage workers much harder than those earning higher wages, and those low-wage jobs have been the slowest to return:[14] "The demographic characteristics of the displaced low- and mid/high-wage workforce also reflect the fault lines in our economy. The displaced low-wage workforce is far younger, more racially and ethnically diverse, and have completed less formal education than the displaced mid/high-wage workforce."[15] Even as the economy started to recover, "several key demographic groups have recovered more slowly, including mothers of school-age children, Black men, Black women, Hispanic men, Asian Americans, younger Americans (ages 25 to 34) and people without college degrees."[16] Job losses due to the pandemic have affected all workers, but the most severe impact has been on those without a college degree.[17] In fact, the data indicates that

> almost 65% of workers with a bachelor's degree or higher reported teleworking in response to COVID-19. In contrast, only 22% of workers with a high school diploma or less worked remotely due to the pandemic. This difference highlights the structural job vulnerabilities of workers with a high school diploma or less to mandated changes in work environments.[18]

Due to the structural racism endemic in America, BIPOC workers were more impacted by pandemic job losses.

The COVID-19 shutdown also more significantly impacted women than men in a variety of ways. Within the first two months of the pandemic, 12.2 million women in the US experienced job loss, one million more than the 11.2 million men who lost their jobs in this first wave.[19] Service workers and waitstaff, both industries with predominantly women workforces, were some of the hardest hit by the job losses in these early months of the pandemic.[20] Consistent with traditional gender roles and assumptions, the closing of schools meant that mothers were more likely to take on the additional roles of teacher, daycare worker, and home care worker. The impacts of the pandemic on those with varying levels of education was perpetuated along gender lines: "The employment and labor force participation of mothers with school-aged and younger children varied by the mother's level of education and the year and season during the pandemic."[21]

The impacts on women are even more significant when looking at the intersectional impacts on women of color: "Women of color often stand at the intersection of multiple barriers, experiencing the combined effects of racial, gender, ethnic, and other forms of bias while navigating systems and institutional structures in which entrenched disparities remain the status quo."[22] Data shows that Black women are further impacted, regaining only 34% of those jobs lost in the first months of the COVID-19 pandemic. They also work in industries more likely to be at the frontlines of the pandemic: "Nearly 30 percent of Black women work in services, compared with only a fifth of White women."[23] Those services include work as nursing assistants, home health aides, and child care providers, all of which were considered essential, meant that more women and specifically women of color were forced back into unsafe work environments.[24] Recovery has also been slower for women workers. Since 2020, men have regained triple the lost jobs that women have regained.[25]

Additionally, unlike previous recessions and the Great Depression, "nine of the 10 hardest-hit industries in the coronavirus recession are services. They include performing arts, sightseeing, hotels, transportation, clothing retail and museums."[26] The social distancing restrictions and overall fear limiting travel and tourism even once states started to re-open, again disproportionately affected women of color:

> Recent data from the U.S. Department of Labor show that the accommodations and food services industry and the health care and social assistance industry have been among those hardest hit by severe unemployment. Women comprise the majority of workers in both industries... And a separate household survey found that women of color make up a disproportionate share of workers in both industries: 24.3 percent and 30.3 percent, respectively.[27]

As a subset of the service industry, the creative economy, including the arts and entertainment, has been one of the most impacted by the pandemic. In June 2021, the Costume Industry Coalition, a group of small NYC-based costume manufacturers for the entertainment industry, surveyed its members and calculated the gross revenue loss from the pandemic shutdown to be over $26.6 million.[28] The overall impacts of this loss of business are still reverberating nationally:

> Arts, culture, and creativity are one of three key sectors (along with science and technology as well as business and management) that drive regional economies. And the creative sector's role in our life and well-being extends far beyond its direct economic function. Lasting damage to the creative economy will drastically undercut our culture and quality of life.[29]

The arts also significantly affect the quality of life of non-arts workers. During the lockdown, Americans in all parts of the country and all industries turned to entertainment – music, television, movies, streaming services – for comfort and solace. (Who can forget *Tiger King*? Shows that in usual times may have not gotten attention became shockingly popular as people used entertainment as an escape.) As those folks went back to work, entertainment workers were left at home: "Although COVID-19 has impacted the entire arts sector, nowhere has the effect been more direct, deep, and immediate than on the performing arts."[30] These economic impacts would be more lasting than on other fields. By November of 2020, the Census Small Business Pulse Survey reported 61% of businesses in the Arts, Entertainment, and Recreation sector claiming COVID-19 continues to have large negative effects, compared to the 31% national average for all sectors.[31] In August 2020, the Brookings Institution published a report titled "Lost Art: Measuring COVID-19's Devastating Impact on America's Creative Economy." In it, they cited, "The fine and performing arts industries will be hit hardest, suffering estimated losses of almost 1.4 million jobs and $42.5 billion in sales. These estimated losses represent 50% of all jobs in those industries and more than a quarter of all lost sales nationwide."[32]

On June 8, 2020, NYC entered Phase 1 of a four-part reopening plan. Phase 1 included public transportation, construction, manufacturing, wholesale supply chain businesses, retail, landscaping, and agriculture, fishing, forestry, and hunting. Cultural institutions including Broadway were in Phase 4 of the reopening plan.[33]

Several groups conducted surveys of production workers during the Pause and immediately following to try to assess the state of the workers and the industry. In July 2020, January 2021, and July 2021, David J. McGraw and Meg Friedman conducted the Return to the Stage study, "a longitudinal study of performing arts workers in the United States, designed to understand COVID-19 related impacts and to begin documenting a broad future vision for the field."[34] The goal of the survey was to help understand the performing arts workforce's experience with COVID-19 restrictions, their coping strategies, and their hopes for the field.[35] The Return to the Stage study found workers cautious in accepting contracts as the businesses started to reopen: "38% of individuals who have received offers indicate they have declined at least one."[36] Though the most common reason for declining work was due to scheduling conflicts, with 69% of decliners noting this as the top reason they refused an offer, the second most common was compensation, with 46% of decliners citing pay as the reason they refused work.[37] Pay was a primary deterrent for production workers in particular: "Technicians/builders, creative team members, and people who indicated elevated levels of anxiety or hopelessness all prioritized compensation, with over 50% of each group identifying it as a top reason for declining work."[38] Considering the issues of pay equity that are ever present in the gendering of production work, the ongoing threat of burnout and the lack of consistent reasonable wages in the industry, these concerns are hardly surprising. The third reason that workers declined jobs was due to safety concerns:

> Feeling safe figured less prominently, but there are notable variances. Among all decliners only 12% indicated this is a factor. Among BIPOC respondents and people with elevated anxiety and hopelessness, safety is a factor for about 20%, suggesting a need for stronger communication and policy solutions.[39]

For the first time in a long time, it felt like calling for both physical and emotionally safe conditions wasn't going to be shot down. But would those calls for change be answered? And would those answers be sustainable?

In 2021, McGraw also conducted the eighth edition of the Stage Manager Survey, which welcomes participation from anyone across the globe who has served as stage manager or assistant stage manager on at least three live audience productions.[40] The 2021 edition included a number of pandemic-specific questions.[41] The 2021 survey had 1,449 viable responses, 1,163 of those respondents work primarily in the US or on tours originating in the US.[42]

In early 2021, the Actors Fund (now the Entertainment Community Fund) conducted a survey to better understand the profile of those in the performing arts and entertainment community who had participated in the Actors Fund services between 2018 and 2021, and how the COVID-19 pandemic has impacted those individuals.[43] This data includes not only theatre workers but cultural workers from television and film, music, digital media, performance art, radio, dance, cultural centers and performance venues, clubs and theme parks. Of those surveyed, "32% work in technical and support (production crew, backstage, stage management, support personnel, editors, marketers, administrators), 28% work in preparing (writers, directors, choreographers, designers, producers), and 6% work in some 'other' capacity. 83% of survey respondents said they were members of a union."[44]

In 2021, the Sundance Institute released an independent theatre study conducted by theatremaker Jesse Cameron Alick, with the charge to "create an in-depth presentation focusing on how the Institute could learn from the events of 2020."[45] Rather than depend on a survey of anonymous or semi-anonymous participants, Alick conducted an extensive series of interviews with "performance innovators, field leaders, thought leaders and field donors."[46] Unlike the hard data from these other studies, Alick's work creates a human-centric context for these change proposals.

In February 2022, *Stage Directions* published the findings of a survey conducted by Production on Deck (PoD) in collaboration with lighting designer and researcher Porsche McGovern. Production on Deck is a consulting and search firm founded by David Stewart (known as dStew) and Sarah Lozoff that "seeks to expand the traditional idea of the talent pipeline and increase pathways for marginalized communities to access jobs in theatrical production."[47] PoD reached out to production people in the theatre segment to answer the question, "Where is all the production staff?"[48]

So what did these researchers conclude? According to McGraw and Friedman's Return to the Stage survey:

- In July 2020, responses showed over half of the Performing Arts workforce being out of work. 56% of respondents reported being either unemployed, furloughed, or unable to work due to illness. 39% reported still working full-time or part-time, and 5% were students or retired.[49]
- In January 2021, unemployment was still high, with 49% of respondents still being unemployed, furloughed, or unable to work.[50]
- By July 2021, the unemployment and furlough rate had dropped to 24%:[51]

> The winter recovery was driven by part-time work, and only as summer engagements pick up steam have workers returned in significant numbers. The

> momentum of 'return' felt by employers and policymakers may take longer to reach the workforce, as people re-establish professional relationships, get (fully) vaccinated, and restore the personal and household resources that enable a return to work.[52]

Of the various primary occupations reported on the survey, those classified as Technician/Engineer/Fabrication consistently had the highest unemployment rates, going from 78% in July 2020 to 64% in January 2021 to 36% in July 2021.[53]

The financial impacts of the Pause on production workers were manifold. According to the Actors Fund survey:

> As a result of COVID-19, the majority of respondents have been impacted by lost income (76%), followed by loss of part-time or gig employment in the entertainment industry (62%), loss of full time employment in the entertainment industry (49%), behind in rent/mortgage (28%), lost non-entertainment employment (25%), lost health insurance, but replace with another option (16%), had to relocate to different region (11%), lost health insurance and do not have health insurance currently (10%), and lost housing (5%).[54]

As shown in Figure 3.2, the Stage Manager Survey asked US stage managers how their income was impacted between April 2020 and April 2021.[55]

The loss of income had varying levels of impact on respondents, ranging from workers having to use savings for regular expenses to food insecurity, forced housing changes, and sales of large assets:[56] "BIPOC respondents were more likely to experience reduced food security, forced housing change, increased credit card or other debt, and/or to have changed utility usage as compared to White respondents."[57] These impacts are significant and life changing.

There were also obviously massive mental health impacts on all workers living through the trauma of a mass disabling world-wide event. While the Return to the Stage study looked at the overall Performing Arts workforce, for the purpose of this book, the researchers extracted data from respondents whose primary occupation is in theatre production. This includes 3,006 respondents from the July 2020 survey; 2,008 respondents from the January 2021 survey; and 1,303 respondents from the July 2021 survey. These respondents each fall into one of four primary occupation categories: Designer, Technical/Project Management, Technician Engineer/Fabrication, and Other. The survey looked beyond the financial impacts of the Pause at the emotional state and coping strategies of performing arts workers. Unsurprisingly for those of us who lived through it, "respondents report elevated mental distress, particularly among historically marginalized populations. Nevertheless, respondents are using multiple coping strategies and report being motivated

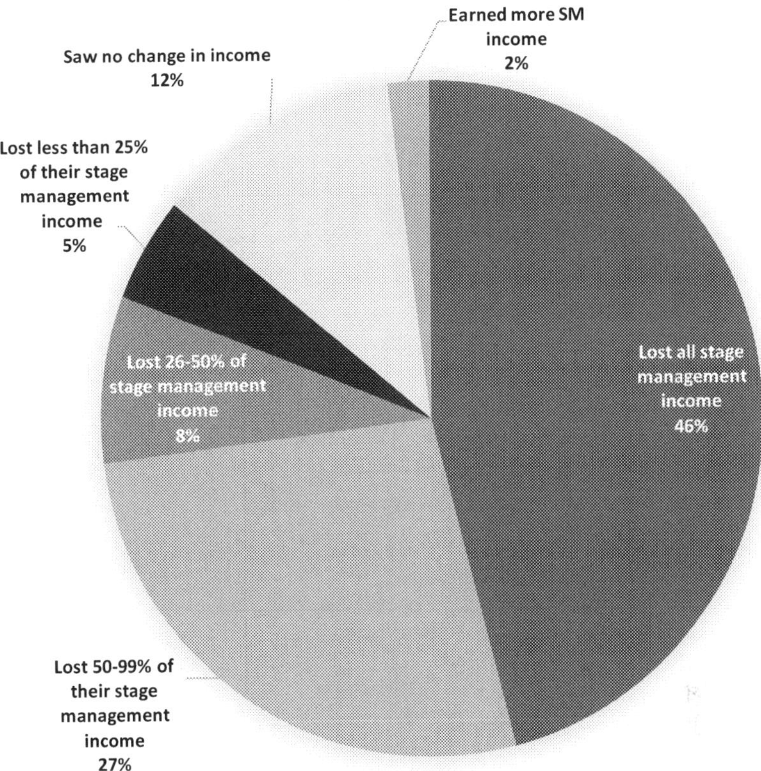

Figure 3.2 US Stage Manager Income (2020–2021)
Compiled from 2021 Stage Manager Study.

by the opportunity to improve not just personal wellbeing, but also to provide more value to the workplace, colleagues, and communities."[58]

The Actors Fund survey data is very clear on the pandemic's psychological impacts on workers: when asked about the impact of COVID-19 on their mental health, 79% of respondents were negatively affected,[59] putting them in a less stable condition to cope with the increasing and manifold traumas: threat of severe illness and death; job loss; pay cuts; loss of housing and food stability; increasing lack of trust in societal protections.

In order to stay relevant and create financial opportunities, many theatres pivoted to creating streaming content or streaming archival production recordings. In order to save themselves from these uncertainties and to keep working, many stage managers pivoted to stage managing that online work. At the time of the Stage Manager Survey, 39% of participants had stage managed an online performance:

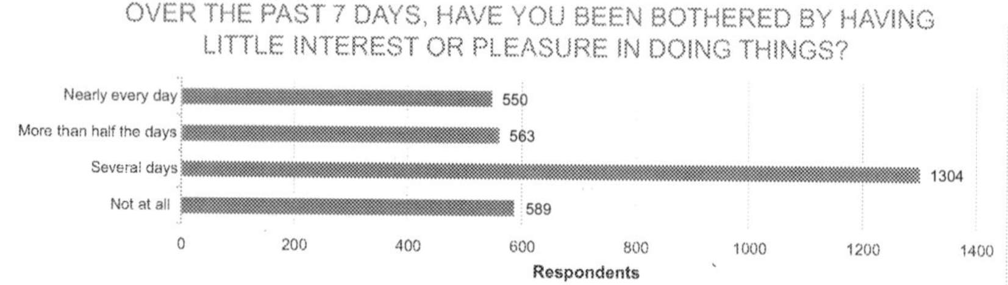

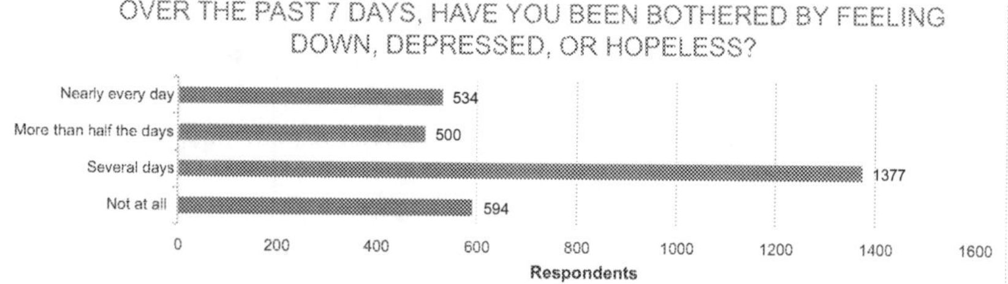

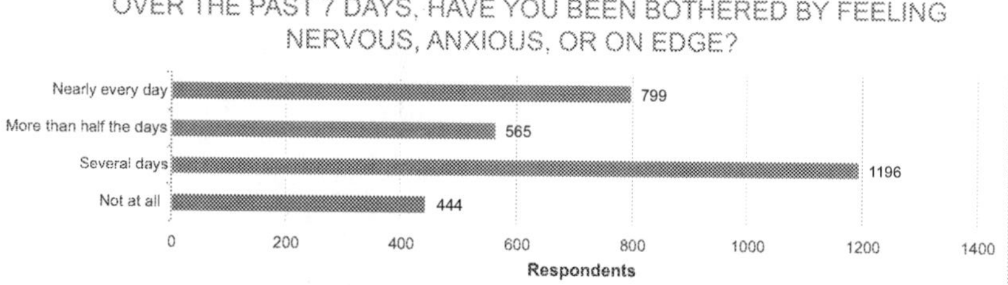

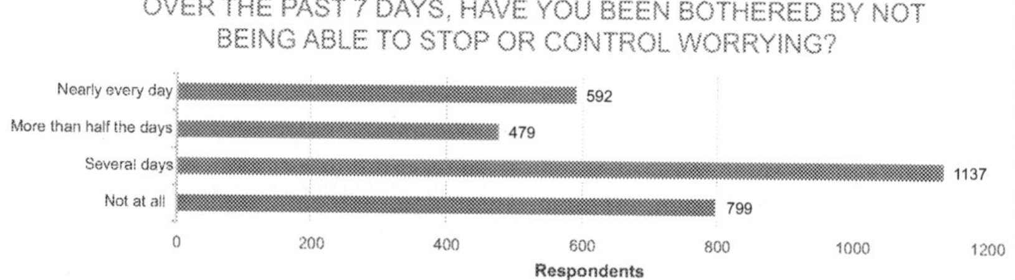

Figure 3.3 Worker responses to four mental health questions; from respondents in the categories Designer, Technical/Project Management, Technician Engineer/Fabrication, and Other; Excluding respondents from this group who did not respond to these questions

Compiled from July 2020 Return To The Stage Survey.

but despite such a large group finding work online, nearly all longed to return to in-person performances. When 1,112 participants were asked, 'In the future, if a stage management job was offered to you either as an online project or an in-person project, which would you prefer (assume same pay, dates, coworkers, and employer),' 94% chose the in-person format.[60]

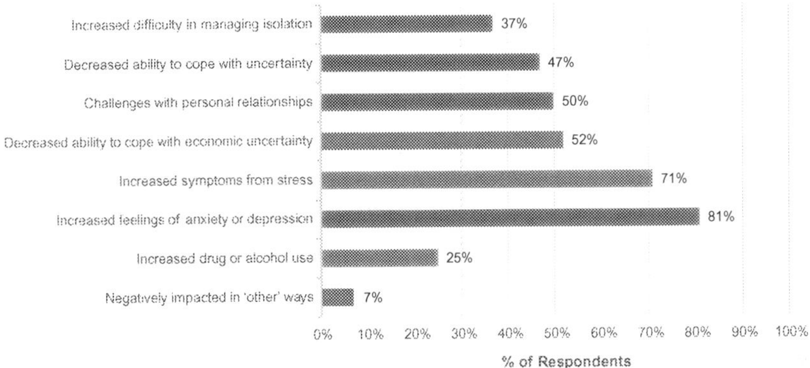

Figure 3.4 Worker responses regarding COVID-19 mental health impacts; Among respondents whose mental health has been impacted slightly negatively or very negatively

Compiled from Actors Fund Survey of Entertainment Professionals.

The shutdown, which we will continue to refer to as the Pause, derailed a lot of workers who ended up leaving the field entirely, at least for the time being. The *Los Angeles Times* profiled NY-based freelance director and stage manager Margaret Baughman:

> Baughman had been following COVID in the news and, in case of a widespread shutdown, contacted a recruiter about a temporary remote position. Now 28, they've since moved back to Chicago and work as a program manager at TikTok – a full-time job with consistent paychecks, affordable health insurance and a semblance of work-life balance. Even the occasional 60-hour workweeks are less of a lift than their years in theater.
>
> 'Before the pandemic, I was so, so close to getting those Broadway credits,' they say. 'But I was in parallel tracks with peers with significant financial privilege, who had so much more time to network and do workshops that didn't pay. I decided it wasn't worth it anymore, and now, I'm finally getting paid my worth.'[61]

Like Baughman, those without work were given the chance to imagine how their work lives could be different outside of the theatre:

For numerous artists and arts workers, the collective pause since 2020 spurred an unprecedented reflection on what they weren't getting from their prepandemic jobs and what precarious elements they had long tolerated for the love of the art form. Some are leaving the door open to return to theatre someday. Others say they'll never go back.[62]

What would these workers even be going back to? Theatre changed immeasurably and perhaps for good during the Pause. In "Emerging from the Cave," Alick pulls findings from a series of 60 interviews with 76 participants and asks what the theatre world looks like in the middle of the Pause. He arrives at four key findings:

- "In these interviews, there were many things people agreed on - especially the notion that during this time period, artists have been innovating like never before. They have been leading the way from their living rooms."[63]
- "The interviewees also expressed deep skepticism when it came to issues of racial equity and the commitment of institutions to addressing them."[64]
- "There was also an almost universal assessment that live performance institutions in the U.S. and in Europe have lost their identities, and are putting themselves into competition for the same projects and the same artists."[65]
- "A final diagnosis is that large institutions, in an attempt to reach national relevance, have failed to make deep investments in local communities and local artists."[66]

From these conversations, Alick also identifies four key themes for how to move forward: collective leadership, holistic artistic support, digital theatre and hybrid futures, and field ideation.[67]

On May 25, 2020, amidst ongoing lockdowns, George Floyd, a Black man in Minneapolis, was murdered by Derek Chauvin, a white police officer. In a moment where Americans weren't distracted by their day-to-day concerns of making a living, this outrageous act of violence sparked a national reckoning and reignited the Black Lives Matter movement. Across the country, Americans took to the streets. And the racial divide that had always been bubbling once again exploded. If it wasn't for the face masks and social media, it could have been 1968 all over again.

The *New York Times* summarized the environment:

> For 2½ months, America has been paralyzed by a plague, its streets eerily empty. Now pent-up energy and anxiety and rage have spilled out. COVID-19 laid bare the nation's broader racial inequities. About 13% of the U.S. population are African Americans. But according to CDC data, 22% of those with COVID-19, and 23% of those who have died from it, are black. Some 44% of African Americans say they have lost a job or have suffered household wage loss, and 73% say they lack an emergency fund to cover expenses, according to the Pew Research Center. 'It's either COVID is killing us, cops are killing us or the economy is killing us,' says Priscilla Borkor, a 31-year-old social worker who joined demonstrations in Brooklyn on May 29.[68]

The demand that Black Lives Matter quickly made its way into the cultural sector. Following statements from companies and leaders across the country, we saw asks by prominent theatre artists across the country demanding that theatres join the call. Director Liesl Tommy posted on Facebook on May 31, 2020:

> Hey American theaters! Please post your statement of solidarity with the Black Lives Matter struggle. Can folks post in comments below the statements from theaters and artists organizations who have already made statements? It comforts and helps us to know who stands in solidarity with us and our pain.[69]

Playwright Jeremy O. Harris "called on six theaters that produce his plays, which he said express on stage the same 'anger, frustration and activism' that are now on the streets of America, 'to articulate to the community you serve why black lives matter to you.'"[70] These six theatres and many more across the country (and world) published statements acknowledging inequalities in their practices and stating their commitments for the future.[71] The Drama Desk Awards and other virtual theatre community celebrations were postponed out of regard for the national unrest. On May 30, 2020, producer Marie Cisco shared a public editable spreadsheet titled "Theaters Not Speaking Out" to track theatres that had not yet made a statement about injustices toward Black people.[72] Over time, this project evolved to include those theatres who had made statements.

In June 2020, sound designer Twi McCallum shared an open "letter to the industry." Consistent with other calls being made by workers, they reiterated that speaking up is the bare minimum for theatres who should be hiring more Black artists to work backstage; creating safe workspaces for them; and offering comparable visibility that they do to the white headliners.[73]

An Open Letter to the Theatre Community from Twi McCallum

Theater Community:

This is an open letter to the arts/entertainment community, including individual artists and the organizations, from a Black femme sound designer who is tired of "inclusion" being exclusive to the actors, writers, producers, musicians, and dancers.

Many regional and Broadway theaters have been silent about the recent Black disparities. Seeing a select few companies speak up is cute – but being vocal is the bare minimum and now we need to see how they will measure up to these sentiments. The next step in showing institutional solidarity is hiring more black artists to work backstage, creating safe workspaces for us, and giving us comparable press/visibility that you give to the headliners.

Many artists I've worked for, collaborated with, or look(ed) up to have been silent. These non-Black sound, lighting, projection, costume, props, and set designers make a lot of money being contracted for these Black stories. Think of the best play/musical you've ever seen and ask yourself how many of the people off-stage were Black. My favorite Broadway production, which opened in 2018, had a majority Black cast and a Black playwright but hired zero Black designers. This is a common practice that nobody publicly talks about and there is no excuse for why companies cannot adequately staff backstage in the same manner they aim to staff onstage. There are several databases that exist where leaders can find the contact information for various demographics of designers, such as Wingspace, Parity Productions, and the Production on Deck website.

Whenever the arts open up for production post-virus, I hope Black and non-Black leaders HIRE Black backstage creatives. Many of us may be faceless to our audiences, but we exist, we are qualified, but we also need safe spaces. I've experienced my share of grotesque racism in my creative workplaces, like being called racist names during a rehearsal and being physically hit during a performance. I've had to resign from productions because the pay wasn't worth the abuse. There are stories we can't tell out of fear of being blackballed, since we lack the platform that the headlining stars have.

I need people to understand that "representation" should extend beyond the basics of seeing a certain Black actor get a starring role in a radical play, or seeing a Black playwright commissioned at a LORT stage. "Representation" should include those who work backstage and aren't asked for autographs or don't receive as much lucrative compensation for their work.

In (Angry) Artistry,
Twi M.

As printed in BroadwayWorld on June 8, 2020

Nataki Garrett, former artistic director of Oregon Shakespeare Festival, explained:

> Data about funding and demographics also revealed an overwhelmingly white leadership and workforce, from artistic directors to marketing and communications – which means theater, inside and out, artist and audience, is a real and perceived stronghold of white prestige and power.[74]

This reckoning demanded that white leaders, artists and administrators began to interrogate their whiteness in new ways and to consider the industry's relationship to white supremacist values.

At this moment, BIPOC theatremakers stepped into the spotlight to demand out loud what they have long needed. On June 9, 2020, 300 BIPOC theatremakers, across various disciplines, published a letter to the American theatre industry entitled "We See You, White American Theater," exposing "the indignities and racism that BIPOC, and in particular Black theatremakers, face on a day-to-day basis."[75] The letter was followed by a series of clearly articulated principles and demands which called for "transformative measures guided by principles of self-determination, presence, joy, access, protection, transparency and integrity in the spirit of independence from our colonized past and present."[76] The cohort demanded a bare minimum of 50% BIPOC representation in programming and personnel, both on and off stage. The writers suggested that eliminating the hiring criteria of years of experience or degree requirements would also foster this 50% minimum in white spaces, as would the development and retention of robust BIPOC student cohorts and faculty in professional training departments with historically less BIPOC representation than performance. We See You W.A.T. demanded structures for the protection of BIPOC workers in white spaces with white collaborators immediately: "Antiracism must become a mandatory, well-budgeted, and explicit core value, with interventionist practices implemented universally and consistently to dismantle white supremacy throughout institutions and project workflow."[77] The letter cites the theatrical motto "safety first," pointing out that antiracism is what makes BIPOC workers safe.[78]

These demands reverberated across the industry, and we will come back to them throughout the book. On June 16, 2020, the formation of Black Theatre United was announced.[79] The organization was launched by a coalition of professionals from across the theatre industry with the mission of reforming and combating systemic racism within the theatre community and throughout the nation.[80] The mission of BTU is to protect Black people, Black lives, and Black theatre.[81] As the *L.A. Times* reminds us:

> Past moments of upheaval resulted in hollow promises from theaters to do better, but this time is different, activists said. If white-dominated institutions can't change, black theater makers will go their own way, joining and cultivating institutions led by people of color. Those institutions are already there, and they are already helping.[82]

In 2021, some of the most powerful players on Broadway signed a pact titled "A New Deal for Broadway," pledging to strengthen the industry's diversity practices as theatres reopen following the lengthy shutdown prompted by the coronavirus pandemic.[83] The New Deal for Broadway outlines the core principles and joint commitments of these Broadway leaders and also breaks out a series of commitments from theatre owners, producers, unions, and creatives, as well as a series of procedural commitments developed in a three-month Commercial Theatre Summit from March to June 2021 hosted by Black Theatre United to establish industry-wide standards around Equity, Diversity, Inclusion, Accessibility, and Belonging with a focus on Black individuals in the theatre.[84] Embedded in the New Deal is an agreement that commits

> Broadway and its touring productions not only to the types of diversity training and mentorship programs that have become common in many industries, but also to a variety of sector-specific changes: the industry is pledging to forgo all-white creative teams, hire "racial sensitivity coaches" for some shows, rename theaters for Black artists and establish diversity rules for the Tony Awards.[85]

Returning to the Production on Deck survey, the results illustrate a handful of themes to answer why production workers have left and don't plan to come back, among them abuse, health, and money.[86] These resonate directly with the "We See You" demands. A white, male worker with 25 to 29 years' experience shared, "I'm considering leaving. The atmosphere created by our industry's reliance on illegal unpaid labor/wage theft, unpaid overtime, unsustainable daily/weekly hours, and the unacceptable emotional abuse that follows is becoming unbearable. Employers abuse, and employees pay it forward."[87] A white female worker with 10 to 14 years' experience explained:

> Covid pandemic, mental health reasons. The lifestyle of working in theater was no longer serving my ability to put my health and happiness first. The pandemic gave space to reevaluate my life and while I want to continue to work in theater, I'm not sure it's healthy for me to do so.[88]

And finally, a white, queer, female worker with 25 to 29 years' experience said, "I love my work. I want to have my career back. But I'm not sure how to do that, be an ally, be a parent and survive financially."[89]

While many workers were hungry to be back at their production jobs, not all were. As Production on Deck shared:

> After a year of survival jobs, it was time to don all-black and make some magic again – an escape from, or maybe an examination of, the past year and a half of trauma. Or so we thought.
>
> After laying off the near totality of their workforce during the pandemic, many theaters began the process of rehiring, only to find a tepid response. And, worse yet, after a year of examining institutional practices that pointed to an

> industry full of racial inequality, those job searches were returning nearly the same homogenous results.[90]

In order to assess why this was happening, Production on Deck surveyed workers about "whether they had left the industry, whether they were looking for work, if they planned to leave, why they would leave, and why they would stay."[91] It is in response to the question "Do you plan on coming back?" that the reality of the current situation unfolds.

As Bear Bellinger wrote for *Projection Lights & Staging News* (*PLSN*):

> Those numbers feel encouraging. The overwhelming majority of people in production are planning on returning. But, if you take the people who are anywhere from 'undecided' to 'absolutely no,' that is almost 28% of the industry. If you add in the people who are 'leaning yes,' 37% of workers are anywhere from tentative to absolutely not returning. In a landscape where nearly every professional theater across the country is looking to fill roles in production, that drastic of a drop in the talent pool becomes debilitating.[92]

As Production on Deck dug into the data, a few more trends appeared. The number of respondents who said they would absolutely not return to the field almost doubled from 5.9% to 10.9% when considering workers with more than 20 years of experience. Women and non-binary workers were 5% and 6% respectively more likely to leave the industry than men, when considered the combined answers of "absolutely no, "probably no," "leaning no," and "undecided."[93] Interestingly, the survey also revealed much about the diversity of the field:

> BIPOC respondents (22%) were 6.5% less likely to leave than our White respondents (28.5%). Though, when placed beside the fact that BIPOC respondents are already drastically underrepresented, if 22% of BIPOC respondents did, in fact, leave the industry, BIPOC share of total production representation would drop between 2–3%. Given that BIPOC folks already only made up 11% of the field, dropping those numbers down 2–3% would have disastrous results for furthering diversity goals.[...] This all points to a job field with potential substantial losses in overall talent, as well as a specific reduction in talent from communities who have been historically marginalized in our industry.[94]

The Production on Deck survey illustrates the combined impacts of the COVID-19 pandemic and the nation-wide dialogue about systemic racism (newly) acknowledged in institutions of all sizes and scope.

The events of 2020, the Pause and the racial reckoning, changed theatre workers' lives. There was no work. And without work, there was time. Time to reflect. Time to discuss. Time to reimagine. And from that, perhaps the

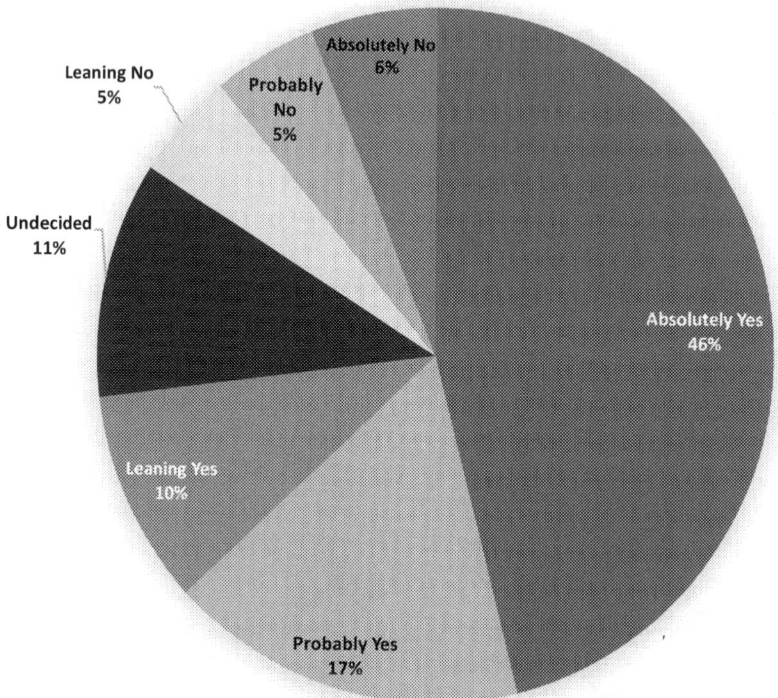

Figure 3.5 Worker responses to "Do you plan on coming back?", referring to returning to the field following the pandemic

Compiled from Production on Deck "Where is all the production staff?" survey, published by Stage Directions.

beginnings of a new way of working begins to emerge. But as Jesse Green of the *New York Times* says:

> Like certain old plays, those old stories are falling out of favor. In part because the 18-month shutdown gave theater people the time to scrutinize their circumstances, and in part because other equity initiatives were at the same time roiling the field, a consensus for change has begun to emerge. Prestigious institutions are being forced to alter or eliminate their unpaid internship programs, smaller companies are voluntarily restructuring their compensation packages and a movement to make fair pay practices standard if not compulsory is gaining traction in Chicago and spreading to other cities.[95]

NOTES

1 COVID-19 RSFLG Data and Assessment Working Group and Argonne National Laboratory, "Analysis: COVID-19's Impacts on Arts and Culture," COVID-19 Weekly Outlook, January 4, 2021, 4, https://www.arts.gov/sites/default/files/COVID-Outlook-Week-of-1.4.2021-revised.pdf.
2 Ryan McPhee, "Broadway Will Officially Remain Closed Through 2020," *Playbill*, June 29, 2020, https://playbill.com/article/broadway-will-officially-remain-closed-through-2020.
3 Associated Press, "3 of the Biggest Broadway Shows Reopen with COVID Rules," *NPR*, September 14, 2021, https://www.npr.org/2021/09/14/1037194157/3-big-broadway-shows-reopen-with-covid-rules.
4 Abbey White, "Broadway's Return Is Triumphant, But Uncertainty Looms: 'Humans Have to Be as Important as the Show,'" *The Hollywood Reporter*, November 22, 2021, https://www.hollywoodreporter.com/lifestyle/arts/broadway-reopening-pandemic-new-york-city-1235046751/.
5 Rosie Brownlow-Calkin, "To Be or Not to Be: Theatres Brace for Another Season of Uncertainty," *American Theatre*, October 26, 2020, https://www.americantheatre.org/2020/10/26/to-be-or-not-to-be-theatres-brace-for-another-season-of-uncertainty/.
6 Brownlow-Calkin.
7 COVID-19 RSFLG Data and Assessment Working Group and Argonne National Laboratory, "COVID-19's Impacts on Arts and Culture," 9.
8 Diep Tran, "What the Save Our Stages Act Means for You," *Backstage*, March 13, 2021, https://www.backstage.com/magazine/article/save-our-stages-act-actors-performing-artists-72354/.
9 COVID-19 RSFLG Data and Assessment Working Group and Argonne National Laboratory, "COVID-19's Impacts on Arts and Culture," 8.
10 Tran, "What the Save Our Stages Act Means for You."
11 David McGraw and Meg Friedman, "Return to the Stage January 2021 Survey," Return to the Stage, February 2021, 24, https://www.returntothestage.com/uploads/6/4/6/6/6466686/return_to_the_stage_february_2021.pdf.
12 Meg Friedman, email message to authors, September 6, 2022.
13 Heather Long et al., "The Covid-19 Recession Is the Most Unequal in Modern U.S. History," *Washington Post*, September 30, 2020, https://www.washingtonpost.com/graphics/2020/business/coronavirus-recession-equality/.
14 Nicole Bateman and Martha Ross, "The Pandemic Hurt Low-Wage Workers the Most– and So Far, the Recovery Has Helped Them the Least," Brookings Metro's COVID-19 Analysis (Washington, D.C.: Brookings Institute, July 28, 2021), https://www.brookings.edu/research/the-pandemic-hurt-low-wage-workers-the-most-and-so-far-the-recovery-has-helped-them-the-least/.
15 Bateman and Ross.
16 Long et al.
17 Mary C. Daly, Shelby R. Buckman, and Lily M. Seitelman, "The Unequal Impact of COVID-19: Why Education Matters," *FRBSF Economic Letter*, June 28, 2020, https://www.frbsf.org/wp-content/uploads/sites/4/el2020-17.pdf.

18 Daly, Buckman, and Seitelman.
19 Liz Elting, "The She-Cession by the Numbers," *Forbes*, February 12, 2022, https://www.forbes.com/sites/lizelting/2022/02/12/the-she-cession-by-the-numbers/?sh=1a0f417d1053.
20 Elting.
21 Claudia Goldin, "Understanding the Economic Impact of COVID-19 on Women" (Cambridge, MA: National Bureau of Economic Research, April 2022), https://doi.org/10.3386/w29974.
22 Jocelyn Frye, "On the Frontlines at Work and at Home: The Disproportionate Effects of the Coronavirus Pandemic on Women of Color" (Washington, DC: Center for American Progress, April 23, 2020), https://www.americanprogress.org/article/frontlines-work-home/.
23 Long et al.
24 Frye.
25 Elting.
26 Long et al.
27 Frye.
28 Michael S. Eddy, "Industry Advocates: Costume Industry Coalition," *Stage Directions*, June 2021, 23.
29 Richard Florida and Michael Seman, "Lost Art: Measuring COVID-19's Devastating Impact on America's Creative Economy" (Washington, DC: Brookings Institution, August 2020), 21, https://www.brookings.edu/wp-content/uploads/2020/08/20200810_Brookingsmetro_Covid19-and-creative-economy_Final.pdf.
30 COVID-19 RSFLG Data and Assessment Working Group, "COVID-19's Impacts on Arts and Culture," 5.
31 COVID-19 RSFLG Data and Assessment Working Group, 6.
32 Florida and Seman, 3.
33 Jen Carlson, "A Guide to New York City's Reopening," *Gothamist*, June 8, 2020, https://gothamist.com/news/guide-new-york-city-reopening-phases.
34 Meg Friedman and David McGraw, "Return to the Stage: A Performing Arts Workforce Study," Return to the Stage, accessed May 16, 2023, https://www.returntothestage.com/.
35 Friedman and McGraw.
36 McGraw and Friedman, 10.
37 McGraw and Friedman, 10.
38 McGraw and Friedman, 10.
39 McGraw and Friedman, 10.
40 David J. McGraw, "2021 Stage Manager Study," January 2022, 1, https://www.smsurvey.info/uploads/6/4/6/6/6466686/2021_smsurvey.pdf.
41 McGraw, 1.
42 McGraw, 5.
43 Actors Fund, "Survey of Entertainment Professionals Helped by The Actors Fund" (New York, NY: The Actors Fund, March 2021), https://drive.google.com/file/d/1LlCjCTsl7jUFx0DYok59YDRa-EH7plHx/view.
44 Actors Fund, "Survey of Entertainment Professionals," 4.
45 Jesse Cameron Alick, "Emerging from the Cave: Reimagining Our Future in Theater and Live Performance" (Park City, UT: Sundance Institute, August

2021), 9, https://drive.google.com/file/d/1AGGaIDFdh_pTT92RewhSLOfZWEYhSHo0/view.
46 Alick, 8.
47 "Consulting," Production on Deck, https://www.productionondeck.com/about.
48 Bear Bellinger, "Production on Deck: Eliminating Excuses," *PLSN: Production Lights and Staging News*, February 4, 2022, https://plsn.com/articles/stage-directions-articles/production-on-deck-eliminating-excuses-2/.
49 McGraw and Friedman, 14.
50 McGraw and Friedman, 7.
51 McGraw and Friedman, 8.
52 McGraw and Friedman, 8.
53 McGraw and Friedman, 9.
54 Actors Fund, 6.
55 McGraw, 17.
56 Actors Fund, 6–7.
57 Actors Fund, 7.
58 McGraw and Friedman, 17.
59 Actors Fund, 8.
60 McGraw, 19.
61 Ashley Lee, "In-Person Theater is Back. A Lost Generation of Artists Chose Not to Return with It," *Los Angeles Times*, March 24, 2022, https://www.latimes.com/entertainment-arts/story/2022–03–24/pandemic-artists-theater-lost-generation.
62 Lee.
63 Alick, 13.
64 Alick, 13.
65 Alick, 13.
66 Alick, 13.
67 Alick, 15.
68 Alex Altman, "Why the Killing of George Floyd Sparked an American Uprising," *Time*, June 4, 2020, https://time.com/5847967/george-floyd-protests-trump/.
69 Liesel Tommy, "Hey American theaters! Please post your statement of solidarity with the Black Lives Matter struggle," *Facebook*, May 31, 2020, https://www.facebook.com/liesl.tommy/posts/10157195311500887.
70 Jonathan Mandell, "Theater and Black Lives Matter. Reopening Fears and Plans. Project Pride," New York Theater, June 1, 2020, https://newyorktheater.me/2020/06/01/theater-and-black-lives-matter-reopening-fears-and-plans/.
71 Mandell.
72 Jessica Gelt, "The Spreadsheet that Shook the Theater World: Marie Cisco's 'Not Speaking Out' List," *Los Angeles Times*, June 9, 2020, https://www.latimes.com/entertainment-arts/story/2020–06–09/theaters-not-speaking-out-list-george-floyd-protests-black-lives-matter.
73 Stephi Wild, "Twi McCallum Shares an Open Letter to the Theatre Community on Hiring Black Designers and Creatives," *Broadway World*, June 8, 2020, https://www.broadwayworld.com/article/Twi-McCallum-Shares-an-Open-Letter-to-the-Theatre-Community-on-Hiring-Black-Designers-and-Creatives-20200608.

74 Nataki Garrett, "The Threat of an Inclusive American Theatre," *The Root*, October 28, 2022, https://www.theroot.com/the-threat-of-an-inclusive-american-theatre-1849715600.
75 Olivia Clement, "300 BIPOC Theatre Artists Call for Reckoning in the White American Theatre," *Playbill*, June 9, 2020, https://www.playbill.com/article/300-bipoc-theatre-artists-call-for-reckoning-in-the-white-american-theatre.
76 "Principles for Building Anti-Racist Theatre Systems," We See You, White American Theatre, https://www.weseeyouwat.com/statement.
77 We See You, White American Theatre.
78 We See You, White American Theatre.
79 "Timeline." Black Theatre United, https://www.blacktheatreunited.com/portfolio/timeline/.
80 "Announcing Black Theatre United," Audra McDonald, https://audramcdonald.com/announcing-black-theatre-united/.
81 "Who We Are," Black Theatre United, https://www.blacktheatreunited.com/portfolio/who-we-are/.
82 Gelt.
83 Michael Paulson, "Broadway Power Brokers Pledge Diversity Changes as Theaters Reopen," *New York Times*, August 23, 2021, https://www.nytimes.com/2021/08/23/theater/broadway-diversity-pledge-reopening.html?action=click&module=RelatedLinks&pgtype=Article.
84 Black Theatre United, "A New Deal for Broadway: Equity, Diversity, Inclusion, Accessibility & Belonging in the Theatrical Industry," 2021, http://www.blacktheatreunited.com/wp-content/uploads/2022/05/BTU-New-Deal-For-Broadway.pdf.
85 Paulson.
86 Bellinger.
87 Bellinger.
88 Bellinger.
89 Bellinger.
90 Bellinger.
91 Bellinger.
92 Bellinger.
93 Bellinger.
94 Bellinger.
95 Jesse Green, "When Paying Dues Doesn't Pay the Rent, How Does the Theatre Survive?" *New York Times*, July 6, 2022, https://www.nytimes.com/2022/07/06/theater/pay-equity-salaries.html.

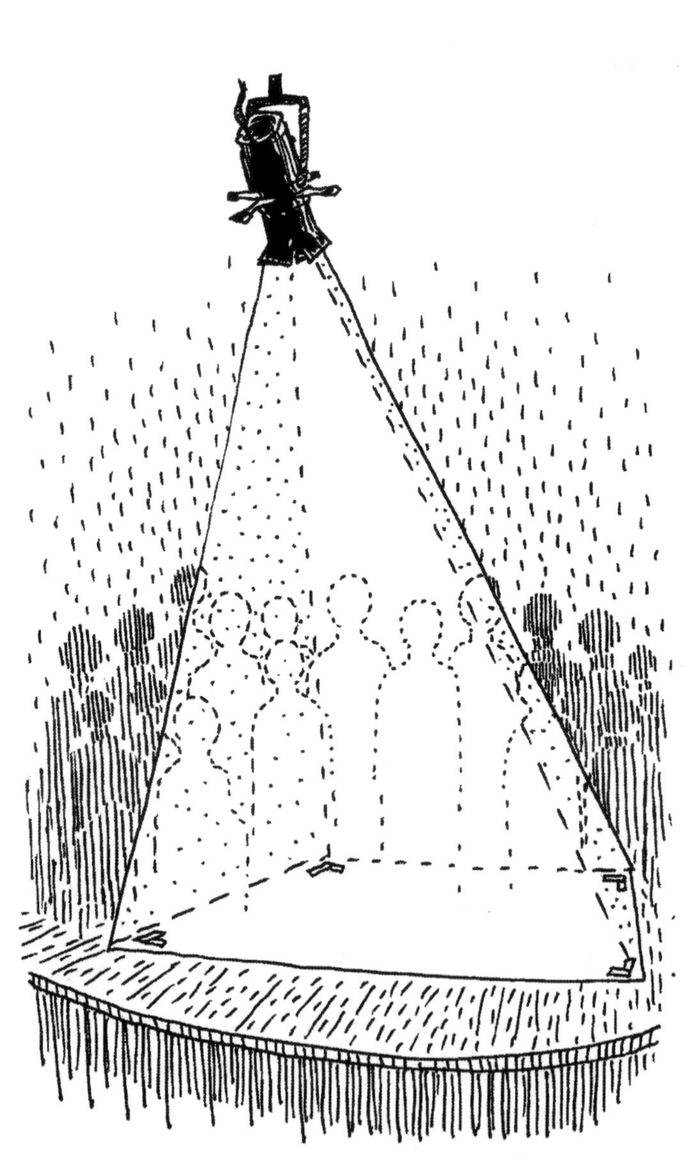

4

OUR RESEARCH

Embarking on this project began with an attempted understanding of the existing research surrounding theatrical production workers. The history of representation frames the research in historical context. And the impressive work by other researchers provides a strong foundation. But central to our questions are: Where are the production workers now? What do they currently need? What is and is not working? In order to even begin to answer these questions, primary research was necessary.

We began our research with a series of assumptions. We suspected that theatrical production included many unsustainable work practices; that racism, misogyny, and bias were endemic; and that barriers to successful careers were keeping the field mostly white, mostly financially privileged, and mostly male. We had seen the research that came out of the Pause, showing the decrease in workers interested in going back after the theatres reopened.

Early in our research process, we spoke with Saru Jayaraman, Co-Founder and President of One Fair Wage, about her leadership in the national labor movement for restaurant workers, employers, and consumers. Restaurant work is similarly precarious to theatrical production labor and, in fact, shares aspects of its transient workforce. Long hours, dangerous conditions, movement between employers and wages out of scale with the labor are reminiscent of our own experiences in theatrical production.

DOI: 10.4324/9781003330394-5

The early organizing of restaurant workers included data collection in ways that inspired our own work. Jayaraman explained that the early participatory research study OFW conducted helped them develop leaders, generate data, and also realize the breadth of the issues:

> It obviously gave us data, it elevated the issues that workers were facing, and it helped us identify what workers' top priorities were at a meta level. So what we heard from workers over and over again, wherever we did the same survey, and we ended up doing like 15,000 of that same survey, was that wages were the top priority everywhere. And that's what really helped us define that–that's what we were going to work on and created that led to the creation of the One Fair Wage campaign.[1]

This early surveying of workers also revealed blind spots in the industry, ways in which the workers themselves didn't know how to process their experiences because they had been so normalized, much like some of the abuses we see in production. Addressing these issues in the long fight for restaurant workers hasn't been a straight line towards success: "It's been an iterative process. It's not just like, do the research, that leads to action. It's an iterative process of research, to action, to research, to action."[2] Jayaraman emphasizes that in her over 20 years of organizing, continually asking the workers about their experiences and their needs is necessary to really understand the roots of the struggle. The strategies, successes, and losses she shared with us inspired our deep dive into the theatrical labor workforce.

Building on the existing theatrical research, including but not limited to "Who Designs and Directs in LORT Theatres By Pronoun," "Return to the Stage: A Performing Arts Workforce Study," "Emerging from the Cave," and the "Where is all of the production staff" survey, we set out to gather data on the current state of the professional theatre production labor landscape in the US.

We conducted a series of worker and employer surveys followed by several interviews to identify the here and now of the production work environment as well as to investigate what advocates, industry leaders, and workers have done to improve their own working conditions. In this chapter we share the methodology for our research and some overarching findings.

Our goal in the primary research was to survey the landscape of professional theatre production workers in the US, including those currently working in the field and those who have left. In the surveys, we were looking for quantifiable data that could lead to a statistical analysis as well as seeking qualitative answers that would allow us to identify and measure people's experience in theatrical production. Using long-form survey questions as well as interviews, we set out to expand our understanding of people's unique experiences and opinions. This part of our research aligns more with the interpretivist research philosophy, based on the assumption that reality is subjective, multiple, and socially constructed.

For the surveys, we worked with data analyst Wayne Carino to collect ethnographic research about theatre production workers in the US in 2022. We were seeking to know more about people's experiences working in theatrical production; ties between identity and experience; and intersections of race, gender, class, work title, and life in the field. The survey was built in Google Forms and included 19 sections. While there were many sections that all participants accessed, there were a handful of sections that participants only accessed depending on their answer to certain demographic questions, such as whether or not they are a caregiver or identify as a person with a disability or neurodivergence. The specific questions and methodology used for data analysis can be found in the appendices.

We shared the survey with over 700 workers directly and reached many more via social media, forums, and email newsletters. The survey was shared with the subscribers of Nothing For The Group; the Production Managers' Forum; USITT Weekly News; the United Scenic Artists, Local USA 829, IATSE e-news; and Facebook groups including Intimacy Choreographers, Coordinators, and Educators Resource Group; Lift The Curtain – End Unpaid Arts Internships; NYC Union Sisters in the Arts: On Our Team; Stagehands; Stage Managers & More; Stagehands Unite; Theater Professionals of Underrepresented Genders; Theatre Sound Designers and Engineers; TWC IATSE LOCAL 798 NYC; United Scenic Artists, Local USA 829, IATSE; USITT Women in Theatre Network; and Year of the Stage Manager. We shared the survey with many educators, requesting they share it with their students and alumni. We also shared the survey frequently on social media, and many individuals and collectives re-shared it. The worker survey was open to participants from July 1, 2022 until August 1, 2022.

We also sought a snapshot of the employer perspective on workplace practices for production employees. In Google Forms, we built an employer survey similar to the worker survey. Seeking data from companies who hire production personnel – professional theatre organizations, general and production management firms, and fabrication shops – in the US we contacted production employers and requested a single response per organization. We contacted 51 shops, 208 theatre producing organizations, and 18 general management and/or production management companies. In addition to this outreach, we posted in various forums such as the Production Managers' Forum and Facebook groups including New York Film and Theater Network, Theater Professionals of Underrepresented Genders, Theatre Beyond Broadway: The Community, USITT Women in

Theatre Network, Women in Film, TV and Theatre, and Year of the Stage Manager. The employer survey was available from July 11, 2022 through August 12, 2022. We received a total of 23 responses to our employer surveys. This was a lower response rate than we were aiming for, and we recognize this as a limitation in attaining a snapshot of the range of employer perspectives. From the collected data, we went on to create a qualitative content and thematic analysis.

The final component of our primary research was a collection of interviews with which we sought to find out more about specific individuals' experiences with particular topics relevant to the book. We conducted the first round of interviews in summer and fall of 2022, coinciding with the early stages of writing the book. We began by identifying people in theatrical production or related fields with specific relationships to the topics we were hoping to discuss. In spring 2023, after completing drafts of the first and second sections of the book, we conducted another series of interviews pertaining to the third and final section of the book. Across both rounds of interviews, we attempted to include geographic, gender, racial, and organizational diversity in our selection of interviewees to represent the breadth of theatrical production work. We interviewed:

Fatima Bunafoor, Director of Talent and Equity, Pittsburgh HR/Equity Arts Cohort
Ineke Ceder, Advisory Board Member, Parent Artist Advocacy League
Sarah Clare Corporandy, Co-Founder and Producing Artistic Director, Detroit Public Theatre
Jessa-Raye Court, Co-Founder, Costume Professionals for Wage Equity
Robert Barry Fleming, Executive Artistic Director, Actors Theater of Louisville
Nataki Garrett, then Artistic Director, Oregon Shakespeare Festival
Angela Gieras, Executive Director, Kansas City Rep
Jon Harper, then Managing Director, Abrons Arts Center
D. Joseph Hartnett, former Co-Director, IATSE Stagecraft Department
Linette S. Hwu, Board Member, Woolly Mammoth Theatre Company
Elsa Hiltner, Co-Founder, On Our Team
Saru Jayaraman, President, One Fair Wage
Beth Lake, Co-Chair, Off-Broadway Assistant Designer Advisory Group
Pat Landers, Business Representative for Health & Safety, United Scenic Artists
Sarah Lozoff, Co-Founder, Production on Deck
Michael Maag, Resident Lighting Designer, Oregon Shakespeare Festival
Anyania Muse, Interim Chief Operating Officer, Oregon Shakespeare Festival
Lauren Parrish, Associate Director of Production, Abrons Arts Center
Rachel Spencer Hewitt, Founder, Parent Artist Advocacy League

David 'dStew' Stewart, Co-Founder, Production on Deck
Stephanie Ybarra, then Artistic Director, Baltimore Center Stage.

Prior to the interviews, we developed a series of questions specific to each interview, including introductory and contextual information about the interviewee(s) and a set of questions based on their particular expertise. We maintained three questions across all interviews:

- What does equitable labor in theatre production look like to you?
- Who do you see bearing responsibility for theatre production practices being accessible, inclusive, and sustainable?
- What do you see as the biggest current challenge for production labor?

All of the questions were shared with the interviewees in writing prior to our interview. The interviews were held via the Zoom platform, typically with two interviewers, though a few had only one. All of the interviews were recorded via Zoom. Transcriptions were then generated using the Otter.ai automated service and then checked against the recordings by research assistant Delaney Teehan. Each interview lasted about forty-five minutes. All of our interviews were conducted between August 2022 and April 2023.

We faced several methodological limitations in our primary research. Our own identities and personal biases have been present throughout the research and writing process, and particularly in relation to building survey and interview questions. As two white cis-women with master's degrees from prestigious institutions, bringing our own experiences and interests from our individual relationships to the field, we approach this material not as outsiders, but as a lighting designer and a manager, with extensive experiences in professional and academic theatre.

We were limited by the reach of our worker survey: there are hundreds of thousands of workers in theatrical production in the United States of America, just over a thousand of whom completed the survey. Membership of the IATSE (which includes film workers as well) is over 160,000 alone, and we don't know how many non-union workers there are. Our reach was limited by our personal networks, our knowledge of allied groups and organizations, and the limited timeline of the survey itself. As mentioned, the reach of our employer survey also limited our generation of a holistic snapshot of the employer perspective. Both surveys were quite long, taking an estimated 15–25 minutes to complete, which may have limited who had the time to engage with them. They also relied on literacy and access to the necessary technology to complete an online form.

We were also limited by the reach of our interview engagement. In our interview outreach, we were not able to connect with all of the subjects we had originally identified and have not included as wide a range of institutions and perspectives as we initially hoped.

Given these limitations, the research itself has been illuminating. We received a total of 1,037 responses to the worker survey. The demographic breakdown from the worker survey assists in contextualizing our research. Respondents were living in 45 states plus Washington DC, with the majority of respondents residing in New York: 338 respondents or 32.6% of the total. There were no respondents from West Virginia, North Dakota, South Dakota, Wyoming, or Mississippi. Our respondents spanned ages from under 20 through 79. The majority of worker respondents fell between ages 25 and 29 (17.65%) and between 30 and 34 (16.68%) (See Figure 4.2 for the age breakdown.).

In regards to race and gender, we asked respondents to self-identify. When asked how they would describe themselves, the majority of respondents answered white (857 or 84.38%), followed by those who identify as multi-racial (84 or 8.10%). (See Figure 4.3 for the breakdown of responses.)

Regarding gender identity, the majority of respondents answered cisgender (850 or 81.97%) followed by "Other" (94 or 9.06%). Many respondents wrote in how they identify, which we have grouped together into categories based on commonalities in the write-in responses.

When asked where on the gender spectrum respondents place themselves, 510 (or 49.18%) of the respondents chose Female; 418 (40.31%) chose Male; and 85 (8.20%) chose Genderfluid/Genderqueer/Non-Binary. Again, many respondents wrote-in their responses, and we have categorized them in order to generate quantitative data (see Figure 4.4). Finally, when asked if they identify as part of the LGBTQIAA+ community, 565 (54.48%) of those who answered said no; 422 (40.69%) said yes; and the remaining chose "prefer not to answer." Both the racial diversity and gender diversity are relatively consistent with other studies of theatrical production workers.

Interested in the relationship between education level and financial success, we asked workers for their highest level of completed education (see Figure 4.5). The vast majority of respondents (561 or 54.10%) reported having completed a bachelor's degree, followed by 378 workers (36.45%) who completed a master's degree.

We asked about neurodiversity and disability statuses, as we were interested in experiences specific to these two identities. When asked if they identify as neurodivergent, 215 respondents of 1037 (or 20.73%) responded yes. When asked if they identify as a person with a disability, 880 workers (or 84.86%) responded no, and 114 workers (or 10.99%) responded yes. We do acknowledge that some people see neurodivergence as a disability.

Interested in how workplace practices impact workers with caregiving responsibilities, we asked workers if they serve as caregivers, in what sort of caregiving unit; and 199, or 19.19%, of the respondents identify as caregivers (see Figure 4.6).

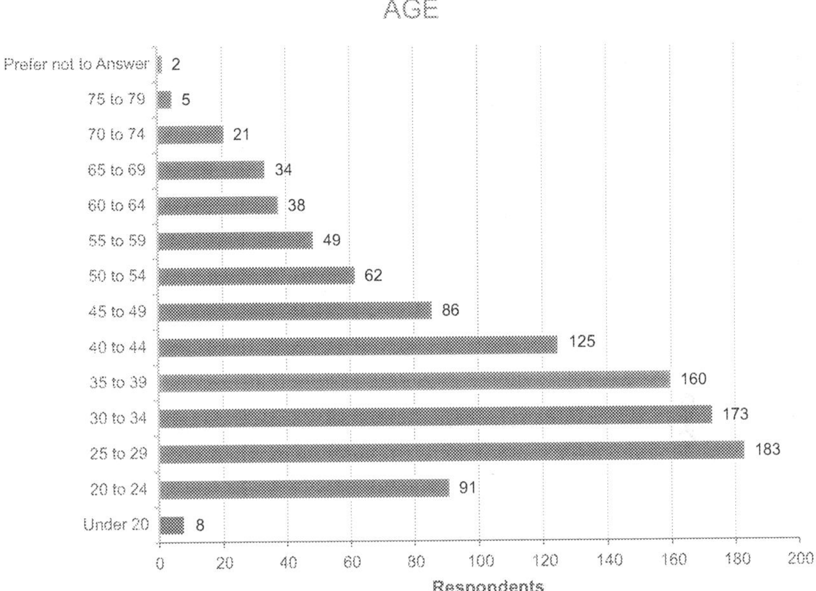

Figure 4.2 Worker responses to "What is your age group?"

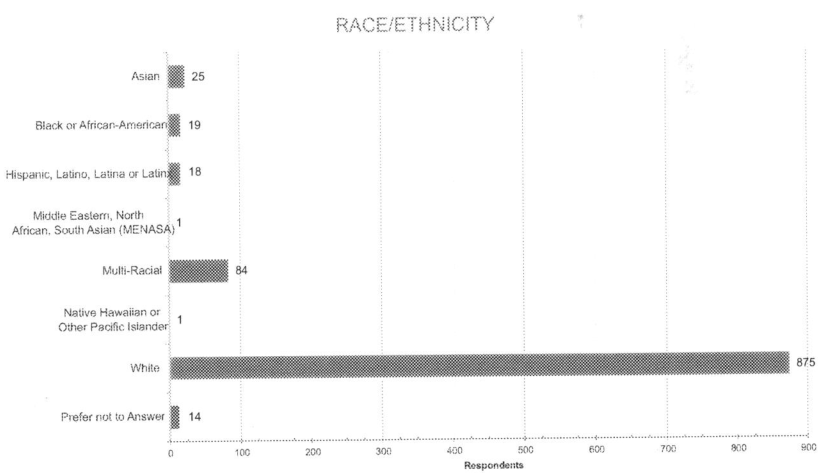

Figure 4.3 Worker responses to "How would you describe yourself?"

When asked to provide their primary roles in theatrical production, the workers' answers were widespread and specific.

We also asked a variety of questions surrounding the style of respondents' worklives. Approximately half of the respondents, 529 or 51.01%,

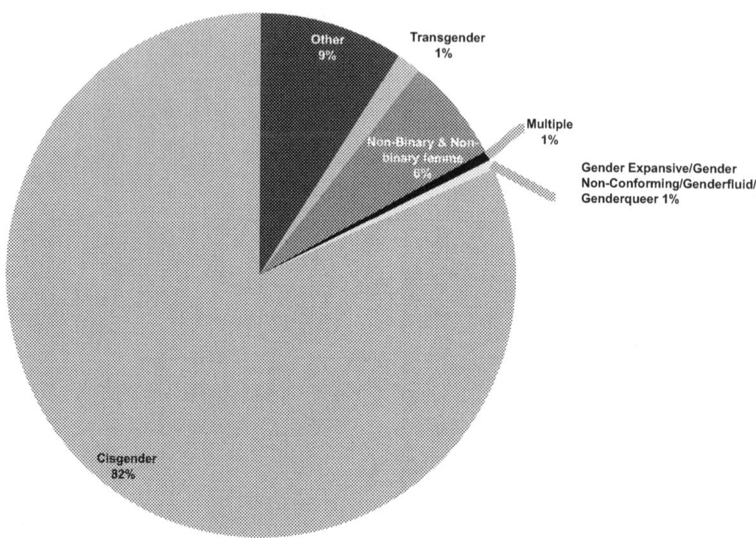

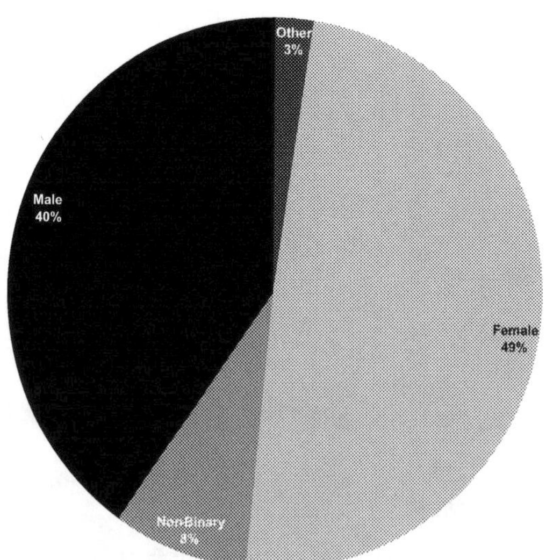

Figure 4.4 Worker responses to "Do you identify as:" and "Where do you identify on the following spectrum?"

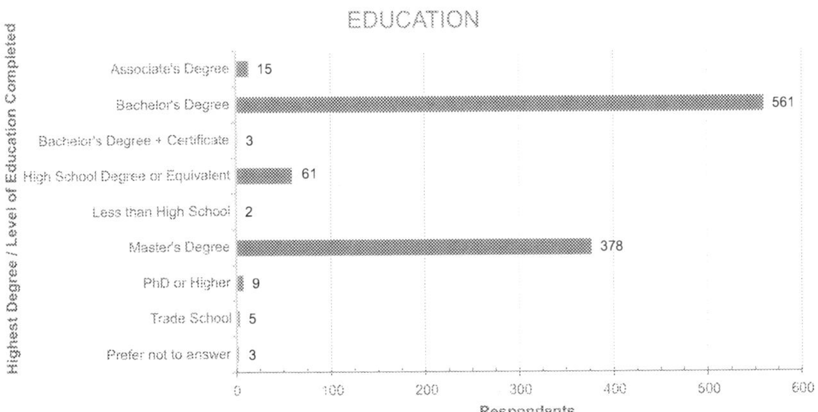

Figure 4.5 Worker responses to "What is the highest degree or level of education you have completed?"

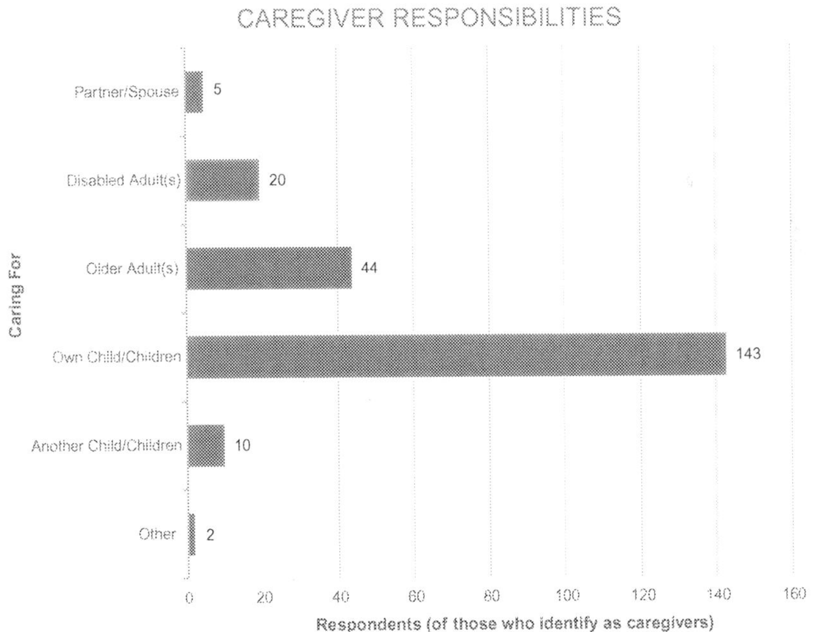

Figure 4.6 Of respondents who answered yes to "Are you a caregiver?", breakdown of worker responses to "Are you caring for:"

worked primarily as freelancers. 285, or 27.48%, worked primarily as a staff member. And the remaining 223 respondents had a relatively equal mix of work as staff members and freelancers. 448 worker respondents (43.20%) were union members. Unions represented included:

- the International Alliance of Theatrical Stage Employees (176 or 16.30%);
- United Scenic Artists Local USA 829, IATSE (191 or 17.79%);
- Actor's Equity Association (77 or 7.13%);
- American Guild of Musical Artists (18 or 1.67%);
- Screen Actors Guild and the American Federation of Television and Radio Artists (2 or 0.19%)
- the American Guild of Variety Artists (1 or 0.09%).

Some respondents indicated membership in multiple unions.

Because we knew that workers responding to our survey were likely to be significantly affected by the COVID-19 Pause, we asked about 2019 and 2021 income. In both cases, workers provided their total individual income including non-theatrical work. In 2019, the majority of workers made between $40,000 and $60,000 annually (248 or 23.92%) or between $20,000 and $40,000 annually (242 or 23.34%), 172 respondents (16.59%) reported making less than $20,000, and only 35 workers (3.38%) reported making over $160,000. By contrast, in 2021, a larger majority of workers, 304 or 29.32%, made $20,000 to $40,000, and 220 workers (21.22%) made less than $20,000. 238 (22.95%) workers made $40,000 to $60,000 in 2021, around 1% fewer than in 2019. Additionally, 13 respondents (1.25%) reported a 2021 income of over $160,000. These numbers support the lack of fully restored theatrical production work following the Pause.

Unsurprisingly, union members in theatrical production make more money than non-union members. For 2019, of the 448 union member respondents, 348 (or 77.7%) reported a production-related income of $40,000 or more. Of the 589 non-union respondents, only 275 (or 46.7%) reported similar income. For 2021, even with the significant financial impacts of the Pause, 289 (or 58.7%) of union members reported a production income of $40,000 or more, in contrast to just 250 (or 42.4%) of non-union members (see Figure 4.9).

Several themes emerged from the respondents' answers to our long form questions. Here we share many of these themes, which we interrogate and elaborate on in Sections Two and Three. Those sections also include extensive research from both the employer surveys and interviews.

Theatrical production is exploitative.

Workers are expected to work exhausting hours in often unsafe conditions for inappropriately low compensation. Survey respondents expressed this exploitation in a variety of ways. When asked if one's identities

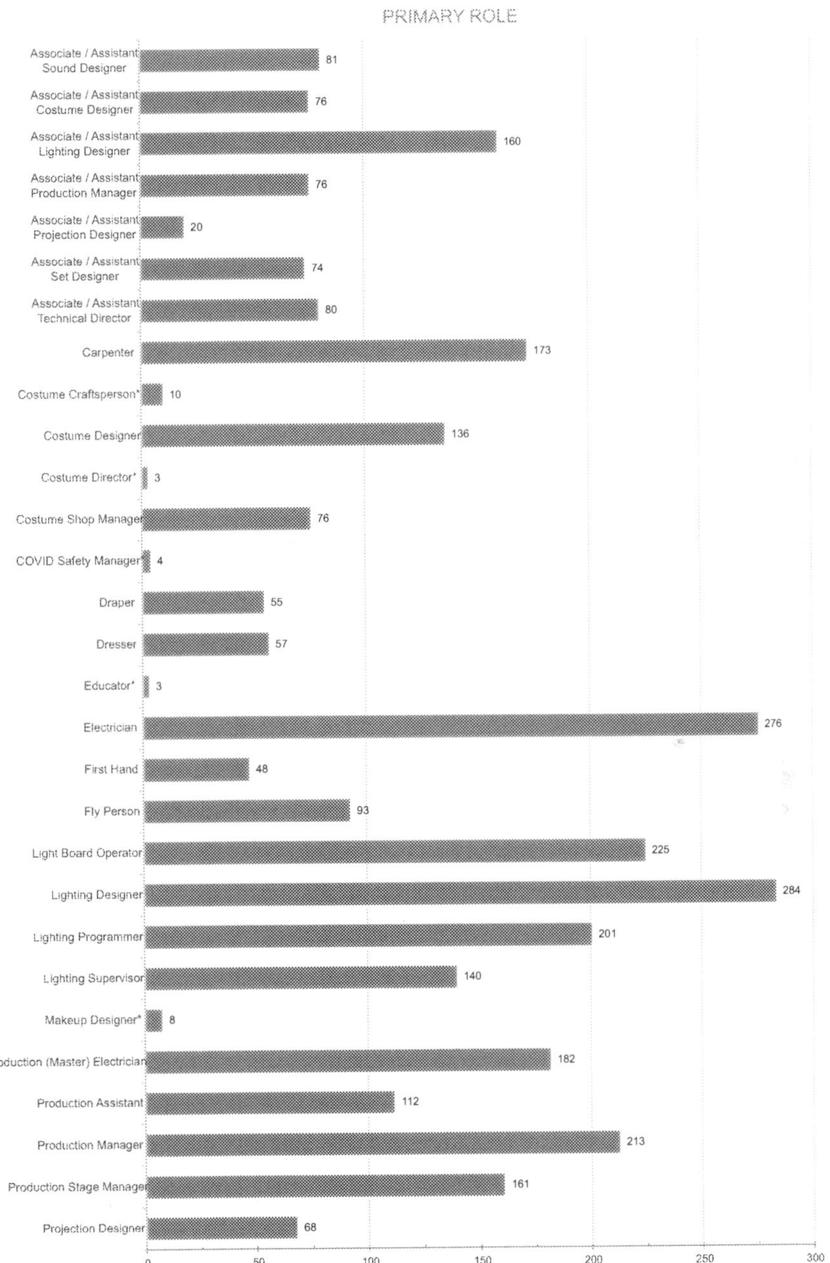

Figure 4.7 Primary Roles, 1 of 2. Worker responses to "Primary Role(s) when you work/worked in theatrical production"

Respondents could check multiple roles and/or self-describe. Responses marked with an asterisk (*) were self-described by respondents. It's important to note that these options were not listed; so there may have been other people who shared these but did not write them in.

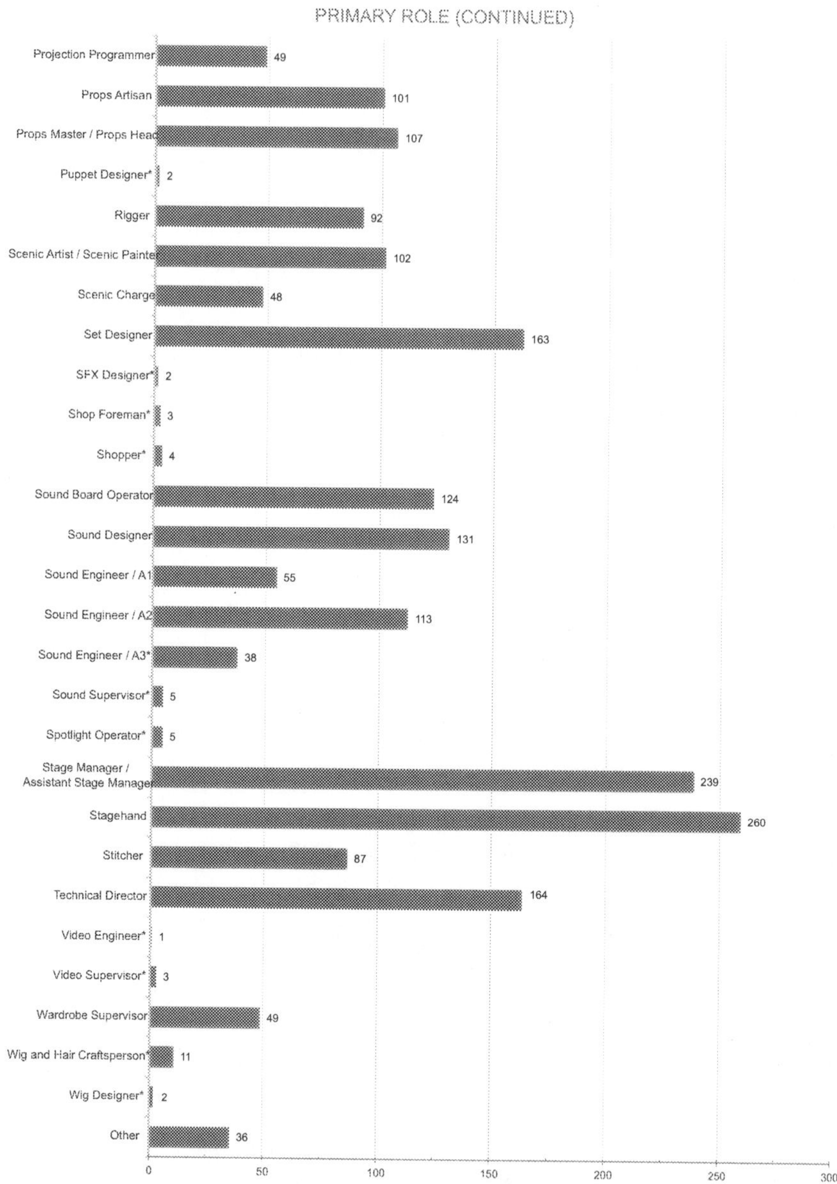

Figure 4.8 Primary Roles, 2 of 2. Worker responses to "Primary Role(s) when you work/worked in theatrical production"

Respondents could check multiple roles and/or self-describe. Responses marked with an asterisk (*) were self-described by respondents. It's important to note that these options were not listed; so there may have been other people who shared these but did not write them in.

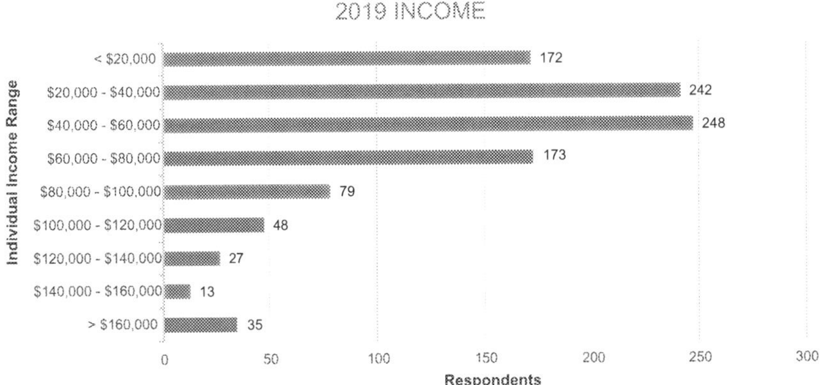

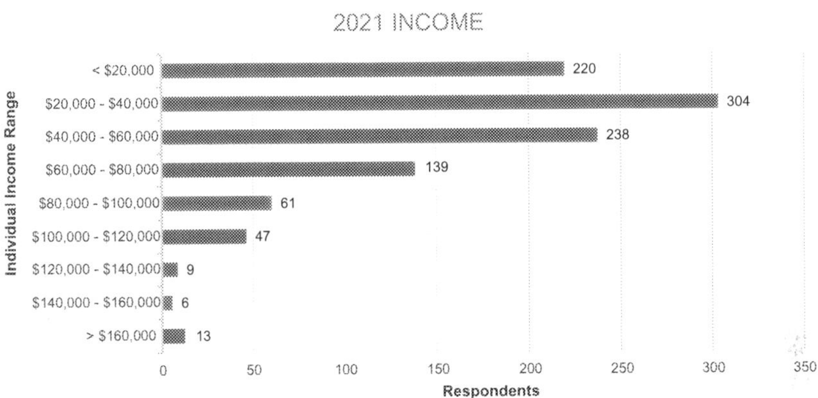

Figure 4.9 Worker responses to "What was your individual income in 2019 (pre-pandemic)?" and "What was your individual income in 2021 (during the pandemic)?"

impacted their decision to leave a theatre production job or the field, one worker shared the unreasonable demands on individual workers:

> I don't want to work in an industry that doesn't value ALL its staff. [...] There's not enough money for the lack of respect and lack of safety respect to do any of these shows. There are just more demands. And after 15 years of that, it wears on you. Hauling 40 sheets of 3/4" cdx ply up the stairs to the theater wears on you when you can't afford to hire help. And this is common. It's not a one off ask, it's not a just this time – it's at all times. And I'm putting myself at risk for $20/hr – which is barely enough to cover rent. It's not worth it.

Another worker explained that the practices of the field led them to leave: "The culture of technical theater is a recipe for burnout and I was toasted.

I was done. I had a chance to change fields and took it. The long unpredictable hours for less that [*sic*] cost of living pay mixed with dealing with microaggressions and the feelings of being other as well as being treated as replaceable was too much burden to handle." Another worker shared the challenges of finding financial stability in production: "One of my identities is that of a blue-collar kid from a blue-collar family – I have had no monetary safety net other than the work that I do in the morning so that I can get to rehearsals/sewing at my kitchen table/tech at night. My parents are aging, I'm in my mid-thirties and didn't have a savings account until 2021 – I've left the field because it was fiscally untenable." Another responded to this question by sharing their safety concerns, "I've left due to sexual harassment that went unaddressed. I've been fired for speaking out about workplace safety issues. I've been called out and my job threatened for bringing up abuse by a designer (as a subordinate)."

There is an endemic reality of low pay and financial barriers in theatrical production. It's often assumed that successful production workers can make quite a lot of money. And, while some can, many can't. In 2022, the USA 829 minimum fee for a lighting designer on a League of Resident Theatre C-1 production was $3,812. A designer is likely to be contracted on the project for several months, with the most intense period from lighting focus through opening to likely be two weeks of more than 60 hours each. A professional designer living in Philadelphia, a city with four local LORT theatres, would have to design ten shows to reach the MIT calculator "living wage" of $36,000. A LORT C theatre like the Wilma Theatre only produces four shows a year. That designer would have to design nearly all of the LORT C productions in Philadelphia in a given year to achieve that living wage, a highly unlikely situation. As one worker responded, "It is increasingly difficult to rationalize staying in the theater industry as a freelance designer when the pay is so atrocious, you need to work at least ten jobs a year to make a minimal living wage and the jobs always overlap, the system protects the theaters and their staff before the designers." These financial realities privilege those workers with financial safety nets:

> I kept seeing male counterparts being paid more for the same amount of work, kept seeing people who came from wealthy families being selected for jobs because they could pour their own money into the production (e.g., a $500 budget would get supplemented by a $1,000 donation from the designer or their parents). After struggling for eight years to make ends meet, constantly working and still falling farther and farther behind on paying off my student loans, I looked around and realized I could not keep up with this competition and one day have a family or life of my own. I know of several other designers who similarly felt 'priced out' of continuing in their field.

The financial barriers carry into workers' work/life balance and family priorities. Many respondents shared that their work in theatrical production limited their ability to have the kind of family lives they hope for, as in this response: "I am leaving theater in order to start a family. The schedule, commitment level, and health insurance would never make that possible while working in theater. My employers would also likely not make accommodations for me to take time off, pump, or be able to raise my child." For workers whose partners also work in production, these concerns are further complicated. One worker shared,

> My partner makes significantly more money as a production rigger than I ever did as a PE [Production Electrician] or SM [Stage Manager]. My identity as the primary caregiver to our children and my partner's frustration any time I had work and he had to turn down more lucrative jobs to be the caregiver led me to decide that the stress of working in the field was too little return for too much emotional, logistical, and financial labor.

Theatrical production is racist.

Consistent with the work done by BIPOC professionals and researchers, our research also showed consistent bias and exploitation directed at BIPOC workers. The majority of respondents to our survey (84.38%) are white. As we acknowledged, that speaks to the reach of the survey, but also is consistent with the overwhelming dominance of white workers in the field as shown in other census-type research. With fewer responses from BIPOC workers, our results have fewer substantial examples of bias but the numbers do speak for themselves.

Most of the experiences shared by BIPOC respondents show a proliferation of microaggressions: "I have had someone come up to me and say, 'Wow, I've never seen a Black woman in your role before.'" Or, "Sometimes designers will pair me with the only other Asian actors in the show or expect me to be the expert in all things Asian." Workers referenced experiences of working on projects where the experiences of folks with marginalized identities were appropriated or told by white artistic leaders: "I have left two productions that ended up with all White creative teams and were focussed on BIPOC experience." These experiences show after show and year after year wear down a worker's desire or ability to advocate for themselves and work through the situation:

> Very few Black women work in costumes that are not the designer. I have found myself being the only Black woman working in most of the shops I have worked. Things can get a bit....out of hand during ED&I training speaking with those colleagues. I have been affected by it greatly and I become tired of trying to change people's mindset, thought process, etc. Even when I don't want to talk about it, I will ultimately have to because I'm the only one around.

As another worker shared, "I left broadway [*sic*] largely because of the workplace culture that felt endemic to the entire field, regardless of individual directors or management. The Blatant Misogyny and Racism was overwhelming. It felt like there was no way to 'move up.'"

There are fewer BIPOC voices in the survey than there should be. This isn't because there aren't BIPOC workers. This is because BIPOC workers have been excluded and silenced. But as the writers of We See You W.A.T. describe,

> What began as a conversation between three theatremakers concerned about the devaluation and violence against Black bodies in the world, quickly evolved into a Zoom call with 30 people, discussing the way racism and white supremacy have also shaped and corrupted our theater institutions, ranging from the universities to not-for-profit and commercial houses.
>
> That three that became 30 then became a mighty 300+ of BIPOC theatremakers who added their signatures to our testimonial letter, demanding a more equitable and safe space for BIPOC communities in our nation and inside of the American Theater.[3]

These voices do exist.

And the theatre industry has begun to listen:

> Since our call to action on 7:00 pm June 8, 2020, within 24 hours our website, weseeyouWAT.com, received 80,000 unique visitors and 50,000 signatories have signed a petition demanding substantive change in the American theater – that number continues to grow by the minute. This outpouring of support is a testament to the widespread and systemic problem of racism many BIPOC continue to face in their field.[4]

This proclamation of 300 became a visible movement, finally saying out loud what had been felt by so many before: Racism is endemic to theatrical production and continues to harm workers every day. Our findings support this claim.

Theatrical production is rife with gender bias and harassment.

We heard from a number of women who cited example after example of ways in which their gender presentation impacted their work environments: "One time I asked a TD for material and when he said no and I said why not he said 'because you're a girl.' This was 2011 but things haven't changed that much; it's just more hidden now." Another worker explained further:

> Sometimes, being a woman means having work taken out of my hands. Sometimes, being a woman means getting sexual talk thrown at me or questions about 'why a pretty lady like you would do this work', etc... Mostly this has happened to me when working as an electrician. Sometimes, being a woman means being doubted by the client and even sometimes by those who hire me. This hurdle can usually be overcome, but it has to be overcome far too often.

> Occasionally, being a woman is useful, especially when working with women artists who are sometimes very happy to work with a female production manager.

Women workers spoke about being taken less seriously, about being sexualized repeatedly at work, about being assumed to be younger or weaker or more fragile than their male coworkers. It's easier for people to not have to adjust their world view. As one worker said, "as a cis-het white man, I fit the 'norm' for a TD or a carpenter in my region. So my identities made it easier for me to get work because people did not have to adjust their expectations of what I could do based on my presentation." These kinds of sexist actions and comments also go un-acted upon by management and leadership: "As a mid-level manager, I reported a member of leadership for microaggressions against myself and other female members of my team. Instead of investigating, the theatre pushed the issue down the road as long as they could and then the pandemic hit, and instead of addressing the issues, they opted to permanently terminate me from my position." And sometimes these microaggressions become actively dangerous: "I have been threatened by male stage hand colleagues, insulted by male directors and harassed by male conductors/singers." Male workers also cited events where they noticed this endemic misogyny:

> Again, I can see that my identity as cis white man lends to different treatment. Not trying to sound profound or anything. I just see it everyday. I've had many female identifying Associate/Assistant PMs and I've been the Assistant/Associate to many badass female identifying PMs (some of whom were younger than me at the time) and have frequently had vendors, designers, contractors, etc. turn to me, ignore my partner's authority, or outright disrespect them right in front of me. I once had a building contractor straight up say to me, 'I don't listen to anything she says.' I f***ing lost it. That's the only time I've ever yelled at work.

Another self-identified straight white male worker shared, "Frankly, many people have been taught to defer and listen to me. For example, if I'm working with a female director and she and I want the same note to happen on stage, the technical team is more likely to do the note if I request it."

Those who occupy non-binary or trans identities also see the ways that perceived gender affects their treatment in workplaces: "I think it took a very long time for me to be taken seriously as a scenic designer while I presented as a woman – after transitioning, my identity became largely irrelevant in comparison to the quality of my work." Another worker shared the other side of a similar coin: "I think that, as I have transitioned to presenting as a woman, some folks in theatre have stopped trusting my thoughts/opinions as much as before. It takes them longer to see that I'm experienced and sometimes they give me less credit for the work I have done." Surviving these environments is exhausting for workers, and the industry loses qualified passionate workers because of the bad treatment:

> After a while, you get tired of trying to prove you know what you're doing. [...] It wears you down, especially when you try to create an inclusive safe working environment and you even get pushback about that because it's the way things have always been done. Some theatres don't care if they burn you out and I learned no one was going to advocate for me (even from leadership) so I left.

Theatrical production, though often seen as a safe haven for LGBTQIAA+ people, still has significant LGBTQIAA+ bias. Repeatedly, workers shared, "I have faced active workplace discrimination as a queer person." Assumptions around the values of a "typical" LGBTQIAA+ workers infiltrate the industry as well: "As a gay person, venues would decide I was a good hire because I was not going to get formally married and have kids so I could work the long hours and cover for others who do have kids. And that I would tolerate rudeness from the white males without complaint." LGBTQIAA+ folks also shared moments of being exploited for their identities, just like BIPOC workers did: "I did a production that was telling transgender journey stories, but was the only trans person on the creative team and the institution was not practicing what it preached on stage, so I left the production after realizing I was being exploited for my identity as trans."

Theatre production workers also experience ageism and ableism. The ageism is felt in both directions – workers who present as younger not being recognized for their experience or expertise, and workers who present as older being "phased out" or not considered due to their age. One worker shared, "I have had to fight against both ageism and sexism in my career – often I am treated by default as if I'm brand new to the industry when I have 12 years of experience under my belt." Another worker shared, "A producer asked me if I knew of any designers 'who were young with fresh ideas,'" implying that older designers couldn't perhaps present as exciting work. And another worker shared their disappointment in aging in an industry that values youth; "This is not an easy answer as I now am 35 + years in the business. I'm now looking at ageism – I have constant concern that my years of experience will not be an advantage."

Workers spoke of disabilities, neurodivergences, and age being a factor in being treated as "incompetent" or "unable" to do the work. Workers shared that theatres prioritized accessibility for audiences and actors without consideration of those working backstage. Few physical accommodations were made in often-hazardous workplaces. And physical fitness was assumed to be a requirement even in those jobs which didn't explicitly demand it.

And, as in all experiences of bias, those workers who occupy multiple marginalized identities experience multiple forms of bias. One male, gay Jewish worker shared:

> I once had a carpenter in a lift tell me that I'm 'going to hell' because I was at work on a Saturday with a Kippah on. I try to wear an alternative head covering (like a baseball hat) because of this and general antisemitism.
>
> I've had supervisors and colleagues tease me about not eating bacon, since some come to work every morning with a Bacon Egg and Cheese. I'm not good about standing up for myself and brush it off and always say it's ok when the teasing crosses the line.
>
> Also – I've had the same prop guy tell me 'Oh, your wife should see you doing that' when I have been running around with a swiffer cleaning small moving lights on an automated wagon during a work call. I jokingly responded both times 'Yeah, my future husband will love it.'

Another worker shared, "I have had derogatory comments directed at me because I'm a cis female and because I'm Asian American. I have had derogatory comments directed at me because I'm a dresser."

In Section Two, we investigate these themes further and get into some of the more specific findings from the worker survey, as well as findings from the employer survey and interviews. We look at issues surrounding access to education and careers; hiring practices; pay equity; production operations; people operations; and labor and safety. We examine how the roads to career access are affected by inconsistent arts education and the expectation of unpaid and underpaid labor, and we investigate how historical hiring practices have led to a place where the majority of people in the field are cis-men and white. When hiring is based on the norm of using word-of-mouth and referrals for candidate searches, access is limited from the beginning. Even once workers have secured jobs in the industry, vast pay inequities affect those of marginalized genders and those working in traditionally gendered parts of the field. The experiences of these workers and others shape a narrative of the current circumstances facing production workers following the Pause and raise a number of questions around if, and whether, there are ways for the theatrical production industry to be more accessible, inclusive, and sustainable.

These questions, and this struggle, are not unique to theatrical production. As Saru Jayaraman reminds us:

> I think right now we're in such a fantastic, historic, incredible, exciting moment of worker power, and where workers are inspiring each other across industries. And so we just need more and more and more of the same. [...] This is the moment to think big, go big, move policy, and share information across sectors so that workers can be inspiring each other.[5]

NOTES

1 Saru Jayaraman (President, One Fair Wage), interview by the authors, September 2022.
2 Jayaraman, interview.
3 "About," We See You, White American Theatre, accessed September 8, 2022, https://www.weseeyouwat.com/about.
4 We See You, White American Theatre, "About."
5 Jayaraman, interview.

Section Two

WHERE WE ARE

What do you see as the biggest current challenge for production labor?

Capitalism. Period. We need to shift from scarcity thinking to abundance thinking. And we have the people, we have the resources, we have the creativity to do what we do. Instead, we are choosing profit.

Michael Maag, Resident Lighting Designer, Oregon Shakespeare Festival

It's inherently exploitative.

Pat Landers, Business Representative for Health & Safety, United Scenic Artists

We have to get out of our own way. Gone should be the days of shouting down people. I know that the buck has to stop someplace, but I think that it can be a gentle tugging of the reins rather than a slap in the face to get there. I think people are really wanting a sense of belonging. They want to take pride in their work. They want to share it with their family and friends. And I think that's when we've arrived when we're able to do that.

David "dStew" Stewart, Co-Founder, Production on Deck

I mean, we talk about COVID and the mass exodus of theater workers, but we also need to recognize that it's not just COVID, it's the precarity that the system has supported for decades and decades and decades. And the lack of people's ability to have savings or any kind of safety net for themselves. That's obviously exacerbated by COVID, and the shutdowns, but the precarity was always there. So because of that, people have left the industry and we as an industry are directly responsible for that. We set up the system, we've been working within it, we haven't done much or enough to address it. Knowing that those two things are directly tied is important.

Elsa Hiltner, Co-Founder, On Our Team

Burnout.

Jessa-Raye Court, Co-Founder, Costume Professionals for Wage Equity

Expectations of the work not changing. There is a paradox between 'we are going to be a kinder, gentler industry, but we're still going to have all these deadlines and this sense of urgency. We are trying to shift out of that mindset to a new one.' It's a major shift. And we all have to be a part of that solution.

Angela Gieras, Executive Director, Kansas City Rep

I would like to say it's the tight labor market, but I'm not necessarily buying that these days. We've lost quite a lot of folks. And we have relied so heavily on our own internal navel-gazing way of inviting folks in. I think that we haven't replenished those pathways in quite a while. And that is not the sole responsibility of Executive Leadership. That's actually our collective responsibility, including individual Lighting Directors, Master Electricians, Shop Supervisors, and so on...

that invitation and workforce development work actually needs to happen by other technical practitioners as well.

Stephanie Ybarra, then Artistic Director, Baltimore Center Stage

Money.

Sarah Clare Corporandy, Co-Founder & Producing Artistic Director, Detroit Public Theatre

Wages. Too long hours for too little pay, literally not enough to live on.

Sarah Lozoff, Co-Founder, Production on Deck

It's that 'this is the way it always is'.

Anyania Muse, Interim Chief Operating Officer, Oregon Shakespeare Festival

Lack of training and clarity on how to gain a job.

Lauren Parrish, Associate Director of Production, Abrons Arts Center

I don't think we're having these transparent, authentic conversations in or asking these kinds of questions as a field. I think what's happening is, there's still a little bit of: *I'm going to keep trying to do it the way that we've done it before. I'm going to make some adjustments. But I'm not going to ask some of these crucial questions of – if I'm going to corporations, foundations and individuals who benefit from this hierarchy, why would they invest in something that's potentially destabilizing it?* And letting that question linger in rooms. It comes down to what dialectic is going to be centered and what's behind pursuing funding from those who benefit from centering narratives that maintain or distract from discourse centered in reifying an inequitable status quo. The patron arts model means someone's on top giving and someone's at the bottom receiving because of the giver's power and largesse. The charity model is not sustainably rooted in equity like a solidarity model. It does not nurture equity. It's not based in operating assumptions that equity is a benefit to the ecosystem. So, the question is, why do we keep prioritizing going to those parties, when we know it's not based in mutual interests? Maintaining privilege for a monolithic group of the world's wealthiest and those in proximity to that requires extraction from and exploitation of someone, an underclass. Going for support there for what we do, obligates us to tell stories that center perspectives and ideology that compromise much needed social transformation; narratives that disenfranchise and gaslight rather than comprehensively liberate people. Why are we not centering those questions and actively initiating more grassroots social justice and anti-racist philanthropy, cultivating donors of color and the smaller but, perhaps, more culturally aligned donor? Then we might have discourse resonate, engaging and inspiring enough to capture people's attention, imagination, curiosity, to show up and support the work at a scale that offsets the increased production costs that are currently making our work economically unsustainable.

Robert Barry Fleming, Executive Artistic Director, Actors Theater of Louisville

WET PAINT
NFG
WELCOME

5

CAREER ACCESS

To think about who works in the arts, we have to start with who *can* work in the arts. And to think about who has access to a career in the arts, and specifically, in theatrical production, we must think about the following questions:

- Who has access to arts education?
- Who has access to higher education in general, and the privilege of pursuing the arts in higher ed?
- What is the relationship between internships and careers in theatrical production?
- How does underpaid work impact production career trajectories?

Digging into these four questions provides some context about the barriers to careers in the arts overall, and, specifically, to those in theatrical production.

WHO HAS ACCESS TO ARTS EDUCATION?

The benefits of arts education are well documented in social and emotional development, as well as part of a satisfying and holistic education. Starting

DOI: 10.4324/9781003330394-7

at a very early age, not all children have equal access to arts education. Access is often affected by race, socio-economic status, location, school funding models, and other factors outside of the child's, or family's, control.

Though "an overwhelming majority of the American public (88 percent) agrees that the arts are part of a well-rounded K-12 education – including 56 percent who 'strongly agree,'"[1] the funding doesn't reflect this: according to the National Endowment for the Arts' Survey of Public Participation in the Arts (SPPA), the last three decades have seen a decline in access to arts education, which many account to schools' increased emphasis on subjects that can be measured for test-based accountability.[2] The declining funding for arts education also perpetuates racial inequalities: "Though white students have experienced virtually no declines in arts education since the mid-1980s, African American students have experienced reductions of 49%, and Hispanic/Latinx students have experienced reductions of 40%. Numerous local audits have found that schools serving low-income students often provide no arts education or lack an arts teacher."[3]

In many school districts, especially those with limited funding, arts education is outsourced to local arts and culture organizations. For example, studying challenges to access and opportunity for arts education in Jacksonville, Florida, specifically, Alarie Gibbs found:

> The challenges include: lack of funding, lack of resources, oversaturation of existing arts and culture programs, the forgotten middle-income schools, and the need for arts to reach all demographics. Additionally, the lack of support from policymakers and the need to respond to mandates concerning K-12 schools are also challenges to access to and opportunity for arts education.[4]

These barriers are common throughout many communities across the US. This inequity prevents some students from gaining not only the social and educational development granted by arts education but also from exposure to the arts themselves. According to the American Academy of Arts and Sciences:

> Students in high-needs schools and historically underserved populations have been hit the hardest. This is especially troubling and bitterly ironic, as the same students experiencing declines are those who rely most on public schools to provide enriching arts experiences. More affluent families are twice as likely to provide such experiences for their children outside the school system. As a result, families with fewer resources are much less likely to have arts experiences if schools fail to provide them.[5]

Parents may have to seek out arts organizations; there can be geographical hurdles like living far from the well-funded and well-known organizations; and there are often financial deterrents including the high cost of private classes. Actress and arts educator Elasia Gray explains that for the handful of kids of color who do join these predominantly white spaces, their talents and skills can't always be fully realized as they often face many additional challenges, from disconnection with the material being presented, to teaching artists' implicit bias, to fear of speaking up and being labeled, to navigating racial microaggressions from their predominantly white peers or teachers. These things can start early in one's education, and as students continue to middle and high school and the social status layers deepen, these challenges heighten.[6]

Young people must encounter successful models who look and sound like them, doing the things they want to do. Gray insists, "Having diverse educators in performing arts is crucial, not only to provide support and guidance for students of all backgrounds, but also for the predominantly white workspaces they occupy."[7] Students of color who are able to access arts education are still not meeting that education with the same privileges of their white classmates. Gray continued, "There also needs to be more spaces strictly for kids of color, with educators of color, so the kids can explore their creative ideas comfortably and freely – utopias, if you will."[8] Clint Ramos, a Filipino-American costume and set designer, advocate, and educator, has seen the impacts of the lack of representation first hand: "There is a dearth of young artists of color going into design for the theatre," says Ramos. "And part of that is because they don't see themselves in it. I never saw people who looked like me. I was never exposed to them. I had to seek them out." It creates a vicious cycle, he explains. "How can we address the problem when we can't attract young artists of color into the design field?"[9]

Young people might see potential futures for themselves if they are able to see theatre as audience members. If they aren't seeing theatre, then they aren't gaining familiarity with the art form or seeing theatremakers who look like them. A 2019 State of the Field Report from Theatre for Young Audiences finds that young people across various regions of the US have significantly differing levels of access to theatre performances.[10] Students in schools without arts programs are likely more affected by the accompanying lack of access to professional performances.

These inequities continue through primary school and high school. When beginning her college studies at Savannah College of Art & Design, Black lighting designer Amber Whatley saw that she was at a disadvantage compared to her white peers who had access to high school theatre training. Her passion for theatre and design had been ignited at an early age. Raised in Montgomery, Alabama, she

> remembers being fascinated at an early age by how colors played together and how objects reflected light differently depending on their environment. She was lucky to have guidance counselors advocate for her to attend George Washington Carver Elementary Performing Arts and Magnet School through fifth grade. This is where she was introduced to the theatre, stage management, and lighting. In a lucky twist of fate, Amber's first drama teacher, Ms. Stewart, just so happened to be a Black female, a rare occurrence that ended up making a big difference in Amber's future career goals.[11]

But her high school training didn't include theatre. And that made her success in college and beyond even more hard won. She explains, "I knew my peers in my program came to college with four full years of theater experience, and the last time I had any theater involvement was when I was 11."[12] This has become her primary motivation in helping to create educational opportunities for future BIPOC theatremakers.

Longtime friends and colleagues David Stewart (known to friends and colleagues as dStew) and the late Tayneshia Jefferson dedicated time and energy to these same questions. Jefferson, a stage manager and production manager, was a member of the USITT Board of Directors who began volunteering for USITT's Stage Management Mentoring Project in 2005 and served as the USITT Vice-Commissioner for Stage Management and chair of its People of Color Caucus.[13] She and dStew, also a production manager, found common goals in advocacy for BIPOC students. In their work, the two looked into the question of why fewer BIPOC students might pursue careers in theatrical production. Similar to Whatley's experience, they pointed out that the need for recruitment efforts begins at the middle school level and that myths about the industry are impacting recruitment. They explained:

> Many minority students hail from families who are unwilling to invest thousands of dollars in a theatre education because they don't understand the potential for sustainable employment in the field. Like many parents, they desire a more practical course of study for their progeny, presuming that the choice to pursue theatre will lead to a future fraught with chronic poverty. A theatre layman will automatically assume that the rate of employment for our end of the business is comparable to that of a performer, when the truth is exactly opposite; because we are not performers our employment ratio is much more encouraging. With the exception of a few, brief, stints, we both have been consistently employed as working theatre professionals for 20+ years.[14]

Jefferson and dStew suggested that there needs to be a focus on building awareness that careers in theatre production are viable and not as risky as perceived, and that this needs to start early.

WHO HAS ACCESS TO HIGHER EDUCATION IN GENERAL, AND THE PRIVILEGE OF PURSUING THE ARTS IN HIGHER ED?

In their Howlround essay "Not a Pipeline Problem, a Problem with the Pipeline," lighting designers and authors Amber Whatley, Sherrice Mojgani, and Calvin Anderson explore the key role that education plays in reforming and reimagining the culture of theatrical design.[15] Citing the frequent claim that the lack of diversity in the theatrical production field is due to a supposed "pipeline" problem, the authors point out this assessment implies a single path into professional theatre, and the false claim that the reason there are not more production workers of the global majority is that they don't exist. The authors argue that the traditional education system does not create a clear path to success for all designers who do not fit the mold of the dominant culture. They suggest that the education system is simultaneously a symptom and a source of this problem and that much of the education system reinforces the systemic issues that have led to an inequitable field.[16] As we discussed, access to arts education and exposure is closely tied to issues of race inequity:

> Extensive research has conclusively demonstrated that children's social class is one of the most significant predictors – if not the single most significant predictor – of their educational success. Moreover, it is increasingly apparent that performance gaps by social class take root in the earliest years of children's lives and fail to narrow in the years that follow.[17]

These inequities continue into the college years and beyond. As it stands right now, "about 61.3% of workers in careers related to theater obtain at least bachelor's degrees."[18] Of workers who completed our survey, 91.8% have at least a bachelor's degree. In an industry without explicit educational requirements, the presence of this many workers with degrees puts those without the resources to obtain even a bachelor's degree at a distinct disadvantage. According to DataUSA, "tuition costs for Technical Theatre Design & Technology majors are, on average, $7,070 for in-state public colleges, and $37,396 for out of state private colleges."[19] More specifically, as of the writing of this book, the cost of attendance, which includes not just tuition, but cost of living and supplies, ranges from $30,710 per year for an undergraduate degree at Cal State Fullerton[20] to $96,608 per year for a BFA at NYU's Tisch School of the Arts.[21] This is a prohibitive cost for many students and families or, potentially, creates a lifetime of student debt for those who cannot front the cost of this education. As the authors of "Not a Pipeline Problem, a Problem with the Pipeline" suggest, we must analyze and revisit traditional theatre education, and accept that there are multiple paths for entry into a career in theatrical design.[22]

In the case of those students who can afford the degree, what are they getting for it? Former co-director of the IATSE Stagecraft Department, D. Joseph Hartnett, who served as the Master Electrician and union steward for the Pittsburgh Public Theater before moving on to a career in touring and then in union work, explains how he sees this change:

> When I first joined – I have a degree in history from Duquesne University in education – but I was one of the few people working backstage who even had gone to college. And now more and more people are coming out of these training programs. [...] I would say that there are steps within academia that need to be made to actually understand how the industry works and functions. And when the vast majority of the college programs are not providing additional training to actually work within the industry, if you're not becoming a designer, for instance, there's a lot of universities where set construction, or even light hangs and focuses are done by subcontracted employees, and everything along those lines. And typically, they're not getting a lot of the hands-on direct training beyond, you know, lab work and everything along those lines.[23]

If the expectation is that production workers have access to higher education, how can the inequities to that access be addressed? Is higher education the answer at all?

WHAT IS THE RELATIONSHIP BETWEEN INTERNSHIPS AND CAREERS IN THEATRICAL PRODUCTION?

Perhaps because of its deep connection to the trades, a lot of theatre training outside of academia has historically been through work experience. Alexandre Frenette, a major contributor of scholarly writing about artistic workers and the intern economy, explains:

> The intern economy is the latest iteration of a millennia-old tradition of work-based learning. As apprenticeships were part of a social and economic system marked by guild and state control in lieu of widespread schooling, internships today are greatly facilitated by institutions of higher education as a complement to classroom learning (and, in some cases, a stepping stone to employment). Despite a decrease in work-based learning earlier in the 20th century, internships made a considerable ascent, notably because of government initiatives, economic and demographic factors, and a favorable intellectual assessment of experiential education.[24]

Internships, and other work-based learning opportunities, have come to be expected for young people pursuing careers in theatrical production in particular. They provide early career theatre practitioners with access to the kinds of opportunities that Hartnett described, where they can hone their skills, familiarize themselves with the inner workings of professional theatres, build relationships with more experienced workers, and access a network of current and former interns from the given organization.

Employers in the US must comply with the Fair Labor Standards Act (FLSA) to ensure that their unpaid internship programs meet the law. The FLSA establishes standards for minimum wages, overtime pay, recordkeeping, and child labor. The Act permits the employment of certain individuals, including vocational education student learners, at wage rates below the statutory minimum wage under certificates issued by the Department of Labor.[25] Under the FLSA, any employee of a for-profit company must be paid for their work. However, interns and students may not be considered employees under FLSA. Unpaid internships are deemed legal as long as the intern, not the employer, is the "primary beneficiary" of the work arrangement.[26] These standards apply to for-profit companies specifically. Unpaid internships for public sector and non-profit charitable organizations, where the intern volunteers without expectation of compensation, are generally permissible.[27]

In Frenette's dissertation "The Intern Economy: Laboring to Learn in the Music Industry," he explores how internships really function, and if and how they benefit interns and companies. Frenette examines how people succeed within the intern economy, finding that it is possible for interns to elevate their status and move beyond the characteristics and constraints of the role, though notions of race, class, age, and gender inform the selection and evaluation of interns. Frenette notes that there has been public and media outcry around the variation in the educational content and oversight of internships, precarious legal standing, and uneven opportunities they grant, but reports of the unpaid internship's imminent death are highly premature.[28]

Frenette also analyzes how the intern economy reproduces social inequality. He finds that interns typically experience "a very informal intern selection process, which accentuates a vetting process during the internship as opposed to before."[29] Many employers who hire interns lack clear criteria for intern selection; since the candidates don't have a lot of professional experience, it's difficult for employers to maintain a consistent list of background experiences they're seeking. This leads those hiring interns to trust their "gut."[30] In most cases, hiring decisions are prone to cultural matching or homosocial reproduction,[31] "the tendency of people to select incumbents who are socially similar to themselves."[32] Informal hiring decisions are particularly prone to these types of biases.[33] Frenette points out that "the informality of intern selection belies and facilitates a series of taken-for-granted assumptions and conventions that obscure the reproduction of social inequalities."[34] If those in management are already members of the dominant social group or groups, then so too will the people they hire.

I, Brídín, have often been responsible for managing the intern application and selection process at theatre organizations where I've worked. More than once I've received "guidance" from executive leadership, encouraging me to hire a relative of their own, of a board member, or of a friend. To some, the idea of doing someone a favor and offering their nephew an unpaid internship may not seem as problematic as the same process for an actual paying job. But each of these steps are impactful, contributing to an inequitable ecosystem.

In 2015, the Strategic National Arts Alumni Project (SNAAP) published findings from a national study that confirmed the value of internships for arts students. Interestingly, the study suggests that "paid internships are more effective than unpaid internships in leading to professional success."[35] In 2021, SNAAP published a special report titled "Growing Divides: Historical and Emerging Inequities in Arts Internships," a revealing deep dive into the efficacy, popularity, and growing inequities that are reshaping the intern economy.[36] The report looks at internships in architecture and design; art education, history, or administration; fine or studio arts; media arts; and performing arts. Consistent with the pressure on students to obtain hands-on experience, the study shows that recent graduates are more likely to indicate that they interned for career-oriented reasons, whereas graduates from earlier decades are more likely to indicate that they interned for educational reasons.[37] Corresponding with the research surrounding access to early arts education:

> first-generation college graduates are significantly less likely to support themselves during their internship through private wealth or family support than are non-first-generation college graduates. Recent graduates are increasingly more likely than prior graduates not to intern because they cannot afford to do so.[38]

The career access barriers here are clear.

Many of the early career opportunities in the theatre are unpaid or underpaid even though the interns are in fact doing necessary work. In part, this is because the theatre industry, as it currently operates financially, can't function without the unpaid labor. Theatres haven't budgeted for labor they have never paid for. From the beginning, education was embedded into the goals of the resident theatre movement. Young artists learned by doing, working in all aspects of production as they received opportunities to train with established artists and take on small performance or production roles. Over time, this foundation morphed into a dependence. Theatres provide education to early career professionals, and they are dependent on the labor of those early career professionals to staff their productions, offices, box offices, and concession stands. Those students-as-workers are then expected, if not required, to be able to work for free or for very low wages. Often they are even given crucial tasks which put the safety of their colleagues and audiences in the hands of those deemed too unskilled to be paid. This is far removed from the traditional guild or union apprentice model where student-workers learn a craft alongside a teacher-master.

Through our worker survey, we found how common the experience of unpaid and underpaid work is for theatre production workers. Of the 1,037 production workers who completed the survey, 478 of them, or 46%, participated in an unpaid theatrical production internship at some point in their career. Of that group, 49% had completed more than one unpaid internship, suggesting that about a quarter of theatre production workers participate in more than one unpaid internship. In addition, 69.7% of respondents who had completed unpaid internships said that the internships directly affected their career trajectory in ways that they can identify.

The relationships and mentorship that can be gained from internships are crucial steps toward establishing a network in live production work. In a field where word of mouth gets most workers hired, who you know really matters. One of the respondents to the worker survey shared:

> All of my opportunities came out of the unpaid internships I did. The first paid a $100/wk stipend, and the person I worked for got me my first job in New York at a Broadway audio shop and supported me as a mentor for years after I worked for him. The second unpaid internship was on a Broadway show and allowed me to meet a designer and other colleagues that I still work with. That designer still gives me work regularly, including several of my Broadway Associate credits. He also acted as a mentor and helped me when I was starting out in New York.

Building a new network is a huge advantage given to those who can take on an internship. In *Working Backstage: A Cultural History and Ethnography of Technical Theater Labor*, Essin describes how some early career technical theatre professionals in NYC gain professional training and find work:

> If they grew up in the tri-state area and are related to IATSE members, they might have learned their skills from industry mentorships. Otherwise, it is likely that they gained skills by participating in the staging of plays, musicals, operas, and dance in high school and college theater departments. New York City transplants looking for technical theater work – costume crafts, dressing, hair and makeup, carpentry, lighting, sound properties, or child guardianship – quickly encounter a complex web of rules and industry relationships that regulate their employment opportunities. Those who arrive without a local connection, a family member or friend established in the industry who can guide their job search and recommend them to prospective employers, might advance more slowly.[39]

Many workers who responded to our survey shared that these networks created clear future job opportunities. One in particular said:

> I was able to jumpstart my career in a way that I would not have been able to, because I was able to take these unpaid long positions. One of the hardest parts of working in technical theater is how difficult it can be to break into the scene, especially as a freelance designer, and having the connections from my internships and apprenticeship gave me a real advantage over people who were not given the same opportunities.

In recent years, the Williamstown Theater Festival has been the focus of much discussion around this dependency on intern and underpaid labor and the harm it causes. In early 2021, an anonymous collective called WTF, Williamstown?! brought attention to the inequitable and exploitative labor model at Williamstown in a broadside they shared with the festival's board of directors. The collective claimed that "Williamstown Theatre Festival's producing model, primarily built on the unpaid labor of young artists, discriminates against, dehumanizes, and historically harms artists – specifically, the marginalized communities of Black, Indigenous, POC, LGBTQ+ and non-binary people, disabled people, women, and those at these communities' intersections."[40] The *Los Angeles Times* ran an exposé on the workings of the institution, which named this harm in a variety of ways:

> 'Young, unskilled labor are trusted to perform safety-driven tasks, and it's scary,' said Barbara Samuels, a former associate lighting supervisor who, as an intern, almost fell from a truss structure. 'And it gets normalized, because we're taught that "accidents happen," as if it's a single accident and not an entire, unsafe work environment.'[41]

In July 2021, in the midst of the first season after the Pause, after weeks in this abusive environment, things came to a head. The staff and interns were paid much less than a living, or in some cases a minimum, wage. They had been working long hours on a production which had been faced with innumerable trials. And it just kept raining. "Whenever rehearsals were paused for intermittent, heavier rain, the cast of actors working under Equity union rules stayed dry under tents or in the museum's auditorium. But others weren't so lucky."[42] In the midst of pouring rain, when asked to resume work in an obviously unsafe environment, the entire sound crew took a stand, walking out of a tech rehearsal for Williamstown's outdoor production of *Row.*[43] No one should be asked to work with electricity and equipment when there is a danger of lightning.

The following day, the festival leadership agreed to provide modest pay increases and improved working conditions to the production team. In response to the festival leadership claiming that the wellbeing and safety of the team is of the utmost importance, one team member shared:

> This is a Band-Aid on the bigger problem that is the way this festival treats its workers, and especially how it abuses the youngest and most vulnerable theater workers who are just entering the industry, and don't know that they can and should stand up for themselves.[44]

Williamstown is just one example of a theatre organization whose producing model relies on intern and unpaid labor. Also in the summer of 2021, actress Sarah Dew wrote an open letter to the Eugene O'Neill Theater Center in response to a job posting for a Production Apprentice. She named the inconsistencies between their stated mission and their institutional practices:

> However, in spite of the bold work you claim to be committed to, it appears you're equally committed to perpetuating a cycle of labor abuse and gatekeeping with your apprenticeship programs and that little has actually been learned from the exposure of systemic oppression throughout 2020.[45]

Dew goes on to point out the the specific position in question is untenable and a perpetuation of systemic gatekeeping:

> For a salary of $150 a week, plus housing and 'experience', you are expecting someone to work 8–12 hrs a day, 5–6 days a week. While you don't require them to have a car, it's considered a plus to their application if they do. Additionally, you have a note that your apprenticeships are a part of an 'On Call' team, a vague point that suggests hours longer and more extensive than you state earlier in the job posting.
>
> This is so far below a living wage, it could almost be read as satire. In spite of your statement on EDI, you've made an entry-level position untenable for anyone whose socioeconomic status requires them to earn a substantial salary to survive. Millennials and Gen Z-ers are saddled with more debt than any other generation in the history of America. To accept a job with these expectations and salary would be fiscally irresponsible for anyone except people whose family or other benefactors could support their lifestyle. [...] Positions like this perpetuate a cycle in which only the already rich have access, and those at an economic disadvantage are forced down another career path.[46]

The O'Neill workers themselves issued a "Call In To the Eugene O'Neill Theater Center" on July 17, 2021. In this letter they outlined a timeline of discussions that had taken place about the ethics of the O'Neill apprenticeship program, shared a list of grievances, acknowledged progress around these issues, and made clear their further demands framed within a call for collaboration.[47] They framed their ask quite clearly:

> This is not a call out, but a call in. Please know this is not meant to be inflammatory. We are writing this because of the potential we see within the institution for growth, collaboration, and improvement, and our desire for the O'Neill to not only be the place where the theatre of tomorrow is created, but a leader in the building of the new, equitable standards of the American theatre. It is also our belief that we can build a better work environment for all of us, together.[48]

Their demands included a living wage based on the CT minimum wage; a regular weekend day off; and a limit of the span of workdays to ten hours, all of which are consistent with legal requirements. They asked that workers be required to clock in and out to maintain these work rules and pay transparency. They also demanded antiracism training; mental health check-ins; subsidies for living costs (like laundry, food, and O'Neill merchandise); and intentionality around the internship and apprenticeship activities. All of these requests line up with a basic list of demands for respect and consideration for interns and apprentices as workers and as human beings. The letter was "Signed, the Apprentices and Writer's Assistants of Summer 2021, with the support of artists on campus."[49]

As a response to these worker demands, as of July 27, 2021, an Instagram post quoted by Dew shares that senior staff at the O'Neill promise a reconsideration of the apprenticeship program plus:

- an increase in pay (from $150/week) to $200/week (including back pay)
- antiracism training for all staff
- hours reduced to 40 hours per week
- a second day off per week
- additional staff hired (and more to come) to support staff in the final weeks of programming this summer
- laundry stipends.[50]

Are these changes, and the ones made at Williamstown, enough? Absolutely not. They are a step but a small one.

These situations provide questions worth digging deeply into. So much of the work in production is dependent on a working knowledge of skills and technology that can't be fully gained from a classroom setting. Even the unsafe practices endemic at summer stock theatres, like Williamstown and the O'Neill, provide skill-building in real world situations. One stage manager who responded to the survey explained:

> I worked as an unpaid intern for a full season, including acting as [production assistant], ASM [assistant stage manager], and rehearsal [stage manager] on

> every show, at Book-It Repertory Theatre, a mid-sized theatre in Seattle that operates under AEA SPT [Small Professional Theater] rules. At the end of my internship, I was offered the (now paid) ASM role on Book-It's next two shows (first contract non-AEA, second contract AEA), which directly came from my intern experience. All of this experience combined launched my stage management career, and without it I doubt I'd be where I am today.

The hands-on experience and resume items show potential employers that a worker has the skills they might need on a job, as another respondent shared:

> I have not had to apply for a theater job since my internship. My skills and qualities proved valuable to those around me and I'm offered every job I've had from the network I made at this internship. I have risen from a costume intern, to a paid costume designer, a wardrobe supervisor, a primary stitcher in a shop, and I have been offered National tours.

Yet another respondent to our survey said, internships "gave me an opportunity to develop my skills and knowledge in a real production setting, generated professional connections with both individuals and institutions that have led to future work and/or mentorship relationships, added to my professional credits." I, Brídín, participated in four internships (a variety of paid and unpaid, as well as for-credit and not) throughout my time at university, which was possible because of financial support from my parents throughout these four years, and housing support from extended family during one of the internships. These internships supplemented what I was learning in school, serving as a bridge between my academic training and my early career work. All of my paid work in my first two years out of school can be directly tied to those internship experiences, and the relationships I developed during those internships have continued to shape my career over the past decade. Internships clearly help emerging production professionals build networks, gain skills, and find future employment opportunities – opportunities which aren't available to those for whom internships aren't feasible.

So what about the early career professionals who can't afford to take unpaid or underpaid work? What about the college students who have to work to contribute to their tuition or living expenses? What about those without family or parental support? Early-career theatre practitioner and writer Ciara Diane asked these questions at the beginning of the COVID-19 shutdown when many aspects of the inequitable system came into sharp focus. Her own experiences shaped her articulate argument:

> We're not only expected to pay our dues to theatre with our willingness to put in hours of low or barely compensated artmaking; we also have to work time-consuming and exhausting survival jobs. It now takes people who are working minimum- and low-wage jobs more hours of work to afford living than it did

> 20, or even 10 years ago. What that means for theatremakers is that we have significantly less time to do anything that isn't sufficiently paying us. As much as we want to be singularly focused on growing our skills and talent, that type of time is often something we simply cannot afford.[51]

Melody Marshall, another young theatre production worker Diane interviewed for a piece in *American Theatre* said, "[Interns] do still have skills and experiences that are useful, and when someone works, they deserve to be paid. Yeah, you have the connections and the experience and the résumé credit, but sometimes eating is nice."[52] Unpaid work is only accessible to those who can afford it. Over the summer of 1999, between college semesters, I, Natalie, interned at New York Theatre Workshop while living at home in NJ. I was paid $50 a week for 3 full days of work per week, which included everything from sweeping the stage to reorganizing the lighting gel stock. And in 2003, I interned at Williamstown, where I paid for housing (luckily, I was able to sublet my room in NYC), and my parents gave me money for food and gas. I worked that summer with exactly one day off, often too exhausted to be safe. Both of these experiences were only possible because of a significant amount of family support. Another Williamstown production worker experienced this divide in their own work as they saw the way various systems perpetrated abuse:

> Classism was the most prominent to me; I was required to pay for housing ($650) and meals (average $15/meal). Events such as portfolio reviews also came at a cost, having to reimburse the supervisor for printing out materials. Even working on shows and being in tech I had to reimburse my supervisor for picking up my meals. All costs fell on me and my family. If I did not come from an upper-middle class family, I would NEVER be able to afford this internship.[53]

Is it ethical to ask people to work for free – or pay to work – even when they can afford it, even in exchange for educational benefits and networking access? It's not. No one's work should be uncompensated, whether they can afford for it to be or not. Another respondent to the survey remembers: "I believe they prevented me from knowing my value and feeling that I should sacrifice my financial security for the sake of making art." And yet another former Williamstown Theater Festival production worker shared:

> Overwork and low pay keeps out people without the financial, cultural, physical/health, etc. resources to allow them to take these 'resume-building' or 'educational' positions, and it burns people out. It's another form of pay-to-play. I ended the summer physically exhausted, depressed, worried about my perceptions, my memory, my hearing, and that I might need knee surgery; certain [*sic*] my time at WTF had damaged my career prospects, not improved them.[54]

Of the 22 producing organizations that completed our institutional employer survey, half of them have production internships, and the majority of those internships are paid in some way. They cited that their rates vary from $350 per week to minimum wage. Some, such as the example cited above, pay a lower rate such as $250 per week plus providing housing, or $11.50 per hour plus overtime, travel reimbursement, and subsidized housing. Three of the 11 organizations responded that they pay their interns minimum wage. One organization shared that their interns work 20 hours per week; the other ten shared that their interns work 40 hours or more, and that for many, the schedule intensifies during the technical rehearsal process for productions. In all of these cases, the interns are making less than a thriving wage.

According to Dr. Stephanie Moser in "A Calculation of the Living Wage," the legal minimum wage does not adequately provide for cost of living:

> Across all family sizes, the living wage exceeds the poverty threshold, often used to identify needs. State minimum wages provide for only a portion of the living wage. For two adult, two children families, the minimum wage covers 59.8% of the living wage at best in Washington and 29.9% at worst in Wisconsin.[55]

Without a living wage, workers' households can't survive. And falling into the gap between poverty and a living wage prevents access to assistance programs. This affects everyone in a community by putting pressure on the education and social welfare systems, as well as on extended family and friends of workers. Once upon a time, the "Fight for $15" – a campaign led in part by Service Employees International Union (SEIU), a union of about 2 million members working in healthcare, education, the public sector and property services – seemed like the answer. Now, ten years after the beginning of that campaign for $15 an hour, that's nowhere near enough. According to the Economic Policy Institute, in 2023 in New York City where a large number of theatrical production workers work, a living wage for a single adult with no children is $64,043 per year.[56] Assuming a 40-hour work week and 52 weeks of work per year, this equals $30.79 per hour, more than double the long fought-for minimum wage of $15 per hour. Also according to EPI:

> The value of the federal minimum wage has reached its lowest point in 66 years, according to an EPI analysis of recently released Consumer Price Index (CPI) data. Accounting for price increases in June, the current federal minimum wage of $7.25 per hour is now worth less than at any point since February 1956. At that time, the federal minimum wage was 75 cents per hour, or $7.19 in June 2022 dollars.[57]

It's no surprise that establishing a living wage that supports all workers would be beneficial. According to Dr. Moser and Chet Swalina, the working poor could achieve financial independence and housing and food security with a living wage and "the living wage might also free up resources for savings, investment, and the purchase of capital assets (e.g., provisions for retirement or home purchases) that build wealth and ensure long-term financial stability and security."[58] This kind of security and wealth building are, arguably, qualities of a thriving wage. A thriving wage is one where workers feel like they have enough; one can not only afford their basic needs, but have some disposable income to afford leisure activities, and can save for the future.[59] This is how generational wealth begins.

Even when accounting for the included housing, a full time worker making $11.50 per hour is making $460 a week before taxes. Additionally, a significant amount of theatrical production work happens in urban areas where an equitable cost of living far outpaces the state or federal minimum wage. As of the writing of this book, in NYC, for example, where minimum wage is $15 per hour, an equitable living wage using the Economic Policy Institute calculator for a single worker with no children would be about $33 per hour.[60] Even in more rural areas, such as Berkshire County, Massachusetts, where Williamstown Theatre Festival is housed and unpaid interns have been expected to pay for housing, the EPI equitable living wage for a single worker with no children would be about $19.50 an hour, still higher than the state minimum wage of $15.

Nine of the 11 organizations with internships shared that interning is a path to potential employment at the institution, a clear benefit for those who have the opportunity to participate in these internships. But interns have to know to look for these opportunities. Of the theatrical production employers surveyed, one agreed that they "don't advertise for or run an application process. They find us and we say yay or nay based on interviews." This is a clear barrier to access, maintaining a culture where only those with a personal connection even know the opportunities exist.

The unpaid internship expectation is not unique to theatre production. In several other fields, the last decade has seen some amount of analysis and, inevitably, backlash against the practice. In "Valuable Experience: How University Internships Affect Graduates' Income," the researchers found that internships increase graduates' incomes and that the skills learned during an internship matter more because internships teach young people to function in a workplace than because they teach any specific process. The researchers suggest this may indicate that internships are less valuable for students with other work experience, as it appears that any experience will do.[61] The study, though, found that internships do increase wages, and they do so by increasing students' marketable skills.[62] This leads us to question whether these skills could (or should) be gained in entry-level paid employment instead.

In other aspects of the cultural sector, there have been several lawsuits filed by un- and underpaid interns. In 2013, Condé Nast closed down its internship program for about four months after two former interns sued them claiming to have been paid below minimum wage for summer jobs at *W Magazine* and *The New Yorker*.[63] In 2014, a group of unpaid interns at NBC settled a lawsuit for over $6 million. Approximately 9,000 interns working on *Saturday Night Live* and other shows brought a suit against the media giant for back wages. According to the interns, they were either paid nothing or less than minimum wage for their time with NBC.[64] In 2019, the board of trustees of the Association of Art Museum Directors passed a resolution calling for art museums to start paying their interns. Jill Medvedow, then co-chair of AAMD's Professional Issues committee and director of the ICA Boston, stated:

> Internships are an important gateway for those seeking careers in art museums, providing incredible opportunities for hands-on experience in many aspects of an institution's operations. Yet by failing to pay interns, we ensure that these experiences are only really accessible to those who are already financially secure and, often, people who have established career networks available to them.[65]

In part because of larger conversations around pay inequity, the conversations around unpaid internships has reached the national stage. In June 2021, President Biden signed an Executive Order directing all federal agencies to reduce their practice of hiring unpaid interns, fellows, and apprentices, and increase the availability of paid opportunities. The order outlined that internship programs should develop individuals' talent, knowledge, and skills for careers in government service, and that federal agencies should improve outreach to and recruitment of individuals from underserved communities for these programs. This all falls under the administration's Government-Wide Diversity, Equity, Inclusion, and Accessibility Initiative and Strategic Plan. One of the goals of the Government-wide DEIA Plan is to eliminate barriers to equity in Federal workforce functions including internship, fellowship, and apprenticeship programs.[66] In June 2022, the Biden-Harris Administration announced the launch of the White House Internship Program. For the first time in recent history, White House interns would be paid. The funds for paying interns come from bipartisan legislation that the President signed earlier in the year.[67]

In September, 2021, a group of lawmakers including Rep. Alexandria Ocasio-Cortez and Rep. Ayanna Pressley signed a letter organized by Rep. Tony Cárdenas of California and activist group Pay Our Interns, calling on the Department of Labor to revolutionize the oversight of unpaid internships by enacting more reporting requirements around unpaid internships and tracking them, as well as collecting data on intern pay.[68] Holding theatrical employers accountable to these same requirements as government departments might help to address at least some of the inequities currently found in, and created by, theatrical production internships.

HOW DOES UNDERPAID WORK IMPACT CAREER TRAJECTORIES?

While unpaid internships are easily recognized, there is also a prevalence of extremely underpaid work in the theatrical production field. Many theatrical production employers pay workers, especially designers and assistants, as independent contractors on a fee-based structure that allows them to avoid minimum wage requirements. Workers are not encouraged to track their hours (or at times even encouraged *not* to) and are often expected to be available for last-minute engagements such as unscheduled meetings or additional rehearsals. All of this unaccounted for work lowers the hourly wages of these workers.

Of the 1,037 production workers who completed the worker survey, 820 of them, or 79.1%, have accepted jobs that they know paid less than minimum wage. Of that group, 565, or 68.9% said those jobs directly affected their career trajectory in ways they can identify. Likely at least in part because of the racial wealth gap, which provides more generational wealth to white workers, 80.6% of white respondents reported having accepted jobs that paid less than minimum wage, more than any other racial or ethnic demographic (except for Native Hawaiian or Other Pacific Islander respondents of which there was only one).

As many workers identified, it is possible for these underpaid positions to provide benefits to those who can afford to take them. One costume professional shared,

> Many of the jobs I took as a costume professional were a stipend job and there is no way that the pay I was given would possibly begin to cover the hours I spent on research, shopping, hunting, altering, tech, wardrobe, laundry, hair, make-up, strike and restocking. However each job taught me a lot - about interacting with a director, with a cast member, about clothing and time periods, about drawing and renderings, about research, about what works for me on a production and what doesn't, how to advocate for myself. Each job was a line on my resume which earned me more lines on my resume. I networked with people and I learned who I liked to work with and who I didn't and when they asked me to work with them again I said yes or no and that led me to the next job and the next.

The financial realities shape workers' careers by determining what work they can and can't take early on. Workers who have to prioritize a living wage are prevented from taking many jobs which are often seen as building blocks to a more traditionally successful career:

> More specifically – the jobs I could NOT take off off Broadway because I literally couldn't pay rent if I did – in many ways inhibited my career growth. I spent much longer working as an associate than I would have liked because I couldn't afford to take on a lot of low paying shows to get exposure/reviews/make contacts.

Workers are often expected to "pay their dues" in low paid work as they climb the theoretical ladder towards financial stability and a successful career. And the cycle perpetuates itself as those who have been fortunate in the current system encourage early career workers to follow the same paths:

> I was encouraged to take assistant and associate positions that would pay me $1000-$1500 total for the entire production period. From pre-production to previews which was often 6/9 weeks' worth of work. I was told that if I stuck with the same designer at the low rate, eventually we would get work that paid better. And we eventually did, and that came at a huge price.

Summer stock workplaces are notoriously known for underpaying production workers. As in some of the internships we mentioned, in this model, employees are often paid in weekly stipends and provided basic housing, and many workers walk away from the summer having barely broken even or even having paid for the opportunity. And yet these workers do see benefits to taking this work: "Contacts I made in these jobs (summer stock) lead to other more stable career opportunities in the future which got me where I am today," said one respondent who also acknowledged their own privilege in being able to take this work. Another worker who had taken low paying summer work said, "I learned a lot and met many contacts who got me jobs later and got me into grad school. I took many embarrassingly low design fees and assistant design fees to work with people and at places I was excited about." Not all underpaid experiences have any clear benefits, even for those who can afford to take them. A production worker who interned for Jacob's Pillow, a dance venue in western Massachusetts, shared,

> My stint at Jacob's Pillow for instance, was paid, but just barely, and NOTHING has ever come of it. I'm told by culture that this is mostly because I didn't work hard enough to make connections there, but I don't think it's fair to put all the blame on me. I wasn't really afforded opportunities to meet anyone other than my fellow interns, many of whom have left the performance world entirely.

Many theatre workers who are able to take underpaid work do so by also working "survival" jobs or by taking as much work as they can:

> Those [underpaid] jobs were the trajectory of my career. I think it's hard to imagine that I took any design job that DIDN'T pay under minimum wage for the first,

> at least, decade of my career. Truly – I just layered them on top of each other as many [*sic*] as I could, and supplemented that with other work (assisting, a little: scene painting or related, a little) to get by.

There is a clear pattern at work here, which puts those without financial support at a distinct disadvantage: to get the job you need work experience; the way to get experience is unpaid and underpaid work. This is a continuous cycle of exclusion.

So how can workers receive these benefits and get paid equitably for their work? Is it even possible in the current fragile ecosystem of not-for-profit theatre?

As the public dialogue around the problematic nature of unpaid internships has increased and organizations begin to feel both the health and economic impacts of COVID-19, some organizations have chosen to make changes or eliminate their internship programs. Williamstown Theater Festival, long known for its dependence on unpaid and underpaid labor, has now put its internship and apprenticeship programs on hold. During her time as Artistic Director of Baltimore Center Stage, Stephanie Ybarra led the sunsetting of the BCS internship program. When we spoke with Ybarra, she explained quite clearly:

> The reasoning was pretty simple – it was just outmoded. It was time. And I was just hearing too often from our interns and fellows about what they couldn't afford. I mean, for starters, they were getting paid a stipend, right, because you can't legally pay workers that little. Now that they're getting a stipend, they're considered volunteers, but that means they're not protected by the sort of labor laws, right? They didn't have access to our health insurance, all kinds of things. So it was pretty outdated, outmoded is a polite way of saying it, exploitative is more apt.[69]

Interestingly, the most pushback Ybarra faced was from stakeholders within the organization, especially from the production staff. This resistance collided with the realities that, in order to support its workers, the theatre needed to reassess how it produced work – how many productions there were in a year, who was expected to do the work to get the shows up, how those people were hired and paid: "I think that what's clear about BCS, what's clear about many institutions, is that if your organization cannot function without interns, then by definition, you are doing it wrong."[70]

Within the theatre industry, there have been many initiatives to address the prevalence of underpaid work and inequities of career access. Advocacy organizations, usually founded by theatre workers, have emerged to spread information and funding to students and early career workers. Lift the Curtain specifically seeks to put the conversation about unpaid internships at the forefront. The mission of Lift the Curtain is to "carve accessible entryways to [the theatre] industry by abolishing the practice of unpaid labor."[71] Founded by a small group of self-identified activists during the Pause, "[they] envision a theatre industry in which socioeconomic privilege is not a prerequisite for success."[72] Lift the Curtain began as a Facebook group, and "quickly saw its numbers balloon on social media, as former intern after former intern shared their stories publicly, many for the first time."[73] From this initial interest, Lift the Curtain surveyed workers and is assembling a database of internships including pay and benefits like housing. Lift the Curtain has compiled a series of resources to use in evaluating theatre internships, including Internship Standards that provide a criteria by which to evaluate the ethical integrity and economic accessibility of an internship position.[74] These standards include a request that interns be given the same protections and compensation as employees; that internships be finite; that interns not be responsible for managing other interns or workers; and that there be a dedicated internship coordinator.[75] The standards conclude with the following statement:

> Internships, in their ideal application, are valuable. They provide early-career professionals the opportunity to practice their skills in a guided, low-risk setting. However, when a program requires an intern to provide free labor, the experience's benefits will be negated by the consequent damage to intern [*sic*], the employer, and the many applicants it ultimately excludes.[76]

There are also a variety of initiatives, such as the Cody Renard Richard Scholarship Program and the Willa Kim Costume Design Scholarship, which aim to enable access to formal education in production and design. Cody Renard Richard is a Black stage manager, producer, educator, and advocate. The scholarship "aims to help students reach their full artistic, academic and leadership potential, by providing a direct financial contribution to help ease the burden of the many costs of attending higher educational learning institutions, such as tuition, housing, textbooks and class fees."[77] Willa Kim was a costume designer for ballet, theatre, opera, and television; the scholarship, designed and administered by the Theatre Communications Groups (TCG) with support from The Estate of Willa Kim, provides financial support that can be used toward tuition, registration fees, supplies, and/or travel expenses for students studying costume design for theatre at a college, university, or professional training program.[78]

Similarly, USITT recently created the Collier Woods Scholarship, which "supports Black and African American students with interests in lighting design and/or theatre production, technology, and associated theatrical fields."[79] There are also institutionally specific scholarships like the Dr. &

Mrs. Edward Gerock Boyette Theatre Production Scholarship at UNC-Greensboro or NYU Tisch Drama's Lenore Doxsee Scholarship, which "was established in honor of professor Doxsee and recognizes upper level design and/or management students who demonstrate the spirit of collaboration that she lived by."[80]

Another advocacy approach is to create alternative education models that aren't dependent on traditional higher education to build networks and skills, as well as awareness of the possible paths in the field. The Open Stage Project is "a free program for female* high school students interested in careers behind the scenes on Broadway and in TV/film."[81, 82] The Open Stage Project's mission is "to close the gender gap in backstage and off-screen careers."[83] The Project teaches job-readiness with an eye toward workforce development, focusing on resume-building and job training to close the gender gap backstage. Programming includes performances, career conversation, studio tours, panels, and mentorship opportunities.[84]

The Studio School for Design (SSD) was founded in 2021 by a community of design professionals in order to pave an innovative new pathway into an education in design.[85] SSD "is an interdependent community of practice where experiential learning is embedded into a curriculum of design storytelling."[86] They offer learning opportunities for professionals, pre-professionals, and educators in the entertainment design professions. SSD was created on "the core principle of de-centering the professions and creating new opportunities for high quality, industry-led, affordable professional training outside of formal educational settings."[87] These classes, which have been offered both online and in person, address a variety of professional skills for a very low cost compared to traditional university or even community college models.

Similarly, lighting designer Amber Whatley created the Blackout Lighting Design and Technology Workshop for Black Youth. Whatley shares that prior to the Pause, she began pondering how to contribute to diversifying the lighting design and technology fields. "From this came Blackout, a free two-week intro to lighting design and technology workshop for Black youth aged ten to eighteen that brings awareness of lighting design and technology to communities that have little to no exposure to theatre education."[88] During the workshop, participants learn basic lighting skills, proper ways to use lighting terminology, and engage in fun, lighting oriented activities.[89] The hope was that participants with further interest in lighting would not enter their next level of education significantly behind students who received theatre training in their secondary schools.[90]

Design Action is "an intergenerational coalition of BIPOC and white designers working to end racial inequities in the North American theater by confronting racism in our workplace and forging new pathways into the industry for rising designers of color."[91] They have focused their energies on advocacy and resource building in the theatre design field. In 2022,

Design Action partnered with the American Theater Wing to create Springboard to Design, a tuition-free program that "aims to provide students with access to theatre education they may not otherwise receive."[92] Through workshops, seminars, and access to theatre, the program "encourages and mentors students from underrepresented populations in the industry to explore the process of theatrical collaboration and the many avenues of American Theatre design."[93]

The Black Theatre Coalition was founded to address "the disparity between the growing inclusivity onstage, versus the almost non-existence of Black professionals off stage."[94] The coalition exists "to remove the *illusion of inclusion* in the American Theatre, by building a sustainable ethical roadmap that will increase employment opportunities for Black theatre professionals. [BTC's] vision is to reshape the working ecosystem for those who have been marginalized by systemically racist and biased ideology."[95] BTC offers six to 12 month fellowships, short-term apprenticeships, semester-long regional fellowships, and project-specific fellowships.[96] As of 2023, 33 fellows have participated in the program.

Created by members of the design field, the 1/52 Project awards grants of $15,000 to "to encourage rising designers from historically excluded groups with the aim of diversifying and strengthening the Broadway design community."[97] The project is funded through donations from "designers with shows running on Broadway … [who] donate one week of their weekly royalties (AWC) to this fund."[98] This kind of funding can help someone who might otherwise be forced to leave the field stay and perhaps even flourish. The prevalence of underpaid work prevents many early career workers without a financial safety net from being able to continue working in theatrical production. For some, $15,000 might be as much or more than they can make from theatrical production work in a given year. The first cohort of recipients included seven designers. While financial support like this can be a gamechanger for young designers, efforts such as this one function within the inequitable system, rather than changing the system itself.

In the essay "Not a Pipeline Problem, a Problem with the Pipeline," lighting/projection designer and production manager Calvin Anderson explains that mentorship outside of the traditional education system can serve as one solution to the "pipeline problem," offering the individualized learning and solidarity that academia is severely lacking.[99] Often people outside the theatre production industry don't realize that these paths can be career-long professions.[100] For Anderson, acting as a mentor has allowed him to form deeply meaningful relationships with the next generation of designers and theatremakers and to remain attuned to what the younger generation is pushing for and what the shifting landscape and priorities look like. He posits that by building these connections, theatremakers can build a web of diversity at every level of production, and in doing so, take care of one another and grow in the process.[101] In addition to being a mentor to his students, Anderson has been a mentor through the Wingspace Mentorship Program. This free, nine-month program is designed to

> broaden access and disrupt barriers early-career designers encounter while advancing their careers in the performing arts. Wingspace seeks to create a learner-centered community that empowers curious and passionate mentees to connect to career opportunities, build connections in the design community, and hone their skills. Mentorships are offered in direction, scenic design, costume design, lighting design, sound design, and projection design.[102]

The Wingspace Mentorship program began in 2015–2016 when there were three mentees. In 2022–2023, there were 11 mentees. Overall, the program has supported 54 early career artists.

Disability arts ensemble Kinetic Light has a mentorship program as well. Designer Michael Maag shared, "And Kinetic Light has a mentorship program, where we very specifically pick disabled designers that are emerging. So I've had the opportunity to have two mentees in that program."[103] Similarly, the Equity by Design Mentorship, founded by members of United Scenic Artist Local 829, creates mentorships for Black, Indigenous, and People of Color (BIPOC) junior high, high school, and college students.[104] The mentorship program attempts to fill some of the gaps created by inequitable access to arts education, theatre and the knowledge about potential production career paths. There are one-on-one mentorships as well as group classes and seminars. In particular, their programs focus on "giving attention to the individual students and fostering a reciprocal relationship between USA 829 and scholastic organizations in an effort to shift the culture of both the schools and the entertainment industry toward values of diversity, equity and inclusion."[105]

Out of Tayneisha Jefferson's work and inspiration came USITT's Gateway Program, which was launched in 2014. This unique, customizable mentorship program fosters opportunities for those who identify with an underrepresented population. It allows an individual to work with a mentor to tailor their learning goals and career development while attending the upcoming conference with the financial support of USITT. In addition, it offers a vast network of industry professionals for mentees to learn and engage with during their time at USITT and beyond.[106]

The range of advocacy work around educational accessibility is impressive, and those seeking to make change are doing amazing work. But these are mostly small independent initiatives, impacting very few students or early-career artists per year compared to the number of people interested in these career paths. Even the largest of the programs can't make a dent in supporting the thousands of theatre workers entering the field each year. And these programs do little to address the needs of the field beyond an individual model. Can we address these questions on a larger scale? How can we get arts education and access to everyone? Could there be widely available alternatives to traditional education models with their high cost barriers? What would a sustainable work-experience model look like? As we evaluate the workplaces of those in theatrical production, these questions of equity in where and how workers enter the field remain crucial to untangle.

NOTES

1 Randy Cohen, "The American Public Says YES to Arts Education," *Artsblog, Americans for the Arts* (blog), March 5, 2016, https://blog.americansforthearts.org/2019/05/15/the-american-public-says-yes-to-arts-education.
2 American Academy of Arts and Sciences, "The Arts and Public Education," Art for Life's Sake: The Case for Arts Education, 2021, https://www.amacad.org/publication/case-for-arts-education/section/2.
3 John A. Lithgow, Deborah F. Rutter, and Natasha D. Trethewey, "The Case for Arts Education Is Strong. Our Commitment Should Be, Too," American Academy of Arts and Sciences, November 4, 2021, https://www.amacad.org/news/strong-case-arts-education-commitment.
4 Alarie A. Gibbs, "The Perception of Nonprofit Arts and Culture Leaders Regarding their Role in K-12 Arts Education" (PhD diss., University of North Florida, 2018), 108.
5 American Academy of Arts and Sciences.
6 Ilasiea Gray, "Why Are There No Great Kids of Color in the Performing Arts?" *Stage Directions*, May 2021, 20–23.
7 Gray, 21.
8 Gray, 22.
9 Pamela Newton, "The Broadway Season Was Diverse Offstage Too Not that You'd Notice," *American Theatre*, June 7, 2016, https://www.americantheatre.org/2016/06/07/the-broadway-season-was-diverse-offstage-too-not-that-youd-notice/.
10 Theatre for Young Audiences, "State of the Field Research Report" (Logan, UT: Utah State University, 2019), https://www.tyausa.org/wp-content/uploads/2019/11/TYA-State-of-the-Field-Report-2019.pdf.
11 Rachel Frederick, "An Interview with Amber Whatley, Lighting Designer," *Et Cetera...: A Blog of Bright Ideas from ETC* (blog), January 27, 2022, https://blog.etcconnect.com/2022/01/amber-whatley.
12 Frederick.
13 "In Memoriam: Tayneshia Jefferson," *Sightlines: The Monthly Newsletter for USITT Members*, September 2013, http://sightlines.usitt.org/archive/2013/09/TayneshiaJefferson.asp.
14 Tayneshia Jefferson and David S. Stewart, "Diversity in the Booth: What it's Like Being a Minority in Technical Theatre," *Stage Directions*, January 2012, 20–21.
15 Amber Whatley, Sherrice Mojgani, and Calvin Anderson, "Not a Pipeline Problem, a Problem with the Pipeline," HowlRound Theatre Commons, September 1, 2021, https://howlround.com/not-pipeline-problem-problem-pipeline.

16 Whatley, Mojgani, and Anderson.
17 Emma García and Elaine Weiss, "Education Inequalities at the School Starting Gate: Gaps, Trends, and Strategies to Address Them," Economic Policy Institute, September 27, 2017, https://www.epi.org/publication/education-inequalities-at-the-school-starting-gate/.
18 "2023 Drama & Theatre Arts Degree Guide," College Factual, https://www.collegefactual.com/majors/visual-and-performing-arts/drama-and-theater-arts/.
19 "Technical Theatre Design and Technology," Data USA, https://datausa.io/profile/cip/technical-theatre-design-technology.
20 "Cost of Attendance," California State University, Fullerton, https://www.fullerton.edu/financialaid/ugrd/coa.php.
21 "Cost of Attendance," New York University, https://www.nyu.edu/admissions/financial-aid-and-scholarships/applying-and-planning-for-undergraduate-aid/tuition-and-other-costs/cost-of-attendance.html.
22 Whatley, Mojgani, and Anderson.
23 D. Joseph Hartnett (Co-Director, IATSE Stagecraft Department), interview by the authors, October 2022.
24 Alexandre Frenette, "The Intern Economy: Laboring to Learn in the Music Industry" (PhD diss., City University of New York, 2014), 218, https://academicworks.cuny.edu/cgi/viewcontent.cgi?referer=&httpsredir=1&article=1038&context=gc_etds.
25 US Department of Labor, "Wages and Hours Worked: Minimum Wage and Overtime Pay," Employment Law Guide, December 2019, https://webapps.dol.gov/elaws/elg/minwage.htm.
26 "Fact Sheet #71: Internship Programs Under the Fair Labor Standards Act," US Department of Labor Wage and Hour Division, January 2018, https://www.dol.gov/agencies/whd/fact-sheets/71-flsa-internships.
27 US Department of Labor Wage and Hour Division, "Fact Sheet #71."
28 Frenette.
29 Frenette, 152.
30 Frenette.
31 Frenette.
32 Lauren A. Riviera, "Homosocial Reproduction," in *Sociology of Work: An Encyclopedia*, ed. Vicki Smith (Thousand Oaks, CA: SAGE Publications, 2013): 376.
33 Frenette.
34 Frenette, 152.
35 "Study: Arts Internships are Important, but Some Are Better than Others," Strategic National Arts Alumni Project, June 18, 2015, 1, https://snaaparts.org/uploads/downloads/Media-Releases/SNAAP-Release-Special-Report-2015.pdf.
36 Alexandre Frenette, Gillian Gualtieri, and Megan Robinson, "Growing Divides: Historical and Emerging Inequalities in Arts Internships," SNAAP Special Report (Providence, RI: Strategic National Arts Alumni Project, Spring 2021), https://snaaparts.org/uploads/downloads/SNAAP-Special-Report-Inequalities-210301_2021-11-09–220850_gmjl.pdf.
37 Frenette, Gualtieri, and Robinson, 9.
38 Frenette, Gualtieri, and Robinson, 4.

39 Christin Essin, *Working Backstage: A Cultural History and Ethnography of Technical Theater Labor* (Ann Arbor: University of Michigan Press, 2021): 23.
40 The WTF, Williamstown?! Collective, "The WTF, Williamstown?! Collective to Mandy Greenfield, Laura Savia, Jeffrey Johnson, Joe Finnegan, Annie Pell, Brad Svrluga, and Donald B. Elitzer; as Well as the Rest of the Staff and Board of Trustees of Williamstown Theatre Festival," https://ca-times.brightspotcdn.com/06/37/5851edc0482387ff1b2fee01b155/updated-williamstown-theatre-festival-letter.pdf.
41 Ashley Lee, "Inside the Battle to Change a Prestigious Theater Festival's 'Broken' Culture," *Los Angeles Times*, September 25, 2021, https://www.latimes.com/entertainment-arts/story/2021–09–25/williamstown-theatre-festival-workplace-safety-culture.
42 Ashley Lee, "Williamstown Festival Crew Walks Off the Job. It's a Cautionary Tale for Outdoor Theater," *Los Angeles Times*, July 20, 2021, https://www.latimes.com/entertainment-arts/story/2021–07–20/williamstown-theatre-festival-sound-crew-walks-out
43 Lee.
44 Lee.
45 Sarah Dew, "An Open Letter to the 'Launchpad of the American Theater,'" *Sarah Dew* (blog), July 2, 2021, https://www.sarahdew.com/post/dear-launchpad-for-american-theatre.
46 Dew.
47 Eotcsummer21, "A Call In To the Eugene O'Neill Theater Center," Medium, July 21, 2021, https://medium.com/@eotcsummer21/a-call-in-to-the-eugene-oneill-theater-center-4cf5c42ea933.
48 Eotcsummer21.
49 Eotcsummer21.
50 Dew.
51 Ciara Diane, "How Do You Pay Your Dues When You Can Barely Pay Your Bills?" *American Theatre*, May 1, 2020, https://www.americantheatre.org/2020/05/01/how-do-you-pay-your-dues-when-you-can-barely-pay-your-bills/.
52 Diane.
53 The WTF, Williamstown?! Collective.
54 The WTF, Williamstown?! Collective.
55 Stephanie Moser, "A Calculation of the Living Wage," Living Wage Calculator, May 19, 2022, https://livingwage.mit.edu/articles/99-a-calculation-of-the-living-wage.
56 "Family Budget Calculator," Economic Policy Institute, https://www.epi.org/resources/budget/.
57 David Cooper, Sebastian Martinez Hickey, and Ben Zipperer, "The Value of the Federal Minimum Wage Is at Its Lowest Point in 66 Years," Economic Policy Institute, *Working Economics* (blog), July 14, 2022, https://www.epi.org/blog/the-value-of-the-federal-minimum-wage-is-at-its-lowest-point-in-66-years/.
58 Moser.
59 Mala Nagarajan, "How Do We Quantify a Thriving Wage?" Vega Mala Consulting, February 6, 2023, https://www.vegamala.com/how-do-we-quantify-a-thriving-wage/.
60 Economic Policy Institute, "Family Budget Calculator."

61 Thomas Bolli, Katherine Caves, and Maria Esther Oswald-Egg, "Valuable Experience: How University Internships Affect Graduates' Income," *Research in Higher Education* 62, no. 8 (December 2021): 1198–1247, https://doi.org/10.1007/s11162-021-09637-9.

62 Bolli, Caves, and Oswald-Egg.

63 Cara Buckley, "Sued Over Pay, Condé Nast Ends Internship Program," *New York Times*, October 23, 2013, https://www.nytimes.com/2013/10/24/business/media/sued-over-pay-conde-nast-ends-internship-program.html.

64 "Unpaid NBC Interns Settle Lawsuit for Over $6 Million," Joseph & Norinsberg LLC: Fighting for Employee Justice, November 10, 2014, https://employeejustice.com/unpaid-nbc-workers-settle-lawsuit-for-over-6-million/.

65 "Association of Art Museum Directors Passes Resolution Urging Art Museums to Provide Paid Internships," Association of Art Museum Directors, June 20, 2019, https://aamd.org/for-the-media/press-release/association-of-art-museum-directors-passes-resolution-urging-art-museums.

66 "Executive Order on Diversity, Equity, Inclusion, and Accessibility in the Federal Workforce," The White House, June 25, 2021, https://www.whitehouse.gov/briefing-room/presidential-actions/2021/06/25/executive-order-on-diversity-equity-inclusion-and-accessibility-in-the-federal-workforce/.

67 "Biden-Harris Administration Announces the First Session of the White House Internship Program, Administration Will Pay Interns for the First Time in History," The White House, June 2, 2022, https://www.whitehouse.gov/briefing-room/statements-releases/2022/06/02/biden-harris-administration-announces-the-first-session-of-the-white-house-internship-program-administration-will-pay-interns-for-the-first-time-in-history/.

68 Juliana Kaplan, "AOC Joins Cárdenas and Other Top Lawmakers in Calling on Biden's Labor Department to Revolutionize Oversight of Unpaid Internships," *Business Insider*, September 28, 2021, https://www.businessinsider.com/lawmakers-call-on-department-of-labor-to-track-unpaid-internships-2021–9.

69 Stephanie Ybarra (former Artistic Director, Baltimore Center Stage), interview by the authors, September 2022.

70 Ybarra, interview.

71 "Our Mission," Lift the Curtain, https://www.liftthecurtain.co/our-mission.

72 Lift the Curtain, "Our Mission."

73 Rosie Brownlow-Calkin, "The Theatre Industry's Internship Problem," *American Theatre*, September 10, 2021, https://www.americantheatre.org/2021/09/10/the-theatre-industrys-internship-problem/.

74 "Resources," Lift the Curtain, https://www.liftthecurtain.co/resources.

75 "Internship Standards," Lift the Curtain, https://drive.google.com/file/d/1plJgSW_6r_jU30fT2WzZKGOMEyt3Ft4q/view.

76 Lift the Curtain, "Internship Standards," 4.

77 "The Cody Renard Richard Scholarship Program," Cody Renard Richard, https://www.codyrenard.com/scholarship.

78 "The Willa Kim Costume Design Scholarship," Theatre Communications Group, https://circle.tcg.org/resources/grant-professional-development-programs/willa-kim-costume-design-scholarship/willa-kim-costume-design-scholarship-description?ssopc=1.

79 "Recipients of the Inaugural Collier Robert Woods, Jr. Scholarship Announced by USITT," United States Institute for Theatre Technology, August 2, 2021, https://www.usitt.org/inaugural-collier-woods-scholarship-recipients-announced.

80 "Tisch Drama Announces Lenore Doxsee Scholarship," New York University Tisch School of the Arts, October 30, 2020, https://tisch.nyu.edu/drama/news/tisch-drama-launches-lenore-doxsee-scholarship.
81 "Program Overview," Open Stage Project, https://www.openstageproject.org/program.
82 The Open Stage Project includes this asterisk and refers to "We use an inclusive definition of 'girls,' 'women,' and 'female.' We welcome trans women, genderqueer women, and non-binary people. We believe in supporting the many intersections of our members' identities, such as but not limited to race, sexual orientation, gender expression, socioeconomic class, and immigrant/indigenous status."
83 "Home," Open Stage Project, https://www.openstageproject.org/.
84 Open Stage Project, "Home."
85 "Studio School of Design Announces Inaugural Classes for June 2021," Live Design, April 21, 2021, https://www.livedesignonline.com/business-people-news/studio-school-design-announces-inaugural-classes-for-june-2021.
86 "Mission," Studio School of Design, https://studioschoolofdesign.org/mission/.
87 "History of Studio School of Design," Studio School of Design, https://studioschoolofdesign.org/history/.
88 Frederick, "Interview."
89 Amber Whatley, "Black Out Lighting Design and Technology Workshop for Black Youth," 2023, https://www.awhatleylighting.com/blackout-workshop.
90 Whatley, Mojgani, and Anderson.
91 "About Us," Design Action, https://www.design-action.com/about-us.
92 "Springboard to Design," American Theatre Wing, https://americantheatrewing.org/program/springboard-to-design/.
93 American Theatre Wing, "Springboard to Design."
94 "Who We Are," Black Theatre Coalition, https://blacktheatrecoalition.org/who-we-are/.
95 "Home," Black Theatre Coalition, https://blacktheatrecoalition.org.
96 "BTC Application Portal," Black Theatre Coalition, https://btc.smapply.io/.
97 "Home," The 1/52 Project, https://www.oneeveryfiftytwo.org/.
98 The 1/52 Project, "Home."
99 Whatley, Mojgani, and Anderson.
100 Whatley, Mojgani, and Anderson.
101 Whatley, Mojgani, and Anderson.
102 "Wingspace Mentorship Program," Wingspace Theatrical Design, https://wingspace.com/mentorship.
103 Michael Maag (Resident Lighting Designer, Oregon Shakespeare Festival), interview by the authors, September 2022.
104 "ETDM Mission," Equity Through Design Mentorship, http://www.etdmentorship.org/about.
105 Equity Through Design Mentorship, "ETDM Mission."
106 "Gateway Program," United States Institute for Theatre Technology, https://www.usitt.org/gateway.

SYSTEM ERROR
No connection.
OK
UNABLE TO JOIN THE NETWORK "Theater_Prod (5G)"
DISMISS

6

HIRING PRACTICES

When one thinks about the hiring process, one often assumes that there will be a public job posting, people will apply, applications will be reviewed, perhaps some candidates will be interviewed, and then a candidate will be selected. In theatrical production, this is rarely the case. As discussed in Chapter 5, hiring in theatrical production is often based on one's personal network – who you know and likely who you have worked with before.

According to our worker survey, the overwhelmingly most common response to how participants hear about available theatrical production jobs is through word of mouth or personal networks. Of the 1,037 respondents, 843 listed word of mouth/personal networks in answer to this question. Comparatively, only 391 respondents (including some who had also cited word of mouth) listed that they typically found out about available positions via public job boards. When explaining how they have gotten jobs, workers' responses included "Entirely word of mouth. I've never gotten any job from dropping an application. It's always been from making a connection and reputation;" "people call me to design for them, I never look;" and "except for one job I cold applied for years ago, I learned about each of the hundreds of individual gigs I've worked through word of mouth (usually at the bar, after the show)." Several respondents also noted that they have found jobs on Facebook, which shows how one's personal network might expand via social media.

DOI: 10.4324/9781003330394-8

In surveying theatrical employers, of the 23 responding organizations, six employers do not publicly post how designers or technicians interested in work might contact them. One employer explained, "[Job information] is publicly available but there is no encouragement or inducement to reach out." This raises the question, why make it available if you don't want people to use it? Some employers also identified that while staff and technical positions are publicly posted, guest artist and designer contract positions are not.

In the case of designer hires, it's common for the team to be assembled from designers already known to the director. And designers are likely to hire assistants or associates that they have worked with before. A high value is placed on long collaborations between directors and designers (or directors and choreographers or designers and other designers). This is true in technical positions as well. The urgency often present in theatrical production demands that those leading the room be able to trust that everyone they work with can "get the job done," which sometimes means that leaders aren't willing to risk working with new people unless they come highly recommended. As we've discussed, urgency, which prevents new ways of thinking, is a white supremacist value we see throughout production. Some of the surveyed producing organizations corroborated the pattern of hiring from personal networks:

> Designers generally are picked by the Director from people they already know, or people who are recommended to them. There is no formalized application process and I cannot remember a time where we created a listing for a Design position. Our list of people we want to work with is generally much longer than our list of available positions.

Even when there is an interview-like process, the designers are often reached through personal networks. As one organization explained, "The designer application process is word of mouth and personal connections only at this time. Everyone needs to submit a resume and website/portfolio to the Director of Production and have a conversation with him." In other words, though designers submit a resume and interview, the opportunity is only open to those already known to those hiring. Simply put by another organization: "We usually take requests and recommendations from directors and then reach out to check availability and interest. We don't usually post nor do we have an interview process." There are, of course, ways to change this practice. As one employer said, "We have been trying to disrupt this process; one such attempt is by offering more Assistant positions to help introduce [the] Director to new people. Our staff directors have been incorporating 1–2 new-to-them people on each show they direct." This kind of check-and-balance is certainly a step towards more inclusive hiring. In a field where the work is deeply reliant on interpersonal connection and collaboration, networking is never going to completely go away. Disruptions like this are merely band aids which don't address the underlying problems of exclusion.

Hiring through personal networks is common beyond the field of theatrical production. In 2011, Matt Youngquist, then president of Career Horizons, shared that "at least 70 percent, if not 80 percent, of jobs are not published." He further explained, "And yet most people – they are spending 70 or 80 percent of their time surfing the net versus getting out there, talking to employers, taking some chances [and] realizing that the vast majority of hiring is friends and acquaintances hiring other trusted friends and acquaintances."[1] This shows a discrepancy between privately and publicly available information which greatly impacts who can even apply for an available position. It's no wonder that limiting the applicant pool limits the diversity of those hired.

There is a direct line from hiring within personal networks to a lack of diversity in the newly hired workers. A 2016 report from the Public Religion Research Institute (PRRI) exploring race, religion, and political affiliation of Americans' core social network found that:

> Fully three-quarters (75%) of white Americans report that the network of people with whom they discuss important matters is entirely white, with no minority presence, while 15% report having a more racially mixed social network. Approximately two-thirds (65%) of black Americans report having a core social network that is composed entirely of people who are also black, while nearly one-quarter (23%) say their network includes a mix of people from other racial and ethnic backgrounds. Less than half (46%) of Hispanics report that their social network includes only other people who also identify as Hispanic, while more than one-third (34%) report having a mixed social network. Notably, nearly one-in-ten (9%) Hispanics report having an all-white core social network.[2]

This instinct towards creating a homogeneous social pool means that word of mouth doesn't travel very far. As we touched on in Chapter 5, cultural matching or homosocial reproduction in hiring perpetuates the ways that workplaces maintain a lack of diversity. Employers and workers in hiring positions are most likely to spread information about available positions within these somewhat closed social groups, keeping the applicant pool limited to workers who look like the employers hiring them.

Socio-economic class and the inherent educational access divide furthers this stratification. Former LinkedIn CEO Jeff Weiner calls the advantage some people have based on who they know "the network gap."[3] LinkedIn data scientists found that:

> If you grow up in a high income neighborhood, you are three times more likely to have a strong network. If you go to a top school or university, you are two times then again likely to have a strong network. If you work at a top company, you are

> two times again likely to have a strong network. If you enjoy all three of those advantages, you are 12 times more likely to have a strong network. And that's the foundation for that nine X advantage.[4]

Weiner explains that:

> this creates a very virtuous cycle for those individuals that benefit from those advantages. And it creates a very, very vicious cycle for those people that have the skills, that have the grit, the resilience, the growth, mindset, that compassion, but don't necessarily have the relationships; who are potentially shut out of those very same opportunities. And the people that have the social capital, create opportunities for people like them. The people that don't have the social capital sometimes can't get access.[5]

White supremacy reinforces the idea that first-generation and BIPOC students are at a disadvantage in the job market. It's not that these students lack a network; it's that they lack the *right* network. Weiner elaborates:

> We should acknowledge instead that those people are usually talking about networks radiating from centers of power and influence in this country, which are overwhelmingly white. We should be explicit in naming the systematic and institutional racism that excludes BIPOC students from predominantly white places of learning and work, perpetuating the concentration of opportunities there.[6]

In "Race and Networks in the Job Search Process," David S. Pedulla and Devah Pager further explore how social networks shape racial disparities in employment opportunities. Their first key finding indicated that "Black and white job seekers receive job leads from their social network at similar rates."[7] However, they found that white job seekers are more likely to see the benefits of these job leads than Black job seekers.[8] Investigating this further, Pedulla and Pager found that

> conditional on hearing about an opening through a network-based channel, Black job seekers are less likely than white job seekers to (1) know someone at the companies to which they are submitting applications, and (2) have their network mobilize key resources on their behalf, specifically contact an employer on their behalf. These two mechanisms – *network placement* and *network mobilization* – assist in explaining approximately one-fifth of the black-white disparity in job offers among applications that are heard about through social network-based channels.[9]

Inequitable hiring practices have contributed to the fact that the majority of the workers in theatrical production are cis-men and white. In our survey, of 1,037 workers, 324 identified as cis-gendered white men.

Pedulla and Pager give terminology – network placement and network mobilization—to the responses we heard time and time again from production workers: that they get jobs through word of mouth. However, some theatrical employers did mention using various job boards when they needed to look for workers outside of their existing networks. In one case, an employer explained, "Once our season is selected, we start with designers we already know and try to fit them with shows/ directors. If we need/ want new designers, we post job description [*sic*] on Offstagejobs.com, Facebook and occasionally Playbill.com."

Job boards and public posts do increase worker access to potential opportunities. However, in a lot of cases, theatrical production job postings lack clarity around the requirements or conditions of a potential job. According to Katrina Kibben, recruiting and Human Resources expert, equitable hiring advocate and founder of three ears media, there are some places to start with every job post:

> Do I know what experiences would qualify someone for this job? If you're posting random years of experience, all you're doing is quantifying candidates, not qualifying anyone.
>
> Are the requirements mandatory? Do you list things like driving a car when it's not required? Do you need that degree? Reconsider if this is bias or what's best for the role.
>
> Is the job title researched or just recycled from the other jobs? Just because you've always done it that way doesn't mean you should continue.[10]

Looking at a range of theatrical production job descriptions across various free job posting websites illustrates a lack of clarity across many of these items. For example, one Set Designer position advertisement lists relevant dates and fee structure but fails to include any information about the skills or experience required. The only requirement explicitly listed is attendance at production meetings and technical rehearsals. Another job listing for a master electrician lists only the following information:

> Seeking to hire MASTER ELECTRICIAN for the Axelrod Performing Arts Center's 2022/2023 season, running from October 2022 through June 2023 for main-stage musicals and concerts. Must live close enough to theater to commute. We are located in Ocean Township and Holmdel, NJ. Job can be ongoing past June 2023, or possibly only through 2022, based on availability.[11]

This listing didn't provide any information about the job responsibilities, the skills needed, the working conditions, or the compensation. These kinds of listings assume that the job seekers either psychically know exactly what the job will entail; make enough of an assumption about the work to be confident in their skills to apply; or are desperate enough for the gig that they aren't worried about the details. Vague and incomplete job listings lead to positions where the scope of work is in fact unclear and workers might be asked to perform tasks not typically assigned to someone in their role. In addition, the lack of pay transparency (more on this in Chapter 7) puts every worker at a disadvantage where they have to negotiate from scratch and may be passed over for the worker who, unknowingly, will accept pay that is lower than the norm. Many job listing sites which have more detailed listings also require a paid membership fee or a cumbersome registration process.

Obviously, none of these examples really qualify as inclusive job postings. In order to write an inclusive job posting, Kibben says employers should eliminate "years of experience" requirements: "Years of experience requirements are made up. We pick numbers out of a hat. You're just looking for people who have applied their skills on similar projects, not years."[12] This points to the idea that years of experience does not necessarily align with number of skills built or level of expertise; a worker could have many years of experience doing a single task, or may have a relatively small number of years of experience, having done many projects and honed many skills in that time. Workers also might apply with some amount of experience gathered in an educational environment, through an apprenticeship or internship or through a variety of shorter term experiences. Secondly, Kibben explains, "College is not affordable for everyone and doesn't make you a better candidate. Experience does. By requiring information about degrees and schools attended, employers may exclude qualified candidates with highly relevant experience."[13] This is a particularly salient point when it comes to theatrical production; perhaps more so than other types of work, production jobs are learned by *doing*, and therefore through specific work experiences. Questions like "Have you crafted a costume piece from a pattern?", "Have you painted a drop from a paint elevation?", and "Have you programmed a show on an ETC board?" are far more telling than what school you attended.

Further, Kibben suggests that employers "optimize your job postings to be more gender neutral by using gender decoders."[14] A gender decoder is a piece of software that searches for linguistic gender-coding (think "bossy" or "aggressive") and alerts the user to their implied bias. We entered a few production job postings from Playbill.com into a gender decoder to see this in action. Most either came back as "neutral" or as "feminine-coded," with words like depending, supportive, and collaborative flagged as feminine-coded words. One wardrobe supervisor posting, for example, was reported "strongly feminine-coded." The decoder flagged the word "independently" as masculine-coded, and the following words from the ad as feminine-coded: commitment (x2), collaboration, honest, interpersonal (x2), and collaboratively.

Another way to be inclusive to LGBTQIAA+ workers, is to "request pronouns during the application process to ensure candidates know they can feel comfortable sharing their pronouns if they'd like, but don't make it mandatory so you can avoid putting candidates in an uncomfortable situation if they are not ready to share their pronouns."[15] Kibben encourages employers to establish clear expectations of their current employees when looking for new hires: "Making sure your team values a positive candidate experience will help candidates feel comfortable and safe each step of the way."[16]

The persistence of advocacy group On Our Team has led to pay transparency on the websites of the League of Chicago Theaters, Playbill, Broadway World, the Minnesota Playlist, and the SCTC job site, as well as a few others.[17] Some additional job boards, including Offstagejobs.com, have added required pay transparency and clear job descriptions to help workers find jobs that support their quality of life.

Organizations like the Oregon Shakespeare Festival are posting more equitable job listings. Their recent post for a Scenic Artist includes:

- A detailed breakdown of the position's principal duties and responsibilities, including specifics such as "Paint, texture, and finish scenery and props according to design information" and "Interpret drawings, paint elevations, and research in order to achieve the look of the set design"
- A list of additional duties and responsibilities such as attending meetings, maintaining supply inventories, and mentoring colleagues as requested
- Reporting chain to and from this position
- Detailed qualifications, including the desired Work Experience, Physical Ability, and Essential Skills and Qualifications
- Compensation and benefits
- A direct statement of application requirements
- An introduction to the organization
- A clear listing of compensation and benefits
- Direct statement of what is needed in an application.[18]

Even if jobs were posted across various platforms and job descriptions were always equitable and inclusive, the pathways for job seekers to apply can create additional obstacles. In order to give workers an equal chance at being hired, employers need to gather the same information from everyone interested in the job. But, in theatrical production, there often isn't a way for workers to provide this information. In the survey we asked production workers how often they have to fill out a formal job application or undergo a formal interview process when seeking theatrical production employment (see Figure 6.2).

The majority of theatrical production workers have rarely or never had to complete job applications for theatre production jobs. So, job seekers outside of the employer's inside circle aren't given equal opportunity to

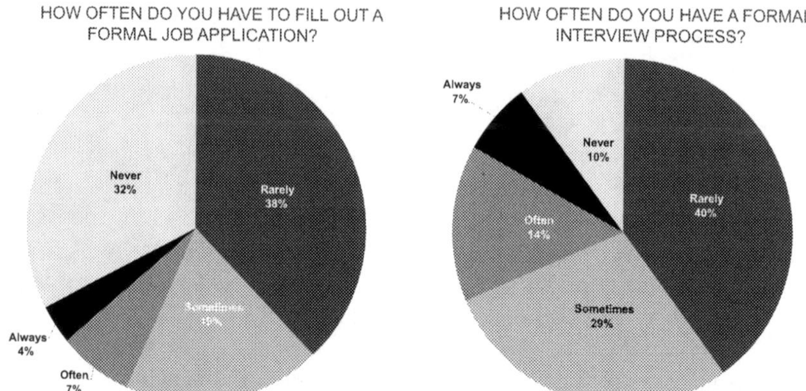

Figure 6.2 Worker responses to "When seeking theatrical production employment, how often do you have to fill out a formal job application?" and "When seeking theatrical production employment, how often do you have a formal interview process?"

present themselves for the positions. Similarly, about half of theatrical production workers have rarely or never had a formal interview process for a theatre production job. One production worker answered frankly, "For production? Never a formal application. For teaching or educational opportunities, frequently though often the HR process is a formality." Another worker said, "All of the production work I've received thus far has been the result of producers reaching out to me directly. I have not done any production work at this point where I have applied for it." For those who did go through a formal interview process, many workers noted that they had not done so for a long time, citing the last time as "Probably 12 years ago. I have only shown my portfolio once in my 15 years as a designer." Or "Depends what we consider an interview. Informal conversation with a director, within the last year. Formal interview with someone in a company: the very first internship I ever had 20 years ago and that's it."

When surveying theatrical production employers, we asked producing organizations whether there is an interview process for their design positions. Of the 23 respondents, unsurprisingly, thirteen employers said no, and only five said yes. The remaining employers provided more extended answers, including "We often have conversations with guest artists before hiring, to make sure they understand the nature of our theatre. At the time of these conversations, we have already determined to hire them if they are interested" and "Interview is a strong word. It's more like an informal match-making chat. It's an opportunity to see if the energies match in order to make for a successful collaboration between the artists." In some organizations, a disproportionate amount of hiring authority is given to the directors of individual productions: "There are usually only designer interviews for new designers. Directors and designers who've worked together previously skip the interview process." This prioritizes art making and the director-designer relationship over modes of working, communication style, time management skills, treatment of design assistants and interns, and interpersonal dynamics with fellow designers, administrative leadership, or technical staff which might be made visible in a process which involved several staff members on a committee. When I, Natalie, have been in a position, as a production manager or academic department chair, to hire designers, especially designers I know or know of, I have seen my role as providing information to see if they are interested – fee, dates, other members of the team, special circumstances of the project – and have almost never asked those designers to provide anything about their own work experience, process, or design aesthetics. I also haven't requested a resume or asked for references. These ways of hiring designers place greater value on the designer's reputation and their final products over how they treat colleagues and subordinates. In regards to if there is an interview for each design position, another employer explains, designer hiring "is up to the artist. We commission the artists but do not tell them how to build their own team." In this case, "artist" seems to mean director or choreographer or conceiver of the project. Again, this takes the decision making power out of the hands of a potentially trained hiring manager or committee.

Discussing how job opportunities are promoted and candidates are selected, one producing organization said, "Job description is provided upon personal contact. We post on our website for local talent. Interview is email then Zoom if needed with Artistic Director and Production Manager." To be clear, an email is not an interview. An email is potentially a one-way street of communication informing the worker of the possible position or offer. An interview is, by definition, a synchronous meeting for people to discuss or consult. An interview allows for nuance and for the worker to ask questions and gain clarity around a job's compensation, expectations, restrictions, and structures. Another employer explains that "Interviews are an informal meeting with [the] show director, Production Manager and Producing Artistic Director [*sic*]." The lack of formal structure assumes a familiarity, and may put less experienced or just lesser known designers at a disadvantage. In yet another case, a leader of a producing organization explained, "We do not have a formal application process for designers. We select designers based on seeing their work, recommendations from directors, and a variety of sessions across the country designed to introduce young designers to more theaters." This means that even if this theatre is seeking to expand its network of designers, only those designers with access to work or these introduction sessions can break into their network. This dependence on non-employees to recommend who to hire removes the pressure on the institution to develop equitable hiring strategies: It just isn't their fault – it's the artist's decision. Several theatres did say that they accept submissions of resumes and materials but this information is not always publicly accessible. This passive behavior allows for some increase in access but still puts the burden on the workers.

Many of these problems with hiring practices aren't unique to the theatre. In "Framework for Fair and Just Hiring Practices," Dr. Aisha Hollands outlines strategies for incorporating equitable hiring practices into a school district's recruitment and hiring processes.[19] While this is written specifically about school districts, the principles transfer to other fields. Hollands outlines ten equitable recruitment strategies that help to create a series of embedded checks and balances, preventing hiring from depending on a single person's opinion and naming the implicit biases which may be present in an individual's evaluation of a candidate. The strategies include developing detailed job descriptions that describe the knowledge, skills, and abilities for the position; posting the job on nontraditional sites such as culture-specific radio stations and newspapers; creating a screening tool based on the preferred skills and required knowledge outlined in the JD; developing a scoring rubric for interview questions; and providing the interview panel with bias and awareness training with enough lead-time that they have the chance to fully engage with the training.[20] Using rubrics and consistent questions helps eliminate these biases. This is consistent with the suggestions made by the institutions like the Harvard Business Review, which suggests similar steps for inclusion and to combat bias. Equitable hiring is often led by a partnership with recruiters and hiring managers, who work together to craft specific job postings based on the actual job to be performed and its role in the organization. The process is transparent and linear, and works through clear documented communication. At this point, theatrical production is far from even approaching most of these practices. So why have theatre employers stayed so far in the past?

Because theatre is creative?

When asked what factors make theatre production hiring potentially different from other industries, Production on Deck co-founder David Stewart shared:

> I think in other industries that you could get really specific, it's like, you need to know C Plus programming, you need to know very, very specific things. And we do have aspects of that, but I think that what we always want is, you know, we always are looking for people-centric creatives first. And that's not to say that those don't exist in other industries, but that seems to be really at our core, we are here to tell stories. So all of us, regardless if you are that stage technician, or you're a producer, or you're Production Manager or Stage Manager, on and on and on. Actors aren't the only storytellers. We production people are the world

> builders in order to tell stories. And so we have to have that kind of analysis as well. So we all share that storytelling gene. And I think that is really unique to our industry.[21]

These unique qualities are part of why traditional data and evidence may not work for theatre hiring managers. How can the storytelling gene be quantified? Does it need to be? On the other hand, hiring managers can create clear and transparent narratives for both what they are looking for and the kind of institution a worker will be entering. They can use their role as storytellers to think outside of the box on traditional qualifications, like college degrees, and see how alternative paths or other experiences might prepare workers for the jobs at hand.

Because theatre is temporary?

In theatre, a person might be hired for a day, a week, a month, or five months. Full-time, long term positions do exist, but the majority of production jobs are not that. Human Resources professionals have various methods for measuring employee worth that attempt to quantify an employee's value over their time in the position. The resources that go into managing a thorough hiring process can be justified by the amount the employee then contributes to the company over many years. In theatre, many workers are hired for limited periods of time, so there is a less obvious financial argument for investing in thorough hiring processes.

Because theatre is historically biased?

Since so much theatre hiring takes place without consistent formalized systems, it is difficult to know how often bias is at play in hiring decisions. However, many workers in production have experienced hiring decisions which they feel are rooted in various types of bias. When asked if they feel that their identities have impacted whether or not they have gotten a theatre production job, 52.3% of respondents to the worker survey said yes.

In response to the racial justice uprising of 2020, we've seen many theatre employers making outward gestures towards racial equity. Respondents to our survey shared instances of both being hired because of their racial identity, and of not being hired or considered because of it. In some cases, this comes as a long awaited recognition of hard work, talent, and skill. As one designer offered, "I do think that I have gotten some design jobs to make a more diverse design team. These are often times theatres who have never called me before. I am happy to take those jobs because it's long overdue that I get to work at some of those theatres."

But in many cases, this practice continues to be harmful. Hiring based on assumed identity isn't inclusive hiring. As one woman shared, "Because diversity is the new theater fad, I become this hot commodity, as a Black woman." Will this hiring pattern be sustained when the so-called fad falls out of fashion? Understandably, some workers are willing to accept the benefits of tokenism. Another Black designer said:

> While getting a job in this way can sometimes be strange/alienating, for the most part I am okay with any reason that helps me get a job that I'd like to have, particularly because I believe that my qualifications in the end will shine above any considerations of my particular identity. Also, while I think it can be a clumsy/awkward way to offer a job, I often do appreciate this kind of thinking as at least an intermediary step as we try to increase DEI initiatives in the performing arts industry.

In other words, maybe something is better than nothing?

Increasingly, producing organizations seek to include members of the production team who share identities with the characters in the play, even if only on the surface:

> I'm Black, and often get hired on shows about the Black experience. That said, I often feel like a token hire so they can say they have a Black person on the creative team (and I am often the only Black person on the creative team).

We heard from many workers about cases in which the employers make assumptions about workers' identities: "I'm Japanese and if the show is about an Asian culture I seem to get offers, even though I'm not familiar with many of the cultures that are in the play (Chinese, Asian American, Bengali etc.)" shared another survey respondent. These practices reveal a significant amount of still deeply embedded bias and continue to function from a place of racist thinking. Another worker shared yet another example of this:

> I know for a fact I was offered an interview at a theatre because they thought I had a Hispanic name and they specifically wanted to hire Hispanic/Latinx designers. I was ghosted after the interview because they discovered I was, in fact, Italian.

In addition to overt racism, other tenets of white supremacy – ableism, anti-fat bias, ageism and gender bias – play a large role in these barriers. A 2021 hiring bias and wage gap report from Actor's Equity Association reported, "While ageism can be waged against people of any age, there is significant data to show that the number of contracts our actors and stage managers receive after the age of 44 significantly diminishes."[22] This is particularly challenging in an industry in which freelance workers often don't have retirement funds. AEA also saw a distinct difference in hiring statistics between members with disabilities and those without:

> 26% of adults in the United States have a disability. However, only 1.5% of the total contracts (6,116 in 2021) went to workers who self-identified as having a disability. This number is skewed by the sheer number of people who did not provide their disability status – 70% of the total contracts in 2021 went to workers who did not share whether they have a disability.[23]

This is consistent with the experiences shared via our survey. One respondent shared, "Having a movement disorder effects [*sic*] my personal physical output in ways that does not sometimes meet director expectations – often expectations outside of what a contract or union agreement states." The 2021 AEA report also illustrates that even when workers with disabilities do get the job, they make less than their colleagues: "For both stage managers and assistant stage managers, workers with disabilities made less on average than their coworkers without disabilities by 2.8%, with stage managers with disabilities making below the average salary rate."[24]

Workers shared consistent experiences of bias surrounding their assumed incompetencies because of their gender presentation. A respondent shared that "In a male dominated field, I was constantly undermined as a fem-presenting non-binary person. I was only really accepted when I presented in a masculine way or over proved my intelligence." Yet another worker said, "I've literally been told that my size will affect my career. Whether we like it or not the entertainment industry cares how we look and how thin we are." We have both witnessed and experienced these biases in hiring. I, Brídín, served on a hiring committee for a props position where there was a single candidate who committee members agreed met the selection criteria more than any other candidate, however because of her gender and age, the majority of the committee assumed she "probably wouldn't help unload a truck." Based on this assumption, she was removed from the candidate pool.

Long held assumptions and biases against immigrant workers also show up in production hiring: "English is not my first language, I feel difficult to negotiate contract and payment sometimes. Also they might lost patience to understand what's my need [*sic*]." Though a violation of equal opportunity employment laws, these biases persist in union membership as well, where some locals still use written exams as an assessment of language proficiency.

Caregivers, who are often those of marginalized genders, are often excluded from hiring for a variety of assumed biases. Of the 199 workers who identified as caregivers on our survey, 127 identified as female, genderfluid/genderqueer/non-binary, or other. One mother shared:

> I know I've been passed over because I'm a woman and a mother. I've been told so, by the men hiring. They perceive me as being not as strong as muscly men ('You can't deadlift 250') and that I can't fully commit to a show position ('You probably have a lot of responsibility at home').

And it should come as no surprise that workers with intersecting marginalized identities feel these barriers the strongest:

> I have been working in the same market/region for 20+ years, and I have always been and have continued to be the ONLY working Female, Production

> Professional of Color. I have also watched young, white men whom I have mentored/trained who are much younger and less experienced than me get hired for positions that I have also interviewed for. Repeatedly.

The localization of hiring within a singular or small group of managers without explicit anti-bias training or oversight leads to these explicit acts of discrimination. Another female caregiver shared a similar feeling:

> I have not gotten scenic design jobs because I am a woman for sure. There have been many times when a TD doesn't think I know how scenery is built. I am not always taken seriously because I am a woman, and it got much worse once I had a child. It was perceived that I would not have enough time to dedicate myself to the show because I was a mother.

Intersectional biases could be limited if inclusive hiring techniques, such as having a hiring committee (with unconscious bias training and a structured process) rather than an individual hirer, were implemented.

Some workers are aware of how they have access that has been kept from others: "I'm a cisgender straight white male. I got hired over women I know are better programmers than I am." Many respondents share this sentiment; one shared, "As a white cis male, I never had to encounter any questioning (overt or otherwise) of my abilities/qualifications beyond my resume and recommendations." But awareness of privilege isn't always that straightforward. Another worker identified her hiring privilege while still citing the misogyny she faces in the workplace:

> I am in the room in the first place because I have been given opportunities due to my racial and socioeconomic privilege. I went to the most expensive college in the country where I studied dance and theater design. The connections I had there led to my internships and jobs. And I got into that college because I grew up in a suburb with a 'blue ribbon' public school. I mean I have benefited from many systems although theater is still a boys club and I have been chronically underpaid and dealt with extreme misogyny.

Workers who have experienced these benefits have sometimes sought to rectify them within their own sphere of influence. One such worker explained, "Unfortunately, being a white male in a white male dominated industry, there is an unconscious bias to hiring me – or someone who looks like me. If that is the case I have made efforts to ensure my associate(s) and crew members have been from diverse backgrounds, when possible."

Across the theatre industry, efforts are being made to improve hiring practices. The North Carolina Theatre Conference (NCTC) has developed a guide for making theatre hiring more equitable, diverse, and inclusive. In the guide, they provide pointers on shifting company culture to promote diversity (before you hire anyone), improving the search process, improving the candidate pool, holding inclusive interviews, and critical steps after the interview.[25]

Making Theatre Hiring More Equitable, Diverse, and Inclusive

A Guide from the North Carolina Theatre Conference

North Carolina Theatre Conference (NCTC) has created a guide for arts organizations to evaluate their hiring practices and move forward with an emphasis on diversity, equity, and inclusion. The following steps are outlined in more depth in the NCTC guide.

5 Steps to Shift Company Culture to Promote Diversity (Before You Hire Anyone)

1) Identify why you want more diversity in your organization
2) Cultivate new personal and professional networks
3) Proactively Identify and recruit talent
4) Cultivate entry level employees
5) Build meaningful community relationships

4 Strategies to Improve Your Search Process

1) Talk about what diversity means to your organization
2) Articulate your hiring goals
3) Diversify your hiring team
4) Discuss bias with your hiring team

4 Ways to Improve Your Candidate Pool

1) Review your job listing language
2) Review how you advertise job openings
3) Consider looking outside your geographic area
4) Don't settle for a pool of all-white candidates

5 Tips for an Inclusive Interview

1) Get on the same page about screening criteria
2) Plan your interview questions in advance
3) Outline the process for candidates in advance
4) Stick to the interview plan
5) Bring up diversity, equity and inclusion in the interview

3 Critical Steps After the Interview

1) Have a full, open debate with the hiring team
2) Personally notify the candidates who have not been selected
3) Keep all job application records for one year

Text courtesy of North Carolina Theatre Conference.

In 2017, the League of Resident Theatres (LORT) published the LORT Equitable Recruitment & Hiring Guide:

> created by the members of the LORT Recruitment Subcommittee to provide useful and constructive suggestions for a more equitable employment process for LORT Theatres with special attention to the recruitment of diverse candidates for leadership positions, primarily people of color and women. With a dearth of representation in key leadership positions at LORT Theatres, this guide seeks to provide a targeted perspective that seeks to expand the candidate pool of future LORT leaders as well as foster a culture that embraces the ideals of equity, diversity and inclusion (EDI) within our member Theatres.[26]

This guide is not specific to production-related positions, but it provides valuable general tips for equitable hiring practices. In line with non-theatre experts, the guide recommends that organizations conduct an internal Equity, Diversity, and Inclusion assessment and apply their values to a process that includes equitable job postings, recruitment strategies, interview processes, and transparent job offers.[27] However, these resources do not address some of the challenges that come up, specifically with technical production positions, such as: Who hires production workers? Is the hiring manager familiar with both the technical aspects of the position (enough so to identify suitable candidates) and with how to facilitate an inclusive hiring process? Is hiring a part of their job, or an add-on? If hiring is an added responsibility, have other responsibilities been diminished so the hirer can devote the time to conducting an equitable process?

The We See You W.A.T. "Principles For Building Anti-Racist Theatre Systems" also address how to make theatre hiring processes more equitable. Their demands address many of the concerns brought forward by workers in our survey and the supporting research. To address the historical exclusion of BIPOC workers from theatrical work, the We See You W.A.T. writers "demand a bare minimum of 50% BIPOC representation in programming and personnel, both on and off stage."[28] Perhaps over time, a 50% representative hiring practice can rectify the exclusion of the last at least century in the American theatre. In addition, the demands include

> eliminating the hiring criteria of years of experience or degree requirements will also foster this 50% minimum in white spaces, as will the development and retention of robust BIPOC student cohorts and faculty in professional training departments with historically less BIPOC representation than performance.[29]

Additionally, they "demand hiring, salary, and budgetary transparency and parity, and an explicit history of theater land acquisition."[30] This budgetary parity includes "compensation for all our work and [a refusal] to engage in unpaid labor through internships, donor cultivation, galas, talkbacks, marketing, or otherwise, as slavery has been abolished. Unless, as the 13th amendment also states, we are being kept as prisoners."[31]

In spring 2023, RISE Theatre was started by Maestra Music with Lin-Manuel Miranda. Maestra is a nonprofit which "provides support, visibility, and community to the women and nonbinary people who make the music in the musical theater industry."[32] RISE, which stands for Representation, Inclusion & Support for Employment, "seeks to build a more equitable and inclusive theatre industry by centralizing DEIA tools and resources through a network of partners and a national personnel directory that supports and amplifies women, people of color, and folks from marginalized communities and underrepresented backgrounds."[33] The RISE Theatre Directory in particular serves as a resource for both workers and employers who have felt trapped by the idea that they can't connect within current hiring practices.

When asked what equitable labor in theatre production looks like to her, Sarah Lozoff, intimacy director and co-founder of Production on Deck, said, "It looks like having informed consent when I apply for a job, knowing what you're gonna get paid, what the working hours are, what the job expectations are, and that being what the job is."[34]

Part of Production on Deck's work with clients is to craft equitable job postings which can reach the right candidates. According to their website, "For too long we have heard 'There just aren't any out there' or, 'we tried, but it just didn't work.'"[35] These are common refrains when theatre organizations are criticized for how homogenous their staff and creative teams are. Equitable job postings are the first step to finding those workers. These listings include pay transparency and an elimination of education requirements. Production on Deck also advocates for a more personal and accessible approach to the job postings, asking Artistic or Managing Directors to speak directly to the potential candidates via video. This has started to catch on outside their direct sphere of influence; as dStew said, "I've been watching a couple of other companies starting to pick up on that and starting to do the videos for their positions."[36] Additionally, Lozoff explains that, as in the case of audition notices, consent begins for the worker with their encountering of a job posting:

> I think it's really the same when it comes to some of the things that we require, which are, you know, pay transparency, a lack of educational requirements, getting rid of things, like, my ever favorite line, 'other duties as assigned,' and I'm like, that could mean anything. That could be going to pick up my kid from school, and that's not what you signed up for as a Production Manager, right? … Even trying to get organizations to be less ableist in their language, just in terms of like – is this person actually going to be required to lift 50 pounds by themselves? On a regular basis? And if that's true, is that okay? Is that sustainable? Why are we asking them to do that, right? And so even just being like, can

> we adjust that language to say team lift? Because, in what instance, if I needed help with something, would I not be allowed to have it?

An equitable hiring process also requires an accessible interview process. Lozoff explains that sending interview questions ahead of time can be crucial to this:

> Usually there are a couple that are kind of 'think on your feet,' but for the most part, especially the ones that we want nuanced answers to, we send ahead, and I think that first and foremost is a part of equitable labor practices. I think it allows for different learning styles, it allows for different personality types, and it allows people to actually think ... And in terms of advocacy, and equitable practice, I do think different learning styles and neurodivergences come hugely into play and we're just talking about the interview process at this point.[37]

Under the artistic direction of Stephanie Ybarra, Baltimore Center Stage became a leader and example for inclusive hiring. They began the practice of putting out an annual open call for designers and technicians, so workers could gain entry to the BCS production hiring network without personal connections. BCS changed their job description and job posting format. But the changes haven't come easy. Ybarra shared that, similar to when BCS sunset their internship program, as they implemented more equitable hiring practices, one of the biggest challenges was pushback from their own production teams. For many who have been employed in the field for a long time, the system works in their favor, so why change it? But Ybarra offered that their evolving process had already opened many doors:

> We haven't gotten away from resumes entirely, but we have sort of expanded our notion of what a cover letter could be. And this gets a little bit to different learning styles and different working styles and different sort of abilities in terms of, you know, communication, but we tend to invite folks to either write or speak or video-submit the cover letter, personal statement, or whatever that is. We give folks as much choice as possible in an agency over the best way they want to communicate about themselves.[38]

As it stands, most of the industry's inclusive hiring is reactive: organizations taking steps to change their processes when specific requests are made. Ultimately, the goal is to get to a place where theatres have holistically integrated the principles of diversity, equity, inclusion, belonging, and accessibility throughout their operations so these are felt throughout the employee lifecycle. As dStew shared:

> I want to retire Production on Deck because there's no more need for it. I want people to have equitable places where I'm just like, 'You all don't need me.' They're the ones knocking down your doors because you have pay that's

appropriate to your location, you are taking care of your staff, your turnover is low, you're cultivating new talent. You don't need me anymore. Actually, I don't want Production on Deck to go out of business. I want it to get to the point where that aspect of Production on Deck could be retired and then we go into something else for the industry.[39]

NOTES

1 Wendy Kaufman, "A Successful Job Search: It's All About Networking," *NPR*, February 3, 2011, https://www.npr.org/2011/02/08/133474431/a-successful-job-search-its-all-about-networking.
2 Daniel Cox, Juhem Navarro-Rivera, and Robert P. Jones, "Race, Religion, and Political Affiliation of America's Social Networks," *Public Religion Research Institute*, August 3, 2016, https://www.prri.org/research/poll-race-religion-politics-americans-social-networks/.
3 Sarah Fischer, "Exclusive: LinkedIn Aims to Close 'Network Gap,'" *Axios*, September 26, 2019, https://www.axios.com/2019/09/26/linkedin-inequality-network-gap-job-opportunities.
4 Nicholas Thompson, "Wired25: The New Networks with Jeff Weiner," LinkedIn, November 9, 2019, https://www.linkedin.com/pulse/wired25–2019-new-networks-jeff-weiner-nicholas-thompson/?src=aff-lilpar&veh=aff_src.aff-lilpar_c.partners_pkw.10078_plc.Skimbit%20Ltd._pcrid.449670_learning&trk=aff_src.aff-lilpar_c.partners_pkw.10078_plc.Skimbit%20Ltd._pcrid.449670_learning&clickid=U1fyToxXAxyJRxS0EkzjZTwgUknQwl3NLU0MR40&irgwc=1.
5 Thompson.
6 Jessica Pliska, "How Our White Networks Exclude Young People of Color from Career Access and Opportunity," *Forbes*, March 31, 2021, https://www.forbes.com/sites/jessicapliska/2021/03/31/how-our-white-networks-exclude-young-people-of-color-from-career-access-and-opportunity/?sh=3160f6932cdd.
7 David S. Pedulla and Devah Pager, "Race and Networks in the Job Search Process," *American Sociological Review* 84, no. 6 (2019): 1006, DOI: 10.1177/0003122419883255.
8 Pedulla and Pager, 1007.
9 Pedulla and Pager, 1007.
10 Katrina Kibben, "Job Postings that Work (And Some that Don't)," *Writing Advice for Recruiting* (blog), April 20, 2021, https://katrinakibben.com/2021/04/20/job-postings-that-work/.
11 Axelrod Performing Arts Center, "Hiring: Master Electrician," Playbill, https://web.archive.org/web/20220927194713/https://playbill.com/job/hiring-master-electrician/752f376f-84ee-4679-b6a0–81fa27dcb814.
12 Pliska.
13 Pliska.
14 Kat Kibben, "Developing an LGBTQ-Friendly Hiring Process," *ERE Media* (blog), July 26, 2022, https://www.ere.net/developing-an-lgbtq-friendly-hiring-process/.
15 Kibben.
16 Kibben.

17 Elsa Hiltner (Co-Founder, On Our Team), interview by the authors, September 2022.
18 "Scenic Artist II: Job Details," Oregon Shakespeare Festival, September 2, 2022, https://recruiting2.ultipro.com/ORE1002OREG/JobBoard/705d9861-cd29-4b49-8d5c-6b35177a1435/OpportunityDetail?opportunityId=17269599-b214-4e00-be09-fa11d43c6064.
19 Aisha Hollands, "Framework for Fair and Just Hiring Practices," *School Business Affairs*, January 2020, 16–19.
20 Hollands.
21 David "dStew" Stewart (Co-Founder, Production on Deck), interview by the authors, September 2022.
22 Danee Conley, "Progress During an Atypical Year: Hiring Bias and Wage Gaps in Theatre in 2021" (New York, NY: Actors' Equity Association, 2021), 33, https://cdn.actorsequity.org/docs/HiringBiasWageGaps2021.pdf.
23 Conley, 38.
24 Conley, 39.
25 "Making Theatre Hiring More Equitable, Diverse and Inclusive: A Guide from the North Carolina Theatre Conference," North Carolina Theatre Conference, https://www.nctc.org/wp-content/uploads/2021/02/NCTC-Hiring-Guide-V5-links.pdf.
26 "Resources for Racial Diversity, Equity and Inclusion," League of Resident Theatres, https://lort.org/edi-resources.
27 Emika Abe et al., *LORT Equitable Recruitment and Hiring Guide* (New York: League of Resident Theatres, 2017), https://lort.org/assets/documents/LORT-EQUITABLE-RECRUITMENT-AND-HIRING-GUIDE_2017.pdf.
28 "Principles for Building Anti-Racist Theatre Systems," We See You, White American Theatre, https://static1.squarespace.com/static/5ede42fd6cb927448d9d0525/t/60262df611ccc800db7defb9/1613114870376/PRINCIPLES+FOR+BUILDING+ANTI-RACIST+THEATRE+SYSTEMS.pdf.
29 We See You, White American Theatre, 1.
30 We See You, White American Theatre, 3.
31 We See You, White American Theatre, 3.
32 "About," MAESTRA, https://maestramusic.org/about/.
33 "RISE," RISE Theatre, https://www.risetheatre.org.
34 Sarah Lozoff (Co-Founder, Production on Deck), interview by the authors, September 2022.
35 "About," Production on Deck, https://www.productionondeck.com/about.
36 Stewart, interview.
37 Lozoff, interview.
38 Stephanie Ybarra (former Artistic Director, Baltimore Center Stage), interview by the authors, September 2022.
39 Stewart, interview.

7

PAY EQUITY

When asked what equitable labor in theatre production looks like to her, sound designer Beth Lake said, "To me, it looks like everyone is being supported in what they want to do, and they're able to be there of their own free will and choice." As she explained, production workers

> want to be there [...] And in order to want to be there, they have to be paid, they have to have the time, they have to want to be a part of it. They have to want that to be their life and their job. So in order for that to happen, we have to all have a living wage, and be able to know and have the security that we're going to be able to pay rent, we're gonna be able to have food, we're going to be able to take care of each other, we're going to be able to take care of anyone that is dependent on us. So being able to make those choices is what equitable theater looks like to me.[1]

In discussing a living wage and pay equity, it's important to make some distinctions. Equity is not giving everyone the same thing; that's equality. Equity is, as Lake described it, giving everyone what they need. Pay equity is not simply everyone making the same money for the same work because not all work is the same. Sometimes, pay equity means that "different jobs with similar elements such as skill, effort, responsibility, training, experience, and working conditions may be rated equally, and therefore must

DOI: 10.4324/9781003330394-9

receive the same pay."[2] Sometimes it means determining pay scales by the job title or responsibilities to acknowledge that the work is different. Sometimes it means taking into account circumstances beyond a worker's identity: "Employers must weigh other factors, like the employee's education and work experience, the responsibilities of the position, and the organization's long-term financial stability."[3] Pay equity, then, is when worker compensation reflects a combination of the work being done and the experience needed to do the work well, within the employer's budget. For example, a USA contract may have a set minimum pay rate for scenic artists, but an artist can negotiate above that rate based on their years of experience or their specific expertise. Someone with excellent wood-graining technique is highly desirable on a production of a realistic period play; a worker with this expertise could negotiate to be paid more.

Prioritizing pay equity helps employers close the wage gap that "affects the earnings of women and minorities, their well-being, the well-being of their families, and the economy."[4] According to the work of the Time's Up Foundation:

> The pay gap is one of the most persistent – yet measurable and, therefore, solvable – indicators of systemic sexism and racism in the United States. While on average, women in the United States are paid 82 cents for every dollar paid to men, Latinx women earn 54 cents, Native American women earn 57 cents, Black women earn 62 cents, and AAPI women earn 90 cents on the dollar of a white man.[5]

Building on these gaps in potential pay and the pre-existing racial wealth gap, which was created through systemic policies allowing white people to accrue generational wealth, explicit pay inequities disproportionately affect people without external support. As we wrote about in Chapters 5 and 6, workers are often expected to gain experience through unpaid or underpaid work. Workers with external support can do that more easily than those without. External support often comes from the kind of generational wealth reserved for upwardly mobile white Americans. Similarly, those same externally supported workers may not be as affected by the pay inequities as those without support. According to Art Omi board member Gavin Berger,

> Underfunded compensation models for arts professionals, especially entry- and mid-level workers, sustain outdated and elitist notions that working in the arts is a privilege that justifies sacrifice [...] The problem with that assumption is that it reserves work in the arts for individuals who have other forms of financial security or are willing to sacrifice financial security for work in the nonprofit sector, limiting the voices and perspectives represented within our sector.[6]

As in many aspects of equitable labor practices, pay equity also benefits the employer: "Employers who implement fair pay policies may be able to: prevent discrimination lawsuits; comply with equal pay regulations; improve productivity and morale; reduce workplace turnover; [and] attract talented new employees."[7] It gives a company competitive advantage; in the information age, workers have more access than ever before to information about what pay and benefits different employers offer, and seeing that a company compensates its workers equitably can impact jobseekers' perception of the company and build trust within employees. A lack of fair pay measures can cause internal tensions and, rightfully so, lower workers' motivation. Well paid workers are also happier at work, more likely to stay with an employer for longer, and more likely to be more productive.

Pay equity has been the subject of various US laws since the mid-twentieth century. Following the National Labor Relations Act of 1935, which guaranteed workers the right to organize and collectively bargain, the Fair Labor Standards Act of 1938 (FLSA) "ensures workplace protections such as the minimum wage and 'time-and-a-half' overtime pay."[8] It's important to note that the NLRA explicitly excluded farm, domestic workers, and public sector workers, which meant explicitly excluding a large number of BIPOC women workers from union protections, including negotiating for higher wages. Unionized workers make more than non-union workers: In 2022, "the Bureau of Labor Statistics reports non-union workers earn just 85 percent of what unionized workers earn ($1,029/week vs. $1,216/week)."[9]

In an attempt to address the gender wage gap, Congress introduced the Women's Equal Pay Act in 1945, which "sought to prohibit employers from paying women less than men for work of 'comparable quality and quantity' on the basis of sex."[10] The law did not pass. Finally, in 1963, Congress passed the Equal Pay Act, which "requires that men and women be given equal pay for equal work in the same establishment."[11] But even the Equal Pay Act has loopholes that allow for the perpetuation of the wage gap. Employers can justify pay disparities by citing:

> A seniority-based pay system based on an employee's tenure with an employer; a merit-based pay system based on employee performance set by criteria established by the employer; a pay system which measures earnings by quantity or quality of production; [or] a pay differential based on a factor other than sex (in some states, like California, it is increasingly harder to rely on this defense).[12]

These loopholes often mean that workers who have had more access to jobs and training or are more normalized workers make more money than their colleagues. In other words, white men still make more than women, non-binary and trans workers, and BIPOC workers. Finally, Title VII of the Civil Rights Act of 1964 prohibits pay discrimination on the basis of sex, race, color, religion, or national origin and, after a later amendment, disability. In 2020, this was interpreted by the Supreme Court in Bostock v. Clayton County, Georgia to include discrimination based on LGBTQ status.[13] These government efforts are significant in the journey to pay equity but still have not solved the problem.

Pay equity alone is not enough. Pay transparency also helps address the gender and racial pay gap. After a pay transparency law was passed in Denmark in 2006, researchers "found that the gender pay gap in the companies affected by the new laws narrowed as a result of the legislation, while the firms' profitability remained unaffected."[14] In 2022, New York City passed Local Law 32, known as the "Pay Transparency Law," which "will require employers hiring in New York City to disclose the minimum and maximum annual base salary or hourly wage for a job, promotion or transfer opportunity in any advertisement for the position beginning on Nov. 1, 2022."[15] And on January 1, 2023, the California Senate Bill No. 1162 went into effect, which requires that companies with at least 15 employees post pay ranges on all job postings. Other states, such as Colorado, Washington, and New York have implemented similar requirements. These laws protect all workers. The culture of secrecy around wages has been promoted by employers and is harmful to workers: "It's enabled companies to keep compensation stagnant even in the face of inflation, or when market rates for talent have risen, and it's prevented individuals from accessing reference points when it comes to the fairness of their own pay cheque."[16]

As costume designer, textile artist, and co-founder of Costume Professionals for Wage Equity, Elizabeth Wisler said, "We can't have equity until we have transparency."[17] Nonprofit arts writer and consultant Alan Harrison writes to nonprofit arts leaders, "you cannot achieve any of your DEI goals without complete pay transparency."[18] In direct response to this need, several advocacy organizations have been doing strong work. On Our Team, a 501(c)3 Nonprofit Organization founded in 2020, seeks to address ongoing labor and pay equity issues, specifically in Costume Design, but including other theatrical design areas as well. On Our Team was founded by Bob Kuhn, Christine Pascual, Elsa Hiltner, and Theresa Ham. According to their mission, "On Our Team builds pay and labor equity in the theatre industry, and is dedicated to creating a united front in requiring equitable pay and support for theatrical designers."[19] As we mentioned, as part of their larger advocacy work, On Our Team has launched a Pay Transparency Campaign. Using social media as a tool for good, in 2020 they campaigned for the League of Chicago Theatres to require pay transparency on their job site. They also joined with Costume Professionals for Wage Equity in a successful campaign asking the same of Playbill, BroadwayWorld, SETC, and Minnesota Playlist's job sites.[20]

Pay equity is also about every worker having a living, or even a thriving, wage. As we mentioned in Chapter 5, a thriving wage allows workers to not only cover their current basic needs, but to plan for the future, to save for emergencies, education expenses, luxuries, retirement, and future generations. Theatrical production workers often do not receive a thriving wage, and are paid in ways that specifically magnify pay inequity. As we have discussed, some production workers are staff members either working as exempt salaried employees or as non-exempt salaried employees who can collect overtime. Some are hourly staff members. Some are hired as temporary or casual employees, paid hourly. Some, like stage managers, are contracted as salaried employees for a set number of weeks. And some, like designers and assistant designers, are often misclassified, and paid as independent contractors in a fee-based system that does not account for the number of hours they work. Only those designers working at the highest levels of production receive weekly payments as well. This extends across all aspects of the industry: "While some theatre companies have equitable production team fees, unequal pay for equal work is not an issue of a few theatre companies. It is a common and widespread problem that our industry currently has no way to measure,"[21] writes Elsa Hiltner, a costume designer, organizer, and co-founder of On Our Team.

These different payment systems create inequities beyond even those created by different pay scales. Set designer, educator, and advocate Kimie Nishikawa explained:

> First and foremost, the flat fee structure just has to go. It's really by taking on that we are already automatically taking on extra labor that we don't even know about ... For example, tech and previews, the institutions tell us to be there at that time for how many days. How is that a flat fee? And then of course it creates a divide between, you know I don't want to think this way but I would think oh the stage manager is getting a weekly and it creates some sort of resentment.[22]

This raises the question of whether fee-based work is ever equitable. Fee-based work rewards designers who work fast. It doesn't take into account potential revisions. It doesn't account for workers who might be hired earlier in the process and therefore attend more meetings and spend more time on a project. It also doesn't account for the invisible labor like script reading or meeting preparation, or even the meetings themselves. This rewarding of efficiency again perpetuates a white supremacist value structure.

According to Minneapolis-based educator and organizer Wu Chen Khoo, compensation is tied up in the assumptions that arts workers are driven by passion, unlike other workers: The

> passion wages of the arts industry is the separation, both systemic but also psychological separation, of the work that's produced, of the end product of the art if you will, and the labor that happens to make that, to make it take place, that somehow those two things aren't linked to one another.[23]

Employers often expect workers to accept artistic satisfaction in lieu of compensation, without regard for the actual work required to get the show on its feet. No one would expect an Amazon warehouse worker to pack a truck for the satisfaction, nor would they expect a coal miner to spend hours underground for the knowledge that someone far away will be warm for the night. But theatrical employers expect that workers will put in more and more and more, above and beyond what they are being compensated for, out of love and care.

This lack of acknowledgment of the labor is exacerbated through the use of a Most Favored Nations payment model. In this model, all workers who share a job title (such as all of the designers on a project) get paid the same amount. The process is meant to address discriminatory practices between disciplines. However, it can often cause more harm than good. This model does not allow for any consideration of the different amounts of time workers might spend on a project. For example, set designers might be hired months before lighting or sound designers and are often expected to attend many more meetings with the director and scenic staff. Costume designers have to do shop visits and attend fittings and possibly perform alterations. They shouldn't be paid less per meeting or per hour than their lighting or sound collaborators. Producers also weaponize favored nations[24] by using them as a tool to prevent workers from negotiating for a higher fee or any additional compensation. When a worker does try to negotiate for a higher wage, producers can cite the Most Favored Nations clause as a way of justifying lack of resources for the higher expense and "fairness" as a way to say no.

In theatrical production, the historical gendering of so-called "women's work" – costumes, wigs and hair, and often props – also greatly impacts the lack of fair pay. Hiltner explains:

> When the modern garment factory was born at the end of the nineteenth century, women were brought in as stitchers, a source of cheap and dependent labor. More than a hundred years later, the labor of garment work is still effectively women's work and is incorrectly considered, much like modern agricultural labor, to be unskilled, disposable, and worth minimal compensation.[25]

There is a long history of gender discrimination in garment work, and it continues to this day. In 1909, more than 20,000 New York City garment workers held an 11-week general strike, now known as the Strike of the 20,000. This worker activism and that which followed the 1911 Triangle Shirtwaist Factory fire led to the creation of sweeping worker protections in the US,[26] but the discriminatory practices have continued as the industry has moved elsewhere in the world, particularly Asia:

> The vast majority of garment workers – approximately 80% – are women. This is not by chance, but the result of discriminatory practices from start to finish.

> Women are desirable in the garment industry because employers take advantage of cultural stereotypes – to which women are often obliged to adhere – that portrays women as passive and flexible. Productive, reproductive and domestic responsibilities such as cleaning, cooking and childcare constrain women's ability to seek other types of employments. they just do not have the time or opportunity to improve their working conditions, or even speak out about the abuses they face on a daily basis, making them the ideal employees in management's eyes.[27]

Although the working conditions in American theatre are not in any way comparable to those in garment factories in Bangladesh, the expectations and assumptions around this type of work are rooted in this history. Costume designers are expected to shop for both fabric and garments, perform fittings, and often sew garments or make alterations, when lighting designers are not expected to climb a ladder to hang a light and set designers aren't expected to paint scenery on the very same projects. Video and sound designers, who are often expected to create original content, and to design the system through which we experience that content, face some of these same issues. However, they are still more likely to have technical support for the execution of said design. In the costume department, this is often not the case. Again according to Hiltner:

> Costume designers are left to their own devices at all but the largest institutions. Without the support of a technician, costume designers have their hands in each step of bringing the design to the stage – measuring actors, drafting patterns, building costumes, shopping, coordinating rentals, fittings, completing alterations, writing up laundry instructions, coordinating understudy costumes, returns, budgets, the occasional mid-run maintenance, and strike. The stitchers and assistants they work with are usually interviewed and hired by the costume designer and are paid from the designer's fee, or occasionally the costume budget if there's room.[28]

Costume staff are often smaller than the staff of other departments: "This imbalance compounds inequities between male and female designers. It relegates costume designers, mostly women, to artisans, while set and lighting designers, mostly men, remain purely artists."[29] In many theatres, the costume shop is not unionized even when the rest of the technical shops are. As Hiltner reiterates, "Costume designers, properties designers, wig designers, and others support the theatre industry with their implied free labor by doing the work of both designer and technician, while other designers on the same production team are given technical support."[30] Costume designers, as we have discussed, are also more likely to be women: "Based on three years of numbers she compiled, Porsche McGovern notes that 76.5 percent of set designers and 80 percent of lighting designers are male, while only 30 percent of costume designers are male in the League of Resident Theatres (LORT)."[31] So what does this mean? Hiltner explains:

> On the surface, the allocation of support and resources within a theatre company is based on the design discipline. Female set designers are offered the same resources as male set designers within an institution, as are male and female costume designers. But this is where our culture's gendered views on garment work come into play.[32]

The gender-based pay inequity problems in production are not isolated to theatre. Workers in film and television face similar struggles:

> In an industry plagued by pay inequity and gender bias, it's no surprise that costume designers are victims of the same issues. 'The majority of costume designers are women, and they are ignored,' says [Salvador Perez, president of the Costume Designers Guild], who's worked as a costume designer on shows like *The Mindy Project*. '[The industry] thinking is, "Well, it's just shopping, my wife can do that."' As a man working in a role dominated by women – the Costume Designers Guild is composed of nearly 90% women – Perez says he's been previously paid more than his female counterparts: 'It's proof that it's a gender thing.'[33]

According the extensive research conducted by the Costume Designers Guild, the current negotiated wages (based on a 60 hour work week) are $8,374 for Directors of Photography; $4,103 for production designer; $4,576 for makeup department heads; $3,140 for film costume designers; and for television costume designers even less at $2,953.[34] Though these numbers are significantly higher than what a theatrical costume designer might make – the minimum rate for a LORT A costume designer is $10,006 *for the entire project* – the discrepancies within the film industry are appalling. According to a study by Local USA 829, costume department coordinators report an average of $1,697.14 per week.[35] Coordinators are considered entry-level workers in the costume department even though they are responsible for tracking and reconciling the massive costume budgets and managing the staff for the entire department. Just like in theatrical production, costume roles in film are predominantly filled by women. Stephen Follows studied the 100 highest grossing films at the US box office for each year between 1994 and 2013, looking at the numbers behind female film crew members. He found: "Women make up only 23% of crew members on the 2,000 highest grossing films of the past 20 years."[36] He continues:

> The jobs performed by women have become more polarised. In jobs which are traditionally seen as more female (art, costume and make-up) the percentage of women has increased, whereas in the more technical fields (editing and visual effects) the percentage of women has fallen.[37]

Which means that overall, women are consistently making less.

All of this combines to mean that costume professionals are doing more work with less support, and, therefore, designers can design fewer shows in a single year. So in a Most Favored Nations model, where all of the designers are paid the same fee, costume designers make less overall. These inequities extend beyond design positions: "For example, skilled stitchers are often paid less than similarly skilled carpenters or even entry-level admin staff."[38] According to the 2019 Broadway League contracts, an IATSE Local 1 stagehand supervisor makes $83 per hour and a Local 764 Wardrobe supervisor makes $45 per hour.[39] Eliminating the nuances between the disciplines creates disparities between the pay structures. Pretending that equity is equality is problematic when folks are doing different amounts of work.

Across the industry, there is inconsistent union representation, which bolsters these differences in pay. For example, in New York City, technicians working on Broadway are organized members of IATSE, but technicians working off-Broadway are generally unorganized, as are those working in even smaller theatres. In many LORT theatres, though most of the designers are members of United Scenic Artists, the actors and stage managers are members of Actor's Equity, and the director is likely a member of the Stage Directors and Choreographers Society, there is no guarantee that the technicians are organized. In Philadelphia, for example, there are four LORT theatres, and the technicians and staff are organized at two of them, the Wilma and Philadelphia Theatre Company, but not at the Arden or People's Light. Similarly, the scenery that is loaded into a union theatre is, in most cases, built in a union shop. But none of the Broadway costume shops are unionized. In fact, it is an unwritten understanding that should those shops unionize, the producers would take their business elsewhere. Inequities range across different producing models as well. And different workers have more power in different markets. In Nashville, for example, musicians hold a lot more power than technicians:

> Tennessee is a so-called right-to-work state, and while Nashville's musicians' union (AFM 257) holds power within the industry, IATSE Locals 46 (stagehands) and 915 (wardrobe professionals) hold significantly less. In Nashville, backstage technicians piece together paychecks from a variety of venues and events, including convention work at the Music City Center and work calls for the national tours of Broadway musicals visiting the Tennessee Performing Arts Center. The city's local theatres hire nonunion staff, and even the civic arts organizations like the symphony and opera that hire union musicians staff their events with nonunion crews, sometimes outsourced from companies like Crew One, Live Nation, or Rhino Staging that pay hourly rates significantly below union wages and offer fewer, if any, benefits.[40]

Until the 2021 Off-Broadway agreement, no Local USA 829 contract in live performance (theatre, opera, or dance) included any language around minimum wage. The inclusion of previously excluded assistant designers and the language explicitly acknowledging an hourly wage is a game changer:

> At the time Assistant Designers are engaged, they shall be provided with a defined amount of total compensation which shall cover a specified term of employment. The Assistant Designers shall be paid not less than the then current New York State minimum wage. Per the Fair Labor Standards Act, Assistant Designers are non-exempt employees and are entitled to receive overtime pay for all time worked in excess of forty (40) hours per work week, which shall be one and one-half times their regular rate of pay.[41]

This was a huge win for production workers. Not only are assistant designers acknowledged to not be independent contractors but instead to be non-exempt *employees*, they are also guaranteed both a minimum hourly rate and overtime. This solution isn't the end of the conversation. At the time of this contract's ratification in 2021, minimum wage in NYC was $15 per hour. A reasonable living wage in NYC was closer to $25 to $28 per hour, but this was a step in the right direction. This agreement is also the first live performance contract that includes assistant designers beyond Broadway.

This agreement is the result, in large part, of a grassroots organizing campaign. Beth Lake, a sound designer USA 829 member and original organizer of the campaign, explained that the work began as early as 2012 when a group of Off-Broadway assistants, including sound designers Charles Coes and Sam Kusnetz, came together casually to meet and talk about the specific challenges facing Off-Broadway assistants. These included low fee-based pay, extremely long hours, and a lack of transparency around the scale of time commitments. In 2019, United Scenic Artists then-Live Performance Business Representative Carl Mulert gathered a group of these workers together because, as Lake explained, "there were multiple people going to the union office with questions and concerns, and trying to figure out how to make it a more equitable and reasonable place to work as an Off-Broadway Assistant."[42]

After years of data collection and individual one-on-one outreach, this grassroots group, now known as the Off-Broadway Assistant Designers Advisory Group (OBADAG), was instrumental in the negotiation and ultimate ratification of the Off-Broadway contract which includes protection for assistants. And their work continues. Though the contract includes minimums, the journey to pay equity and a living wage has been fraught. In the summer of 2022, the assistant and associate designers on the Public Theatre's production of *As You Like It* were pushed to threaten a work stoppage to achieve equitable pay. The Public was offering assistants and associates $15 per hour (the New York City minimum wage) when entry-level electricians on the same show were offered $25 per hour. The lighting team was able to leverage their necessary participation when the lighting designer came down with COVID during tech, after three months of negotiations.[43]

Pay inequity is also perpetuated through systemic wage theft: "Most people think wage theft is not getting paid but it goes way beyond that. Wage theft is defined as underpayment or failure to pay all wages earned."[44] Advocacy group Technicians for Change share information about wage theft and what theatre production personnel can do about it. Among other definitions, wage theft can be seen in situations where workers are shorted pay though subminimum wage or tipping violations, through shorted time worked where workers are working off the clock or are "working far more hours than promised for a flat rate."[45] This all sounds very familiar to theatre production workers. Illegal practices such as manipulated time sheets, delayed or missed payments, unlawful deductions, or entirely skipped payments are also factors. For designers especially, so is the "misclassification of employees as independent contractors."[46] This misclassification confuses how the workers are paid, in a flat untaxed fee versus a taxed salary, with whether or not they are considered employees, a confusion of employment law and labor law.

It's not just the ways that workers are paid that make working in theatrical production hard for so many, but the amounts as well. When asked what she sees as the biggest current challenge for production labor, Sarah Lozoff said,

> I'm going to come back to wages. Too long hours for too little pay, literally not enough to live on. And that makes it hard. That makes it hard to sign up to do the job, and it certainly makes it hard to do it well. When I'm hungry, when I'm tired, when I don't have my own private space, when I haven't seen my friends and family enough.[47]

As we keep coming back to, in the arts, there is a general perception that everyone working in the field is there out of a love for the art. Lozoff shared:

> I would love for theater to make room for the fact that this is work, that it is transactional, that we hope people are here because they love it, we think that people wouldn't dedicate this much time and effort because it is really hard to do something that they didn't love. But that also days and weeks and maybe even months and years can go by where it's really hard and we don't love it. And that that's okay, too, that we are showing up for a paycheck. And that also says something about our dedication.[48]

As we said before, this disconnect between the art and the labor needed to make the art is systemic. And the perpetually underpayment for the creation of the art perpetuates itself. "As designers in theatre we have become so accustomed to being underpaid for our art, so selling ourselves short comes all too naturally," continued Lozoff. "As artists, we are used to being paid in validation when the money falls short because we love our art. But when we look more closely, that validation belies an industry that pays as little as it can get away with."[49] Set designer Kimie Nishikawa reiterated that sentiment, explaining that, even in situations where workers have Collectively Bargained Agreements which state minimum fees for work, "the minimums are becoming our maximums. Not becoming. They are our maximums right now."[50] It is increasingly rare for theatres to offer above the minimum rate when working on a collectively bargained agreement without a fight, and, even then, Most Favored Nations contracts are weaponized against workers as a way to prevent folks from getting paid more for their work.

But at least collectively bargained contracts include minimums. For technicians working Off-Broadway or at unorganized regional theatres, their hourly rates are often individually negotiated or set by assumed industry standards. During the COVID-19 Pause and theatre's re-emergence, workers around the country have been pushing for higher wages and safer workplaces. But there is still a long, long way to go.

As part of her advocacy work, Hiltner conducted interviews with an expansive series of Chicago theatre executives to figure out what they think about pay equity and how, if at all, they are approaching it. Out of that work came the Pay Equity Standards created by On Our Team. According to the On Our Team website:

> The Pay Equity Standards are a rubric and public symbol for equitable pay practices within a theatre company. Designed as a checklist, the Pay Equity Standards lay out a path to establishing equitable pay using a three-pronged approach to pay equity: Transparency, Working Conditions, and Accountability. The program was launched in January 2022. Inspired by the organic and fair trade food labels, theater companies that opt in and meet all certification requirements will be granted use of the Pay Equity Standards badge.[51]

As of April 2023, three companies – 2nd Story, Collaboraction Theatre Company, and Summit Players Theatre – have been certified. The hope is that making this certification visible gives audience members information about where their ticket money is going, funders transparent data about how grants might be used, and workers knowledge about where they might want to apply for jobs. In a Wingspace Virtual Salon, Elizabeth Wisler spoke about how a lack of pay equity can be an indicator of larger concerns:

> My understanding of wage equity, pay equity, also comes with an understanding of labor equity and health and safety equity and that you can't really do one with the others. That they, all three, need to coexist in your organization or in your program. If the wage equity isn't there I can almost always guarantee that the labor equity and the health and safety equity aren't there.[52]

The information being gathered by On Our Team allows workers to look out for these situations and hopefully to avoid unsafe work environments.

Dramaturg and writer Lauren Halvorsen writes *Nothing for the Group*, a weekly newsletter about American theatre. Each week, Halvorsen compiles a round-up of industry news, reviews, links, and her own "salty but never mean" commentary to explore the power structures and dynamics that create and perpetuate inequity in the industry, and to dissect how institutions frame their public narratives.[53] In a series titled "That's Not A Living Wage," Halvorsen shares theatre job listings paired with information about the living wage for a 40-hour work week for one adult with no children in that area. She augments these listings with the institution's most recently available Form 990 organizational tax filing data to contextualize the overall finances and executive compensation of each hiring theatre.[54] For example, she cited that Shakespeare Theatre of New Jersey posted a job listing for a Master Electrician: "$42,000– $47,000 (overtime – eligible after 40 hours/week); Living Wage for Morris County, NJ: $50,300; Revenue (2020): $2.07 million / Net Income: -$45,533; Executive Compensation: $185,000 (Artistic Director)."[55] In the 2023 season, Shakespeare Theatre of New Jersey is producing five mainstage productions and one outdoor production. They cast a combination of union and non-union performers, but their production workers are not unionized, beyond the designers. The actors are similarly paid below a living wage. The AEA actors are on a LORT contract and are paid $739 a week, which would translate to $38,428 annually. It's perhaps useful to note here that the LORT contract bases the salary on the gross box office receipts from the venue in which a show is being produced, not the employer's operating budget. The disparity between the executive compensation and the production worker compensation seen here is common. If institutions were willing to close these gaps, both the executive leadership and the low-paid production workers could earn a thriving wage for their regions. Perhaps this season is out of scope with what is reasonable for Shakespeare Theatre of New Jersey to produce responsibly?

Similarly, a posting for an interim costume shop manager and production coordinator at Imagination Stage in Maryland was listed as the following: "$41,000– $49,000; Living Wage for Montgomery County, MD: $53,074; Revenue (2021): $5.2 million / Net Income: $1.66 million; Executive Compensation: $101,093 (Executive Director) / $87,693 (Founding Artistic Director)"[56] Imagination Stage cites as one of its values: "We value our staff associates and respect their contributions to the achievement of our mission and values."[57] One of the clearest ways to show one's employees that they are valued is by paying them enough to live.

Consistent with the prevalence of unpaid and underpaid internships in theatrical production, the Walnut Street Theatre in Philadelphia advertised for apprentices who would be paid "$350/week ($18,200 annual); Living Wage for Philadelphia, PA: $39,560; Total Expenses (2020): $12.4 million / Executive Compensation: $533,259 (President/Producing Artistic Director)."[58] As a side note, Halvorsen also proclaims: "This remains the *wildest* AD salary in America."[59] Referring to the apprenticeship program, Halvorsen notes:

> WST Apprenticeship contracts vary between 6– 12 months depending on the position. No housing or health benefits provided, but apprentices receive 'a full scholarship' (Not totally sure what that means! But it sounds like the classic apprenticeship narrative: spinning the program as an 'educational opportunity' when it's really just an underpaid full-time job.)[60]

The phrase "apprentices receive a full scholarship to be in the program"[61] implies that participation in the program should come at a cost rather than that it involves labor that should be compensated. It's common that this kind of structure is the first job a worker might have in the industry, introducing the lack of living wage early.

In June 2020, Halvorsen launched a spin-off of her newsletter, *Bills, Bills, Bills*, a monthly series of anonymous money diaries from theatre workers curated by dramaturg Jenna Clark Embrey. The first installment was prominently featured in the *New York Times'* coverage on pay equity and salary transparency."[62] In one example cited in *Bills, Bills, Bills*:

> A woman who has been working for about 16 years in a costume shop at a midsize theater in a midsize city in the Midwest agreed to discuss her job. A typical 40-hour week finds her cutting, draping, patterning, tailoring, altering, stitching, dyeing, distressing, repairing and 'whatever else comes up.' The pay is $18.64 an hour, but only during the theater's nine-month season. During her three-month furlough, she collects unemployment and goes without health insurance, 'praying to Baby Jesus,' she told me, 'I don't hurt myself over the summer.'[63]

In 2020, half of US adults were concerned that a single medical event could land them in bankruptcy.[64] This is an increasingly significant concern for workers who struggle to make a living wage. It is exceptionally hard for production workers to be prepared for any kind of crisis or emergency when they are working in the model we have described. And this became all too clear in the spring of 2020. As designer Nishikawa explains, "I still remember I had $923 in my bank account when the pandemic hit … but

I'm a successful designer. That's what I'm told."[65] Perhaps unique to the arts, then, success is defined by notoriety and visibility rather than by financial stability. This goes back in many ways to the ways in which theatrical production workers are taken advantage of for liking what they do. Wu Chen Khoo connects this to the larger question of the worker's relationship to their own labor:

> I think it's important to think about the way we're alienated in our labor – the very point in so many ways is to separate us from our humanity and to just extract labor from us for the production of something and by not paying us very much and functionally what happens is that workers are subsidizing the industry.[66]

In order to combat this, there needs to be systemic change. Elsa Hiltner offers the difficult answers:

> All theaters will end unpaid internships. Those with annual budgets greater than $1 million will meet minimum-wage rates, and eventually living-wage rates, for all workers. Compensation categories, or each worker's actual pay, will be clearly defined and shared. The highest salary in an organization will exceed the lowest by no more than a factor of five. Schedules will be set 'to the greatest extent possible' to fit within a 40-hour workweek.[67]

Right now, workers are expected to operate in a sort of honor system. Theatre production workers are often expected to begin work on a project before a contract is in place. Even workers protected by a union are often in this situation. We asked workers how often they have started a project without a signed contract or accepted a job without knowing the pay. (See Figure 7.2 for a breakdown of the responses.)

The percentage of workers who, at least sometimes, begin without a contract, are being asked to work without knowing the complete terms of employment and without being paid for that initial work on time is 67.3%. As in many of these inequitable practices, lack of contracts raises the questions: who has the ability to work without an initial payment? And who has the ability to do work for which they may not be compensated? Once again, workers with financial safety nets are the only ones who can participate in this system.

One of the reasons it is often hard to organize artists is because of the mythology around the starving-artist archetype. As Wisler explains, this allows for employers to maintain power over a disorganized workforce:

> The industry promotes a scarcity model that tells artists they should be grateful for the few jobs there are and pits designers against each other with competition and questions of whose job is harder or which area requires more skill, whereby maintaining that designers take what they can get individually and don't organize together on systemic issues like equitable pay.[68]

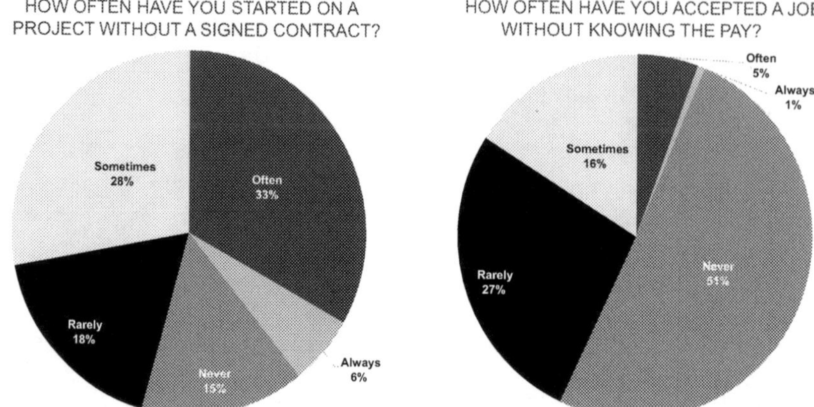

Figure 7.2 Worker responses to "How often have you started on a project without a signed contract?" and "How often have you accepted a job without knowing the pay?"

This also means that workers don't have a sense of what their time is worth or of what they could be asking for. Discussing wages and fees can help resolve this, but often workers aren't comfortable doing so. And the culture of underpaid labor permeates everything. As in any workplace, it's in the employer's best interest to keep workers in the dark about each other's wages: "The less artists know about the pay and terms those around them have been offered or negotiated, the easier it is for those cutting the checks to shortchange designers. This inequity isn't a sign of a broken system, it is the system."[69]

Non-profit theatres benefit from a significant set of myths around workers' pay. As we have discussed, the primary myth is this one: that people work in the theatre because they love it, and that that in and of itself is a kind of compensation. But landlords don't accept happiness in lieu of rent checks. Sarah Lozoff elaborates to say:

> Yet a pervasive story theater people have told themselves forever says that scrounging and sacrificing and 'paying dues,' sometimes indefinitely, are part of the identity, even the glamour of the field. Poverty may be seen as a sign that progress, if it comes, has been earned by suffering.[70]

This shows up in very tangible ways for theatre workers. In the Fair Wage Onstage blog these very myths are discussed:

> For instance, you believe if a particular theatre paid you more, that it might go out of business. You believe that if you were paid a living wage, ticket prices

> would dramatically increase and it would result in smaller casts and less work for actors. You believe that you are easily replaceable. You believe you are 'lucky' to be working. You believe that you work in the theatre for 'exposure.' You believe that your union is weak. You believe that you are powerless to change 'the way things work.' You believe that the work itself is the reward and those lucky enough to have coveted theatre jobs should be grateful and not expect or ask for a fair wage. You believe if you speak up how hard it is to sustain yourself as an artist, you will be seen as a 'trouble-maker' and blacklisted and never work again.[71]

This mentality is incredibly common. It stems in many ways from societal understandings of how hard it is to "make it" in the arts, and in theatre in particular, from stories like *All About Eve* and *42nd Street*. It is a myth that is taught in educational institutions where students compete for the opportunities to work on productions and are encouraged to believe that there is always someone waiting to take their place. It continues to be affirmed through competitive graduate programs that accept an incredibly small class of maybe two designers in each discipline. It's reaffirmed by producers who say that they can just find someone else for the money if you won't take it, by theatres who don't even bother to post job postings because their existing network is so vast. The Fair Wage Onstage blog goes on to explain:

> Fear and anxiousness are symptomatic of a career path that is financially and professionally unstable. [And] these myths are so much a part of the conversational culture of being an actor or stage manager that we unconsciously replay them over and over, literally carving neurological grooves into our brains that form our experience of baseline reality.[72]

These myths don't just apply to stage managers and actors. They absolutely also apply to designers, technicians, and all production workers.

So where do we go from here? How can employers and workers rectify pay inequities across theatrical production? At the heart of the issue is not just understanding the systemic inequities but creating systemic change including, first and foremost, a basic thriving wage for everyone. As Simone Stolzoff writes, "the rhetoric that a job is a passion or a 'labor of love' obfuscates the reality that a job is an economic contract. The assumption that it isn't sets up the conditions for exploitation."[73]

NOTES

1 Beth Lake (Co-Chair, Off-Broadway Assistant Designer Advisory Group), interview by the authors, September 2022.

2 Commission for Women, "Pay Equity" (Augusta, ME: Commission for Women, 1980): 1, https://search.alexanderstreet.com/view/work/bibliographic_entity%7Cbibliographic_details%7C2520364.

3 "Pay Equity," ADP, https://www.adp.com/resources/articles-and-insights/articles/p/pay-equity.aspx.
4 Stephanie R. Thomas, *Compensating Your Employees Fairly: A Guide to Internal Pay Equity* (New York: Apress, 2013): 13.
5 "Gender and Racial Inequity During Crisis: The Pay Gap," Time's Up https://timesupfoundation.org/work/times-up-pay-up/gender-and-racial-inequity-during-crisis-the-pay-gap/.
6 "Berkshire/Columbia Counties Arts Organizations Launch Regional Pay Equity Initiative," Berkshire Art Center November 14, 2022, https://berkshireartcenter.org/news/equitysurvey2022.
7 ADP, "Pay Equity."
8 "Pay Equity 101," Trusaic https://trusaic.com/pay-equity-complete-overview.
9 "The Union Advantage," US Department of Labor, https://www.dol.gov/general/workcenter/union-advantage.
10 Trusaic.
11 Trusaic.
12 Trusaic.
13 Trusaic.
14 Josie Cox, "The U.S. Push for Pay Transparency," *BBC*, September 29, 2022, https://www.bbc.com/worklife/article/20220929-the-us-push-for-pay-transparency.
15 Jennifer Lada and Stephanie M. Merabet, "Seeing Through the Pay Transparency Law," Holland and Knight, October 19, 2022, https://www.hklaw.com/en/insights/publications/2022/10/seeing-through-the-pay-transparency-law#:~:text=NYC%20Local%20Law%2032%2C%20known,on%20Nov.%201%2C%202022.
16 Cox.
17 *WS Virtual Salon 29 Pay Equity*, YouTube video, 2022, 19:24, https://www.youtube.com/watch?v=jTaNBzc1AAE.
18 Alan Harrison, "Nonprofit Arts Boards—Pay Equity Starts with YOUR Nonprofit," *Scene Change* (blog), July 19, 2022, https://medium.com/nonprofits-arts-politics-leadership/nonprofit-arts-boards-pay-equity-starts-with-your-nonprofit-4598441e9a3f.
19 "About Us," On Our Team, https://www.onourteam.org/about.
20 On Our Team, "About Us."
21 Elsa Hiltner, "Inequity by Design," HowlRound Theatre Commons, July 13, 2020, https://howlround.com/inequity-design.
22 *WS Virtual Salon*, 15:35.
23 *WS Virtual Salon*, 6:25.
24 *WS Virtual Salon*, 59:40.
25 Elsa Hiltner, "A Call for Equal Support in Theatrical Design," HowlRound Theatre Commons, November 23, 2016, https://howlround.com/call-equal-support-theatrical-design.
26 "Triangle Shirtwaist Fire," AFL-CIO, https://aflcio.org/about/history/labor-history-events/triangle-shirtwaist-fire.
27 "Gender: Women Workers Mistreated," Clean Clothes Campaign, https://cleanclothes.org/issues/gender

28 Hiltner, "A Call for Equal Support in Theatrical Design."
29 Hiltner, "A Call for Equal Support in Theatrical Design."
30 Hiltner, "Inequity by Design."
31 Hiltner, "A Call for Equal Support in Theatrical Design."
32 Hiltner, "A Call for Equal Support in Theatrical Design."
33 Frances Solá-Santiago, "Costume Designers Are Stars on Social Media. So Why Aren't They Being Paid That Way?" *Refinery 29*, September 17, 2021, https://www.refinery29.com/en-us/2021/09/10676505/costume-designers-pay-inequality-social-media.
34 Fawnia Soo Hoo, "The Real Reason Costume Designers are Paid Less than their Peers," *Fashionista*, May 5, 2022, https://fashionista.com/2022/05/costume-designers-pay-equity-wage-gap.
35 IATSE Local USA 829, "The Case for Costume Department Coordinators: An Equitable Path for United Scenic Artists, Local USA 829 Costume Coordinators" (New York, NY: IATSE Local USA 829, December 2022), 12, https://mcusercontent.com/cd56c12d8cc5b412b582b737f/files/44d02bd0-a237-b7bd-566a-903daddda37f/CDC_Pamphlet_12_22.pdf?fbclid=PAAaZHl7WD39UnfjgRjHuvJAbFJuERQh_BmqNonrrnXtLeMcO00LI_DkgYgS4.
36 Stephen Follows, "What Percentage of a Film Crew Is Female?," *Stephen Follows: Film Data and Education* (blog), July 22, 2014, https://stephenfollows.com/gender-of-film-crews/.
37 Follows.
38 Hiltner, "Inequity by Design."
39 ia_costumes (@iatse_costumes), "While pay equity is on everybody's lips, here are the statistics sent to us regarding local 1 (NYC Broadway stage crew) and Local 764 (NYC Broadway wardrobe)," Instagram photo, March 30, 2022, https://www.instagram.com/p/Cbv_GCJufmL/?igshid=YmMyMTA2M2Y%3D.
40 Christin Essin, "Coda from Working Backstage," *Theatre Design & Technology*, Winter 2022, 28.
41 Agreement by and between The Off-Broadway League and United Scenic Artists, Local USA 29, IATSE, April 22, 2021, https://static1.squarespace.com/static/60be748b0b55be0c7e119dab/t/62bdb8fac461613318df8da1/1656600826797/USAOBLAgreement+21–25+FE-compressed.pdf.
42 Lake, interview.
43 "Asst Coverage Enters 2nd Season & Rate Increase WIN at Public Theater," Off-Broadway Assistant Designer Advisory Group (electronic mailing list), August 26, 2022.
44 Allana Olson, "Wage Theft and What You Can Do About It," Technicians for Change, January 2022, https://techniciansforchange.org/2022/01/05/wage-theft/.
45 Olson.
46 Olson.
47 Sarah Lozoff (Co-Founder, Production on Deck), interview by the authors, September 2022.
48 Lozoff, interview.
49 Hiltner, "Inequity by Design."
50 *WS Virtual Salon*, 38:32.

51 "The Pay Equity Standards," On Our Team, https://www.onourteam.org/pay-equity-standards.
52 *WS Virtual Salon*, 1:52.
53 Lauren Halvorsen, "About," Nothing for the Group, Substack, https://nothingforthegroup.substack.com/about.
54 Halvorsen.
55 Lauren Halvorsen, "The Week of November 5–11, 2022," Nothing for the Group, Substack, November 11, 2022, https://nothingforthegroup.substack.com/p/the-week-of-november-5–11–2022?utm_source=substack&utm_medium=email.
56 Lauren Halvorsen, "The Week of October 1–7, 2022," Nothing for the Group, Substack, October 7, 2022, https://nothingforthegroup.substack.com/p/the-week-of-october-1–7–2022?utm_source=email.
57 "About Us," Imagination Stage, https://imaginationstage.org/about/.
58 Lauren Halvorsen, "The Week of May 2–6, 2022," Nothing for the Group, Substack, May 6, 2022, https://nothingforthegroup.substack.com/p/the-week-of-may-2–6–2022.
59 Halvorsen, "Week of May 2–6."
60 Halvorsen, "Week of May 2–6."
61 "Professional Apprentice Program," Walnut Street Theatre, https://www.walnutstreettheatre.org/about/apprenticeships.php.
62 Halvorsen, "About."
63 Jesse Green, "When Paying Dues Doesn't Pay the Rent, How Does the Theater Survive?," *New York Times*, July 6, 2022, https://www.nytimes.com/2022/07/06/theater/pay-equity-salaries.html.
64 Dan Witters, "50% in U.S. Fear Bankruptcy Due to Major Health Event," *Gallup*, September 1, 2020, https://news.gallup.com/poll/317948/fear-bankruptcy-due-major-health-event.aspx.
65 *WS Virtual Salon*, 45:22.
66 *WS Virtual Salon*, 13:19.
67 Green.
68 Hiltner, "Inequity by Design."
69 Hiltner, "Inequity by Design."
70 Green.
71 "Myths That Keep Actors and Stage Managers Exploited and Broke," Fair Wage Onstage, September 3, 2017, https://fairwageonstage.org/myths-keep-actors-stage-managers-exploited-broke/.
72 Fair Wage Onstage, "Myths."
73 Simone Stolzoff, "Please Don't Call My Job a Calling," *New York Times*, June 5, 2023, https://www.nytimes.com/2023/06/05/opinion/employment-exploitation-unions.html?searchResultPosition=4.

YOU GOT THIS!
CALL SHOP
NOTHING for the GROUP
M T W Th F S S S S
BID ONLY

8

PRODUCTION OPERATIONS

While creative processes develop and evolve differently, theatrical production typically follows a relatively standard order of operations to get a show up on its feet. Once a producing entity has selected a show, they generate a budget, create a calendar, and staff the team. We will use the term "production operations" to refer to the creation and continued management of the budget, schedule, and production staff for the project.

Budgets are value statements for a producing organization. The more one values something, the more resources one is willing to put towards it. For many organizations, production budgets are just a part of a larger institutional budget. Budgeting for a production includes considerations of materials costs, equipment rental costs, and, of course, labor costs. In many cases, the cost of materials and equipment is much higher than the funds dedicated to human labor, implying that the humans are more temporary or replaceable. Looking at who articulates the institution's values, we surveyed producing organizations, asking who makes the production budget. The most common answers were the production manager, general manager, or artistic leadership. In some cases, members of the artistic team on a specific production may have input into how resources are distributed. For example, when we asked the management of HERE in New York City who creates the budget, they responded:

DOI: 10.4324/9781003330394-10

> the General Manager in collaboration with the commissioned artist. We allow the commissioned artist to lead the budgeting process, but we guide them through that and we impose certain restrictions upon them (like adhering to certain hourly caps, pay minimums, and benefit minimums).

In general, employers who responded to our survey said that production budgets vary – from moderately to drastically – depending on the production, and they cited several reasons for this variation. At Spring Green Wisconsin's American Players Theater, considered the country's second-largest outdoor theatre devoted to the classics, leadership cited the specific needs of the production as room for varying budgets: "the size, scope, and scale of the production. Number of costumes has the largest impact of changes from show to show." Other theatres, including Abrons Arts Center in Manhattan, the Kitchen Theatre Company in Ithaca, NY, and InterAct Theatre Company in Philadelphia, cited the number of humans, especially those working under Actor's Equity contracts, engaged on the production, and, for InterAct specifically, "participation of out-of-town artists (which typically require higher fees/salaries, along with travel and local housing), scenic fabrication, and special design elements (original music, projections, fight choreography, culturally specific dramaturg, etc.)." This is a clear example of how a theatre can be responsive to a production. Some theatres use more of a formula, which can ignore the specific needs of a script or of a group of humans engaged on a project. All of these factors, and their relative importance, reveal values of these institutions.

Budget flexibility often relates to an organization's size. Sarah Clare Corporandy is a co-founder and Producing Artistic Director of Detroit Public Theatre, whose annual budget has grown from $425,000 to $2 million.[1] She explained that organizational scale greatly impacts how much budgetary choices can reflect artistic values. In her previous role at Chautauqua Theater Company, the resident theatre company of the Chautauqua Institution in upstate New York, it was very different:

> We couldn't really do our own fundraising, and you're basically reliant on them to give you a subsidy to make your budget work, right? [...] So we're always making a case to an organization that has 30 departments under it, and they're trying to decide where they want to spend their money. And so we're advocating for that, and for me, it always came down to – we were a summer theatre company, we brought in a ton of people to do a ton of shows.[2]

Being at a smaller institution has offered more control and more dialogue between values and budget. She explained:

> At DPT I had the power to say, 'Well, we can't work that way.' So this is what it costs. I don't have to fight first for that with someone else. It's easier for us to

> establish. I imagine in an organization that's been around for 100 years, if people are being underpaid, or the hours are screwed up, and the whole model is based on that, once you pull one string, all the dominoes fall.[3]

This is consistent with the pushback other organizational leaders have encountered when efforts have been made to change the schedule and labor structure of long-standing institutions. For Corporandy at Detroit Public, the priorities have remained relatively clear:

> If you make it a priority first, you'll figure out how to make it happen, but if it's not a priority, then spending an extra $100,000 a year feels super crazy when there's five other things to spend $100,000 on and if it's been working, if the product has been coming out for years, if you're fighting for it, it's hard for the people to understand that they're not going to get it. That's hard in those institutions, and I've been in that situation before, and I feel like I'd been moderately successful, but not as successful as I am at DPT right now because I just don't have a ceiling pushing me down.[4]

In part, that seems to be a result of their shared leadership model. Corporandy serves as Co-Artistic Director with Courtney Burkett and Sarah Winkler. Playwright Dominique Morriseau is the Executive Producer, collaborating on artistic leadership. Together, these four leaders have kept humans at the center of those priorities. As Corporandy continued, "We don't really ever have a fight about the budget. We're all half-artistic, half-administrative, [...] And so we have a responsibility to the budget, because if we fucked that up, we can't pay people."[5]

Stephanie Ybarra, then at Baltimore Center Stage, shared her experience with this production budget and organizational values alignment. She had been working to increase design fees to be the same across both spaces at BCS, slowly stair-stepping them over time with an approach she calls "relentless incrementalism."[6] She explained that one of the spaces is LORT D and the other is LORT B, but actors were already getting paid at LORT B rates for both spaces. These LORT designations are determined by Rule 13 of the LORT-Actor's Equity Association (AEA) Agreement, and are based on number of seats and budgetary considerations. Under Ybarra's leadership, BCS incrementally raised the wages for directors and designers to be the same across both spaces as well. This has led to the need to keep physical production expenses lower because the organization has a finite amount of financial resources. As she explained to designers that higher fees means smaller production budgets, and told them why, she was amazed by some of the positive responses she heard from designers, such as, "Well, this is the first time I've been so inspired to bring a show in on a budget."[7] Transparency is a tool towards progress; people often are open to these changes when they understand the reasons.

The scarcity of arts funding increases the sense of urgency and the impulse to push through because "the show must go on." There is just never enough – never enough crew, never enough money, never enough time. Like many aspects of theatrical production, this started to be re-evaluated during the Pause. In a HowlRound conversation with producers Sophie Blumberg, Ben Johnson, and Jonathan Secor, Blumberg said:

> Financial security has always been a big piece of the artistry puzzle. We sacrificed our own safety in the name of creating and producing work and keeping a roof over our heads. I think part of the urgency is that we've all realized this past year that we just can't work that way anymore. It is unsustainable.[8]

When we discuss production scheduling, there are a variety of types of schedules involved: the overall production calendar, the weekly rehearsal schedule, the load-in and tech schedule, the preview and performance schedule. Production calendars can vary wildly, but generally include some form of the following phases: pre-production, rehearsals, design and construction timelines, load-in, technical rehearsals, performances, and strike. Production workers are involved in all aspects of these timelines. This entire process can fit into a few weeks, months, or several years, which shapes the impact on the workers.

During pre-production and the design process, the focus of work is on those workers involved in conceptualization and budget and time estimations. Designers work with the director, choreographer, and music director to create and submit designs for the production. Production managers and production department heads such as technical directors, costume shop managers, production electricians, and the like, review these designs for feasibility and then estimate both material and labor costs. Designs are revised and resubmitted until everything can theoretically be executed within the time and material and labor budgets allotted.

Once designs are accepted, the various shops – scenic, costumes, lighting, sound, projection – work to execute the designs. At some point in this process, sometimes simultaneously, the directing and stage management staff begin rehearsals with the performers. Designers are expected to continue to work closely with both those executing the designs and the rehearsal room to be sure that the production continues on track. This process can take weeks or months or, in something like Broadway or large opera, years.

Once the project nears the end of rehearsal and moves into the technical rehearsals, the time crunch and expectations typically increase. In our production employer survey, we asked employers to describe their typical production schedule. The range of answers represents in many ways the range of institutions who completed the survey. Cortland Repertory Theatre is a summer stock theatre in upstate New York with a full-time, year-round staff of three. Their respondent shared:

> We typically have a 2 week build for all shows. We strike shows on Saturday night at end [*sic*] of the show. All hands on deck until Midnight. At Midnight, we feed everyone and then most people leave. Scenery works overnight to install set for the next show. Lights / Sound have the space on Sunday morning, dry tech Sunday afternoon and then scenery returns Sunday night. Monday is 10 out of 12 tech. Tuesday is afternoon rehearsal and then invited preview Tuesday night. Wednesday night is opening.

The model described here is consistent with many summer stock theatres and, as we described in Chapter 5, can put an intense burden on often underpaid and under trained workers. InterAct Theatre Company, a Small Professional Theater[9] in Philadelphia which produces three to four professional productions in an average season, follows a typical schedule for many non-LORT professional theatres outside of New York City:

> Load-ins typically take 2–5 days, usually Monday-Friday. Light hangs typically take 1–2 days, usually on Monday–Wednesday. Prior to tech rehearsals, we typically dedicate up to one full day for light focus and one half day for quiet time for our sound designers. Our tech rehearsals typically take place on weekends and we never schedule 10-out-of-12s (we haven't done one in more than 15 years). Following tech, we typically have three days of dress rehearsals, followed by five previews over six days, prior to opening. In most cases, we do not require our designers to be at all five previews (most notably, on Saturdays, when we have two performances).

Another Small Professional Theater, the Intiman Theater in Seattle, which has a similar operating budget to InterAct, explained that their schedule is typically a "3 week build, 1 week load-in, 3 week rehearsal, 1 week tech, 3 week run, 3 day strike."

In contrast, the Santa Fe Opera, which has an operating budget of about $25 million[10] techs their entire five-show summer season in a single month: "We start rehearsals and techs the first week of June and work through all 5 shows to open the first two the first weekend in July, the 3rd the third week in July, the 4th the 4th week in July and the 5th the following weekend." Of the employers who shared their schedules with us, this is one of the most intense for the technicians, as they are asked to work in their highest-stress environment for the longest stretch of time.

Functioning inside an academic institution, which is where many production workers first get exposed to their future careers, the production manager at the Williams College '62 Center for Theatre & Dance explained that, in creating their production schedules, they are conscious about keeping to eight-hour work days. They described the typical schedule:

> For Theatre, in terms of on-site work: there is typically a 6–8 hour dry tech the Friday before first performance, 8 hours of tech on the Saturday, 8 hours of tech on the Sunday, dark day Monday, 4–6 hour tech/dress Tuesday, 4 hour dress Wednesday with performances Thursday, Friday, Saturday. For Dance, in terms of on-site work: 4 hour tech/dress Monday, 4 hour tech/dress Tuesday, Wednesday off, 4 hour final dress Thursday with performances Friday and Saturday.

This schedule might seem lighter than other professional models, but the expectation, of course, is that some of these workers are also attending class or teaching, so the production work has to fit in with other responsibilities.

In part because of these drastically different schedule structures, there are often drastically different expectations of work hours for production workers depending on where a project is in the process and the worker's role. In order to get a sense of the range of schedules workers are subject to, we asked workers how many hours they work in a typical work week. Rather than listing multiple-choice answer options, we asked workers to write in their responses because we recognize that for many, there is not a consistent single response. Of the 1,037 survey participants, 468 gave us a single number of how many hours they work in a typical week. These ranged from 0 hours to 100 hours:

- 128 respondents said they work 40 hours in a typical work week;
- 90 respondents said they work 50 hours in a typical work week;
- 85 respondents said they work 60 hours in a typical work week.
- The other 569 respondents shared ranges or long answers.

Many of these write-in responses highlighted how drastically the "typical" work week can vary. One worker explained that they work, "0–60. Feast and famine. Nothing is 'typical' or everything is 'typical' depending on time [*sic*] of year." With no exaggeration, another respondent offered that they work "10–100 [hours per week], it varies wildly." Another worker explained that it "varies widely, based on number [*sic*] of productions coming up/ when I'm in tech/previews. Anywhere from 5–85."

For some it depends on the part of the season. For one worker, they explained that for "16 weeks a year – 80hrs/wk, [for] 26 weeks a year – 60 hrs/ wk, [and for] 10 weeks a year – 40 [hours per week]." Other production workers employed in various roles explained that their hours in a given week depend on the phase of the production process. These answers ranged from one worker who cited "10–72 [hours] depending on pre-pro, tech or previews," and a designer who answered:

> This fluctuates wildly – my most recent tech I worked ~90hr [weeks]. In my upcoming tech I'm scheduled for ~54hrs in the theater over 5 days and will have to work outside of those hours on paperwork as well, but I get 2 days in the calendar week 'off.' When I'm keeping studio hours I work 30–45 hrs a week usually.

Several workers mentioned something in the range of "45 when we're not in production, and between 70 and 100 when we're in production."

Some respondents to the worker survey explained that the schedule varies depending on the role they are in on a given project. For one prop technician, "It depends – if I'm an artisan it's usually 40. If I'm the prop master it's usually more like 50–60." One audio professional said, "I take all sorts of jobs. When I'm a Production Audio, 60–70, when I'm a designer 30 in pre-production, 60 in production." This worker has chosen to leave theatre completely, in part because they "work on average 28 hours a week in my new line of work and make a little over 1.5x what I was making in theater." For freelancing workers, the expectations of work hours can also vary based on whether or not they are on contract. One costume professional explained, "As a freelancer, [how many hours] varies as to the show/cast size/budget, etc. but generally 60+ since so many budgets do not include budget for over-hire or jobbing out designs to costume houses. As a manager, generally 50–60+ hours a week but I am paid for those hours." And yet another worker shared, "It completely depends on the job I'm doing. When I'm in rehearsals, it's probably around 60 hours a week, but in tech, that could be upped to 70–80 hours a week. But if I'm freelancing and in-between large contracts, I'll probably be working around 20–30 hours a week."

We also asked employers what hours they expect production workers to work at various points in the process of putting on a theatrical production. Designers, in particular, have a wide range of commitments. They are almost always contract employees so are not subject to the institution's typically structured week. According to the Off-Broadway Atlantic Theater Company, designers commitments are as follows:

> Pre Tech is probably about 40–100 hours depending on show needs. Tech is typically 12+ hour days even for an 8 hour rehearsal day but that depends on which department they design for and the needs of the show. Previews still [*sic*] about 10–14+ hour days until the last post-preview production meeting. Tech can be as little as 1 day or as many as 12 days here depending on the needs of the show.

At the Delaware Theatre Company, a LORT theatre in Wilmington, Delaware, the expectation is similar:

> Pre-production, Designers make their own schedule; we do not have good insight into their schedules other than the meetings we call. There's usually 3–4 pre-tech production meetings, and assorted other design/creative meetings. During tech, designers usually work 11am–10:30pm, when you include pre-tech notes/cueing and post-tech production meetings.

These companies produce comparably scaled shows and the expectations for both time and quality are high. At the same time, all of these employers cite hours in excess of the standard 40-hour full time work week.

As was evident in the production schedules, the amount of days in technical rehearsals, and thus the amount of time a designer and their team spend in the theatre, is often directly proportional to the budget of the company or production. The bigger the show, the more technical rehearsal days. In downtown Manhattan at HERE, "We are trying to commit to 8 hours tech days with call times reduced within that to allow for designer and stage manager work. No more than 40 hours per week." InterAct responded:

> Prior to dress rehearsals, our work hours for designers are typically daytime. Tech hours are typically weekend days from 10 am–6 pm, but sometimes start and end later due to artist conflicts. We typically have brief production meetings at the end of each tech day. After tech our hours shift to afternoon/evening, and once in previews only evenings and weekends.

At Santa Fe Opera, on the other hand:

> If they are designing one show, their rehearsals are 10a–5p Mon-Sat for 3 weeks. In that time they will have 3 tech rehearsals (8:30p–2a). There will be a shift rehearsal or 2 at some point in the process, sometimes during the day and sometimes in the evening. They have 3 days onstage, one run through on stage in daylight and 3 dress rehearsals at night starting at 8:30p. Though they are often hired as freelancers (and misclassified as independent contractors), designers and their assistants don't have control over how much time they spend in tech.

Assistant designers, especially in non-Broadway theatres, are typically younger, earlier career workers. Their hours are less within their own control and even more at the mercy of both the theatre and the designer they are assisting. Prior to technical rehearsals, scenic and costume assistant designers often are employed by the designer to work in their studios. Assistant projection designers and assistant sound designers may work on content creation or system design, or both, and are likely to be present for all of tech and previews as well. Assistant lighting designers may spend less time on a project prior to being in the theatre but are often there through the most preview rehearsals and performances.

Once in the theatre, the Atlantic Theater Company cites that assistant designer commitments vary: "Depends on the department. For Lighting and Sound, about double what the designer's hours are. Costumes and Projections, equitable or double depending on the stature/caliber of designer. Scenery, usually a little less than the designer." The Intiman Theatre agreed that "Assistant designers' hours are not tracked outside of tech." In order to protect the assistants, HERE agrees that they didn't know how many hours assistants were working; their hours are "unknown, but we have started to hire them directly as employees of HERE to ensure that they can come to us with problems. They often work on their own schedules in collaboration with the designers." This vague response is indicative of the ever-expanding scope of assistant designers' commitments to a project. When I, Natalie, was first assisting Off-Broadway, I regularly spent six days a week for up to five weeks of tech and previews in the theatre. I was expected to be there both when the designer was present and in their stead when they had other commitments or had moved on to other projects. I was rarely, if ever, paid more than $1,500 for this work.

For production staff and technicians, work hours can be very different from those of designers and assistant designers. Off-Broadway theatres often have a mix of full time and casual technical staff. At the Atlantic Theater Company, the schedule "depends on what part of the process. Typically 8–10 hour days for load in, 40–50 hr weeks. Tech can be as little as 4 hours per day or as much as a 60+ hour week." HERE doesn't have full time technicians so they are hired for each production. Their hours "depend upon the production. 10am–11pm are the work days, but we try to keep any individual work calls to no more than 8 hours per day and no more than 40 hours per week." The Naples Players in Naples, Florida employs a mix of technicians, interns, and volunteers to staff their shows. Their Production Stage Manager/Internship Director explained the various departments' hours as:

> For me ... probably an average of 50–60 hours a week, most days working 11a–11p. More when I'm in production. Very rarely do I get two days off in a row. Other on staff technicians: Scene shop is the most consistent = Tuesday–Saturday 9a–4p. Costume Shop = Monday–Friday 10a-8p with staggered shifts. Lighting and Sound are at the mercy of the Scene Shop and have to have flexible hours when they don't have the stage, so Mondays and weekends and/or before and after shop rehearsal hours.

InterAct Theatre Company also does not employ technicians or designers outside of production-specific hires. Their workers have the following schedule:

> During load-in week, our technicians typically work daytime hours of anywhere from 1–5 days. Tech hours are typically weekend days from 10 am–6 pm, but sometimes start and end later due to artist conflicts. After tech our hours shift to afternoon/evening, and once in previews only evenings and weekends. We don't typically need technicians, other than run crew, for many hours post-tech.

At the Intiman, where many of the technicians work under IATSE contracts, everyone works a 40-hour week. Similarly at the Old Globe, technicians in the shop work eight to ten hours a day while the onstage crew typically works 12 to 13 hours a day. During load in, the crew typically works ten to 12 hours a day and during technical rehearsals, their days extend to 13 to 14 hours onstage. At the Santa Fe Opera, when productions are in tech, the hours become extremely long: "A tech (8:30a–2a) into a changeover (2a–5a) into a run through the next day (11a–ish)." It's important to note that in the case of most professional theatres, technicians and designers are working a six-day work week.

The rehearsal schedule is typically determined based on the contractual guidelines negotiated by Actors' Equity Association (which as we've mentioned is the labor union representing American actors and stage managers in the theatre). The rehearsal schedule, based on the AEA criteria, then often dictates the hours production staff, including designers and technicians, work. And so, unless the crew is unionized as at the Intiman, the performers' union determines the schedule, without any guidelines protecting the needs of other production personnel. This can play out in many ways, such as the designer being expected to work during the break in order to be ready for the actors and stage managers returning and picking back up after ten minutes. One particularly contentious aspect of the technical rehearsal scheduling is the ten out of 12. A ten out of 12 refers to the longest rehearsal day set out by AEA guidelines in which actors and stage managers are called for a 12-hour day inclusive of two-hours of breaks, making for a ten-hour work day. In order for technical rehearsals to progress efficiently, production staff members, including technicians and designers, have to arrive before the rehearsal starts to prepare and stay after to clean up and prepare for the next day. According to designer Matt Kizer:

> The [10 out of 12] mandate was created to protect the well-being of actors. In the hurried world of the theatre industry, it has created an expectation that most likely was not intended. Actors are called for ten-out-of-twelve hours and are expected to be dismissed promptly when that time is complete. Around this, the designers, technicians, director, stage management, and other contributors are typically ready and waiting to ensure that those ten hours of time with actors are used to their fullest.[11]

Designers and non-union production workers might work a 14- or 16-hour day to be prepared to best use the ten hours with the actors. This often disproportionately affects assistants who are likely to be expected to be at the theatre before and after the designers or stage managers they are assisting and to complete paperwork which may require even more work outside their time in the theatre. Some workers will arrive as early as eight o'clock in the morning and not leave the theatre before one o'clock in the morning the following day, only to be expected to do it all again for several days in a row. This allows for very little time for workers to sleep or eat between shifts, especially when accounting for commute times which could easily include an hour plus subway or bus ride each way when traveling outside of typical commuting hours. There is something ironic about a mandate that was originally meant to protect the workers now being a way to abuse them.

These work days are incredibly common. We asked production workers if their typical jobs use the 10-out-of-12 (or 10-out-of-11-and-a-half as determined by some specific AEA schedules). Of the 1,013 who answered this question, 53.8% said yes. On a Broadway production contract, a production can schedule seven 10-out-of-12s in the week leading up to the first public performance. And on a LORT contract, "In the seven days prior to the first paid public performance, the total workweek shall not exceed 52 hours,"[12] but, during that same period, "the Theatre may schedule two days of '10 out of 12' consecutive hours for each production."[13]

According to Actors Equity contracts, breaks must be taken for ten minutes after 1 hour and 20 minutes of work, or for five minutes after 55 minutes of work. IATSE breaks are typically 15 minutes and some musician union breaks are twenty minutes. Even within a five-day work week, the standard ten-minute break schedule can be a hindrance for workers. Designer and wheelchair user Michael Maag explains, "Equity breaks are only ten minutes. It is not enough time to get to wherever the accessible restroom is, to deal with catheters and what all. Here is another way we can adjust our working methods to be more inclusive and humane."[14] What would the downside be of extending breaks to accommodate everyone?

New Standard of Care for Caregivers

From Parent Artist Advocacy League for Performing Arts + Media (PAAL)

The New Standard of Care for Caregivers is a movement of ethical support for caregivers expected of all institutions for 2021 and beyond.
About: The three pillars of justice uphold and run through the 11 action steps, prioritizing Anti-Racism as the central pillar to caregiver support as lack of caregiver support impacts Black, Indigenous, People of Color communities uniquely and exponentially. Prioritize and center anti-racism in all practices, including caregiver support.
Make It Standard.

3 Pillars of Justice | 11 Action Steps

1. You cannot have an anti-racist organization without formal caregiver support.
2. You cannot have gender parity or gender inclusion without formal caregiver support.
3. You cannot support reproductive rights without formal caregiver support.
4. Provide caregiver support for all departments and contributors in the organization - regardless of status in the employment hierarchy and family design.
5. Provide financial childcare support/caregiver fund/stipends as a formal budget-line item.
6. Implement family leave structures for administrators and contributing artists.
7. Abolish the 10/12 to achieve caregiver support that is also humane for everyone.
8. Implement the 5 day rehearsal-week and/or progressive work and rehearsal hours.
9. Support the health and well-being of families through inclusive sick day policies that extend to children/dependents and through remote work opportunities
10. Make the workspace/rehearsal space accessible for caregivers and their child(ren)/dependents as needed.
11. Create a plan for accessible remote-work options for caregivers who do not feel safe bringing their children into the workspace.
12. Create accessible and compliant spaces as well as remote work/call-in opportunities to support caregivers in the disability community and/or with children/dependents with disabilities.
13. Stop firing pregnant people through AEA loopholes of change in appearance, or refusing to adjust work task lists for pregnant people on crew or physical labor roles backstage, in design, stage management, and other departments.
14. Educate staff, managers, and representatives on the socio-economic realities and legal obligations.

"The New Standard of Care", © 2023 Parent Artist Advocacy League (PAAL); for additional information, contact: www.paaltheatre.com/contact-subscribe.

The Parent Artist Advocacy League (PAAL) published the New Standard of Care, described as a movement of ethical support for caregivers expected of all institutions for 2021 and beyond.[15] These standards address workplace conditions which would benefit all workers, not just caregivers. One of the eleven action steps they expect of institutions is to "abolish the 10 [out of] 12 to achieve caregiver support that is also humane for everyone."[16] They cite that "excessive hours can create great logistical, financial, and physiological obstacles impeding employment and/or sustainable, healthy employment."[17] Considering that workers who have to complete ten out of 12s are possibly away from their homes by upwards of 16 hours at a time,

> the financial cost of 10/12 rehearsals for caregivers is exorbitant and does not justify artistic and productive time in the space; the financial costs of 10/12 – when considering childcare, meals, time management, and scheduling for support – often result in great debt or the inability to justify accepting work all together for parents and caregivers in the performing arts.[18]

It's important to note that the majority of workers who are expected to reduce their work time for caregiving responsibilities are women and folks with uteruses. PAAL points out that "school systems and work expectations were designed around white male workflow that expected free caregiver labor to run school pickups, weekend support, and supply endless, round-the-clock food, rest, and childcare support."[19] Unsurprisingly, there is also an increase in obstacles to work for those caregiving for adults or people in the disability community who might have less access to traditional caregiving resources like nannies or daycare.

Empowered by the We See You W.A.T. demands, organizing around the elimination of 10-out-of-12s has taken hold in many parts of the industry. Tanner Richardett's thesis "No More 10 out of 12s: Considerations for a more Equitable Theatre Rehearsal Structure in Philadelphia," found that "Since the introduction of demands from We See You, White American Theatre and No More 10 Out of 12's arose, theatres across the country have made strides to improve upon prior shortcomings and antiquated practices."[20] Though some theatres are admirably eliminating 10-out-of-12 rehearsal days, these efforts do not always entirely address the harms caused by the 10-out-of-12s. If the quality of production is meant to be the same, how are the "lost" hours made up? Some theatres are adding additional days to the technical rehearsal period without adding additional compensation, thus lowering the hourly wage of contract employees who receive a project fee. Some theatres are expecting production values to remain the same with less time, putting even more of a burden of urgency and perfectionism on production workers. Some theatres are making no changes at all.

Why No More 10 Out of 12s

From the NO MORE 10 Out Of 12's Working Group
10 out of 12's and six day workweeks are detrimental for the following reasons:

Upholds white supremacy

A 12+ hour work day, back to back on multiple days, with only one day to recover is a severe impediment for anyone trying to live and make a living. It is a racist practice disproportionately impacting BIPOC folx who do not have the privilege of other family support (social, financial, or otherwise) or built-in network, nor the benefit of being the most represented voice in the room. For indigenous communities who are trying to rebuild their population after generations of genocide and mistreatment, the choice of picking between family, work/life balance and a career takes on an entirely different meaning. Any discussion of equity, diversity and inclusion is built on a false premise if the work conditions preclude certain races from ever being able to get in the door. We encourage you to read more about dismantling these oppressive practices at www.weseeyouwat.com.

Anti-safety

Studies have repeatedly shown that sleep deprivation and mental exhaustion can cause physical deterioration over the long term, but even more importantly, it can immediately cause people to be less aware and less adept in crucial moments. In our current theatre climate, where stagecraft is increasingly complex and imposing, mistakes can cost money, time, and even people's lives.

Continues Ableism

Extended hours create a barrier for those who struggle with disabilities, forcing them to either hide their symptoms or push themselves to keep up. Many times, these people are left with a choice to either worsen their conditions or leave theatre behind altogether in order to survive.

Anti-Caregiver

Long work hours and six day workweeks are particularly difficult for parents and caregivers who frequently have to choose between their dependents and their careers due to physical, financial, logistical, and relational impact. Visit PAALtheatre.com for more on caregiver impact and support.

Negative effect on quality of life

A 10 out of 12 day is not just a twelve hour day for most theatre workers. For designers, technicians, stage managers and other theatre workers, it can easily be a 16 hour day or longer. Most theatre workers are freelance, are not paid hourly, but work until the job is "done". In some cases, the additional house that they work reduce their wages to minimum wage levels or worse. Furthermore, a six day workweek creates a situation where there's not enough time to rest and recover from those long hours, and provides less opportunities for theatre workers to build personal lives of their own. If you know someone who works in theatre, then you know someone who has had to miss a wedding, a funeral, a birthday or some important personal engagement because they had to work a six day workweek.

Text courtesy of the NO MORE 10 Out Of 12s Working Group.

For theatres where many production workers travel in to work on the show, eliminating the 10-out-of-12 and shifting to a more equitable days-off schedule can have impacts on the worker's personal expenses. Many theatres base their per diem allowances on the federal minimum for covering meals and incidentals; often, the meals that the workers have access to in close proximity to the theatres and within their meal break time constraints cost more than what they are receiving as per diems. Some theatres only provide per diems for working days, so having more days off means more days when the worker is away from their home without having meal and incidental expenses covered. Some workers would prefer fewer days off and longer working hours, so they get home sooner. There is not a one size fits all solution.

Working conditions for production workers are unprotected if the workers aren't members of a labor union. Of the workers who completed our survey, 43.2% are members of at least one labor union. In cases where workers are working under an IATSE (for technicians) or Actor's Equity (for stage managers) contract, collectively bargained labor protections may limit these long days and hours and offer limited control over working conditions. But in non-union theatres, there aren't mandated limits on the number of hours a worker can work; there aren't mandated breaks; there aren't even mandates guaranteeing that workers are hired as employees and thus qualify for overtime or time-and-a-half pay.

Because of the scarcity mentality in production staffing across the industry, there is a default to understaffing. Typically, even in theatre production departments with some full-time staff, the expectation is that at least some, if not the majority, of the labor will be completed by over-hired technicians.

The industry has been dependent on the availability of production workers willing to take on temporary, casual, and contract work. Workers are then on their own to assemble enough work to make a living, often taking on the extra complications of buying their own health insurance (something that has gotten somewhat easier since the advent of Obamacare) or to go without, to deal with complicated taxes full of a mix of W2s and 1099s, and to always live with the knowledge that there just might not be enough work. The availability of over-hire technicians in large urban centers has made this somewhat possible. But, as workers post-Pause are leaving the industry, employers are faced with a lack of sufficient workers. This puts an increased burden on the remaining freelancers and those in staff positions as the workload remains the same with fewer folks to do the work itself.

The theatre industry benefits from a cycle that begins in middle and high school extracurricular theatre. For many students, from their first experience in the theatre, there is an expectation that students will put aside everything else (including school work) during "hell week," when the production is finally prepared for audiences. Hours are long, there is a lot of waiting around, and a game of pride develops around who works harder, sleeps least and "cares the most." I, Natalie, remember staying at school until all hours painting scenery and steaming costumes after four or five hours of watching rehearsals just so I could be the "most" involved. Theatre work is presented as the creation of a family for which sacrifice is both expected and valued. The show must go on, right? These models prepare people for unsustainable production schedules and even establish them as a source of self-worth. Production employers can then depend on their workers' supposed love of the job to carry them through the unreasonable working conditions.

As we discussed in Chapter 5, there is a long history of dependence on unpaid and underpaid labor in theatrical production. As producing organizations develop staffing plans to maintain their budgetary and artistic goals, this dependence figures in significantly. For example, one employer explained, "It is up to the individual designer to establish working hours for their assistants. On staff designers typically don't have over hire assistants and will use interns." This is a clear misuse of the educational experience, taking advantage of the intern labor instead of hiring professional assistant designers.

The reliance on intern labor to fill the gaps is harmful for production workers across the board. In addition to potentially harming the interns and the other workers, it is a self-perpetuating system which teaches exploitation. A former Williamstown Theater Festival worker explained:

> Historically, not only does Williamstown depend on pay-to-play funding from apprentices in exchange for their 'learning experience,' but WTF simply would not function without relying on young, mostly unpaid, untrained laborers to push their bodies through intense physical stress for an unsafe number of hours.[21]

Perhaps because the system has worked this way for so long, and because it is working as designed, overhauling the existing structures has been hard. Stephanie Ybarra, then Artistic Director of Baltimore Center Stage, shared the pushback she received from the longtime production staff in response to ending their internship program. After announcing the plan to "sunset" the internship program, she was met with resistance from the staff to come up with other solutions to fill the labor gaps. Though additional full-time positions wouldn't be possible, Ybarra was surprised at the lack of interest when she suggested expanding the pool of casual employees.[22] This resistance to change harms the institutions as well as the workers. Without adaptation and support for workers, they will burn out and leave the industry or, worse, they will be unable to keep up with the pace of work and will get physically or emotionally hurt. A lack of safe workplace conditions prevents the work from being done, harming the production goals of the employers.

Theatrical production work is very demanding on workers' bodies. In addition to long hours and a lack of sleep, workers are likely to be subject to various work injuries. Several costume designers have, anecdotally, spoken about incurring shoulder injuries from carrying bags of costumes. Lighting, sound, and video designers, as well as stage managers, often sit hunched over temporarily constructed tech tables for hours on end, causing back and neck strain. Carpenters, electricians, and riggers risk injuries from falls, power tools, and badly maintained equipment. The urgency often caused by a combination of inadequate budgeting, staffing, and scheduling contributes to all of these situations. In addition, the focus on the audience has taken precedence over the physical protections of the production workers.

Theatrical production spaces are typically created for able-bodied workers which means that there are increased dangers for workers with disabilities. In her thesis, Mallory Kay Nelson writes about the inclusion, or lack thereof, of disabled American theatre artists both onstage and backstage: "Presently, in American theatre, one does not come across many disabled actors, designers, and technicians working professionally."[23] There is a lot of visible acknowledgement and accommodation made for audience members with disabilities: physical access, ASL-interpreted performances, access to visible descriptions, relaxed performances. Nelson illustrates the disconnect between these efforts and the workplace environment: "Even when the front of the house is being renovated to accommodate differently-abled audience members, the theatre community does not think about the same issue occurring backstage for its technicians, because these are not public spaces."[24]

Backstage theatrical workplaces are often full of narrow hallways, steep staircases, and overfull storage areas. They are regularly dark, especially during performances, making movement a challenge for many workers. Many theatre organizations, including Broadway landlords, cite the historical nature of the theatre spaces as a reason for the lack of physical accessibility and architectural improvements. But these accessibility issues make working in production an even bigger challenge for workers with disabilities. Nelson spoke with a costume designer who has a mobility disability from an injury, who shared that they encounter accessibility issues when shopping for costumes in stores, and also are usually not able to dig through a shop's costume stock. The designer has to rely heavily on their assistants, far more than they did before becoming disabled. Their job options are limited simply by whether or not they can access the theatre's shop; many costume shops (as well as scene shops, backstage areas, stages, and booths) are not wheelchair-accessible.[25]

Lighting and projection designer and wheelchair user Michael Maag shared his own experiences working in spaces designed for able-bodied performers:

> For a wheelchair user, getting from the house to the stage might involve going outside, around to the loading dock or wherever the ramp is, then through the typical backstage maze of elevators, hallways, and narrow doors. Once you get on stage the platform where the actors perform is a number of steps up! It would be comical if it wasn't so frustrating.
>
> When lighting for folks who can stand, I must position myself to focus the lights from a seated position so that the hot spot is at eye level to the taller folks. Sometimes I can't get to a place to indicate shutter cuts – to control the shape of the beam of light – with my arms, so I use a laser pointer.
>
> Folks with disabilities are fantastic in the theatre; we have to be creative, innovative, and adaptable just to get through the day. We are not living in an equitable world.[26]

Annie Wiegand is, as far as she knows, the only Deaf lighting designer currently working in the American theatre. In a HowlRound Theatre Commons piece, Weigand looks back on her career and notes ways in which her access to the on-the-job training and low-hanging fruit of job learning hasn't been accessible. Her specific needs are unconsidered in the typical workplaces for a lighting designer, particularly around communications which happen primarily over headset or in the dark:

> ASL interpreters are utilized to assist in communications – they interpret what is being said to me through the headset. Not only do I have to use a headset, I have to use my voice and speak into it. While I am comfortable using my voice, the next Deaf lighting designer might not be as comfortable. With voice recognition experimentation, I hope to eventually find a way for future Deaf designers to be less reliant on ASL interpreters and more independent in tech.
>
> Also, my theatre and lighting design vernacular might not appear as strong as the next lighting designer, because I'm not able to pick up different words.

> I'm not able to hear the different vocabulary usage on the job, so that's something I have to figure out along the way. It took me years to figure out what a cube tap – a three-way Edison plug – was. It's the small things like that that most people take for granted, things I had to learn and pick up through trial and error. There's also the fear of being perceived as stupid when you don't know the vernacular.[27]

Theatres often budget for the potential for one or two ASL-interpreted performances for their Deaf and hard-of-hearing audience members, but what happens when a designer or crew member is Deaf? Often, nothing.

And what about when a production worker gets sick? Designers and technicians are often casual or contract hires with no paid sick leave. Pressure is put on workers to show up even when they are sick because they are supposedly irreplaceable. The egregious problems with these policies have become increasingly obvious as theatres have reopened during the COVID-19 pandemic. When I, Natalie, was asked to design a show without an assistant in 2022, I asked the production manager what would happen if I caught COVID and had to miss tech. The production manager's response was to offer $200 to pay an assistant for what would have been up to 14 days of work. I found a local assistant with the theatre's help and paid them out of my own fee so that the show would be protected. By subsidizing the cost of my own assistant, I reduced my fee (originally $3,400) for the show to a total of $2,900 ($2,508 after paying my agent and union dues) for a project which included 15 days in residence, six studio days, and several months of meetings and conversations. Without paid time off, workers risk either their own health and that of those around them, or not making enough money to pay bills and support their households.

So, why are these budgeting, staffing and scheduling practices problematic for production workers?

The long hours of theatrical production, a result of both schedule and understaffing, put workers at increased risk. According to human factors researchers Dr. Ashleigh Filtness and Anjum Naweed, "Fatigue is an important and unique issue for workplace risk management."[28] Studying train driver fatigue in the rail industry, Filtness and Naweed found "consistent evidence that fatigue increases the risk of safety critical events."[29] Fatigue is not just a lack of sleep over a night or two but is much more than that: "Within a clinical environment, clear distinction is made between sleepiness and fatigue. Where sleepiness is caused by insufficient sleep and fatigue includes sleepiness as a symptom but expands to wider physical and psychosocial impairment."[30] Theatrical production workers who are prone to fatigue – due to the working conditions – are often climbing to potentially dangerous heights or dyeing fabrics in vats of boiling liquid or using power tools while at work inside these exhausting work schedules. According to Richardett:

> Physical and psychological fatigue can lead to a decrease in awareness, reactivity, and coordination. Especially in stagecraft, when moving certain objects, set pieces, or operating fly rail systems, the lack of adeptness can lead to serious costs of money, time, or the safety of human health and life in the worst circumstances.[31]

The six-day work week doesn't provide adequate time for rest away from the workplace. Workers often use one day of a weekend for family and household tasks, and with only one day off, rest is likely to get pushed aside. In live performance, and embedded in the AEA and IATSE collectively bargained contracts, it is still the practice to have a six day work week with, typically, a Monday or Sunday off. On weeks that include a holiday, sometimes that holiday then is the only day off, as is often the case with Thanksgiving or Christmas. In spite of the availability of the five-day work week in most Actor's Equity contracts, producers rarely use them. According to research done by the Parent Artist Advocacy League (PAAL):

> Time for rest, especially that includes separation from the workspace, contributes to improved mental health and support; sustainable pace of rehearsal better sustains energy and physical resources leading into the demands of tech, previews, and performance; more human time off can reduce injury and improve bounce-back.[32]

PAAL has determined that, in order for institutions to ethically support caregivers, and as a result all workers, they must move to the five-day work week or, in some cases, progressive work hours. PAAL aims to elevate the national standard of care for caregivers in the performing arts and media.[33] Their work with caregivers has made it clear that, "without the adjustment to the workweek, only the privileged can sustain the hours demanded in the theatre, which perpetuates the imbalance of leadership and employment demographics, creating barriers to work, particularly for Black, Indigenous, People of Color communities."[34]

Producers hesitate to make this move for a number of reasons. Equity members are paid a weekly salary and so a decrease in working days per week could create an increase in number of weeks hired. Similarly, rent on theatres and some rehearsal spaces is calculated weekly so an increase in days off means more time paid for "unused" space. According to PAAL, the AEA contracts allow for shifting to the five-day work week, and:

> if the producer/theatre insists on having the lost hours, then the option of adding a week will cost in terms of salaries (and potentially space). Adding hours can cost in overtime both daily/weekly, but may be less than an entire salary. Overtime hours may be preferable to an entire extra week because of space rental, etc. However, grant funding or support can go directly to this week when the goal and its benefits are communicated clearly.[35]

In the HowlRound essay "Hold, Please: Addressing Urgency and Other White Supremacist Standards in Stage Management," the writers look at the ways that typical production workplace structures uphold the white supremacist value of urgency, which forces workers into the dangerous state of fatigue. Building on historical practices, "theatres have a complex history of pushing against labor laws to continue working long hours – things like state requirements for days of rest or, recently, California's Assembly Bill 5."[36] Avoidance of those practices intended to protect workers is a direct result of prioritizing urgency and production over safety and consideration. A well-budgeted institution builds in room for contingencies and change. This allows for a project to evolve artistically. It accounts for last-minute changes, which alleviates pressure on the workers to do the impossible and allows them to maintain safer conditions. As is the case in many other aspects of the nonprofit industrial complex, theatre employers often depend on workers' love of their jobs, the presumed scarcity of work, and the prioritization of profit-as-art over people:

> Our industry has instilled the expectation of artists to put the show ahead of everything else, and it's taking a massive toll on our safety and well-being. According to the Center for a New American Dream, people who work eleven or more hours a day are two and a half times more likely to develop depression and sixty times more likely to develop heart disease. In addition, multiple studies have shown long work hours and work-related stress to have adverse effects on a wide range of health impacts, including anxiety, sleep quality, substance use, mental health, physical health, and injuries. Prioritizing quantity over quality is a colossal tentpole of white supremacy that works to put organizational revenue before the physical and mental impact on the workers.[37]

There is a lack of sufficient time for production to always be completed safely. This also limits the time that staff technicians can spend being trained on new tools or technologies and on updating their current training. Freelance workers have to take these types of trainings on their own time, potentially losing work and covering their own costs. This increases the likelihood that production workers and those around them may be unsafe. These practices also contribute to the lack of sustainable careers in theatrical production and, from there, the lack of diversity in the industry:

> For people with multiple jobs, people with disabilities that prevent long working hours, people with religious and cultural events outside of the Christian calendar, parents, students, and so many others, a capital-driven production schedule could be the final barrier barring them from a career as a theatre artist.[38]

How can systems for production operations be reimagined to include all workers?

NOTES

1 Sarah Clare Corporandy (Co-founder and Producing Artistic Director, Detroit Public Theatre), interview by the authors, September 2022.
2 Corporandy, interview.
3 Corporandy, interview.
4 Corporandy, interview.
5 Corporandy, interview.
6 Stephanie Ybarra (former Artistic Director, Baltimore Center Stage) interview by the authors, September 2022.
7 Ybarra, interview.
8 Sophie Blumberg, Jonathan Secor, and Ben Johnson, "Perspectives on Safety and Sustainability for Venues and Cultural Spaces," HowlRound Theatre Commons, October 5, 2021, https://howlround.com/perspectives-safety-and-sustainability-venues-and-cultural-spaces.
9 Small Professional Theater is a designation of those theatres who are members of the SPT collectively bargained agreement with AEA.
10 Propublica, "The Santa Fe Opera," Nonprofit Explorer, https://projects.propublica.org/nonprofits/organizations/850131810.
11 Matt Kizer, "The Ten out of Twelve: It's a Lie," *Matt Kizer: Scenic and Lighting Design* (blog), August 16, 2021, https://scenicandlighting.com/article/the-ten-out-of-twelve-its-a-lie/.
12 Actors' Equity Association, "Agreement and Rules Governing Employment in Resident Theatres" (New York: Actors' Equity Association, 2017): 69.
13 Actors' Equity Association, 72.
14 Michael Maag and Annie Wiegand, "Illuminating the Careers of Disabled Lighting Designers," HowlRound Theatre Commons, February 25, 2021, https://howlround.com/illuminating-careers-disabled-lighting-designers.
15 "The New Standard of Care," Parent Artist Advocacy League for Performing Arts and Media, https://www.paaltheatre.com/new-standard-of-care.
16 Parent Artist Advocacy League for Performing Arts and Media, "New Standard."
17 Parent Artist Advocacy League for Performing Arts and Media.
18 Parent Artist Advocacy League for Performing Arts and Media.
19 Parent Artist Advocacy League for Performing Arts and Media.
20 Tanner A. Richardett, "No More 10/12s: Considerations for a More Equitable Theatre Rehearsal Structure in Philadelphia" (master's thesis, Philadelphia, PA, Drexel University, 2021), 37, https://drive.google.com/file/d/1C0YdONhCUwzE6DSSfXlmtHkH1p507Zem/view.
21 The WTF, Williamstown?! Collective, "The WTF, Williamstown?! Collective to Mandy Greenfield, Laura Savia, Jeffrey Johnson, Joe Finnegan, Annie Pell, Brad Svrluga, and Donald B. Elitzer; as Well as the Rest of the Staff and Board of Trustees of Williamstown Theatre Festival," https://ca-times.brightspotcdn.com/06/37/5851edc0482387ff1b2fee01b155/updated-williamstown-theatre-festival-letter.pdf.
22 Ybarra, interview.

23 Mallory Kay Nelson, "Inclusion of the Disabled Theatre Artist" (master's thesis, Pittsburgh, PA, Carnegie Mellon University, 2010), 1, https://mallorykaynelson.files.wordpress.com/2019/03/inclusion_of_the_disabled_theatre_artist-nelson.pdf.
24 Nelson, 26.
25 Nelson, 32.
26 Maag and Wiegand.
27 Maag and Wiegand.
28 A.J. Filtness and A. Naweed, "Causes, Consequences and Countermeasures to Driver Fatigue in the Rail Industry: The Train Driver Perspective," *Applied Ergonomics* 60 (April 2017): 12, https://doi.org/10.1016/j.apergo.2016.10.009.
29 Filtness and Naweed, 20.
30 Filtness and Naweed, 19.
31 Filtness and Naweed, 19.
32 Parent Artist Advocacy League for Performing Arts and Media, "Using Five-Day Rehearsal-Week Contracts, Negotiation, and Execution," *Parent Artist Advocacy League for Performing Arts and Theatre* (blog), https://www.paaltheatre.com/post/five-day-rehearsal-week.
33 "About Us," Parent Artist Advocacy League for Performing Arts and Media, https://www.paaltheatre.com/about-us.
34 Parent Artist Advocacy League for Performing Arts and Media, "New Standard"
35 Parent Artist Advocacy League for Performing Arts and Media, "Five-Day Rehearsal-Week."
36 Miguel Flores et al., "Hold Please: Addressing Urgency and Other White Supremacist Standards in Stage Management," *HowlRound Theatre Commons*, October 15, 2020, https://howlround.com/hold-please.
37 Flores et al.
38 Flores et al.

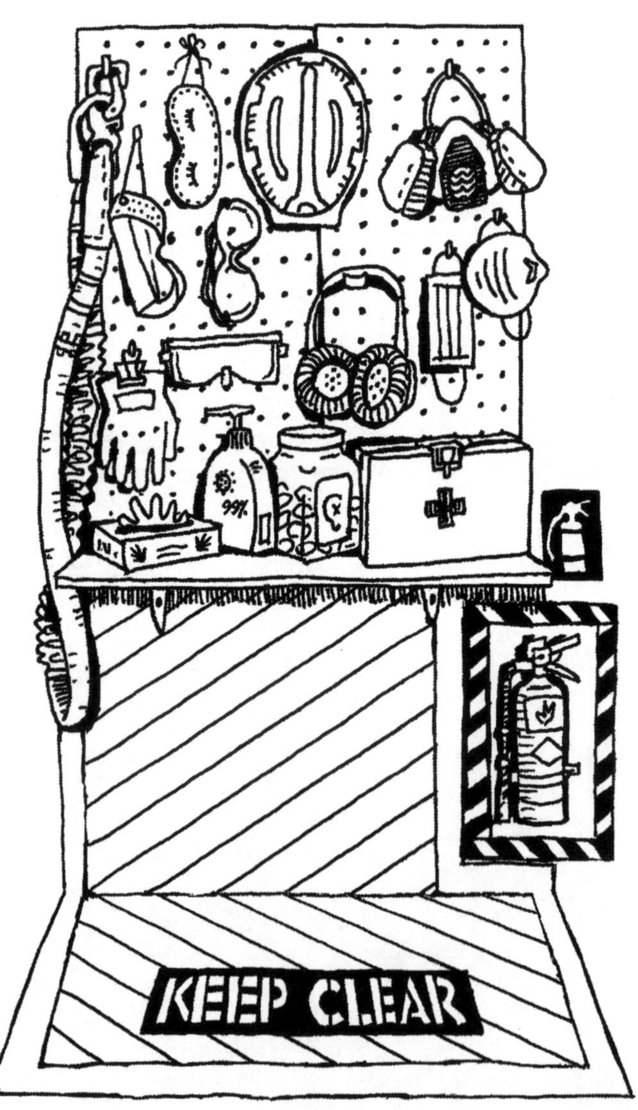
99%
KEEP CLEAR

9

WORKER SAFETY

Perhaps the most basic assessment of equitable labor practices lies within an assessment of worker safety. In theatrical production, where there is an uneven distribution of acceptable safe work practices and an unequal distribution of worker protections, this is even more true. For our purposes, safety is inclusive of both physical and mental, emotional, and psychological safety. As organizer Wu Chen Khoo points out, "It doesn't take malicious intent to make for an unsafe or unwelcoming work environment."[1] It does, however, take mindfulness and intentionality to create a safe and welcoming one.

Theatrical workspaces are rife with potential physical dangers. Many technicians learn their crafts on the job, often working under significant time and budget constraints. The training is often ad hoc and haphazard. Budget constraints may lead to badly maintained and rarely updated equipment. A perceived lack of time can contribute to this lack of maintenance. Shortcuts and improvisation are the norm. Often safety practices are considered at best an inconvenience and at worst completely disregarded.

Even when work is done in the safest possible environment, there are physical hazards inherent to theatrical production work. Carpenters use power tools; set designers build models using sharp blades; electricians work at heights; riggers hang scenery above other workers' heads; tailors squint at hand beading for long hours; scenic artists breathe in paint fumes

DOI: 10.4324/9781003330394-11

and other possibly toxic chemicals. Active construction continues in the theatre throughout the technical rehearsal and preview period, introducing a number of other hazards.

On a recent show at a LORT D theatre where the electricians were dangling from catwalks by their ankles with no fall protection, the production manager reassured the guest lighting designer, me, Natalie, by saying that the crew was top notch and would be fine. I wasn't commenting on the crew's skills when I asked about fall protection. But apparently it was just too inconvenient. Similarly, while designing a show at a major New York nonprofit theatre during the period when the crew was starting to be required to wear harnesses, there was a lot of grumbling above me about how much longer it took. Again, the safety measures were seen as inconvenient. According to the US Bureau of Labor Statistics assessment of the Entertainment industry, though, safety is an obvious and real concern: "In 2016, there were 57 fatal injuries and 5,570 estimated nonfatal injuries and illnesses, resulting in days away from work, among this industry."[2] And those are just the ones that have been reported.

As we discussed in Chapter 8, an embedded sense of urgency makes the normal risks of theatrical production work even more dangerous. Working quickly increases the dangers and invites easy mistakes into the equation. One of the byproducts of this urgency is that workers are being overworked. Fatigue can lead to unsafe work practices. As Tanner A. Richardett explains:

> Fatigued operation or installation of heavy or dangerous equipment, including speakers, stage lights, set pieces, fly rail systems, scaffolds, and ladders pose a risk to everybody in the room. If, for example, a sound technician does not properly clamp down a speaker, or a fly rail operator loses their grip on a rope or neglects to lock down a rail, everyone on stage in that moment is at serious risk of injury from a heavy object falling to the stage. This risk exists not only because of the prolonged nature of work hours that 10 out of 12s create but also by the rushed, must-get-done nature of these tech days. Also paralleled is the stop-and-start nature of both conducting and technical rehearsals, requiring short bursts of work and occasional long stretches of waiting for the next task.[3]

Theatrical production puts workers in a near-constant heightened state – navigating a lack of time, a lack of resources, an imminent crisis – in a high-risk environment. This combined with the intense schedules and lack of time off prevents normal rest cycles where their bodies can reset. This perpetuates the onset of fatigue and invites more room for error.

And, as we introduced in Chapter 5, another way that worker safety is compromised is by expecting underpaid and undertrained interns or workers to perform necessary tasks. To exaggerate that problem, interns are often expected to complete these tasks within the pressure and culture of urgency which invites even skilled workers to do dangerous things. In the letter from the WTF, Williamstown?! Collective workers to the Williamstown leadership, they cited this exact problem:

> Multiple apprentices reported being seriously injured on the 'job,' and then being forced to do similar labor the following day. This violates government regulations around workplace safety as well as unpaid educational experiences, and left many former apprentices feeling that their significant financial hardship was neither justified nor respected.[4]

We asked production workers if they have ever felt physically unsafe in their theatrical production workplace(s). A clear majority of 681 of the 1,037 survey participants, or 65.6%, said yes, they have felt physically unsafe in their theatrical production workplace(s). Looking at how this broke down across the gender spectrum, of people who identify as female, 63.9% have felt physically unsafe in the workplace; of people who identify as male, 64.4% have felt physically unsafe in the workplace; of people who identify as genderfluid/genderqueer/non-binary, 77.6% have felt physically unsafe in the workplace; and of people who listed "Other" for how they identify on the gender spectrum, 83.3% have felt physically unsafe in the workplace. Perhaps for a variety of reasons, theatrical workplaces seem to be more dangerous for gender non-conforming workers, consistent with the realities faced by these workers throughout the workforce.

Workers with union representation are more likely to be working in conditions with explicit rules around safety. There is no way for us to know the exact number of unrepresented production workers in America, but if the approximate 4:6 ratio we saw in our survey (four workers with union representation for every six without) is anything to go off, it's likely many more than the roughly 170,000 IATSE members working in theatre, film, and television. Production managers aren't represented by any union.

Union representation is a path to a more safe workplace. As discussed in Chapter 8, IATSE contracts often include breaks, maximum span of day and minimum turnaround times to address fatigue and burnout. There are minimum staffing provisions, especially in cases where overhead rigging or work might be involved to protect both those overhead and those on the ground. It is, according to the law, an employer's responsibility to provide a safe work environment. Workers may require additional safety training, which employers pay for. Employers are typically required to provide safety equipment, including Personal Protective Equipment. Stage managers are protected by the same contractual protections as actors when working under an Actor's Equity contract. These also include limits on span of day, weekly hour maximums, mandatory breaks, limitations on certain aspects of physical space (like a maximum change of height on a raked or tilted stage), or use of chemicals like theatrical fog and general workplace safety precautions. Union contracts also provide grievance procedures which give workers a secure and consistent method of airing complaints and receiving support.

Even with union support and representations, workers are not always guaranteed safe conditions. USA live performance designer contracts have no workplace safety language. This means that workers only benefit from contractual safety if there are other unionized workers with more comprehensive safety language in their contracts on the same project. Union stewards, as protected by the National Labor Relations Act, are workers empowered to act on behalf of the union on a worksite. Their work often centers around handling grievances against employers and offering the protections granted to workers by their Weingarten Rights, in which union members are guaranteed union representation in any disciplinary investigation. Stewards also protect workers by making sure workplace safety rules are followed. As of early 2023, United Scenic Artists also does not have a functioning and robust steward program. This lack of on-site support can be really detrimental to the safety of designers, especially in toxic work environments where no other union is represented.

Outside of union protections, all workers benefit from a variety of institutional protections within and beyond the theatrical production industry. The Occupational Safety and Health Act of 1970 was passed:

> to assure safe and healthful working conditions for working men and women; by authorizing enforcement of the standards developed under the Act; by assisting and encouraging the States in their efforts to assure safe and healthful working conditions; by providing for research, information, education, and training in the field of occupational safety and health.[5]

OSHA, the Occupational Safety and Health Administration, has been writing safety regulations since 1971. OSHA regulations often require both written and hands-on training, as well as regular training renewals, to teach safe work practices. The existence of OSHA training is extremely useful and important but also presents some challenges. It is the responsibility of the employer to provide safety training. But who pays for the training for the freelancers? Safety is expensive and often unplanned for. As Monona Rossol, chemist, artist, and industrial hygienist and then USA 829 Health and Safety Director, wrote in a 1997 OSHA Rules and Scenic Arts data sheet:

> Budgets for production companies and shops should have allocations for meeting the OSHA regulations. And each year, these allocations should have been steadily increasing. In fact, most good sized companies and shops should have a full time professional to address safety, OSHA, EPA, and fire regulations.[6]

Often employers are content to assume that production workers have the appropriate training, and workers may not want to admit that they don't have specific training at the risk of losing their jobs. In theatrical production, this is most likely to be true of workers and employers surrounding the OSHA 10 training. Specifically created for the entertainment industry:

> The OSHA 10 training covers general [entertainment] industry safety and health principles and OSHA policies, procedures, and standards. Modules are customized for the entertainment and exhibition industries and include: Introduction to OSHA; Personal Protective Equipment; Materials Handling, Storage, Use, and Disposal; Mobile Elevating Work Platforms; Walking and Working Surfaces; Hazard Communication; Electrical Safety for the Entertainment Industry; Ergonomics; Exit Routes, Emergency Action Plans, and Fire Protection; Fall Protection; Hand and Portable Powered Tool Safety.[7]

Obviously workers benefit from this training, which benefits employers. Fewer on-site injuries lower costs in both insurance premiums and lost productivity. If employers aren't taking up the mantle to provide the training, though, who is?

There are service organizations doing a lot to provide additional safety support to those workers who need it. In order to explicitly address access to safety training for workers, in 2013, the United States Institute for Theatre Technology (USITT) and IATSE established an alliance with OSHA. This alliance, renewed in 2018, provides OSHA training to members of both USITT and IATSE.[8] The priorities of the program are "raising awareness of OSHA's rulemaking and enforcement initiatives; training and education; [and] Outreach and communication."[9] Pat Landers, the United Scenic Artists' Business Representative for Health & Safety, credits this collaboration between USITT, IATSE, and OSHA with a shift in the culture towards prioritizing safety. He has seen safety practices improve over the last 20 years of his career:

> There are just so many people now that are interested in being safe on the job. There are a lot more people that are less interested in wearing the badge of being overworked. And you know, taking risks, climbing up on truss that's hanging over a stage or an arena floor without any fall protection. There's still plenty of people that do that kind of stuff, but it's not cool now, the way it used to be, which is good.[10]

Not only are workers better informed and thus using safer work practices, the trainings have also empowered them to speak up.

Arts, Crafts & Theater Safety (ACTS), founded by Rossol, is a not for profit which provides services to arts organizations like museums and theatres. These include health, safety, industrial hygiene, and technical services as well as safety publications. Rossol has created a myriad of worker-focused trainings that help to spread awareness and actionable steps to those who encounter dangerous situations, including workshops on hazardous chemicals, working practices to handle contagious diseases like COVID-19 and MPX, and conducting OSHA inspections.[11] With a focus on all types of live events, the Event Safety Alliance is a member-driven organization that aims to help event professionals put "life safety" at the center of their work.[12] Started in response to a 2011 live event tragedy which left seven dead and more than forty injured, they offer resources such as standards and guidance for weather preparedness, audience control and structure and fire safety; an event safety podcast; and events and training.[13]

These support systems are great for workers but only skim the surface of worker safety. As we know from Chapter 8, different workers have different needs in regards to accessibility, and this is the same with questions of safety. As producer Sophie Blumberg said:

> Safety looks different depending on who a person is and where they are making work. So, the real question is, who is safe in this moment? What might make me feel safe might not make my colleague, or the Black artists I'm working with, feel safe. What are our assumptions about safety? This is about being intentional in how one builds safety and security for the people they're working with and the communities they're working in.[14]

Perhaps less tangible and often less recognized aspects of worker safety are psychological and emotional safety. Harvard leadership scholar Amy C. Edmondson coined the term psychological safety in a 1999 journal article exploring the relationship between psychological safety and team learning and performance.[15] Edmonson defines psychological safety as "the belief that one will not be punished or humiliated for speaking up with ideas, questions, concerns or mistakes, and the team is safe for interpersonal risk-taking."[16] She explains, "Psychological safety means an absence of interpersonal fear. When psychological safety is present, people are able to speak up with work-relevant content."[17] This ability to take risks and speak up for both themselves and their colleagues gives workers more agency in their work. They can be more creative and are more likely to make valuable contributions. According to Dr. Timothy Clark, workers need to feel four kinds of safety to achieve this level of comfort in the workplace:

> Stage 1: Inclusion safety. You feel safe and accepted for who you are. Connecting and belonging is a human basic need!
> Stage 2: Learner safety. At this stage, you feel safe asking questions, learning new things, experimenting, and making mistakes. Giving and receiving feedback is a crucial part of learning!
> Stage 3: Contributor safety. You feel comfortable and safe enough to make contributions using your skills and knowledge to make a difference.
> Stage 4: Challenger safety. At this stage, you feel comfortable challenging certain notions when you see an opportunity to improve or change something.[18]

In a not particularly surprising recent study, Workhuman found that "women experience less psychological safety than men, and working parents had lower levels of psychological safety compared to those who aren't parents. Looking at race and ethnicity, white employees experienced the highest levels of psychological safety, with other races falling behind."[19] According to a parallel Gallup poll, "One crucial misconception among business leaders is that psychological safety will be present in any reasonably healthy work environment, like freedom from harassment or a commitment to keeping workers injury-free are. In fact, psychologically safe work environments are rare."[20] Unsurprisingly, Gallup found that improving psychological safety in the workplace leads to reduction in turnover, reduction in safety incidents, and an increase in productivity.[21]

There are several common practices in theatrical production that endanger psychological safety: harassment; mistreatment from leadership; lack of reporting structures; the culture of urgency; and a historical acceptance of abuse. There are seemingly endless examples of these dangerous environments. One such example occurred at the Washington, DC company Spooky Action Theater. In 2022, Spooky Action Theater was cited by DC Theater Arts as the site of harmful leadership practices by the artistic director Richard Henrich. The workers at the theatre shared

> numerous examples of Henrich's leadership that they felt to be toxic including: refusing to speak in group meetings, pressuring individuals to side differently with him once group consensus had been reached on a topic, cornering individuals outside the women's restroom, repeatedly entering occupied dressing rooms even after he was asked not to, and waving his hand in front of women's faces to stop them from talking during group meetings.[22]

Speaking of the artistic director's role on the wardrobe crew:

> 'The power dynamic of the artistic director taking on these duties is wrong and dangerous,' [the *Man Covets Bird*] director says. She repeatedly received texts and calls from the actors asking her to help get him out of the dressing rooms. 'I told him repeatedly to stop doing that and he claimed that it was "his theater" and he "has to" be allowed access to that area to do his work.'[23]

This kind of abuse of power removes the avenues of safety workers should be guaranteed. Workers at Spooky Action were also not protected by union contracts. More well-known examples of this kind of abuse of power centered around producer Scott Rudin who once "pegged the number of assistants he burned through in the previous five years at 119."[24] Similarly, citing the cases of abuse by Kevin Spacey, Harvey Weinstein, and the Gate Theatre's Michael Colgan, Dr. Karen Morash writes in *The Conversation*, "It is worth querying whether there is something in the nature of the performing arts industry which creates conditions conducive to exploitation."[25] Theatre, by its very nature, depends on bodies and emotions to tell stories. This currency of storytelling leads to mistreatment more often than it should, in the exhaustive hours, the exploitation of physical and emotional intimacy, the blurring of lines between personal and professional. In order to see the impact of these events, and their relationship to the prevalent culture, the UK newspaper *The Stage* published a survey of 1,050 theatre employees in 2018:

> The results of the survey, which were published last week, revealed that more than 40% of theatre professionals and students said they had been bullied, with one in three experiencing sexual harassment. Nearly 8% said they had been sexually assaulted at work. The survey also recorded several accounts of rape. Those most affected were backstage staff, creative staff and females. The harassment included inappropriate comments, unwanted sexual advances, touching and sexual intimidation.[26]

In our own survey, we asked production workers if they had ever felt mentally or emotionally unsafe in the workplace. Of the 1,037 survey participants, 804, or 77.5%, shared that yes, they have felt mentally or emotionally unsafe in the workplace. Our research shows that at least some of this lack of safety is connected to gender identity:

- Of those respondents who identify as female, 84.1% have felt mentally or emotionally unsafe in the workplace.
- Of people who identify as genderfluid/genderqueer/non-binary, 91.8% have felt mentally/emotionally unsafe in the workplace.
- Of people who listed "Other" for how they identify on the gender spectrum, 75.0% have felt mentally/emotionally unsafe in the workplace.
- Of people who identify as male, 66.7% have felt mentally/emotionally unsafe in the workplace.

Though more than half of any gender group has felt unsafe, there is a distinctly higher incidence of these feelings from non-male identifying workers.

So who do production workers talk to in situations where they might not have formalized reporting structures? We asked workers who they talk to in inequitable situations. Of our respondents, who were able to give multiple responses:

- 678 said colleagues;
- 521 said a department head or supervisor;
- 415 spoke to a production manager;
- 110 spoke with a union representative;

- 85 specifically spoke with a union steward;
- 20 workers cited organization leadership, general management, producer, company management, agent, stage manager, director, and other;
- 38 workers cited that they spoke to someone in their personal network;
- 134 workers said they spoke to no one.

For the 134 workers who spoke to no one, is this because there isn't a system in place or because the existing system didn't serve the worker or didn't feel like it would serve them?

When we asked employers who workers could report to in case of unsafe situations, the responses were similarly varied. At HERE:

> Workers have three options for reporting. They can report to their manager, to a representative on the HR Committee, or to the Business Administrator. They are also welcome to report it to the Producing Director or General Manager, though the first three options are recommended to begin the process.

At Williams College, which has the benefit of university institutional structures, "Workers should report first to their supervisor or the supervisor of the work but they also have access to Human Resources and the Environmental Health & Safety department at the college." Philadelphia-based theatre company InterAct has

> created an accountability flow-chart for all who use our venue, including staff, artists, technicians, audiences and other theatre companies renting the venue. Depending on who it is who feels unsafe, and the nature of the concern, there is a protocol for who to report to.

This flexibility is admirable as it addresses situations where the person to whom they can report is also the cause of the harm. Azuka Theatre in Philadelphia similarly offers that workers can speak to the "Co-Artistic Directors or Board president or Board HR person, it's up to them." At Ithaca's Kitchen Theatre Company, they expect workers to report to the "Stage Manager then theatre leadership then 'community support' provided by our Board's HR Committee." This raises some questions for those production workers who may not be comfortable with, or have access to, the stage manager.

The lack of consistent reporting structures across institutions puts an extra burden on a worker who has already suffered harm. Not only do they have to navigate the harm itself, but they have to navigate a system which may or may not have transparent protocols and is almost definitely a different set of protocols than the last institution or production where they worked. Simply reporting the harm is only the first step. How are workers who report, outside of union grievance procedures, protected from retaliation or continued harm? What happens when a temporary employee is abused by full time staff or leadership? Are they just not hired back? Production workers are very vulnerable to these kinds of situations. There is also the question of the accumulation of harm. An isolated incident may not seem to warrant reporting, but years and years of microaggressions and small abuses add up and have a significant impact on an individual worker.

Of those workers who had spoken with someone about unsafe situations in the workplace, we asked if the situation changed after speaking up:

- 15.0% said yes, the situation changed;
- 54.5% said sometimes the situation changed;
- 30.6% said no, the situation didn't change.

For those for whom it did change, the majority (53.2%) of changes happened on both the institutional and personal level. 28.2% of respondents said the changes were institutional. But 18.7% of the workers said the changes were solely personal. This begs the question of whether the change exists beyond the employee lifespan of that individual worker.

Harassment and threats to workers' psychological safety are often tied to the identities of the worker being harmed. To see the impact of this, we asked production workers how often they felt affected by actions or words directed at them personally, based on their identity. Of those who responded, only 17.7% said never. When asked how often they felt affected by indirect actions or words or other cultural aspects of a workplace, again only 18.2% said never. In both cases, the majority of workers have at some point been affected by the environment they work in ways directly related to their own identity. The majority of respondents have experienced microaggressions in the workplace. When asked how often they have been so affected, 4.3% said always; 18.2% said often; 33.6% said sometimes; 27.3% said rarely; and 16.6% said never. As a theatre worker, I, Brídín, have often had production colleagues confide in me about harmful actions they've experienced in the workplace, actions they perceive to be based on their identity. Their supervisor made a distressing comment about their parental responsibilities, a coworker's frequent microaggressions make them uncomfortable, or the one I am always the most unsettled by – the friendly warning about that one colleague with whom you should just avoid ever being in a room alone. They may tell me these things in the workplace, but it's always with the clarification that they are telling me as a friend and they do not want to formally report it. People tend to brush off the actions – whether due to the culture of urgency, lack of confidence in recourse, fear of blame, or the assumption that it's only impacting them and they can just deal with it – and keep going. But this data shows us that these instances are not isolated; the industry has a culture of harassment.

Beyond their employers, there are a number of resources that can provide additional support to workers. The Entertainment Community Fund, formerly the Actors Fund, for example, provides access to social services and financial assistance, social workers, health care providers and insurers, financial planning, tax preparation, career development, long and short term residential care, housing, and senior support to all those working in the entertainment industry. United Scenic Artists is one of many entertainment unions who have partnered with the ECF to create a Member Assistance Program which provides these services specifically curated and focused on the needs of designers and scenic artists. This, in part, comes from an acknowledgement of the potential of psychological harm caused in the workplace. Pat Landers explains:

> The pandemic has really illuminated issues of mental health and how it's a real thing. Especially in our industry, I think a lot of people are also viewing that not as its own thing, but along the same lines of wearing your safety glasses, people are recognizing when there are workplaces or employers that create poor mental health.[27]

USA has provided mental health first aid training to their staff to be able to identify concerns which might arise in a typical interaction with a member:

> The intent of that training is to kind of identify people like having panic attacks or that are suspected or visibly suicidal, and get them to appropriate care. But then, in addition to that, that provides staff tools to be able to recognize different levels of mental stress, and how to facilitate getting people where they need to go.[28]

This training is in addition to anti-harassment, antiracism, and implicit bias training for the staff. Landers continues:

> And that, of course, those things spill out into the work we are doing when we write contract language, when we negotiate contracts, when we have conversations with producers, when we have to deal with different situations on a worksite. Like, if there's a worker that is experiencing harassment, or is experiencing some sort of mental distress. We can use these tools. I think that's a pretty big step.[29]

The unions themselves can also provide protection and support for their workers in their collectively bargained contracts. Landers explains that there usually isn't pushback to requests for physical and occupational safety language, but:

> It's more challenging to negotiate contract language that deals with things that are more related to mental health or respect in the workplace. While we have

> developed language that we are working to negotiate into every new contract that does deal with those things, it's language that's sort of hard to enforce because there's not concrete points. It's like, you have violated this piece of the contract and this sentence is a violation and like you owe a penalty now. This kind of language isn't enforceable that way. Employers are certainly interested in it conceptually because most people are. Sometimes it can just be hard to enforce.[30]

There have been actions to address this. In one such move, the IATSE has explicitly added anti-bullying language into its constitution. At the 2021 IATSE Quadrennial, the assembled members approved an amended version of Constitution Article 16, which now reads:

> Section 31. Discrimination, Harassment or Bullying Behavior Certain rights are set forth in this Article when charges are preferred against a member alleging discrimination, harassment or bullying behavior, which shall include a charge alleging discrimination based on race, religion, gender, age, disability, sexual orientation, and other protected categories under any federal, state or local law or a charge alleging bullying behavior, defined as repeated inappropriate behavior that is threatening, intimidating, or humiliating, or involves work sabotage, either direct or indirect, whether verbal, physical, or otherwise, by one or more persons against another or others, at the place of work or in the course of employment.[31]

The addition of this language makes clear that not only the employers, but also the union itself, are responsible for protecting its members from emotional and psychological harm at work.

Working to support production workers, the Behind the Scenes Charity provides financial support to entertainment technology workers or their families who have been seriously injured or ill. The Mental Health Initiative promotes mental health and psychological safety. These tools include the Mental Health First Aid Training (those cost of which IATSE reimburses) and resources for workers who may be struggling.[32] One of which is sample text for production personnel to use in their "toolbox talk," equipping workers to lead conversations about difficult topics such as mental health and psychological safety in a stressful workplace.

Put Together Your Toolbox Talk

From Behind the Scenes' Mental Health Initiative

Behind the Scenes discusses why it's important to talk about mental health and psychological safety and what your Toolbox Talk can look like. This information is meant to be incorporated into your current safety or toolbox talks and is not meant to replace other safety briefings.

Sample Text for Toolbox Talks

Examples of language on each of the topics are shown here, and more are provided in the Behind the Scenes resources at btshelp.org/mentalhealth (or btshelp.org/mentalhealth/toolboxtalks). Workers are encouraged to select the topics and statements that are appropriate for your workplace and use the statements as written or put them into your own words.

How to talk about Mental Health and Psychological Safety

Explain why mental health awareness is important in the workplace

Examples:

- We want you to feel safe working here, and to do that you need to be both physically safe and psychologically safe.
- Working to protect your mental health is as important as protecting you from physical injury.
- Stress can contribute to accidents
- Talking about mental health challenges isn't easy, but we have to start somewhere.

Describe Psychological Safety

Examples:

- Psychological safety means being able to:
    - Make mistakes and receive constructive feedback, not be ridiculed or punished
    - Say "I don't know" or "I don't understand"
    - Have a voice regardless of your position
    - Feel respected and valued
- Psychologically safe teams accept and respect all their members.

Acknowledge stressors and challenges in the workplace

Talking openly about potential stressors and anxiety triggers can lessen their impact

Examples:

- Today is going to be long with a lot of stress and we've all been working long hours and we're tired. This can negatively affect your mental and physical health.
- If you don't feel physically or psychologically up to a particular task, tell your supervisor or someone you trust. It's better to say something than to hurt yourself or someone else.

Excessive and/or sustained pressure can result in stress that is harmful

Examples:

- We all feel stress on the job and some days are worse than others. Everyday stress can be helpful in motivating us on the job, but when it's unmanageable it can be dangerous for ourselves and others around us.
- This work can be really stressful, if you start feeling overwhelmed let somebody know.

Take a 90 second "time out"

Examples:

- If you are feeling overwhelmed, angry, or things are really tense, take a 90 second time-out if it's safe and walk away. It just takes 90 seconds to reset your brain's stress levels.
- If you can, take a 90 second break to help reduce your stress level.

Offer tools and tips

Examples:

Here are a few things to do to help you if you are struggling. Pick the one that works best for you:

- Take a few deep breaths – and make your exhale longer than your inhale
- Use a calming exercise such as observe and name 5 objects around you
- Think of a place that brings a sense of calm and go there for a moment
- Close your eyes, start breathing deeply, and mentally walk the path to your nearest emergency exit.

Text courtesy of Behind the Scenes Foundation's Mental Health Initiative "Put Together Your Toolbox Talk", © 2023 Behind the Scenes Foundation; for additional information, contact: http://behindthesceneschar‌ity.org/mentalhealth.

Pat Landers explained that United Scenic Artists shares these resources with its membership, including the incredibly useful online therapist finder:

> One of the bigger issues that we found within workers in the industry is that they have to spend the first couple sessions just explaining what the heck we do. So

> these are all therapists who are familiar with the industry in some way, shape, or form. Some are former technicians, some are former actors, directors, designers, or they've worked specifically within groups within the arts. And that way, it's a pool of resources for not just individuals in certain major markets, but also in every state and every province in Canada and also the territories.[33]

Trained as an Intimacy Director, Sarah Lozoff from Production on Deck brings consent-based practices into the production workspaces to increase worker safety. She encourages production managers to check in with their staff and workers, to make sure that there are content disclosures given to the production staff, to consider understudy-type arrangements if someone has to step away:

> I think production people often don't have a voice in what they are witnessing and partaking in, and especially at theatres like OSF where they're living with these shows for 120 performances for eight months. It's a long time. Right? A lot can happen in someone's life during the better part of a year [...] Something that I felt that I was going to be okay witnessing several times a week backstage, you know, simulated assaults and blood and murder and misogyny and racism and everything else might start to wear on me six months in, or you know, something happens in my personal life that makes it so that suddenly it feels very triggering or too heavy or like maybe I just need a break from.[34]

This kind of consideration and agency makes for a safer workplace overall, one in which communication allows for the concerns of workers to be heard and addressed.

As part of our survey of workers, we asked workers to provide their own definitions of safety. Overwhelmingly workers mentioned both physical and mental or psychological safety. There were several shared themes including proper equipment, safety training, access to PPE, reasonable work hours, and proper staffing. As we discussed in Chapter 8, questions of accessibility also enter into safety needs: an accessible space is a safer space. Workers mentioned variations of understanding that

> a safe environment is one in which employees have the right and expectation that they will come forward immediately with any physical safety concerns and they also have the right to come forward with any personal or emotional abuse, threats, etc. to their supervisor. That supervisor also needs to act promptly and professionally to resolve the issue at hand.

Importantly, many workers mentioned being recognized for their humanity: "Being seen as a human, and putting those needs before the needs of the show." One worker put it clearly:

> Safety is all-encompassing; physical, emotional, and mental. It's not just about whether or not you're too tired to climb a ladder or too strained to lift and hang a light. It's about whether or not your needs are being met, if your ideas are being supported by your peers and supervisors, if you are being validated rather than neglected or belittled for your work. Theatre is at its core a collaborative process, and safety in all forms is central to that collaboration.

And another worker shared that safety is:

> Eliminating risk where possible, mitigating risk where necessary, and educating all crew about the nuances and details of the risk so as to eliminate general fear and instead promote a precise understanding, and healthy respect, of the danger.
>
> In other words, you should never fear something you don't understand, nor fear it because you don't understand it. If there is a risk we cannot mitigate away, we must become experts on why it is dangerous, how it can hurt us, and methods to avoid that happening.

Production work does have risks, and as this worker thoughtfully points out, being familiar with the risks is in itself a safety measure.

When we asked employers "How does your institution define workplace safety?" many of the answers reflected a focus on physical safety and a lack of awareness of mental or psychological safety. Management at one NYC venue answered: "Proper PPE for the job being done. Cleaning up after yourself so that the next person can safely do their job." Another theatre replied: "We use OSHA as a guide for defining workplace safety." Similarly, another NYC theatre is providing "More available types and sizes of PPE. Trying to get to hard hats, but it's an uphill battle. Enforcing crew minimums so that no one works alone."

Consistent with their other policies around reporting, InterAct Theatre Company has a more holistic view of safety:

> We define workplace safety in both physical and spiritual terms. Physically, we seek to have a fully-accessible venue for artists, technicians, staff and audiences alike. And with the exception of our tech booth, which is only accessible via stairs, all other spaces are fully accessible and ADA compliant. Spiritually, we seek to cultivate a venue that feels safe for artists, technicians, staff and audiences alike. We have created quiet, private spaces for all of the above to go, if desired. We have ten all-gender bathrooms to make all people feel welcome.

This consistency is reflected across other organizations: the more expansive an organization's ideas about structure and support, seemingly the more expansive their definitions of safety. At the Kitchen Theatre Company:

> Every [worker] is taken care of physically and mentally and is able to focus on tasks at hand, while receiving the necessary support to do their jobs. Literally, this means hard hats and appropriate tools for technical positions, and open, transparent communication for all jobs.

This contrasts our previous concerns about their reporting structures.

Everyone – workers, employers, unions – are responsible for workplace safety. As D. Joseph Hartnett shared, from a union perspective, though it is incumbent on the employers to provide safe workplaces:

> We need to be listening to the membership as well, and trying to strive to make the better workplaces that people want. And ultimately, you know, our role as a labor union is to negotiate those terms and conditions with the employers. And the key part of that sentence is negotiate.[35]

Several of the employers we surveyed offered ways that their organizations have been working to further address worker safety. American Players Theatre has created a safety committee of several staff members and stakeholders which meets monthly. Delaware Theatre Company shared their Safety Manual, which has in-depth coverage of general workplace safety procedures, emergency action plans, first aid protocols, and many specific protocols for physical safety.[36] It does not, however, address psychological safety. Kitchen Theatre Company explained that they are "putting in place a conflict resolution path for all employees, creating active anti-racism support, active shooter guides, and purchasing hard hats/knee pads/braces, etc. to support the physical safety in the room." And, finally, Seattle's Intiman Theatre shared their process: "Walk through shops with OSHA compliance officer and improve layout and equipment to improve physical safety, install air filters to add to the filtration of spaces. Have a safety committee represented by each department where issues can be documented and resolved."

When asked what he sees as the biggest current challenge for production labor, USA 829 Business Representative Pat Landers shared:

> It's inherently exploitative. I think that the mentality of 'the show must go on,' I believe in it, but I think it has been taken too far. In most cases. I think the nature of work in live production, a lot of times is so sporadic, but also, a lot of things happen in a very short amount of time, and it's easy to take advantage of people when that is the case. [...] Maybe the pace of it could slow down a little bit, that would probably be helpful. I've never been part of a road crew for a Broadway show or traveling music act, but I know it's brutal. It's brutal to race from one venue to the next. When the only rest that you get is maybe on the six hour bus ride from Chicago to Minneapolis. That doesn't make for good habits.[37]

This really sums it up. Workers need time and space to be safe. They need access to the right tools and the right training. They need protections and clear communication with supervisors. Employers need to put people before productions or profits.

NOTES

1 *WS Virtual Salon 29 Pay Equity*, YouTube video, 2022, 23:15, https://www.youtube.com/watch?v=jTaNBzc1AAE.
2 IATSE, "Performing Arts and Motion Picture Hazard Information" (Occupational Safety and Health Administration, August 2018), https://www.osha.gov/sites/default/files/IATSE_2018.pdf.
3 Tanner A. Richardett, "No More 10/12s: Considerations for a More Equitable Theatre Rehearsal Structure in Philadelphia" (Thesis, Philadelphia, PA, Drexel University, 2021), 24, https://drive.google.com/file/d/1C0YdONhCUwzE6DSSfXlmtHkH1p507Zem/view.
4 The WTF, Williamstown?! Collective, "The WTF, Williamstown?! Collective to Mandy Greenfield, Laura Savia, Jeffrey Johnson, Joe Finnegan, Annie Pell, Brad Svrluga, and Donald B. Elitzer; as Well as the Rest of the Staff and Board of Trustees of Williamstown Theatre Festival," https://ca-times.brightspotcdn.com/06/37/5851edc0482387ff1b2fee01b155/updated-williamstown-theatre-festival-letter.pdf.
5 Occupational Safety and Health Administration, "Workers' Rights" (Washington, D.C.: United States Department of Labor, 2019).
6 Monona Rossol, "Data Sheet: OSHA Rules and Scenic Arts," IATSE Local USA 829,1, https://www.usa829.org/LinkClick.aspx?fileticket=M6xZptQuLvs%3D&portalid=0.
7 "IATSE Training Trust Fund," IATSE Local 524, https://www.iatse524.com/ttf.
8 "USITT-IATSE Alliance Agreement," Occupational Safety and Health Administration, United States Department of Labor, July 16, 2013, https://www.osha.gov/alliances/national/usitt_iatse_alliance-agreement_20130716.
9 Occupational Safety and Health Administration, "USITT-IATSE Alliance Agreement."
10 Pat Landers (Business Representative for Health & Safety, United Scenic Artists) interview by the authors, November 2022.
11 "What is ACTS?" Arts, Crafts, and Theater Safety https://www.artscraftstheatersafety.org/aboutacts.html.
12 "Who We Are," Event Safety Alliance, https://www.eventsafetyalliance.org/ourmission.
13 "Home," Event Safety Alliance, https://www.eventsafetyalliance.org/.
14 Sophie Blumberg, Jonathan Secor, and Ben Johnson., "Perspectives on Safety and Sustainability for Venues and Cultural Spaces," HowlRound Theatre Commons, October 5, 2021, https://howlround.com/perspectives-safety-and-sustainability-venues-and-cultural-spaces.
15 McKinsey & Company, "Is It Safe?," *McKinsey Quarterly*, https://www.mckinsey.com/featured-insights/leadership/five-fifty-is-it-safe.
16 Amy C. Edmondson., "Psychological Safety," https://amycedmondson.com/psychological-safety.
17 McKinsey & Company.

18 Hebba Youssef, "Employees Don't Feel Psychologically Safe at Work and It Stifles Innovation," Workweek, November 21, 2022, https://workweek.com/2022/11/21/employees-dont-feel-psychologically-safe-at-work-and-it-stifles-innovation/.
19 Bryan Robinson, "10 Red Flags that Psychological Safety is Lacking in Your Workplace," *Forbes*, June 13, 2021, https://www.forbes.com/sites/bryanrobinson/2021/06/13/10-red-flags-that-psychological-safety-is-lacking-in-your-workplace/?sh=2e86027810c1&utm_source=Sailthru&utm_medium=email&utm_campaign=IHIH%2011/21/22&utm_term=I%20Hate%20It%20Here.
20 Amy C. Edmondson and Per Hugander, "4 Steps to Boost Psychological Safety at Your Workplace," *Harvard Business Review*, June 22, 2021, https://hbr.org/2021/06/4-steps-to-boost-psychological-safety-at-your-workplace.
21 Jake Herway, "How to Create a Culture of Psychological Safety," *Gallup*, December 7, 2017, https://www.gallup.com/workplace/236198/create-culture-psychological-safety.aspx.
22 Nicole Hertvick, "Under a Cloud: Artists Describe Toxic Work Conditions at Spooky Action Theater," DC Theater Arts, May 20, 2022, https://dctheaterarts.org/2022/05/20/under-a-cloud-artists-describe-toxic-work-conditions-at-spooky-action-theater/.
23 Hertvick.
24 Tatiana Siegel, "'Everyone Just Knows He's an Absolute Monster: Scott Rudin's Ex-Staffers Speak Out on Abusive Behavior," *Hollywood Reporter*, April 7, 2021, https://www.hollywoodreporter.com/movies/movie-news/everyone-just-knows-hes-an-absolute-monster-scott-rudins-ex-staffers-speak-out-on-abusive-behavior-4161883/.
25 Karen Morash, "Acting Unpleasantly: Why Harassment is So Common in the Theatre," *The Conversation*, November 16, 2017, https://theconversation.com/acting-unpleasantly-why-harassment-is-so-common-in-the-theatre-87374.
26 Jacqui Morton, "Putting a Stop to Harassment and Abuse in the Theatre Industry," *Emmott Snell Solicitors Abuse Survivors Blog* (blog), https://www.emmottsnell.co.uk/blog/putting-a-stop-to-harassment-and-abuse-in-the-theatre-industry.
27 Landers, interview.
28 Landers, interview.
29 Landers, interview.
30 Landers, interview.
31 "Together We Rise: 69th Quadrennial Convention Resolutions, Book 1," IATSE, 2021, 2, https://www.iatseconvention.com/Doc-Page/FileId/3193/Extension/pdf?FileName=Resolutions+Book+1.
32 "BTS Home," Behind the Scenes, https://wp.behindthescenescharity.org.
33 Landers, interview.
34 Sarah Lozoff (Co-Founder, Production on Deck), interview by the authors, September 2022.
35 D. Joseph Hartnett (former Co-Director, IATSE Stagecraft Department), interview by the authors, October 2022.
36 "Safety Manual," Delaware Theatre Company, 2020, https://docs.google.com/document/d/1rC20649OrX4rEDblTlb5EzuR7exwCRHuhYSRDncRGCg/edit?usp=sharing.
37 Landers, interview.

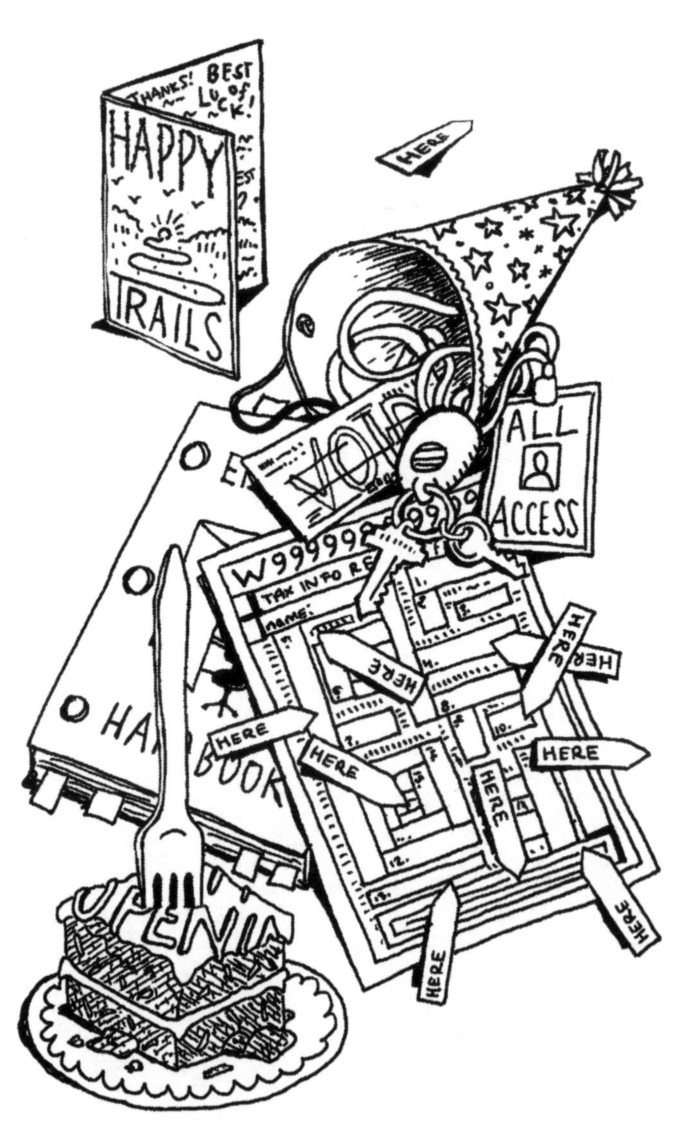

HAPPY
TRAILS
THANKS!
BEST LUCK!
HERE
ALL ACCESS
TAX INFO
NAME:
HERE
HERE
HERE
HERE
HERE
HERE
HERE
HERE

10

PEOPLE OPERATIONS

Employees' bodies, time, and energy are key to the success of a business, or of a production. The treatment of these humans defines equitable labor practices from the start. An equitable workplace guarantees that all people working have the ability to do their job safely and sustainably. Many people find their ideal job in the theatre and want to do it for a long time. And their workplaces should allow for that.

So, what does this entail? First and foremost, workers need financial security and a thriving wage, which includes the ability to plan for a future retirement. They need access to affordable healthcare and benefits, including life and disability insurance. As we covered in Chapter 6, workers need to understand the scope and responsibilities of their job. While accurate and thorough job descriptions and inclusive hiring processes are steps toward this, once hired, workers need regular communications about expectations and feedback. They also need ongoing training and education. Workers need a respectful and safe work environment, a reporting structure for grievances, and to believe that those in charge will address their concerns. Workers need a workplace that is physically accessible, in ways beyond mere compliance with the Americans with Disabilities Act, and welcoming to all workers regardless of identity.

DOI: 10.4324/9781003330394-12

As we consider the details of the factors – recruitment, onboarding, accessibility, performance management, retention, grievances, benefits and compensation, and separation – that make up people operations, it is helpful to look at how traditional human resources practices do and do not fit into the theatrical production framework. In many work environments, once a worker is hired and some semblance of a contract is agreed to, there is an onboarding process which includes goal setting with the supervisor. As the worker begins their day-to-day work, they expect to receive feedback, recognition, and regular performance evaluations. Milestones are celebrated. When it is time, the worker resigns, retires, or is promoted. All of this is overseen by a human resources staff or department. These formalized processes don't necessarily apply to theatre production workers, much as they don't apply to restaurant workers and other service workers. There is a much higher employee turnover rate, as workers move between multiple employers or expect their employment to be for a limited time. The work is precarious and inconsistent. Workers are often unclear about clear accountability and management structures. A career in the theatre often doesn't look like working the same job at the same location until retirement. It might look like a constant ebb and flow of moving between productions, shifting roles and employers and work circumstances.

Regardless of its presence or absence in the theatre, for our purposes, "human resources" refers to those aspects of management often covered by "the process of employing people, training them, compensating them, developing policies relating to them, and developing strategies to retain them."[1] Many believe that human resource departments are a tool of the employer originally created to limit worker-driven power. Oftentimes employers create HR departments to address the same needs that workers seek unionization to establish and protect. The key to prioritizing the worker-focused policies that can increase productivity without causing harm is to remember that:

> Human resources, or employees, are perhaps the most critical resources a firm possesses because human capital underlies any organizational capability in the sense that organizations do not make decisions or allocate resources; people do. Organizations actually capitalize on the employees' ideas to leverage the financial and physical resources to create financial returns [...] By increasing the extent of human capital through the use of strategic human resource practices, employees' skills and capabilities can be developed to meet the demands of unpredictable environmental changes.[2]

The employer benefits from a people-first human resources approach because it "saves time and therefore money; minimizes risk of claims and fines; clarifies company ethos and culture, attracts professional staff through professional environment and standards; [and] retains staff, giving them clear career progression opportunities through clarity of process."[3] In other words, it makes the employer's life easier.

The theatrical workplace clearly needs to have some sort of policy in place to ensure that employment practices are inclusive, equitable, and sustainable for all workers. However, theatre is not the same as "typical" workplaces. Theatrical workplaces often benefit from some of their differences. The theatre has long been seen as an accepting and welcoming workplace. Its non-traditional hierarchies, active pace, creative environments, and unorthodox schedules have made it a field where workers who cannot find a place in the "normal" workplace can often thrive. The self-directed nature of much theatre work, paired with the erratic hours, can really be ideal for many workers. This is perhaps why there are quite a number of neurodivergent workers in the theatre. Many people find theatre because of the uniqueness of the way of working – the fast-paced nature of it and the pressure that goes with it, the combination of physical engagement and technical thinking, and the flexibility it can allow. All of these things can be seen as perks, but they also can create limitations, feeding a workplace that is not accessible or sustainable for all workers. These limits also make traditional human resources policies an uneasy fit.

If, as recent studies increasingly show, having happy employees increases productivity,[4] then human resources departments can be seen as potential collaborators in the creation of equitable labor practices. That being said, it's important to remember that human resources departments are designed to interact with employees for the employer that they serve. Contract and temporary workers are often not considered in employee policies and so don't often have the benefits of human resources offered to full time staff.

A people-centered operations approach includes an in-depth onboarding process for new hires. According to Karla Gutierrez, an Inbound Marketer at Aura Interactiva, onboarding "is an entire process by which new employees acquire the skills, knowledge, and behaviors that will permit them to become effective contributors within an organization."[5] Onboarding establishes expectations for both employee and employer. Effective onboarding communicates company values and culture and aligns these with performance goals and expectations, all of which are key to setting the new employee up for success. Structured onboarding is proven to increase employee retention.[6] This is also the time when detailed information about an employee's location within an organization is established: "During the onboarding stage, new employees cover more in-depth aspects of their position, identify the attitudes, knowledge, skills, and behaviors that are required to function effectively within the organization."[7]

But how does onboarding work for contract or casual employees? In the case of many theatrical production employers, short term or temporary employees do not benefit from this process at all. We asked theatrical production employers about their processes for onboarding designers and technical staff. The range and kind of responses was telling of the lack of consistency or equity between staff and non-staff production workers.

Again and again employers cited incomplete onboarding processes for production workers. San Diego's Old Globe Theater said that their onboarding process is "haphazard" and "ad hoc." However, they shared that the institutional HR staff does support production personnel, and that production staff receive feedback at least once annually. At Kansas City Repertory Theatre, the onboarding for production staff is limited to a need-to-know system. This implies that there may be instances where resources are only offered to employees after an incident has occurred. They shared: "We are developing a 'welcome week' for all staff, to review organizational culture, values, and expectations. Additionally, production management works with designers and technical staff to flush out these expectations, as needed. Department heads work directly with designers and technical staff."

There is a clear disconnect between the attempts at onboarding staff and the inclusion of short term or temporary artist employees. At Abrons Arts Center on NYC's Lower East Side, the director of production shared that for technicians – casual and full-time – "there is an in-depth HR onboarding which has very little to do with their actual jobs. I give new folks a venue tour, hand them a walkie talkie and expect them to do the job I hired them for." Though Abrons prioritizes equity in many aspects of their employment, this reflects a lack of commitment to casual employees. InterAct Theater Company in Philadelphia has a process to handle the tangible onboarding for their non-staff production workers: "After setting up their payment processing with our Managing Director, they are given tours of our facilities and theatrical equipment inventory, and an overview of our typical production schedule and process." This onboarding doesn't seem to include discussion of organizational culture or expectations, nor any team building or process focused conversations. HERE goes on to name a misclassification of workers that is common in many theatres: "Designers are contractors, so we require them to read and review our code of conduct, but do not provide onboarding. Technical overhire generally does not receive onboarding either, as they are merely day laborers." As we have discussed, this misclassification, considering these workers independent contractors, is in contradiction to the labor laws classification of these workers as employees. None of these onboarding processes fully invest in the short-term production workers.

In contrast, Delaware Theatre Company has a much more robust process for their production workers for at least the practical components of onboarding:

> Upon acceptance of a job offer, designer and technical staff receive a contract, payment paperwork, and a welcome letter from DTC. The welcome letter has

> links to the employee handbook, the production guide, feedback channels, Equity, Diversity, & Inclusion resources etc.
>
> When first on site, each person gets a building tour which includes a safety walkthrough (pointing out first aid, emergency exits, fire extinguishers, etc.)
>
> During the first production meeting and first rehearsal, DTC reviews the above information, as well walks through show resources like the contact sheet, dropbox, and schedules.

But even this process isn't onboarding the way HR professionals describe the processes employers should aspire to.

So why is onboarding different, or even entirely lacking, in production?

Many production jobs are much shorter than a typical expected employee lifecycle. According to Natasha Dilena of Factorial HR:

> A thorough onboarding program often begins from the very moment a recruit accepts the job offer and can last up to a year. Within this time frame, new employees can expect to take part in the orientation, actively participate in presentations, and take on new projects. Regular meetings with their managers and Human Resources are also scheduled to monitor their progress. It's clear why more than a month is required.[8]

Many non-staff production workers have completed their commitment long before that kind of process, or even the minimum month that Dilena references, would allow. It is also important to differentiate here between short term employees like actors or stage managers, who are likely contracted for weeks or months prior to the start of performances, contract hires like designers and directors who are regularly misclassified as independent contractors, and over-hire technicians who are typically considered to be casual employees who work in a day laborer model. Each of these employment models presents a different set of challenges for onboarding. And not everyone starts at the same time.

Even if there were an onboarding process, who would oversee it for production workers? A human resources professional or administrator who knows very little about the production work, as seems to be the case at Abrons? Or a supervisor with production expertise but who may not have interest in, experience with, or capacity for cultural onboarding? Would the onboarding be the same as it is for full-time staff or even between various production departments? How can workers in these non-traditional but certainly common situations be served? Would workers be paid for their onboarding time? What would it even include? A one-size-fits-all model is unlikely to serve all of these different workers.

Rather than trying to force the current onboarding processes into a new form, perhaps there is another way of approaching this for production workers. Even with temporary or short term contracts, there must be a way for productions and organizations to engage employees in some form of expectation-setting around role, communication strategies, feedback loops, working styles, and job goals. For a stage manager hired on their first professional job, for example, having a clear list of job duties and scope allows them to understand the employer's specific expectations of how they see the position within this production and team. Even a seasoned stage manager benefits from the clarity a detailed description provides – as different organizations, producers, general managers, and directors may have varying preconceived notions of the role. This shared understanding between the stage manager and other leadership will also serve all other collaborators.

Another component of people operations, in order to both support the worker and maximize organizational capacity, is ensuring that all workers are able to do their work. As we have discussed, feelings of physical and psychological safety in the workplace are greatly tied to questions of accessibility. Having an accessible workplace is vital to worker productivity. We asked production workers if and how they felt supported in the workplace, and, specifically, to describe how theatres they've worked in facilitate an accessible working environment. Many respondents said that they haven't found accessible production workspaces. Consistent with many responses, a worker said of the theatres they work in: "Most I've worked in aren't even ADA compliant let alone facilitating an environment that accommodates people who are neurodivergent or that provides safe spaces for LGBTQIA individuals."

Workspaces are often made increasingly inaccessible by the attitudes of those who work in them. One worker stated, "I often feel like I need to push myself – especially with my physical disability – even when it's not safe, because it's 'all hands on deck' and I might not get hired again in the future if I don't 'pull my weight.'" Another agreed:

> They have a certain expectation that things will be done a particular way, based on old practices, and do not consider how to make the workplace more accessible. It is up to individuals to educate and ask for what they need. In most cases, they see people as being able or not able. They do not ask for input and do not seem open to change.

The collaborative nature of theatrical production creates an environment where the expectations and attitudes of one's co-workers can drastically impact a worker's experience.

As we mentioned in Chapter 8, the focus on accessibility seems to be on the audience or the performers. One worker explained, "I feel like they largely have not been accessible working environments at all, maybe besides allowing for wheelchair seating." Another survey respondent shared:

> I think a lot of accommodations have been made for actors with accessibility needs – in terms of adding wheelchair ramps backstage, providing translators

> for HOH [Hard of Hearing], and a lot of Mental Health support as well as built in PT. I believe staff generally have decent access to these as well. However those accommodations are notably lacking for freelancers in production.

In many cases, accessibility for production workers seems to be reactionary: These accommodations are "largely done on a case by case basis, but it's rare that any company asks what accommodations would help the company. Accommodations are usually made only when demanded." And, in some cases, even when those demands are reasonable and requested, they aren't met:

> A friend of mine has struggled to get access to a fridge for her insulin. They can't even do that. Not to mention if you are vocal about your disability people see you as a problem or as someone who 'can't get the work done' or is 'lazy' (actual comments I've heard about coworkers that did ask for accommodations).

We did hear from workers about the occasional case of producers and institutions providing exactly the kinds of support workers need – providing opportunities for artists to request accommodations, having a wheelchair-accessible booth, offering ASL interpretation for auditions and rehearsals, and taking workers' suggestions to improve accessibility. Another worker shared an experience where an institution invited people to state their names before speaking on Zoom calls, allowing time for sign language interpreters to share who was speaking. Some organizations have offered childcare stipends, and some have provided or places to rest. And increasingly workers are receiving more information about what to expect in terms of access and show needs before the workers begin the project. One manager shared that:

> We are working to meet individual needs of each worker as they are disclosed. Do you need to have written instructions due to audio processing. Do I provide you a box of masks to alter the strings on because we need you to wear N95 masks instead of cloth and the strings on your ears cause too much stimulation. You have use of one hand but we need you to push two buttons – purchase a button accessible with your foot. You are in a wheelchair and can't access the booth? We move the booth to an adjacent room with a camera.

Again, these are small concessions to a larger concern. These actions speak to employers who value inclusion but do not fully address the creation of accessible work environments. Making a workspace accessible to workers with disabilities or neurodivergences will benefit workers overall. Fulfilling the individual needs of a single worker benefits the majority of workers.

Those who are caregivers also may have unique needs that allow them to show up at work as their best selves. Of the respondents to our worker survey, 199 (or 19.2%) of the respondents identified as caregivers. Of those, 62 (or 31.2%) are, at least sometimes, solo caregivers. And 43 (or 24.2%) of caregivers have a co-caregiver who also works in production. When asked if they have any family or community support, more than 20% of the surveyed caregivers said they do not. Unsupported caregiving puts an additional strain on any caregiver, and is particularly strenuous for those working in an already precarious industry without common workplace support.

Supporting caregiving workers supports all workers. As Rachel Spencer Hewitt, one of the founders of the Parent Artist Advocacy League (PAAL) offered:

> Everyone's a caregiver at one point, and here's why investing in care in your organization means that you're investing in those moments when suddenly you need care, and everyone knows how to take care of you. So it's about that reflective model of identifying need as a community conversation.[9]

For parents, who are the majority of caregivers who have been studied, choosing to have a family has had clear impacts on career and work lives. In 2016, Parents in Chicago Theatre (PICT) conducted a survey to determine the effect that having caring responsibilities has on theatre careers. They surveyed a sampling of parents in a wide variety of theatre jobs: actors, directors, designers, educators and administrators.[10] They found that "91% of parents have turned down theatre work because of scheduling or the cost of childcare."[11] It's important to note that the focus of this survey was current theatre workers, so there wasn't data on workers who had left the field. Following that survey, in 2018, PICT surveyed people who took an extended break or stopped working in the Chicago theatre industry after becoming parents to learn about their experiences.[12] PICT's findings included information about education level, showing that

> A significant number of people in Chicago theatre have made a huge investment in their education, yet are finding it impossible to maintain a career in their chosen profession since becoming a parent. This also means that there is a wealth of knowledge and expertise that the industry is missing out on by not supporting parents [and] most of the parents surveyed also had a significant level of experience – an average of 13 years. More than half of respondents have over 15 years of experience. There is of course some attrition in the theatre industry of people who study and 'pay their dues' working in theatre, but find it an unsustainable long-term career.[13]

What specifically makes a career in the theatre unsustainable for these, and other, caregivers? The PICT survey found:

> Of the approximately ⅓ of respondents who are working outside theatre, almost all are working full-time. The two reasons cited the most often were higher pay was more and a schedule more compatible with parenting young children. This is consistent with the findings in last year's report that scheduling, low pay and the cost of childcare are the greatest barriers for parents working in theatre.[14]

Similarly, in 2020, UK-based organization Parents & Carers in Performing Arts carried out the Backstage Workforce Survey. The survey revealed significant challenges faced by backstage workers in the UK, particularly women and those with caring responsibilities.[15] Unsurprisingly, the report cites working conditions shared by many workers: poor work-life balance; not feeling listened to; feeling disenfranchised.[16]

When we asked, "Are there instances where your theatrical production workplace has been supportive of your caregiving responsibilities?" the answers were similarly unsurprising. Though there have been theatre companies that have attempted to support caregivers, the overwhelming response is that there is a lack of assistance. One respondent shared:

> I find that the theater world is actively against supporting caregivers. I suppose there have been individual instances where I was given consideration in, say, meeting scheduling, but overall, no, the theater world has not been supportive.

The lack of standard caregiver benefits, like maternity or parental leave and sick leave, make caregiving as a freelancer even harder. Even under the Family Medical Leave Act, most freelancers don't qualify because they have so many different employers. Workers spoke of the expectations that their children and families would be second to their work life: "As a whole, never; the work comes first, not your personal life even if that is a sick kid or parent. I also have health issues myself and to them even making my own doctor's appointments is seen as an inconvenience." And theatre is not free of the typical misogyny that assumes mothers cannot parent and do a good job at work:

> My daughter is adopted from foster care. My pre-pandemic theatrical job gave me no time off. I took 2 days when she moved in and 1 day when she was officially adopted. I took NO maternity leave. At my next review I was told I was 'less effective' since I'd become a mom. What they meant was I wasn't working 13 hour days every day any more but was working 10 hour days and actually taking my weekends off to help my child adjust to my family.

A common sentiment emerged from workers: "[I] left theater because I could not raise my kids and work."

For those respondents who feel they have been supported as caregivers, a number of them noted or implied that their production jobs are full time rather than freelance. One respondent, who benefits from working at a university, says:

> My university is very supportive of children and families and theater which is wonderful. My child has been to many of my classes and is often in the costume shop and tech.

This environment is also home to other workers who welcome children, as the same worker adds:

> I work very hard to make sure we do not impede the work that needs to be done and respect the workplace and given protocols and safety procedures. Many of my colleagues have held or directly interacted with my child when they were upset or trying to interrupt during a meeting etc. without becoming irritated or frustrated and have helped to redirect my child if needed.

Another worker shared the aspects of their full-time job, which allowed them to continue to be successful at work:

> allowing me to work remotely during the entirety of my pregnancy during the pandemic, provided [New York Paid Family Leave], as well as short term disability after birth, flexible with hours when needed for children's doctor appointments or sorting out childcare, and providing time/space for pumping breaks at work.

Many workers mentioned the flexibility of schedules, the ability to work from home, and the ability to bring their child to work.

But not all jobs in production can be done remotely or on an alternate schedule, and not all workplaces are safe for children. Though it appears possible for production employers to create workplaces that are welcoming and inclusive of parents, it seems unlikely that these solutions are sustainable for all workers. These examples beg the question: If parents bring their children to work, who ends up doing the caregiving? Theatrical production spaces are much like construction zones. Is it really safe to have children there? And, again, what about those who are caregiving for adults who cannot be served by a simple childcare solution?

There have been cases where institutions, like Merrimack Rep or Playwrights Horizons, or individual productions, like Broadway's *Lifespan of a Fact*, have provided childcare for the designers and workers who needed it. But most of these models ceased after a season or show, unable to be sustained financially by the institutions. How can the industry more holistically support all workers as people? Again, fulfilling the needs of individual workers creates a more supportive ecosystem for all workers.

Once workers' immediate needs have been met, employers must provide the space and ability for workers to grow. Developing workers is a tool that employers use not only to continue to provide an increasingly strong product for less cost but to also increase employee retention. What does professional development look like in an environment where the employer providing the development might not employ that worker in the future? In Chapter 9, we touched on safety training requirements for employers. Workers carry these skills from job to job, but there is additional cost associated with providing the training itself. Partnerships like the IATSE/ USITT OSHA trainings alleviate some of this pressure on employers. Unions provide training and professional development opportunities that might typically come from employers:

> The IATSE Entertainment and Exhibition Industries Training Trust Fund is the result of a partnership between the IATSE and Signatory Employers. The IATSE Training Trust Fund facilitates training opportunities for IATSE workers to achieve and maintain the skills, ability, and knowledge necessary to meet the ever changing technologies in the entertainment and exhibition industries.[17]

Through the Training Trust, which is available to all active members of IATSE and those working under an IATSE agreement, workers have access to OSHA trainings specifically created for the entertainment industry, AVIXA Partnership courses, safety trainings, and Linkedin Learning, an "online library of high-quality, instructional videos across a wide spectrum of technologies,"[18] among other opportunities. Individual locals provide additional training specific to the needs of their members; Local USA 829 offers training ranging from drafting classes to workshops in ergonomics and hazardous chemicals. Is that enough?

Another type of professional development that many organizations are now offering is training around inclusion, diversity, belonging, equity, and accessibility. Many arts organizations require this sort of training for full-time employees, but often overlook this for production workers who engage with an organization in less permanent ways. As we saw in the worker survey data, many folks experience identity-based discrimination and harassment in the production workplace. Finding ways to facilitate this kind of learning is important in evolving the culture in the production workplace.

In addition to professional development opportunities like trainings and classes, employees can be developed through performance management, which is defined as the "ongoing process of communication between a supervisor and an employee that occurs throughout the year, in support of accomplishing the strategic objectives of the organization. The communication process includes clarifying expectations, setting objectives, identifying goals, providing feedback, and reviewing results."[19] According to the Chartered Institute of Personnel and Development, performance management includes activities that:

> Establish objectives for individuals and teams to see their part in the organisation's mission and strategy; Improve performance among employees, teams and, ultimately, organisations; [and] Hold people to account for their performance by linking it to reward, career progression and termination of contracts.[20]

Performance management is essential in helping employers distribute their resources (human, material, and financial) to meet their business goals. It can also alert employers to impending concerns and allow management to adjust.[21]

Effective and equitable performance management includes a "formal, structured process used to measure, evaluate, and influence employees' job-related attitudes, behaviors, and performance results."[22] Well planned and organized performance management "can enhance employee motivation and productivity, support the achievement of the organization's strategic goals, and facilitate strategic planning and change."[23] Performance management has the potential to empower employees to grow within their positions and explore the various ways in which they can support the organization. On the other hand, ineffective performance management can lead to low morale, high inability to achieve strategic objectives, decreased employee productivity, increased employee turnover, and can have a negative impact on the organization's financial performance.[24] When implemented poorly, performance management is often seen by workers as a pointless assignment that detracts from people's actual work.

Goal setting is a key part of effective performance management. According to McKinsey research, "when done correctly, goal-setting can help improve employee engagement in a way which elevates performance and benefits organizations overall."[25] On this note, in Jackson, Schuler, and Werner's *Managing Human Resources*, they explain:

> There is a large body of research showing that goal setting can enhance productivity. Specifically, goals that are clearly defined, difficult but achievable, and accepted have a positive effect on productivity and performance. When goals have a direct and obvious link to strategic goals and to the firm's success factors, two benefits occur. First, employees better understand their organization's strategic focus and how their jobs fit with it. Second, the goals direct employee behaviors toward activities that are consistent and supportive of the organization's strategy.[26]

McKinsey suggests keeping in mind the following when establishing effective employee goals:

- involve employees from start-to-finish;
- link individual goals to business objectives;
- adapt goals in real-time.[27]

So what does performance management mean for production workers? We asked production workers if they have clear performance development goals in their theatrical production workplaces. (See Figure 10.2 for the breakdown of responses.)

The variance between full-time and freelance workers underlines the differing processes revealed by the surveyed employers. Arguably, if one is unsure of their performance development goals, those goals are neither achievable nor effective. How achievable are well-articulated goals within

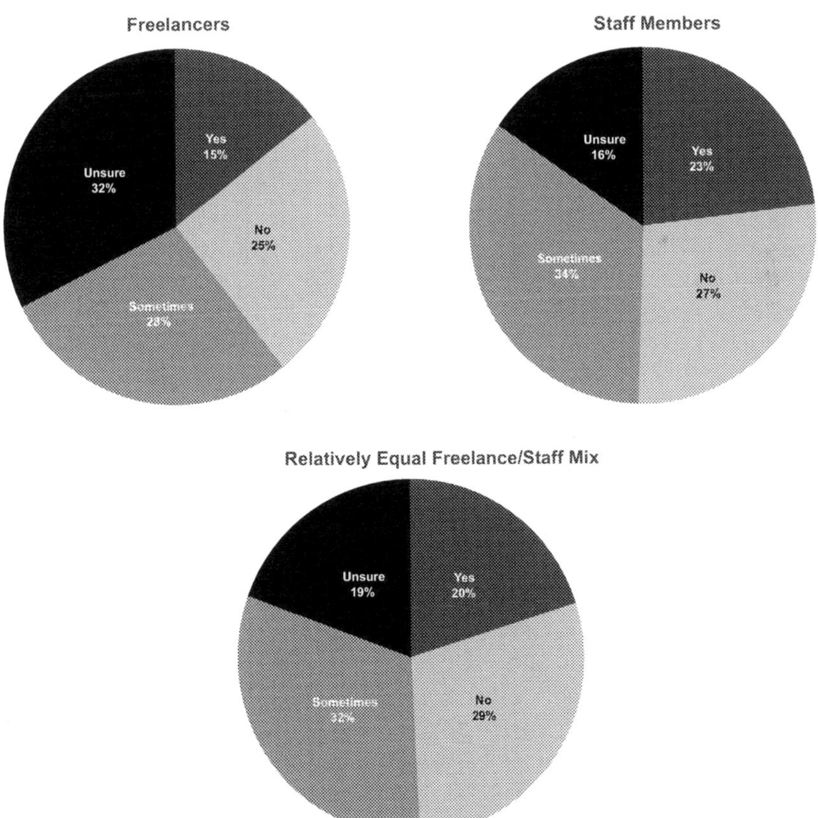

Figure 10.2 Worker responses to "Do you have clear performance development goals in your theatrical production workplace(s)?"

such a pressure-cooker, short-term environment? Why would employers invest this time and energy in short-term workers anyway? And would workers even be open to this?

What if, at the top of each project, designers talked with their teams about their long-term goals? And what if at the top of each work call, crew leaders had each worker set their goals for that day? A worker might establish a goal which they will continue to work on throughout their work at various venues on different productions. Perhaps a technician is hoping to improve their intelligent lighting programming skills or their proficiency with video editing software like After Effects, or a costume designer is trying to work on how they communicate design research to collaborators, or a production assistant wants to get more comfortable asking for help on a task. Being aware of their goals, their supervisors and colleagues in these various workplaces could support the worker's progress. If all employers prioritized establishing time and systems for this sort of goal setting, then all employers would benefit, though this benefit may be less direct than in other types of workplace. The ecosystem is strengthened. If a supervisor at The Public supports this worker's goal on Monday and Tuesday, then Playwrights Horizons will benefit when the worker is on their roster on Thursday and Friday, and the Wilma will benefit when the worker does a project with them three months down the line.

Who sets these performance goals for production workers? Obviously, workers can set some for themselves. But how might supervisors be involved? We asked production workers if they have a clear supervisor in their theatrical production workplace. Of the workers who responded, 52.8% of respondents said yes, 36.3% of respondents said sometimes, 1.8% of respondents said they were unsure, and 9.1% of respondents said no. According to Weingarten rights granted to all union members, a worker is entitled to union representation in any meeting where they might be questioned or reprimanded. What if you don't know if the person in the meeting has the authority to reprimand you? If a worker can't identify their supervisor, is that because they aren't receiving feedback on their work? There's also the complex organizational structure of a production or arts organization. If a set designer is hired by the general manager, is the GM the designer's supervisor? Is the director? Likely the answer to both of those is no (or it's not that simple). With whom does the worker set expectations and goals, and who gives feedback? What about for assistant designers? What about for technicians? According to research by Caitlin Mazur,

> 65% of employees desire more feedback. Companies that invest in regular employee feedback have 14.9% lower turnover rates than organizations where employees do not receive feedback. Four out of ten employees who receive little to no feedback are actively disengaged from their work. 69% of employees say they would work harder if they felt their efforts were being recognized through

> feedback. 43% of highly engaged employees receive feedback at least once a week. 98% of employees disengage from their work when they receive little or no feedback.[28]

Following along this line of research, we also asked production workers how they receive feedback in the workplace. Respondents were able to choose all that applied to their experiences in their answers (see Figure 10.3).

Based on this data, staff members are more likely to receive written feedback. This is consistent with the existence of clear structures for setting measurable performance goals for full-time employees. What sort of goal setting is effective with temporary or short-term workers? Is goal setting something that workers should do on each gig, or could there be structures consistent to the worker across their various projects? How can goals be established or evaluated without consistent oversight or management? Expectations at different institutions are likely different and without clear and tangible goals workers might improve in one location to the detriment of their progress somewhere else. How can freelancers improve at their jobs? And what does improvement even look like? Freelancers often take pride in being their own boss, but what does that imply for professional growth?

One question we did not ask is whether those in supervisory roles have received training in managing teams, goal setting, or giving feedback. From our own experiences, people are often expected to take on a supervisor role without these sorts of trainings. We have both been in this position. So how then can workers, especially those in non-staff positions, be best served?

Of those workers who said they do receive feedback, we asked if this feedback is primarily artistic.

So, from this, we know that feedback for staff members has less to do with the artistic goals of an individual production and more to do with their overall performance in their role in relation to the employer's larger undertaking, while feedback for freelancers is most often artistic.

This likely means that workers are not being given the tools they need to be as successful as possible. The lack of consistent feedback against a clear and articulated scale negatively affects production workers and perpetuates increased inequity between freelancers and staff members. Part of this lack of consistency comes because "the three most common approaches to timing performance measurement and feedback are focal-point, anniversary and natural time span."[29] These approaches cannot be applied to workers who are not with a single employer for consistent or enough time.

> With the focal-point approach, performance measurement for all employees occurs at approximately the same time. The major advantage of focal-point approach is that supervisors find it easier to make direct comparisons among employees. They consider everyone at once and get a sense of how their performances compare during the same specific period.[30]

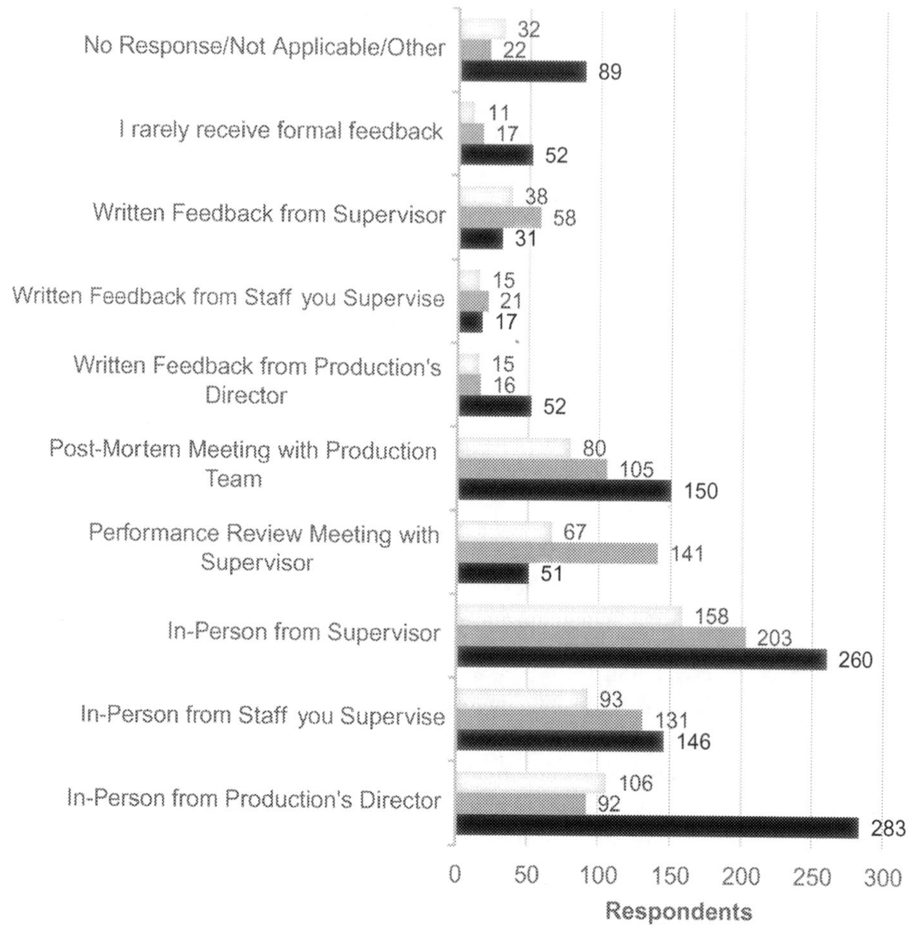

Figure 10.3 Worker responses to "How do you receive feedback on your work?", sorted by work type

The first eight options were provided on the survey and respondents could select more than one, or select "Other" and write-in an answer. "I rarely receive formal feedback" was one of the most frequently written in answers, so those responses have been compiled into a category (but it's important to note that this option was not listed; there may be other people who shared this answer but did not write it in). Besides write-in responses that were sorted into this category, all other respondents who selected "Not applicable," "Other," or did not respond have been grouped together.

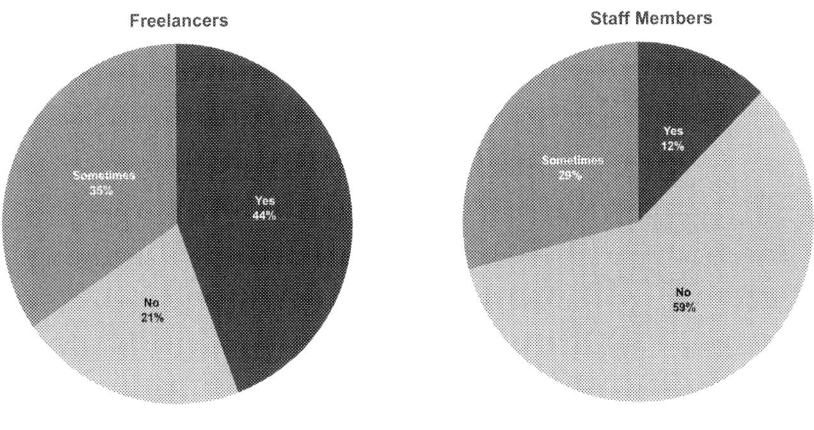

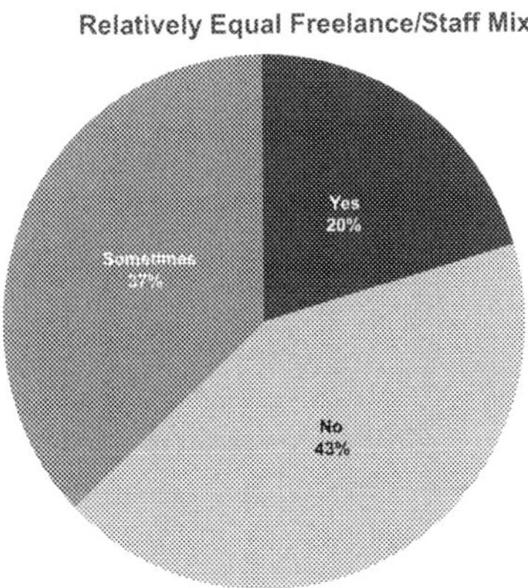

Figure 10.4 Worker responses to "Is this feedback primarily artistic?", a follow up question to "How do you receive feedback on your work?"

Sorted by work type.

How would that work for a mix of employees who might have been at the organization full time for months or years, some who have been casual over-hire technicians on and off for a decade but perhaps for only a few days at a time every few months and designers and directors who might come and go several time over the course of their careers or work there only once. Similarly, "the anniversary approach distributes the task of reviewing performance, and providing feedback over the year. Often, employees' performance reviews are timed to take place on the dates they joined the organization."[31] But short-term workers don't have anniversaries of significance. Interestingly:

> Some experts argue that a better timing rule is to schedule reviews to correspond to the natural time span of the job. If performance is assessed too soon in the

> natural time span, it cannot be reasonably measured due to lack of information. If performance is measured too late, motivation and performance may suffer because the feedback comes too late to be of any use. Feedback that comes too late is particularly detrimental to a poor performer, who will likely not know how to improve performance until it's too late.[32]

This model might work in theory for stage managers or designers but also may be challenging to incorporate into short-term production contracts or applying to casual over-hire workers who might work only a shift or two, and continues to raise the question of who is equipped to facilitate the feedback process.

Another integral aspect of feedback is the ability for workers to give feedback to their managers or supervisors. The Parents & Carers in Performing Arts' 2020 Backstage Workforce Report revealed that working cultures backstage present challenges for positive interaction and dialogue between employers and managers: "The findings suggest that dialogue and negotiation between employees and managers about work-life balance and flexible working issues is not commonplace and largely ineffective."[33] We asked production workers if they have a way to give feedback to their supervisor.

So not only do production workers receive feedback inconsistently, many also do not have a way to give feedback to their supervisor. Freelance workers in particular often do not have a way to provide feedback to the people they report to on jobs. Some theatres have instituted production post-mortems. These are group discussions, typically between the full-time production staff and guest designers and directing staff to evaluate what was successful, and not successful, about the production process. These are a way for designers and technicians to get feedback to the employers, but they aren't private, and they may create a feedback loop depending on whether the decision makers are actually present.

All of this makes it difficult for workers to get support for their own development, and means they often don't have a way to voice challenges they are facing in the workplace. Again, we come to the question of how to bring the benefits of performance development processes to production labor, when the timespan of employment is so variable. Having systems for goal setting and feedback clearly can benefit workers and employers alike, but in the everchanging production landscape, how can these systems be sustainably integrated?

The integration of goal-setting and feedback systems creates a more sustainable environment where workers might be more willing to stay or, in the case of freelancers, to return. The employer's role in creating such environments is considered retention.

> Retention – a Definition: The ability to retain your staff. High retention means that fewer people leave. It is considered important because the cost of high turnover can be significant in terms of time, productivity and stability.[34]

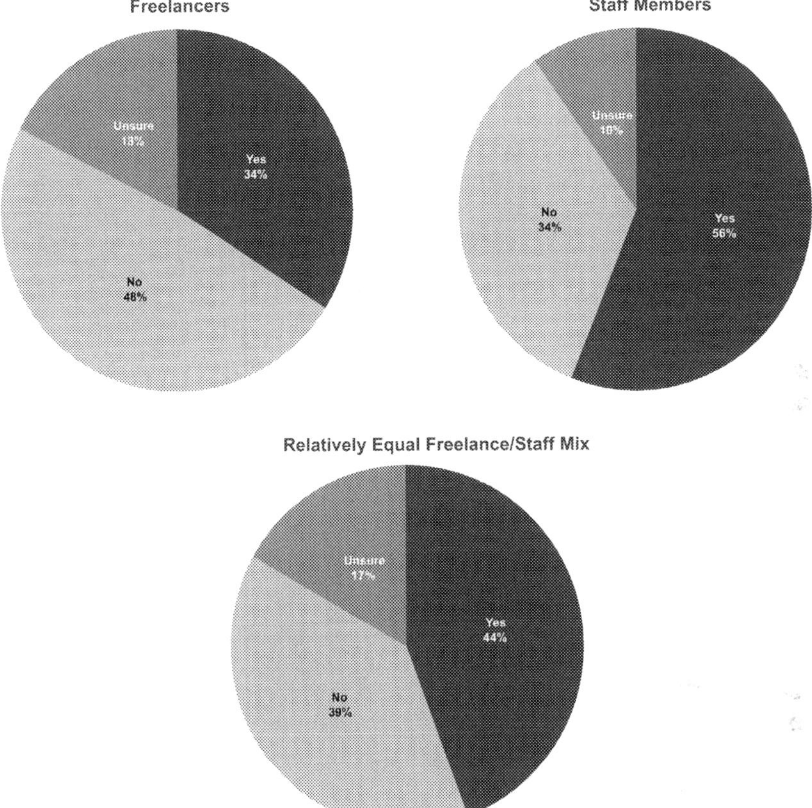

Figure 10.5 Worker responses to "Do you typically have a way to give feedback to your supervisor?"

Sorted by work type.

Retention allows the employer to celebrate their employees: "Great businesses find a way to identify and celebrate the employees who are going above and beyond, and then take deliberate measures to nurture and groom them to continue working for the company."[35] For some in full-time production jobs, retention may be more similar to other fields. But defining retention for freelance workers is more nuanced. For some workers, it may mean returning to the same employer for multiple projects over a period of time. For others, it may mean choosing to stay in the field as a whole, committing to the uncertainty and instability of gig work. As we discussed in Chapter 3, following the industry shutdown of the Pause, the Production on Deck survey showed that 28% of production workers were reconsidering whether they wanted to return to working in the field. This is a significant factor in assessing the successful retention of the field.

Burnout has a direct impact on how and why workers might leave a job, a career, or an industry. Burnout happens over an extended period of time, which in a freelance career will likely include several potentially overlapping projects each with potentially different employers. When an employee is only with you for a short time, does an employer care whether or not they burn out?

Another challenging piece to thinking about HR practices for theatre is how to establish and implement equitable policies that aren't experienced as limiting the creative process. According to Danielle Mohlman, a playwright who advocates for theatrical human resources in the wake of #MeToo:

> Theatre is an industry built on human stories that move audiences. So it may come as a surprise that many regional theatres don't have a dedicated human resources professional on staff. But HR, it turns out, can actually have an impact on the quality of the art an organization delivers, mainly by keeping tabs on the quality of life enjoyed by artists, administrators, and theatre staffers.[36]

So who is responsible for HR practices for production workers? This is, to a certain extent, a misstated question. When employed, production workers should benefit from the human resources department and the practices of their employer. The widespread misclassification of contract workers as independent contractors and the lack of investment in temporary or casual workers does not actually remove the responsibility from the employer. That said, in many cases, labor unions negotiate these protections into worker contracts or, in some cases, have found ways to provide some of the HR benefits directly to their members.

Workers often do not bring issues of concern forward due to a lack of trustworthy grievance procedures. Grievances are perhaps when workers and human resources departments are most at odds, as the HR professionals are required to protect the employer, even in cases where workers have been harmed. Grievances are mostly likely to be related to working conditions or interpersonal interactions. In theory:

> The grievance procedure is a way in which an employee or worker can raise issues about which they feel aggrieved. Most often, if an employee has an issue of some sort, they will have a chat with someone or send an email about it, and the manager or HR representative will help to resolve it. In some cases, however, an employee may feel that the matter has not been resolved to their satisfaction and they may choose to raise a formal grievance.[37]

According to Kate Marks, the common principles for disciplinary and grievance procedures include: Confidentiality, Documentation, Reasonableness, and Consistency.[38] All of these steps, while seemingly logical, protect the employer in the case of future legal actions. They also depend on the "reasonableness" and "fairness" of the HR professional whose interests lie explicitly with the employer rather than the worker. This can lead to obvious cases where equitable labor practices are pushed aside or ignored. When we asked production workers how their identities have impacted their treatment in the workplace, an overwhelming number of respondents mentioned bias and discrimination in production workplaces, most frequently mentioned were sexism and ageism. (Again, it's worth noting that, consistent with other census-type research in the field, the majority of survey respondents were white.) Many female-identifying respondents mentioned being talked down to, not being respected, and the frequency of male colleagues doubting their physical abilities:

> If I had a nickel for every time [somebody] made a comment about my ability to lift something heavy, told me I couldn't do something because it was heavy, or straight up grabbed something out of my hands because it was heavy, I would actually be getting the same pay as the men on the work calls. Especially as a woman in live events, you have to be twice as good just to be taken seriously, and even then you have to fight for it.

Even more upsetting than the number of people who spoke about these biases is the number of respondents who spoke about sexual harassment. "Sexual harassment is still rampant in the theatre," one worker shared.

Under the National Labor Relations Act, which grants unions the right to negotiate on behalf of members, union representatives known as stewards are granted rights to engage with employers on workers' behalf under equal footings. Rather than depending on HR to handle grievances, union members have the right to union representation: "The National Labor Relations Act protects employees who file grievances in good faith."[39] A grievance is initiated when something is broken in the contract. In a union workplace, this usually involves designated steps including arbitration. Arbitration is a path to restitution in which a third party arbiter decides whether the contract is broken. The enforcement of grievance resolutions is legally binding. But, as with any other protections, these grievance procedures only apply to those workers working under a union agreement. This leaves thousands of other workers with no recourse or clear system to access.

Another important component of people's operations is benefits. In addition to a paycheck, in what ways does the employer support their employees? Providing benefits demonstrates that employers value their employees. Having discussed the lack of a thriving wage, we know that workers need to be able to save for the future. One way that workplaces can be accessible is by assisting workers in planning for the time when they can no longer work. But this is often outside of the scope of what theatres provide for production workers. According to the 2019 TYA State of the

Field Report: "Of the fifty-four theatres that responded to questions about employee benefits, a minority (46%) offered retirement plans for their staff."[40] So workers are, in many cases, neither making enough to save for retirement, nor assisted in that saving by their employers. Other financial benefits such as health, dental, vision, life and disability insurance; paid time off; paid family leave; retirement contributions; professional development and education benefits; and a flexible work schedule also contribute to employee satisfaction and retention. Many union members receive health insurance, pension and retirement benefits, and access to life insurance through plans controlled or partially managed by their unions. Contributions on behalf of the union members are made to these funds by the employers, but rather than being employer provided, the union-provided plans allow workers to easily move between employers and work environments. Non-union workers are on their own, often uninsured or having to pay for independent insurance. Many workers do not have any retirement funds in place. And many have cited the need for stable benefits as a reason that they left the field. One worker shared that they left theatre production for this reason:

> I could not afford to be disabled and work in theater because I had no retirement or health insurance and I need both because my medical conditions will progress to where I can't work anymore. I also felt like I was going crazy as a neurodivergent person.

Benefits are typically only offered to full-time staff members who work a minimum number of hours. This puts a large number of non-staff production workers out in the cold once they are no longer able to work.

Non-employer resources do exist for production workers, but they require time to take advantage of. As we've previously mentioned, one of the most commonly used is the Entertainment Community Fund (formerly known as the Actor's Fund), which is "dedicated to keeping our community healthy and insured through personalized health insurance counseling provided nationally, guidance and enrollment support; referrals to health care resources; and more."[41] The ECF provides access to insurance resources, mental health support, as well as the Friedman Health Center for the Performing Arts; Stage Managers National Health Directory; Women's Health Initiative; HIV Initiative; and The Dancers' Resource.[42]

The final stage of the employee lifecycle is separation, when a worker moves on from a company. This is another process that most often applies to staff members. Employers are encouraged to use separation procedures, known as "off-boarding" to learn from the departing workers:

> Off-boarding typically consists of exit interviews and evaluations. But before seasoned and experienced employees leave, it is important to put in place

> mechanisms where they can share or distribute their knowledge, skills, and behaviors with the employees who replace them. This process ultimately mitigates organizational knowledge loss and completes the employee lifecycle, with exiting employees contributing to the development of new employees.[43]

Exit interviews or evaluations are rare in production; yet again, the valuable feedback that could improve future production operations is lost. In our worker survey, we heard so much valuable feedback about workplace experiences; it seems like a great loss that production employers rarely receive this feedback in an organized way that can impact future worker experiences. With the form and pace of production jobs, are there innovative ways that information could be gathered and passed on between workers?

As is evident, because the production worker's employment is often short-term or irregular, involving multiple employers and multiple types of employment, typical HR practices cannot always apply. As we have shown, "Unique to the regional-theatre model is the mixed employee base: year-round and temporary, union and non-union, staff and contractors. Navigating those moving parts can be particularly challenging for folks who are also trying to do their own work or run a department."[44] In actuality, this applies to all theatrical production employers. This mixed model does not successfully allow for HR practices to be applied to the engagement with all production workers.

So where does all of this put the people operations in theatrical production? Many of the benefits of traditional practices do serve the full-time staff production workers. But what about the temporary and short-term workers? Mohlman's dream of an HR department that supports the quality of workers' lives is likely to leave out the production workers. How can these practices be expanded to include everyone? Is that even possible?

NOTES

1 "What is Human Resource Management?" *Human Resource Management* (Minneapolis: University of Minnesota, 2011), https://open.lib.umn.edu/humanresourcemanagement/chapter/1-1-what-is-human-resources/.

2 Sabarudin Zakaria and Wan Fadzilah Wan Yusoff, "Transforming Human Resources into Human Capital," *Information Management and Business Review* 2, no. 2 (February 2011): 48, DOI: 10.22610/imbr.v2i2.882.

3 Kate Marks, *HR for Creative Companies* (Newcastle upon Tyne: RIBA Publishing, 2016), chap. 8, O'Reilly Online.

4 Camille Preston, "Promoting Employee Happiness Benefits Everyone," *Forbes*, December 13, 2017, https://www.forbes.com/sites/forbescoachescouncil/2017/12/13/promoting-employee-happiness-benefits-everyone/?sh=4fb6f1ea581a.

5 Karla Gutierrez, "The Importance of Training at Each Stage of the Employee Lifecycle," *SHIFT eLearning* (blog), https://www.shiftelearning.com/blog/training-in-each-stage-of-the-employee-lifecycle.

6 Chuma Chukwujama, "A Guide to the HR Lifecycle," LinkedIn, November 30, 2018, https://www.linkedin.com/pulse/guide-hr-lifecycle-chuma-chukwujama/.
7 SpriggHR, "6 Stages of the Employee Lifecycle," August 13, 2020, https://sprigghr.com/blog/360-degree-continuous-feedback/the-6-stages-of-the-employee-life-cycle/.
8 Natasha Dilena, "Onboarding vs. Orientation – Is There Really a Difference?," Factorial HR, June 1, 2022, https://factorialhr.com/blog/onboarding-vs-orientation/?utm_source=Sailthru&utm_medium=email&utm_campaign=IHIH%2010/24/22&utm_term=I%20Hate%20It%20Herehttps://factorialhr.com/blog/onboarding-vs-orientation/?utm_source=Sailthru&utm_medium=email&utm_campaign=IHIH%2010/24/22&utm_term=I%20Hate%20It%20Here.
9 Ineke Ceder (Advisory Board Member, Parent Artist Advocacy League) and Rachel Spencer Hewitt (Founder, Parent Artist Advocacy League), interview by the authors, September 2022.
10 Lydia Milman Schmidt, "Barriers to Work for Parents in Chicago Theatre–Survey Results," PICT: Parents in Chicago Theatre, April 6, 2017, https://parentsinchicagotheatre.wordpress.com/2017/04/06/first-blog-post/.
11 Schmidt, "Barriers to Work."
12 Lydia Milman Schmidt, "2019 Report–Lost Voices," PICT: Parents in Chicago Theatre, July 21, 2019, https://parentsinchicagotheatre.wordpress.com/2019/07/21/2018-research-in-chicago-theatre-lost-voices/.
13 Schmidt, "Lost Voices."
14 Schmidt, "Lost Voices."
15 Parents and Carers in Performing Arts, "PiPA Backstage Workforce Report" (Sheffield, UK: Parents and Carers in Performing Arts, February 2020), https://pipacampaign.org/uploads/ckeditor/PiPA_backstage_workforce_survey_Feb2020_v11.pdf.
16 "Backstage Workforce Report," Parents and Carers in Performing Arts, April 23, 2020, https://pipacampaign.org/research/backstage-workforce-report?referrer=/research.
17 IATSE Entertainment and Exhibition Industries Training Trust Fund, "Providing Training Opportunities for the IATSE Workforce," https://www.iatsetrainingtrust.org/about.
18 IATSE Entertainment and Exhibition Industries Training Trust Fund, "Individual Courses: LinkedIn Learning Subscription," https://www.iatsetrainingtrust.org/lil.
19 Berkeley People and Culture, "Performance Management–Definition" in *Guide to Managing Human Resources* (Berkeley, CA, University of California Berkeley), https://hr.berkeley.edu/hr-network/central-guide-managing-hr/managing-hr/managing-successfully/performance-management/concepts.
20 Chartered Institute of Personnel and Development, "Performance Management: An Introduction," August 17, 2022, https://www.cipd.co.uk/knowledge/fundamentals/people/performance/factsheet#gref.
21 Raffaele Carpi, John Douglas, and Frédéric Gascon, "Performance Management: Why Keeping Score is So Important, and So Hard," McKinsey and Company, October 4, 2017, https://www.mckinsey.com/capabilities/operations/our-insights/performance-management-why-keeping-score-is-so-important-and-so-hard.

22 Susan E. Jackson, Randall S. Schuler, and Steve Werner, "Conducting Performance Management," in *Managing Human Resources*, 10th ed. (Mason, OH: Cengage, 2009): 314.
23 Jackson, Schuler, and Werner, 315.
24 Jackson, Schuler, and Werner, 314.
25 Sabrin Chowdhury, "How Effective Goal-Setting Motivates Employees," McKinsey and Company, December 27, 2017, https://www.mckinsey.com/capabilities/people-and-organizational-performance/our-insights/the-organization-blog/how-effective-goal-setting-motivates-employees.
26 Jackson, Schuler, and Werner, 317.
27 Chowdhury.
28 Zippia, "20 Essential Employee Feedback Statistics [2022]," June 29, 2022, https://www.zippia.com/advice/employee-feedback-statistics/.
29 Jackson, Schuler, and Werner, 329–330.
30 Jackson, Schuler, and Werner, 330.
31 Jackson, Schuler, and Werner, 331.
32 Jackson, Schuler, and Werner, 331.
33 Parents and Carers in Performing Arts, "Backstage Workforce Report."
34 Marks, chap. 5.
35 Chukwujama.
36 Danielle Mohlman, "Why You Need an HR Department," *American Theatre*, January 2, 2019, https://www.americantheatre.org/2019/01/02/why-you-need-an-hr-department/.
37 Marks, chap. 7.
38 Marks, chap. 7.
39 Robert M. Schwartz, *The Legal Rights of Union Stewards*, 6th ed. (Detroit, MI: Work Rights Press, 2017): 37.
40 Theatre for Young Audiences, "State of the Field Research Report" (Logan, UT: Utah State University, 2019), https://www.tyausa.org/wp-content/uploads/2019/11/TYA-State-of-the-Field-Report-2019.pdf.
41 "Stay Healthy and Insured," Entertainment Community Fund, https://entertainmentcommunity.org/services-and-programs/healthcare-and-health-insurance.
42 Entertainment Community Fund, "Stay Healthy and Insured."
43 Gutierrez.
44 Mohlman.

Section Three

WHERE WE GO

What does equitable labor in theatre production look like to you?

Everyone is being supported in what they want to do, and they're able to be there of their own free will and choice. They want to be there, to be a part of that creation of this event, whether that means that they are stacking chairs as an usher, running the followspot, or they're stitching clothes. They want to be there, and in order to do that, they have to be paid. They have to have the time. They have to want that to be their life and their job. So in order for that to happen, we have to all make a living wage, and be able to know we have the security to pay rent, to have food, to be able to take care of each other, to be able to take care of anyone that is dependent on us. Being able to make those choices is what equitable theater looks like to me.

Beth Lake, Co-Chair, Off-Broadway Assistant Designer Advisory Group

I wouldn't want anybody to feel like they couldn't take a job in theater because it didn't pay enough for them to survive on.

Linette S. Hwu, Board Member, Woolly Mammoth Theatre Company

Providing an environment for people to work in where they can feel like they are provided for by their work in an emotional way, in a financial way, and a way that they feel safe. And that looks different for every single person.

Jon Harper, then Managing Director, Abrons Arts Center

People being fairly compensated for the work, and defining what that actually means.

Angela Gieras, Executive Director, Kansas City Rep

A consciousness about the work that you do, and its importance and value in totality. Whether that is about the resource that you make in your take home pay, or whether it is about a respect for your time, and acknowledgement for the work that you do, and being intentional about making sure that what you bring to the table is necessary at that table. I think we spend a lot of time in our industry focused on the money. We think that equity is about money. It is; it is. And it's also about value. And it's also about intentionality. And, and I think that we get away with it if we pay people more, but while not being intentional. And we get away with it if we pay people more, but we don't value their work. And I think you have to have resource, value and intentionality come together.

Nataki Garrett, then Artistic Director, Oregon Shakespeare Festival

Making sure that everybody has equitable pay and the same level of labor support for the job they're doing.

Elsa Hiltner, Co-Founder,
On Our Team

We must create the access for everybody to exist in the world and do what they need to do.

Michael Maag, Resident Lighting Designer,
Oregon Shakespeare Festival

Creating transparency, being able to say this is what we pay each position, posting that everywhere, making sure that the standards are clear, if there are unions that are dictating that, that's language that needs to be clear. And if there are ways for us to advocate, to create some balance around that, whether it's the benefits that we offer, or an opportunity we offer, the professional development money that we offer to bridge that gap. There are opportunities to do that, and to move away from this culture where we pay the moneymakers, essentially, like the development department, the marketing department, the directors the most money because they're seen as the most valuable books, but the reality is your front of house staff, your daily managers for these productions – without the shops, without which none of these productions would come to life. Creating parity, I think is a big one for the field; understanding what parity looks like across fields, across positions and roles, but then creating space to hear from staff around what they need.

Fatima Bunafoor, Director of Talent and Equity,
Pittsburgh HR/Equity Arts Cohort

For workers at all levels to be compensated for their work.

Pat Landers, Business Representative for
Health & Safety, United Scenic Artists

It's not just minimum wage, but a thriving wage. There it is. And thriving can mean different things to different people, but I think it's enough to sit there and go, I can put a roof over my head, I can put food in my belly, I can pay for my car payment, and I have some money to put into savings.

David "dStew" Stewart, Co-Founder,
Production on Deck

Creating a culture of belonging that starts with the hiring process. Starting the conversation with what do you need, do you have any access needs?

Rachel Spencer Hewitt, Founder,
Parent Artist Advocacy League

I liken it to STEM. You've got all of these brilliant people in the world who have these mathematical minds, and these logistics and logic models in their brain that they play out, and they can build a thing based on that. But usually, the people who get access to that are the people with the money and the ability to go to school, and be certified, and get degrees, and and, and, and, and. What it looks like for me is taking people who are not privileged in that way and creating space for them to belong, even if the learning is longer, even if it takes longer for them to – and the longer is usually not an understanding, it's a deficit of privilege and access that holds people at bay from being able to be in STEM, in the same way that I think it holds people at bay and being able to be in theater. Privilege also often sees creativity as one thing produced by one group of people in certain ways. My experience with theater is that we hold to who and what we like and name it as tradition, while excluding the brilliance and artistic genius of those we don't see as worthy, or holding to the traditions we respect.

Anyania Muse, Interim Chief Operating Officer,
Oregon Shakespeare Festival

It looks like having informed consent when I apply for a job, knowing what you're gonna get paid, what the working hours are, what the job expectations are, and that being what the job is.

Sarah Lozoff, Co-Founder, Production on Deck

Prioritizing the needs of the worker. And knowing that will always be changing.

Stephanie Ybarra, then Artistic Director, Baltimore Center Stage

WE'RE
BACK!
SOLD OUT
SMASH HIT! BEST!
MUST SEE

11

IMAGININGS

What is unique about the theatre community is that we have a shared goal. The people that are working in it, we're all interested in this idea of support, lifting each other up, and bringing something into existence. We are creators. We are creators and storytellers. We have this amazing process: we gather together as a group of people, we have a purpose in mind, we give birth to something that's often painful and challenging. Then we live with it, and then it closes, and we strike it. And so we are ultimately well positioned for dealing with grief because our children run and then die to never be done again. I think that there's something that's powerful in that for us as theatre people. And then I also think that the other thing that we uniquely have is the ability to deal with change. Change is everything, there is always change, it is the only constant, and it is especially true in theatre and the production side of theatre. And we have to be flexible to be successful, we have to do that. And so that's the support structure that we have that is amazing in theatre – we've got people that are ready to quickly pivot. And when we change our priorities to make the show better, or to make it more accessible, we can do that. I know that's a real optimistic point of view of all of this.[1]

Michael Maag, Resident Lighting Designer,
Oregon Shakespeare Festival

DOI: 10.4324/9781003330394-14

Even as we write and research this book, the landscape of American theatre continues to change. We are, it seems, finally seeing the financial crisis hinted at during the Pause. Across the country, not-for-profit theatres have not seen their audiences return, some citing as much as an 85% drop in subscribers. And supply chain issues combined with inflation have led to a significant increase in production costs. In July 2022, New Orleans' Southern Rep Theatre announced its plan to close: "After a tumultuous few years, the theatre had struggled to keep up with expenses while meeting the needs of its community and audiences."[2] The overwhelming hardships of the Pause and slow restart were too much to overcome and the theatre exhausted its resources before it could get back on stable footing. In early 2023, NYC's New Ohio Theatre, a laboratory for experimental work and longtime home to many nomadic NYC companies, announced it would conclude operations on August 31, 2023.[3] According to statements:

> The theatre cites [Artistic Director] Lyons's intention to step down as artistic director, the shifting landscape and dynamics of the field, and increased financial pressures as contributing factors to the decision, as well as a desire to step aside and make space for the next generation of theatre-makers.[4]

It's interesting to consider the life of a theatre being tied to the life of a leader or founder. What happens when the leader is no longer there? Are we creating a model where theatres expect to be carried by a single charismatic figurehead? The New Ohio was, as is the case with many underfunded institutions, home to many inequitable practices, specifically centering an underpaid and exploited production labor force, so maybe it isn't such a loss after all.

In early 2023, amid rehearsals for *Into the Woods*, Dallas Theater Center informed 37 staff members, including the entire acting company, that they would be laid off following the company's gala in May.[5] The timing, lined up with what should be a celebratory launch of a large production, feels particularly fraught. These layoffs, which were not labeled as temporary, have cut their labor force in half. And yet, while the workers are in a place of uncertainty, the organization is touting a robust upcoming season. In a recent press release, artistic director Kevin Moriarty is quoted:

> Our 2023–24 season is the biggest, most exciting season we've produced since 2019. It's a season filled with music, laughter, and great performances from DTC's Diane & Hal Brierley Resident Acting Company, who will be joined by outstanding artists from Dallas and across the country.[6]

What does it mean to produce the "biggest" season following layoffs which are blamed on a financial crisis?

In April 2023, Oregon Shakespeare Festival (OSF) announced a $2.5 million emergency fundraising campaign, labeled "The Show Must

Go On: Save Our Season, Save OSF," in order to complete their current season, programmed through December 2023. OSF has already canceled its winter offering *It's Christmas, Carol!* to focus on the already-in-progress repertory season. Like the other theatres in crisis, OSF has been suffering from lost revenue and donations: "All across the theatre industry, attendance and donations are down significantly. Because we are a destination theatre where people often have to spend thousands of dollars to reach our stages, we have been especially hard hit by the twin impacts of COVID and inflation."[7] The financial impacts of the Pause and the wildfires affecting the Ashland area have led to this financial crisis on the verge of the company's 90th anniversary. But this crisis has been likely long in coming:

> According to an Oregon Shakespeare Festival employee [...] the organization's leaders said they need to correct more than 15,000 incorrect entries in its financial ledger, the result of antiquated systems that were not properly maintained. The leaders told employees they're still trying to precisely determine cash flow numbers, bills owed and overall expenses of the organization.[8]

This revelation brings into relief questions of institutional stewardship and fiduciary responsibility. For an organization for whom, "according to tax filings obtained by ProPublica, total revenue for the OSF Association plummeted from approximately $45 million in fiscal year 2019 to approximately $25 million in fiscal year 2020,"[9] can it be claimed that no one saw this coming?

In the summer of 2023, this pattern continues. Triad Stage in Greensboro NC announced it would be closing. The Westport Country Playhouse announced a campaign to make up an urgent $2 million gap in funding to "save" the Playhouse.[10] And, perhaps most indicative of the larger problem, Center Theatre Group in LA announced that it would be ceasing production in its midsize theatre, the Mark Taper Forum, and Brooklyn Academy of Music announced layoffs of 13% of its staff, eliminating 26 positions. Things are not ok at the regional theatres:

> 'We've been putting on a brave face, saying, "we're back, we're strong,"' said [Meghan] Pressman, referring not only to CTG but to the theatre field writ large. 'We need to send the message that, no, actually we're hurting. We're not back to normal. We need your support.'[11]

All of these examples make something very clear: the current operating systems are failing us. As Nataki Garrett, then Artistic Director of OSF, explains

> All the pandemic did was accelerate something that was already moving, and all of the things that were actually failing in the American theatre, it moved them

up very quickly. So we're at the end of something where we thought we had a little bit more grace; we don't have the grace. We actually have to be conscious of how our theatres are structured, and how they are actually going to be able to survive.[12]

As of the writing of this book, Garrett, who oversaw the institution through these crises, has left.

In order to imagine a future for theatrical production workers that is sustainable, equitable, and inclusive, we have to look at how these failing systems impact the workforce and imagine a new way forward toward new systems in and around producing live theatre. This section of the book focuses on these imaginings for the field as a whole.

When we first approached Carmen Morgan about writing the foreword to this book, she, rightfully so, challenged us about whether we – Natalie and Brídín, two white women – should be the ones writing this book, examining practices that have been harmful to BIPOC workers particularly, and exploring the work that is happening to improve production workers' lives. We are writing about it not because we have ownership of the work itself, but because we have many privileges that allow us to spend time on the research and the writing. This is, in her words, an "in the meantime" solution. This section of the book invites a series of grand imaginings for disruption and re-creation, as well as a series of smaller, potentially more manageable "in the meantime" solutions or potential actions for a more incremental approach.

As the number of theatre institutions in crisis visibly accumulate, we ask: Is this ok? Can we live without these institutions? Is this a sort of Darwinian emergence of the strongest and fittest? Are these sacrifices we can accept? Is the American Theatre structurally able to avoid this crisis?

In April 2023, Jesse Cameron Alick published an essay titled "The Spirit of the Thing: Why the American Theater Can't Change." This follows Alick's research study *Emerging from the Cave*, which, as we discussed in Chapter 3, looks at the future of theatre after the re-emergence from the Pause and which has also been influential in our reimaginings. Questioning why the American Theatre can't, or won't, change, Alick shares the concept of the egregore: "In brief, an Egregore is a non-physical entity that is made material and brought to existence by the collective belief of a people [...] The Egregore is consensus made manifest."[13] He uses this metaphor to contextualize one of the primary conundrums of this moment in American theatre:

> There is an Egregore living in your walls. There is an entity that IS the institution that you work at. It has interests and desires, it has moods and issues that are unique unto itself. It was created long before you arrived there and it will be there when you are gone. You could replace every single person at your institution,

> and the institution would behave in the same way. Because the Egregore is more than the people. You can have endless meetings about cultural transformation and not change a single thing about the way you do business. The Egregore wants to be itself. This 'Spiritus Instituti' was summoned into existence to do a job in a certain manner and it will not rest until that job is done.[14]

This institutional spirit, as it were, is deeply invested in capitalistic consumption, in the pillars of white supremacy that holds up the American Theatre (Yes, capital A and capital T are intentional here), in the oppressive and exploitative work practices that make sure that the show does, indeed, go on. The way it has always been done.

When asked what he sees as the biggest current challenge for production labor, lighting designer Michael Maag shared, "Capitalism. Period. We need to shift from scarcity thinking to abundance thinking. And we have the people, we have the resources, we have the creativity to do what we do. Instead, we are choosing profit."[15] Because we, as theatre workers, are working inside of American capitalism, we are required to reckon with the limitations of capitalism as we imagine opportunities for future change. This includes the question: how can institutions, leaders, producing organizations afford the things that are more equitable? Embedded in this question is a series of other questions: what do we need to make these changes? How can these changes center the most historically marginalized workers? How can these changes be sustainable? As part of this analysis, we encourage the use of adrienne maree brown's Emergent Strategy assessments.

brown offers many resources for shifting how we see and feel the world and therefore how we can transform the world, including tools for reflecting on how we are adapting, our interdependence, and our engagement in resilience and transformative justice. In her Assessment of Adaptation, brown encourages us to reflect on how we respond to changes: what are our intentions, and how we keep our intentions present during changes.[16] Change is daunting; our ways are ingrained in us. The institutional dependence on "how we have always done it" travels from theatre to theatre on the backs of its workers:

> And as you go from one institution to another, can you feel how the Egregores seems to be very familiar? Same same [*sic*], but different? The tensions between the production and the administrative departments? The stress of tech week? Ways in which we must bite our tongue and sometimes engage in distasteful conversations with donors? The problems there are the problems here. They don't change. The spirit is the same. Imagine with me, that the American Theater has an Egregore as well. [...] Remember, it wants to continue to exist – and existence for an Egregore, means existing as it currently exists – eating the same food, making the same things, working with the same people. Egregores don't want to change. This is the reason why, ironically, even as systems begin to fail

> it, even as the flow of donations dry up, even when audiences stop responding to kinds of art, even as the Egregore begins to starve to death, it has great difficulty adapting. And it will stop you from adapting too.[17]

But we must change. And we must do it radically. This isn't going to be easy or smooth. This is a call not just for dreams but for disruption. For an examination and diagnosis of theatremaking which may end with a theatre field that looks very different from the one we have now. In order to move forward, we will have to address the harm that has been done. This includes reparations. How can we heal those workers who have been harmed by this field? This is the invitation to the entire theatre field: Reimagine how we do the work to make the art.

This work is not the work of individuals. Though we must hold each other accountable, we must look to systemic, not personal or institutional change.

Do not fall for the promise of the plastic straws.

According to Jim Leape, co-director of the Stanford Center for Ocean Solutions, "Our oceans are currently swimming with plastics. It is estimated that there are now 150 million metric tons of plastic in the ocean. We add another 8 million tons each year."[18] We have been told that plastic is one of the causes of climate change. We, as individuals, have been told that we need to recycle. We need to lower our individual consumption. We need to stop using plastic straws. But this isn't a problem stemming from plastic straws: "Plastic straws are only a tiny fraction of the problem – less than 1 percent. The risk is that banning straws may confer 'moral license' – allowing companies and their customers to feel they have done their part."[19] What really needs to be addressed is the massive impact on the climate caused by global industries, by reliance on fossil fuels, by capitalistic selfishness. We need to move the onus of repair away from the individual human or individual institution and embrace it as a field, in which together we can make great change.

In other words, we need to kill the Egregore. Because it won't let us change it.

The change feels, at times, unimaginable because it is radical. This invitation for radical change is consistent with the approach we hear from many leaders, especially those who occupy historically marginalized identities: Black and Brown leaders, Women of Color leaders, LGBTQIA+ leaders. These leaders who we interviewed, in particular, graciously shared their time and energy and hope, and with the spirit of collaboration, invite us to envision a better future. Interestingly, many of the white leaders we spoke with seem more inclined to be mired in a feeling of hopelessness around forward-looking, radical change. The ways in which we may benefit from a broken system are often the ways that have the tightest hold on us.

We, Brídín and Natalie, feel this tension as well. Quite literally as we have worked on this book, we have come up against our own resistance to these shifting practices and the ways that the harmful practices are deeply ingrained in us as theatre workers. Are the things that drew us both to theatre work part of the problem? With a more equitable approach to resource allocation, how do we keep up the quality of the art? Would these systemic changes destroy the theatre culture that draws many people in? Is it really that broken?

Yes, it really is.

Our inspirations for radical change come from work that has been happening in various movement spaces for generations, work led by BIPOC workers, women, and those of historically excluded identities, including but not limited to Feminist organizational structures, Anti-capitalist resistance, and the Afro-futurist movement. We hope to build on and contribute to this work by weaving existing ideas, new ideas, and questions together in relation specifically to theatrical production labor.

We hold close the ideas of adrienne marie brown as we pick our way through the rubble we are hoping to rebuild. In *Emergent Strategies*, brown shares: "My vision is changing our *how*, more than seeing clearly our *what*. I see a how where we are all much more comfortable with change, and with our personal power to change conditions."[20] We are questioning the *how*.

> We need to do this together. Organizations need to invest in 'co-evolution' – the idea that changing can change each other. Nothing happens, or should happen, in a vacuum. And it won't happen in a clean order. For real change to occur, mistakes will be made. As brown says: Transformation doesn't happen in a linear way, at least not one we can always track. It happens in cycles, convergences, explosions. If we release the framework of failure, we can realize that we are in iterative cycles, and we can keep asking ourselves – how do I learn from this?[21]

And, as in the case of the plastic straws, no radical enough change can happen from the individual human, or institutional, level. Changes have to be co-created and co-supported.

Anyania Muse, Interim Chief Operating Officer and Director of Inclusion, Diversity Equity, and Access (IDEA) at Oregon Shakespeare Festival, situates the changes the American theatre needs in a lens of co-liberation. This idea, too, is borrowed from groups such as Black Lives Matter, the queer Chicana movement, Bioneers, and the Women's March and aims to connect each individual's freedoms to the freedoms not only of other people but of the whole community.[22] Co-liberation is a kind of antidote to the individualistic and demonizing tendencies of White Supremacy. As Muse explains:

> It's like that scene in *The Matrix* where everybody's in the hallway. And the guy has all the keys to every door. And there's the door that you walk through, there's all the doors in the hallway, and then there's the door at the very end of the hall. Co-liberation is all four of us, in that hallway, trying to get from the door we walk

> through to the door on the other side. We don't give a damn about what's in these other rooms. But what we know is that what's going to come out is racism, misogyny. All of the nasty stuff that we deal with on a daily basis is going to come out.
>
> Co-liberation is not me looking at you and saying, 'Really, look, I don't like clowns.'
>
> And you go, 'Well, you're gonna have to deal with the clown.'
>
> I may say to you, 'I'm not afraid of the KKK, I'll handle the KKK, you got to get the clown.'
>
> [...]
>
> So our goal together is to attack the things that we each hold fear around together to get to the other side, to get through that door.
>
> [...]
>
> Co-liberation is: Bring all your crap. I don't care what your crap is. And let's go together to get through this. Because it is literally the only way. That's the work I do.[23]

As theatremakers, we should be good at this. Collaboration is in the DNA of our work. And what we have heard from the majority of workers is that they are all in. Rachel Spencer Hewitt, co-founder of the Parent Artist Advocacy League, embraces this collaboration towards radical change:

> I think what scares a lot of people is that a lot of the radical change is going to get messy before it gets cleaned up. Some of our systems are actually designed to break people. And some of them can be like a support can be added to make this an equitable structure, but some of them will just need to be reimagined. [...] There will need to be a collective acceptance that we will need to deconstruct to rebuild, even as we practice and make mistakes, for there to actually be the equity that we talked about wanting. [...] The good news is, we've all been uncomfortable for a very long time. So if you continue to let the people with access needs lead the conversation, we can also help guide us to your discomfort as well. Because we're here for the collaboration. We're not here because we hate the art. We're here because we believe it can work in a different structure.[24]

Robert Barry Fleming, Executive Artistic Director of Actors Theatre of Louisville, is a Black queer man leading a theatre in Kentucky. As one might imagine, he frequently encounters tensions between his executive leadership and the culture of white supremacy that is deeply rooted in our nation. Still, he welcomes the opportunity for a collaborative approach to radical change:

> It's an invitation to work collaboratively with others because you're not going to solve it, I'm not going to solve it, it's going to take all of us together as a brain trust. It is inherently a socialistic enterprise. And I know that's really

> disappointing for those who live in a plantation capitalism framework, but that isn't really a sustainable model based on historical precedent. It ultimately backfires and falls apart. So I'm not a Socialist, I'm not a Capitalist. I don't know enough about any of that. I'm an artist – I know just enough to be dangerous. But I know what trends in the way of falling apart and what trends in the way of sustainability.[25]

As Maag said, at the heart of the issue is the structure of capitalism. Capitalism breeds inequitable operating systems; designing systems that prioritize the people over the product is inherently at odds with capitalism.

Every person should have access to educational opportunities that lead to and enhance careers in production.

We need just hiring practices which address the varying needs of workers.

All work must be paid equitably. Production operations, including budgets and schedules, must be human centered.

Labor and safety standards must expand to include all aspects of physical and emotional health, and must be taught and followed.

Careers should be sustainable and healthy, where everyone feels a sense of belonging and safety.

In this section, we imagine approaching these challenges not one by one but through expansive big picture approaches to workplace culture. A holistic approach to addressing workers' needs can better serve them than a bunch of individual band aids to seemingly isolated problems.

This change is hard. But it is possible and it can be sustainable. Ybarra's work at Baltimore Center Stage is an example of how significant progressive work can happen:

> Ybarra's accomplishments included raising salaries for staff members and adopting the industry-leading policy of paying playwrights for attending rehearsals. While theaters nationwide are struggling financially due to the effects of the coronavirus pandemic – including many that have ceased operations – Center Stage's balance sheet is sound.[26]

Ybarra cites the support of some of the board as a reason progress could happen, but she also speaks about the resistance she faced. Board members resigned, one "in part because he thinks Ybarra prioritizes politics over production quality."[27] Production workers also experience these sorts of changes in different ways. Radical change can be clunky. Deconstructing our systems of inequity will involve disruptions to the lives of production workers. There will be growing pains as we evolve. In OSF's recent restructuring, scaling back drastically impacted employment: "12 layoffs and seven employee furloughs, as well as a stop or delay on hiring for 18 open positions. And this year's season is down to six in-person productions, down from last year's eight. (Pre-pandemic seasons at OSF included as many as 11 productions)."[28] The reduction in the season means fewer production positions–fewer designers, fewer assistants, fewer management roles, fewer over-hire or short-term technicians. OSF is at the forefront of making progressive changes in the way they manage their productions and, yes, they are also, according to some metrics, failing because of all of the existing systemic challenges. And the audience-benefactor-donors don't like change. Garrett shared with *American Theatre*:

> I got a really nasty note in the mail a week ago that said, 'Go woke, go broke.' And he put his member number down next to his name and said, 'Former member, 33 years.' I was like, let me analyze this language here for a moment: He doesn't want to be awakened. He wants to be in the dark. He wants to be asleep. And if choose [*sic*] to wake people up at OSF then then we're going to lose our resources – that's the threat, you know, 'Go broke.' And I think: Thank you for letting me know in advance. What I need to know now is, who's coming behind you? And how do I make a connection to them? And then maybe you'll come back?[29]

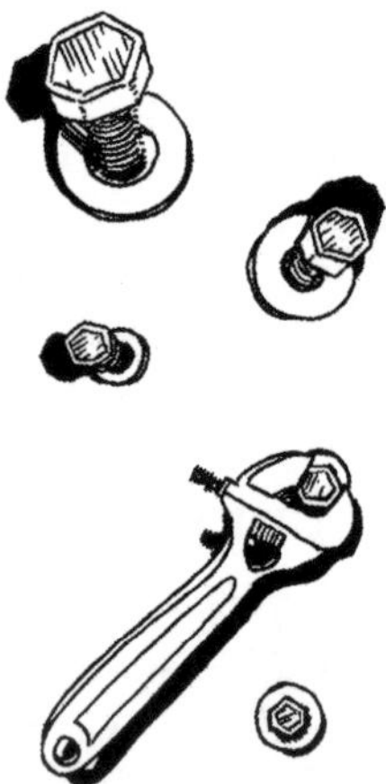

We need to apply a universal design lens to theatre production operational systems.

The workplace must work for every worker. Universal Design is one framework we can use to organize this shift. Also known as "design for all," "life span design," or "inclusive design," Universal Design is "the design of products and environments to be usable by all people, to the greatest extent possible, without the need for adaptation or specialized design."[30] One of the primary tenets of Universal Design is the elimination of the term "special needs." Instead, the invitation is to implement a "people first" approach, in which users "should not feel that this is designed especially for me; which is an uncomfortable feeling for the disabled person."[31] The "universal" in Universal Design refers to an "understanding [of] the diversity in people [and] responding to that diversity with informed design decisions."[32] Bringing a universal design approach to theatre production workplaces would mean reforming how we hire, budget, schedule, and operate in a way that recognizes every potential worker, welcoming workers of any age, size, ability, race, ethnicity, and gender.

In *Universal Design: Creating Inclusive Environments*, the authors begin by examining barriers as an experiential and intellectual phenomenon, to demonstrate the potential scope and importance of universal design.[33] Since we have established the barriers – to arts education; to career access; to a sense of belonging in the workplace; to equitable pay; to a healthy work environment; to sustainable careers in theatre production – we can start to imagine universal design-minded solutions.

Universal Design is not (only) accessible design: "Universal design is focused on all people's needs, including users with disabilities. In other words, universal design aims to make products, services, and environments more accessible for everyone."[34] Universal Design includes not only functionality but aesthetic satisfaction: "The aesthetic usability effect states that users tend to find designs more usable if they have a nice visual appearance."[35] Universal Design is not an add-on: "Universal design is not a set of guidelines that can be applied at the end of the design process – it is a set of principles that should be integrated into your process from the very beginning."[36] Universal Design is culturally appropriate, respecting and reinforcing cultural values, and the social and environmental contexts of any design project. Classic examples of successful universal design are "Sidewalks with curb cuts and doors that automatically open when a person moves near them are examples of universally designed products. They benefit people with disabilities, parents with baby strollers, delivery workers, and others."[37]

Universal Design Principles

From The R.L. Mace Universal Design Institute

The authors, a working group of architects, product designers, engineers and environmental design researchers, collaborated to establish the following Principles of Universal Design to guide a wide range of design disciplines including environments, products, and communications. These seven principles may be applied to evaluate existing designs, guide the design process and educate both designers and consumers about the characteristics of more usable products and environments.

[...]

Universal Design

The design of products and environments to be usable by all people, to the greatest extent possible, without the need for specialized design.

Principle One: Equitable Use

The design is useful and marketable to people with diverse abilities.

Guidelines:

- Provide the same means of use for all users: identical whenever possible; equivalent when not.
- Avoid segregating or stigmatizing any users.
- Provisions for privacy, security, and safety should be equally available to all users.
- Make the design appealing to all users.

Principle Two: Flexibility in Use

The design accommodates a wide range of individual preferences and abilities.

Guidelines:

- Provide choice in methods of use.
- Accommodate right- or left-handed access and use.
- Facilitate the user's accuracy and precision.
- Provide adaptability to the user's pace.

Principle Three: Simple and Intuitive

Use of the design is easy to understand, regardless of the user's experience, knowledge, language skills, or current concentration level.

Guidelines:

- Eliminate unnecessary complexity.
- Be consistent with user expectations and intuition.
- Accommodate a wide range of literacy and language skills.
- Arrange information consistent with its importance.
- Provide effective prompting and feedback during and after task completion.

Principle Four: Perceptible Information

The design communicates necessary information effectively to the user, regardless of ambient conditions or the user's sensory abilities.

Guidelines:

- Use different modes (pictorial, verbal, tactile) for redundant presentation of essential information.
- Provide adequate contrast between essential information and its surroundings.
- Maximize "legibility" of essential information.
- Differentiate elements in ways that can be described (i.e., make it easy to give instructions or directions).
- Provide compatibility with a variety of techniques or devices used by people with sensory limitations.

Principle Five: Tolerance for Error

The design minimizes hazards and the adverse consequences of accidental or unintended actions.

Guidelines:

- Arrange elements to minimize hazards and errors: most used elements, most accessible;
- hazardous elements eliminated, isolated, or shielded.
- Provide warnings of hazards and errors.
- Provide fail-safe features.
- Discourage unconscious action in tasks that require vigilance.

Principle Six: Low Physical Effort

The design can be used efficiently and comfortably and with a minimum of fatigue.

Guidelines:

- Allow user to maintain a neutral body position.
- Use reasonable operating forces.
- Minimize repetitive actions.
- Minimize sustained physical effort

Principle Seven: Size and Space for Approach and Use

Appropriate size and space is provided for approach, reach, manipulation, and use regardless of user's body size, posture, or mobility.

Guidelines:

- Provide a clear line of sight to important elements for any seated or standing user.
- Make reach to all components comfortable for any seated or standing user.
- Accommodate variations in hand and grip size.
- Provide adequate space for the use of assistive devices or personal assistance.

Text courtesy of NC State University, Center for Universal Design.

Perhaps the most obvious implementation of Universal Design does lie in the physical environment and objects that production workers encounter. So we begin with "flexibility in use:" by accommodating a wide range of individual preferences and abilities in technical theatre equipment, we can create an environment that puts less physical strain on workers: "An employee who is comfortable in [their] environment is more likely to be productive."[38] In the theatre, this can mean different needs for different bodies doing different jobs. Office workers may need modular and adjustable furniture that they can adjust to their own specific needs. Attention should be paid to having spaces that are more conducive to collaboration and those where one can work in quiet if they need. Workers who do demanding physical tasks on and backstage need places to rest. More often than not, the furniture in crew lounges and green rooms are cast-offs, used in shows and then stuck backstage: mix-matched chairs, couches with broken springs, the bare minimum required for an "equity cot." This does not necessarily create a comfortable rest area accessible to all workers.

Similarly, when considering "size and space for approach and use" it's necessary to think about production workers as much as we think about audiences and performers. Production workers are not all the same size or shape. They shouldn't have to duck under or climb over or squeeze through their typical workspaces to get their jobs done. And yet they do. Many of our theatrical spaces were not originally built and designed as theatres but have been converted from banks or community venues or retail spaces into theatres. Even those that were designed as theatres were often designed without interest in explicit accessibility. Backstage spaces are often essentially inaccessible – dark, cramped, full of props and quick-change sets, and often ladder or equipment storage. Accessible ramps are nearly unheard of. Booths are often accessible only by ladders or steep staircases and certainly rarely accessible via an elevator. But why? Why can't we renovate these spaces to be able to accommodate workers of different sizes, with different mobility needs? An elevator or ramp doesn't only help a wheelchair user; it helps a costume shop worker moving racks of clothes. A well-lit access point with suitable masking to keep the light from leaking onstage helps both the actors and the backstage crew, regardless of whether any individual has vision needs.

Lighting designer Dawn Chiang introduced an opportunity for Universal Design for production workers in a 2017 blog post where she revisited the functionality and comfort of the tech table. For many stage managers and lighting, sound, and projection designers, a significant amount of time is spent working at temporary workstations set up in a theatre's audience area during the technical rehearsal process. As Chiang explained:

> For generations, the tech table has been treated [as] a temporary afterthought, with little consideration devoted to human comfort. At its most basic, a tech table can be a single slab of plywood, painted black, thrown over a couple of rows of seats near the rear of the orchestra level. Sometimes, it is a temporary tabletop with supporting legs.[39]

As one can imagine:

> Auditorium seats are typically too low in height for the creative staff to work comfortably at the tech table, and so far away from the table that I constantly have to lean forward to work. After a few short hours, my back starts to hurt from leaning forward and nothing that I do at that point can shake the muscle and nerve pain that has set in. Sometimes a 'butt board' – a piece of ¾" thick board, about 12" wide is thrown over the seat armrests, to prop me up higher. Unfortunately, this arrangement leaves me too high and too far away from the tech table, and I still need to lean and hunch forward.[40]

None of this allows the worker to be in an ergonomically neutral position. Instead, a physical strain is added on top of the intellectual strain of the work, especially on long 10-out-of-12 rehearsal days. Chiang acknowledges that there has not yet been a solution to this problem. And it's an excellent example of seemingly small ways that production workers' bodies aren't prioritized in their workplaces.

It is enough to add accessibility into spaces even if that accessibility is only necessary for someone with a disability. We provide ASL interpreted performances because we know there are likely audience members with hearing impairments who want to attend the show; why don't we budget for ASL interpreters for the backstage workers we know might want to work on the production? Michael Maag expanded:

> I think that the people that are in the organizations, for the most part, are 100% on board with the idea, right? I've never gone to a stagehand at some place in New York City, a Local One guy, and said 'hey, I need to get up on the stage' and have them go, 'yeah, tough shit wheelchair dude.' You know, that's not been the attitude. It's like 'Oh, I will build you a ramp. What ratio would you like it? Okay, it'll be here in three seconds.' That's the attitude from the people. The problem is the resources. The problem is the built environment. It is the focus. We're going to present a thing, and I would like ASL interpreters, but we don't have the budget for that. Well, why not? Right? When you're building your budget, these are the basics, right? And we need to change our mindset that accessibility in all of its forms is not an add-on. It is where we start. [41]

Access isn't only physical. Universal Design initially has been focused on physical spaces and items. But we can expand the theory to the worker experience at all stages of the employee lifecycle. By considering all the ways a person interacts with the field of theatrical production, how can we think about each of these phases through a universal design lens?

Accessibility can also be connected to information, and thus, power hoarding. Looking at ways to present perceptible information in simple and intuitive ways in a workplace begins with job descriptions and the hiring processes. We have cited a variety of barriers to the ways that workers even get to a job interview (if there even is one), let alone get hired for a job. Hiring managers need to eliminate unnecessary complexities. Job postings should be spread widely in public forums which do not depend on group affinity or access. The internet makes information universally accessible and also creates innumerable ways to limit that access. Hiring managers should not only post equitable job postings on their own websites but should reach beyond their own networks to share opportunities with community groups, labor federations, unions, education institutions. The job postings themselves should be clear and easy to understand. The workers should be able to opt in to the process they are entering. As Sarah Lozoff shared, equitable labor practices "looks like having informed consent when I apply for a job, knowing what you're gonna get paid, what the working hours are, what the job expectations are, and that being what the job is."[42] Lozoff also discussed how important it can be to send questions in advance of a job interview:

> Usually there are a couple [of questions] that are kind of 'think on your feet,' but for the most part, especially the ones that we want nuanced answers to, we send ahead, and I think that first and foremost is a part of equitable labor practices. I think it allows for different learning styles, it allows for different personality types, and it allows people to actually think, and, you know, well, yes, some of our job has to be performed under pressure, often we are able to come up with a

> plan with a little bit of time rather than knowing the answer right away. So I also think that it allows for people to show their true colors in a really beneficial way because they aren't under the pressure of 'I just gotta give an answer. I just gotta give an answer. I just gotta give an answer. I just gotta give an answer.'[43]

These antiquated interview techniques where people are forced to think on their feet do not assess the interviewee's skills for the job at hand, and exclude workers with particular learning or information processing styles. We can use the Universal Design framework in developing hiring processes that are attentive to the different ways people receive information and communicate. How can job expectations and workplace communication also be simple and intuitive? How can hiring managers and supervisors create an environment in which any person coming into the role has the opportunity to succeed? Does everyone share the expectations for each role?

Similarly, the Universal Design approach can be used to consider workplace communications. How do workers communicate within production teams? How are these norms established? Are everyone's needs taken into account? Are production workers on short-term contracts as freelancers or overhire workers included in the communication systems of an institution? Do they have resources on how to engage with these systems, guidance on the project's communication protocols, and a way to note if these systems are not accessible for them?

The Universal Design principles of "simple and intuitive" and "perceptible information" also come into play when we consider how production workers can report issues in the workplace. We must develop clear, consistent reporting mechanisms that every production worker, even the electrician hired for a single work call, knows how to navigate. The worker should not have to know who to ask, or how to navigate the administrative database, in order to find out how to formally note if they are experiencing bias in the workplace. Like curb cuts in sidewalks, initially designed to serve disabled veterans, making grievance processes clear and navigable will support more people than we can know.

The "tolerance for error" principle clashes with our industry's culture of urgency and perfectionism. We need to find ways to create room for mistakes – in professional training environments, yes, but also in the workplace itself. In rehearsal, working in the shop, or teching in the theatre, it needs to be okay for someone to try again or take extra time to accomplish something. This is how we create safe workplaces. There must be room in the schedule, budget, and culture for mistakes, for missed deadlines, and for a worker to pause on any task that does not feel completely safe.

The Universal Design framework is not a single solution, but it is a mindset that is vital for us to progress to a more inclusive field. We have to start by remembering to include all of the workers in the co-creation of the field. And by making some "in the meantime" changes to improve workers' workplaces and lives immediately.

We need to disrupt the norms of professional training in the field and reimagine how production workers develop their craft.

We acknowledge that both of these things can be true: much of what is done in theatrical production is best taught and learned by doing. And, as we have discussed in Chapter 5, the industry's reliance on and expectation of unpaid labor creates barriers to access to the field and is part of why the labor force is so homogeneous.

One of the largest parallel barriers to access is the cost of higher education. The current system isn't affordable, even to the upper classes. Who can be expected to take on more than $200,000 in debt before entering a career in the arts? If we took out the financial barrier – if cost weren't part of the equation – would we believe that everyone who wants to pursue careers in production should go to university? No. In many cases, the skills needed for a job in production aren't learned in an academic institution: students graduate and are then expected to take on underpaid hands-on work to learn those missing skills. There are, one could argue, more intangible skills and information needed by designers than, say, traditional technicians, which are learned inside of classrooms. But those classrooms don't necessarily have to be part of accredited degree programs.

We believe that a college degree has value but that it is not necessary for many paths within theatrical production. We have both attended theatre programs in universities and have since taught and mentored in specialized production and design programs in those universities and others, and we do see value in them as an opportunity for specialized study, as well as for general studies, personal growth, and relationship building. Liberal arts

programs, including those in theatre, invite students to think and explore through a particular lens, rather than prepare them through a series of hard skills. These programs, generally, do not necessarily seek to create professionals, but rather curate future artists and audience members. Students in liberal arts colleges often discover their interest in theatre, or other disciplines, while in college, in contrast to BFA students who have identified their interest in order to be accepted through an audition or portfolio review process before even graduating high school. BFA, or conservatory-style, programs often focus on training professionals with an emphasis on hard skills. Either types of programs may be the right path for individual students; both often perpetuate professional models which create oppressive work practices. A lot of educators are doing good work to dispel these practices, which start young.

That said, in order to iterate toward a more inclusive field, the theatre industry, the people, and the culture need to divest from the dependency on the higher education system and the diploma, and move toward skill-based training. In order for this to happen, we need to reimagine professional training for production work outside of traditional universities.

We also need to interrogate the existing systems. Many university performing arts programs teach and model inequitable production labor practices embedded into their operating structure. As in all of our other invitations for reimagining, the examples we discuss here are not radical enough but they are "in the meantime" steps toward transformational change grounded in a disruption of the current systems.

There is obvious societal value placed on higher education. According to 2021 statistics from the US Bureau of Labor, with each level of educational attainment, earnings rise and unemployment rate drops.[44] The median usual weekly earnings for a worker with less than a high school diploma is $626 versus a worker with a doctoral degree at $1,909. And, as of 2021, the unemployment rate for those with less than a high school diploma was 4.7% versus 1.5% for those with a doctoral degree.[45] However, according to a 2023 study by Jobsage, "69% of people believe college degrees will be less important for getting well-paying jobs in coming years; 72% would skip college if their ideal job didn't require it [...] Only 1 in 4 say their college degree has helped a lot in their career so far."[46] This move away from the value of a degree might be connected to the upheaval of the pandemic. It might be tied to the unbelievable cost associated with higher education. And it might be an openness to considering the value of practical training over a piece of paper with a fancy seal.

There are close similarities between technical theatre work and the traditional building trades – such as carpentry, bricklaying, plumbing, etc. – that are performed in building construction. The building trade unions have, historically, tied education and practical education together through apprenticeships. Union apprenticeships can be highly competitive and typically follow an earn-while-you-learn model. Apprentices earn a livable wage, usually somewhat less than Journey or Master union members. They receive benefits like health insurance and retirement benefits while working

> side-by-side with highly skilled and highly trained journeymen, who teach them trade. Additionally, apprentices also receive mandatory class education, where they learn more about their trade and particular craft. As apprentices advance through their apprenticeship, they receive pay raises, which reflect their new industry skillsets and education. [...] Instead of racking up massive amounts of student debt, apprentices are paid to work and learn. Some apprenticeship programs allow apprentices to earn free college credits and a select few could even earn an associate's degree.[47]

The apprenticeship fulfills similar functions to an ideal internship, but the training responsibilities are on the union, not the employer. The union is taking on the role of educational institution in place of a college or university while the employer typically contributes financially to some kind of training fund. This is an example of professional training which includes components that are purely education oriented – classes and training – in addition to work experience with job placements. For example, the Joint Industry Board of the Electrical Industry, a partnership between the International Brotherhood of Electrical Workers Local Union No. 3 and the National Electrical Contractors Association, offers an Apprentice Program that includes 35 hours per week of on-the-job training for four years plus four hours a week of mandatory instruction including: "Classroom instruction in Electrical Theory; and Three (3) hours per week in college courses leading to an associate degree."[48] Workers finish the apprentice program both as a union journeyperson and with an accredited associate degree. This kind of apprenticeship creates tangible class mobility in a country that values a college degree.

Apprentice Program Information

From The Electrical Industry of IBEW Local Union No. 3

The Apprentice Program of the Electrical Industry of IBEW Local Union No. 3 includes a minimum of 35 hours per week on-the-job training for four years plus the following requirements:

- Mandatory attendance at related instruction for four (4) hours per week;
- Classroom instruction in Electrical Theory; and

- Three (3) hours per week in college courses leading to an associate degree.
- The fifth and final period will consist of four (4) hours per week of related instruction for 18 months and a minimum of 35 hours per week of work (from 18 months to two years).

  [...]

What is Apprenticeship?

- Apprenticeship is a well organized and supervised method, which industries use to train people with little or no prior knowledge of a craft, or trade, to become capable, qualified craftspersons or journeypersons. It is a "earn while you learn program." The "on the job" portion of the training is a full time, well paid job.
- Gain experience using the most modern practices;
- Work under the direction of a competent journeyman who will teach you the trade in the shop and at the jobsite;
- Attend evening classes a minimum of four hours each week to receive technical instruction and 3 hours each week in college courses leading toward an associate degree;
- Have your work experience reports, school grades and attendance reviewed before each wage increase is granted. Satisfactory progress results in automatic wage increases.
- Have the opportunity to become a member of the most respected and progressive Union in the Building and Construction Trades.
- The opportunity to "earn" a journey level status and certification, which is recognized throughout the United States.

Text courtesy of The Joint Industry Board of the Electrical Industry.

Many IATSE locals have apprentice programs to train and initiate the next generation of theatrical stagehands and technicians. Additionally, United Scenic Artists already has an apprentice program for its Scenic Artist category. But even these existing programs are not as robust nor do they include accredited degree granting like the IBEW program. And there are not yet comparable apprenticeship models for designers or stage managers.

As we discussed previously, both the IATSE and United Scenic Artists also have training trusts that are funded jointly by employers and the unions. These trusts produce skill-based training for union members, as well as reimbursements for various certifications and coursework, which allow members to stay up to date on current technologies and expand their own skill sets as the field continues to grow and expand. But what about for non-union workers? Is there a version of this that could exist outside of unionized labor? Are there partnerships between educational institutions and independent organizations that can expand the IBEW model into theatrical training?

Deepening the conversation about ending unpaid internships, the hands-on training offered by paid internships can be imagined to serve both the intern and the organization. In imagining such a system, we need a model that can work on a scale consistent with the scale of unpaid internships now. We know that unpaid internships are unethical. As discussed in Chapter 5, the FLSA provides guidelines for determining whether or not an employer must pay interns for their work – but we believe that even if they meet the legal requirements for unpaid internships, the structure and history of unpaid internships in the arts is extremely problematic and has created innumerable barriers, and the field should fully move beyond unpaid. That being said, we acknowledge the value of skills-based learning that can occur in on-the-job internship-like opportunities.

Is there an ethical paid internship model? What makes it an internship versus a job? What's the difference between a paid internship and entry-level work? As defined by the National Association of Colleges and Employers (NACE):

> An internship is a form of experiential learning that integrates knowledge and theory learned in the classroom with practical application and skills development in a professional setting. Internships give students the opportunity to gain valuable applied experience and make connections in professional fields they are considering for career paths; and give employers the opportunity to guide and evaluate talent.[49]

NACE clarifies that an internship is "not simply an operational work experience that just happens to be conducted by a student."[50] Many, many of the positions currently named as internships should be reclassified as entry-level work. As we heard in We See You W.A.T., "We demand the dismantling of internship programs, and we demand that paid entry level positions be created in their place."[51]

If equitable internships can exist, the interns must be paid a living or even thriving wage. And the operations cannot be dependent on these interns as workers. So first, we need to really assess: are we talking about paid interns or entry-level workers? In cases where the worker just happens to be a student and they are expected to perform duties with the same accuracy or knowledge as any other paid staff member, we are talking about entry-level workers. If the priority is serving the operations of the production or organization over learning, then the job isn't an internship. But if the focus is experiential learning, then it could be a paid internship.

Learning implies that there is a) guidance available; b) room for error; and c) feedback.

This learning environment obviously benefits the student, but how can it benefit the institution or production, especially those which have historically depended on unpaid or minimally paid intern labor? Though there is a fine line between interns supporting operations and being necessary, interns can support and bolster the existing operational infrastructure. They cannot, however, be the only ones building the show or necessary in the labor matrix to complete the work. And if the interns are there to learn design, it doesn't make sense for them to be supporting operations doing administrative tasks or ushering or bartending. The long-term benefits to the institution include continuing to contribute to the future of the field and continuing to build relationships with the next generation of theatre workers.

What does an educational internship look like? The intern has a clearly identified supervisor. That supervisor must work in the field and specialty the intern is looking to train in so that they can actually help the intern learn. Mentoring the intern is part of the supervisor's job. If this is an added responsibility, the mentor-supervisor is relieved of some other responsibility in order to demonstrate a recognition that mentoring is a part of the job and takes capacity to do well. The supervisor receives training on teaching and mentoring and giving feedback. These feedback methods are consistent across an institution or production regardless of departments. For each intern, learning goals are identified and articulated. There are opportunities to focus on learning: to ask questions, learn about the greater context of the work, and, perhaps most importantly, to make mistakes. There are opportunities to learn by doing. There is consistent feedback offered. At the end of the internship, there is time, space, and structure for reflection and two-way feedback.

What are the budget implications of expanding entry level work and paid internships? If interns or entry level workers are being paid a living wage, what is the trickle up effect on the finances of the institution? This idea of "budgeting from the bottom," starting with the person at the bottom and working your way up, means that interns earn less than their supervisors who make less than their supervisors and so on. It means that the lowest paid workers have to make more than the interns. Ideally, this model closes the gap between the pay of the artistic leaders and the lowest paid employees, as we pointed out in Chapter 7. This also supports the demands of the We See You W.A.T. cohort:

> We demand that the theatre's highest paid executive staff members make no more than 10x the yearly salary of the lowest paid full-time staff member.
> We demand divestment from bloated executive packages and bonuses.

> We demand all incoming executive leadership hires be offered a salary that is equitable to that of the prior hire's offer and consistent with those of executive leadership partners within the institution.[52]

This kind of payment structure doesn't solve the issue for small low-budget arts organizations, but for the larger institutions that currently have massive gaps between what executives are making and what the regular staff are making, this is how it becomes financially feasible.

It seems to us that partnerships across organizations are key to paid internship programs that are sustainable long-term. As we will discuss further, the added financial and structural requirements of this shift might be too much for an institution to take on alone. The Diversity in Arts Leadership internship (DIAL) is an example of a paid internship program administered by Americans for the Arts and national partners; it is run by Americans for the Arts, and the students get placed at arts nonprofits. In addition to the work placement, students are paid $4,500 ($15 an hour for the required hours of work and the required hours of training in the program), and they receive professional development workshops, facilitated discussions, and site visits through DIALogue Fridays, pairing with an individual mentor and membership in a national intern cohort and alumni network.[53] Excitingly, there is also a system for feedback:

> Interns will be expected to meet regularly with both host arts supervisors and mentors to define, review, and evaluate project and personal goals. Interns, host organizations, and mentors will each be required to complete mid-point check-in with staff as well as a final evaluation survey to assess the program.[54]

Working as an assistant designer or assistant stage manager is another way to learn and to be exposed to the work, to "get in the room." Being an assistant is not the same as being an apprentice; being an assistant is its own job and doesn't necessarily place a focus on learning. This is a job, not an internship. On an individual basis, assisting can be a learning opportunity and a way for designers to bring new assistants into the profession, but it is not a systemic fix. Assisting-as-learning puts a burden on the designers who, as production workers, are already perhaps suffering from the systemic problems we have identified.

As with equitable internships, assistantships invite a series of questions around mentorship. Could organizations or unions provide supervisor or mentorship training? Is there structured hiring, goal setting, and feedback for assistants? Can organizations and producers support their designers in developing an equitable system for finding assistants? When the organizations and producers or general managers handle the administrative lift of posting, promoting, and managing the search process, designers and stage managers can expand their hiring of assistants beyond their personal network.

Do observerships satisfy similar training needs? In an observership, unlike in an assistantship or even an apprenticeship, the learner doesn't have any work responsibilities. The best example of this is the SDC Professional Development program, designed for early career directors and choreographers. As of November 2022, the SDC Professional Development program includes three tiers of opportunities: Shadows, Observers, and Fellows:

> Shadows will watch a particular part of the production process via a short-term exposure opportunity. Like Shadows, Observers will also watch the production process; however, observerships are a production-long opportunity from first rehearsal to opening night. Lastly, Fellows will support a director and/or choreographer as part of the artistic team over the course of the production process.[55]

This program, like assisting, provides access to the room and the art making and the network. It also doesn't cross the line into possible entry-level work, except perhaps in the Fellows program. These opportunities do not exist in design or production in the way that they do for directors and choreographers. But this is an excellent example of how unions can partner with institutions to expand education. It would be great to expand this model beyond directing or choreography so that people aren't in a situation where the only way to get into the room is being someone's assistant.

Another way of divesting from traditional higher ed is through a low-cost a la carte education model. This asks that we as an industry divest from this idea of a degree requirement when the skills are what are needed to do the job. What is the value of that piece of paper in relation to the ability to do the work? We acknowledge that in addition to purely skills-based training, designers especially benefit from various aspects of a liberal arts education. But, is there a way to learn the content without incurring the cost of a degree?

There have been versions of this model for many years in theatrical design, though many were oriented around the master-teacher model. Most notable was the Polakov Studio and Form of Stage Design. Founded in 1958 in NYC, "Lester Polakov trained many important designers during its thirty-five-year history. Besides being an esteemed teacher, Polakov designed on an Off-Broadway as well as for opera, film, and industrial shows. Many of the designers of the last forty years of the twentieth century were trained"[56] by Polakov. His legacy lives on in the training at MFA programs like NYU and Yale, whose influential leaders often trained with Polakov or his proteges. The idea of this a la carte model is that interested students, including professionals, can just take classes. They pay for those classes they are interested in without trying to achieve an accredited degree. And the focus is on the learning and not the piece of paper.

Begun during the Pause by lighting designers Clifton Taylor and Mark Stanley, the Studio School of Design has taken up a similar mission. The SSD is

> an interdependent community of practice where experiential learning is embedded into a curriculum of design storytelling. [...] We see lighting design as a creative art form and are deeply invested in the potential of telling diverse and inclusive human stories through the medium of light.[57]

Students are free to pick and choose from the course offerings to build the curriculum that best suits their needs, whether that is one class or a flotilla of classes. The classes themselves range from free to approximately $600 for eight two-hour sessions and include topics like Lighting Live Events for Camera, Vectorworks 3D, Dance Lighting Intensive, Business for Freelance Designers, and more. Cost can be kept low because there isn't a need for accreditation from any kind of qualifying board. Is the SSD sustainable? That is yet to be seen. It was founded by well-established designers and maintains a small scale of programming. But an expanded series of trainings or some proliferation of this model into other organizations serving a wider range of theatre production workers would clearly benefit the field.

And what about traditional higher education? Why are we proposing that universities aren't the answer? In addition to the overwhelming burden of debt from higher ed, it is incumbent on educators to ask what workplace practices we are modeling in educational theatre spaces and what cultural norms we are promoting. Because in many cases, the harm greatly outweighs the good. Academic theatre spaces often train students through a mix of classroom studio training and actualized production work. Historian and labor researcher Christin Essin asks:

> Do our university theatre departments offer educational gains that correspond ethically, if not materially, with the fair compensation and work provisions received by professional unionized technicians? Do our curricular work requirements in technical theatre break ethically, if not materially, with the labor codes that govern industry professionals? In my experience, we promote backstage work as generative learning experiences in which students acquire a range of theatre-specific and transferable occupational skills. But in practice, student technicians receive less guidance, fewer opportunities to experiment, and quicker explanations about how their labor contributes to a production's overall mission.[58]

Following the Pause, many classrooms are holding conversations around antiracism and questioning our practices, but much of what's happening in production is what we see in production elsewhere, perpetuating these problematic practices due to a culture of scarcity and urgency. There is a disconnect between what's being discussed in the classroom and what's happening in production operations. In order to showcase performance students, many schools produce too many shows to maintain a sustainable or even remotely safe environment. I, Natalie, taught at an institution that produced more than twenty productions each school year to serve bloated BFA Acting and Musical Theater programs. That meant that students were teching shows every weekend of the school year. To support this high volume of shows, the small number of design and technology students were expected to maintain a production schedule that gave them little to no time to reflect or learn from a project before being thrown into the next one. Students were expected to take a full load of classes, attend rehearsal, tech and performances and, in many cases, work 20+ hours a week in extracurricular employment to be able to make ends meet. Even as the numbers of performance students receded, the push to produce more, and larger, shows persisted, causing many students to burn out and leave our program citing their mental health needs.

How do we reckon with this disconnect? How can we divest theatre production training from the same emphasis on scarcity, urgency and perfectionism that we want to eliminate from professional theatre production practices? It begins with asking the same questions of academic leadership that we want to ask artistic leaders:

What is the value of art that causes harm to those who make it?
How can we center humanity in the work of producing theatre?
How can we welcome the whole student or worker into the space where theatre is made?
What changes need to be prioritized to value people over productions?

We need to share the proverbial wealth instead of hoard it.

> We have lived through a good half century of individualistic linear organizing (led by charismatic individuals or budget-building institutions), which intends to reform or revolutionize society, but falls back into modeling the oppressive tendencies against which we claim to be pushing. Some of those tendencies are seeking to assert one right way or one right strategy. Many align with the capitalistic belief that constant growth and critical mass is the only way to create change, even if they don't use that language.
>
> There are new strategies emerging, or being remembered— many would describe this as a shift from a masculine to feminine (or patriarchal to feminist) leadership. I see that, and I think it is also about something beyond all of our binaries— evolving in relationship with our hierarchical tendency.[59]
>
> adrienne maree brown, *Emergent Strategy: Shaping Change, Changing Worlds*

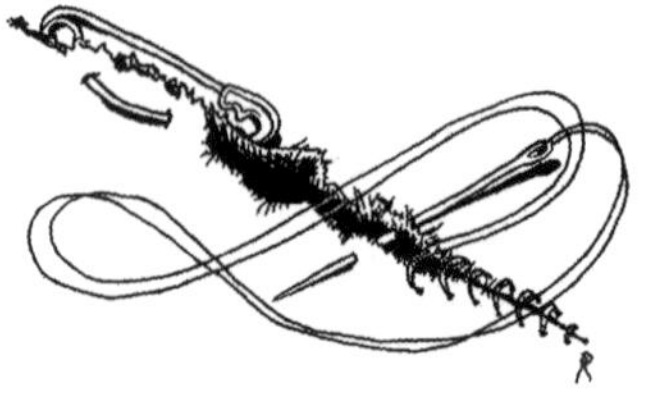

We acknowledge that all of our imaginings for more equitable labor practices require resources not yet allocated. Some of the resources we're discussing are things that organizations and productions need access to constantly. Some of these needs are more sporadic or ad hoc. Some are consistent but not constant. This requires nonlinear organizing. One of the most notable ongoing worker needs that comes up regularly but not consistently is support for caregivers. In an institution, there may be consistent enough caregiving needs from staff to demonstrate a need to support caregivers institutionally. But what about the production workers who have those needs on one show or group of shows? Productions like *Lifespan of a Fact* and companies like Playwrights Horizons have tried to provide these resources for individual artists on individual shows, but the lack of consistent need makes it hard to develop a structure or identify a funding source. Other companies have tried offering caregiving stipends or reimbursements to those workers who needed support. When the money is provided, it still puts the burden on the worker-caregiver to arrange care within that budget. Some may prefer this, but some may prefer that the employer do that work. Alternatively, what if institutions came together to fund either an existing caregiving institution or to start one which served a community of institutions? If all of the theatres, in Philadelphia for example, joined together to fund childcare in the same location, this would also mean that parents and children know the facility and the staff. Using the same principles as a union's multi-employer benefits fund, each of the theatrical production employers could contribute to this institution on each contract, which could mean that even when engaging non-caregiving workers, the employers are contributing to the sustainability of community care.

Where do institutions start? The Parent Artist Advocacy League offers many shared resources including Human Resources Workplace Support, Compassion Training for Organizations, Childcare/Caregiver Fund Consult, Grant Applications Consult, and PAAL Handbook Consult.[60] It's important to know that not all caregivers are caring for children. And that caretaking for adults requires different support. How could institutions come together to provide support to caregivers in various different circumstances? And what about caregivers who need support when they aren't working under an institution – playwrights writing their next play, designers who need time in their studios before getting to the theatre, technicians completing certifications? In some cases individuals have used their own resources to support fellow workers. Could some of these workers be supported by foundation support? Is foundation support even something we want to continue as a practice? (Stay tuned!)

There are a lot of excuses about why these things don't happen – or get tried and abandoned – but there must be a way to do it.

When considering these needs of production and production workers, some can be addressed by outsourcing a solution on a one-time or sporadic basis. But often, the need is consistent enough that a different solution is required. Sometimes that solution is hiring an outside firm to do that work.

There are many situations where this practice is the norm. In cities with a lot of theatre work, productions will often hire General Management and Production Management companies to manage the various aspects of their productions or will hire scene shops to build their scenery. In these cases, the institution does not need to have this full service team all of the time. Often this model is used in commercial productions which lack the infrastructure of a producing institution. But not always. These firms can help to increase the capacity of understaffed producing organizations. When an institution outsources this work, especially the work that includes budgeting and hiring, how are these outside companies supporting the institutional values? Are they? Who is paying attention? It's all well and good for an institution to publicly state its values, but it doesn't work if they outsource the work without an accountability structure.

In some cases, the institution hires a consultant to advise on the necessary work, to set up a system which the organization can continue. The consultant model can be extremely useful to approaching systemic change within an organization. One such area is internship educational oversight. As we discussed above, internship creation and oversight is rarely a fiscal priority. And, in order for a new kind of internship model to work, someone needs to be dedicated to creating the internship system with an eye toward education, supervision, and employee workload. A single person could serve multiple organizations at once, while still maintaining relationships with each to oversee the maintenance and sustainability of the program. Or there's the Production on Deck example, a firm serving the hiring needs of many organizations, while also requiring accountability on the part of the institution.

Similarly, institutions are already often hiring experts to oversee staff trainings. Consultants can provide safety training; inclusion, diversity, equity, and access trainings; leadership and supervisor training, including those around performance goal setting and feedback; and other professional developments. When considering incorporating performance evaluations, goal-setting, and feedback processes for production workers, there might be sharing of ideas and findings between organizations in building out these systems. From our worker survey findings, it is evident that there is very little in the realm of performance measurement and management for production workers; what if arts leaders and managers (producers, artistic directors, executive directors, managing directors, GMs, CMs, PMs, etc.) came together to discuss these sorts of practices in the production workplace? Every theatre may not need a unique system for this type of employee cultivation; the challenges are shared and could be solved together, under the guidance of a consultant.

Freelancers, as we have discussed, often don't benefit from even the benefits of human resources departments. In some cases, unions can fill that role. But even unions don't always have the resources. To address this need, United Scenic Artists has partnered with the Entertainment Community Fund (ECF) through a Member Assistance Program. As we have mentioned, this partnership provides social services to the union membership beyond what the employers will, or the union can, provide. It's much more affordable for the local than hiring specialized professional staff, especially in the wide range of services that the ECF provides. And the ECF can serve various organizations simultaneously.

In some cases, organizations are teaming up with other, seemingly similar, organizations to have a shared hire, someone who is employed by, and works for, all of the organizations individually in a shared time model. This can be an innovative solution, but it can also put the burden of navigating a job with too many needs and too much demand on one's time onto a single worker. This sort of position must be carefully crafted, and the joint hire needs to be given the support and agency to succeed. In Pittsburgh, five organizations known as the Pittsburgh Arts EDIA/HR Cohort, the August Wilson African American Cultural Center, City Theatre Company, the Mattress Factory, the Pittsburgh Glass Center, and the Pittsburgh Public Theater, came together to hire a shared Talent and Equity Director. Since creating the cohort, the Pittsburgh Public Theater has left, leaving the remaining four institutions.

This model holds real promise for a different kind of shared resources. Describing what attracted her to this position, Fatima Bunafoor shared:

> They're willing to invest the money, they're willing to invest the time they've been together for close to two and a half years – meeting regularly as a cohort. I think that says a lot about the leadership that's involved in this cohort. And when you look at different boards, different directors that are doing this work, it's a sort of two, three month plan of how do we get this EDI or HR, whatever PR public campaign to sort of erase the image if they have. Then next year, come back to it whenever there's another crisis. So I saw there's enough promise in this cohort, and I also was really interested in the field.[61]

However, Bunafoor also shared some of the challenges she's encountered serving these very different organizations in this position. She serves as both human resources and DEI staff for the organizations, which have very different needs. This position has been hard to imagine as sustainable. There has also been a lot of leadership transition within the organizations, creating a lot of unanticipated change management. And the day-to-day needs of the organizations have taken away from Bunafoor's focus on larger scale institutional policy work.

As someone coming from outside of the arts, Bunafoor also had a lot of in-depth research to do, as well as taking the time to really understand the specific nuances of each of the four institutions. She has become a conduit for the needs of four groups of staff members. Consistent with our research among theatre workers:

> This idea of critical feedback is not really welcome outside of the theater production process because it's so dramatic in the theater space itself that people take it into their own performance evaluation process, or coaching or management, it's almost unheard of. And it's something that I'm learning and I've been trying to understand and wrap my head around because I've never seen people be so hesitant and afraid of feedback in this way, especially with two theaters that I'm working with. So it's been a lot of relationship building with the directors making sure that they have the resources, but also like shifting their mindset around feedback loops from this like really negative traumatic thing to just an investment that you make in your staff, and it's a space for you to learn from your employees – what's working, what's not working for you – to get that feedback and opportunities to grow.[62]

Another challenge is the misalignment between the organizations, especially between the theatres and visual arts institutions, which function off of different fiscal calendars and organizational structures. All of these challenges aside, Bunafoor sees value in positions like hers:

> I think it brings in sort of a level setting that doesn't exist in the fields around how do we actually learn from one another, especially if people work in silos, and it forces them to listen. I've seen one organization listen to a practice that they've not listened to for years because they've seen it work in another organization.[63]

After some time in the work, she shifted the focus of her position towards better use of the monthly organizational cohort meetings. This included less on-the-ground HR work and more big-picture approach building. As she explained to the leaders, "I'm not going to convince you to adopt values that you've already committed to doing, which saves me time and saves me the capacity, it holds them accountable in one space."[64]

These various shared staffing and support models can be cost effective. They allow for a small group to specialize and offer their specific services while supporting several producing organizations or artists. As in Bunafoor's experience, this work can exceed the capacity of those hired to do it. If a service is supporting multiple institutions or productions, all of them need to conform to similar systems or the service or person needs to be able to divide their time across all the organizations sustainably and equitably. We don't have data on what some of these models look like long-term in this industry and so we don't know how sustainable they are, but sharing resources has a higher likelihood of success than hoarding them.

Most of these examples are ways to share resources between organizations or productions, as a way to use these resources more efficiently. Shared leadership is another way to, as brown describes, evolve our relationship with our hierarchical tendency. Shared leadership models reimagine the structure and sharing of responsibilities in an institution, as a way to decentralize power and have more collaborative leadership. The most ideal shared leadership approaches ask: How do you incorporate multiple, non-hierarchical perspectives into leadership? This begins with embracing an antiracist and, to some extent, anticapitalist approach. Journalist Helen Shaw spoke with then Baltimore Center Stage Artistic Director Stephanie Ybarra about how to introduce ideas of antiracism into the institution in which she works:

> Hierarchy concentrates power, which turns out to be very difficult to give up. In Baltimore, the anti-oppression staff group is decentralized because 'subverting the hierarchical structure and encouraging staff to self-organize in this work creates shared accountability,' Ybarra says. And when it comes to the question of artistic directorship itself, Ybarra is conscious of its perils, no matter how careful the AD might be. 'Centralized power is a form of white supremacy,' she says—and yet the scarcity of top jobs (in all under-resourced fields) leads to narrowing and fear. Few in New York ever willingly surrender a crown; we see very little of the healthy turnover that happens outside of the city. [...] 'Hierarchy reaffirms a supremacist state. And while I never doubted who was the boss of the Public Theater while I worked there,' she says, 'that structure of having multiple program directors driving their own curatorial processes is one of the closest structures I've seen to a major institution with some element of decentralization operating inside of it.'[65]

One seemingly progressive leadership model, that of Dual Executive Leadership, actually enforces hierarchy and concentrates power in a different way. The Dual Executive leadership model places two people, typically an artistic leader – seen as a creative individual – and an operational leader – seen as a more practical one, at the head of an organization. Both typically then report to the board. This model is seen to ease the amount of responsibility on an individual leader, but in doing so, it separates the art and the money. This is a silo-ing and hoarding of wealth that precipitates opportunities for tokenizing of artistic leadership. More often than not, even when a theatre organization's artistic executive is BIPOC or a woman, the executive leader primarily responsible for the organization's finances is a white man. This creates an opportunity for the organization's community members to avoid placing their trust in the artistic leader. Robert Barry Fleming named how this manifests in his experience as a Black artistic director:

> I feel like [Actors Theatre has] made enough changes to be the future-for organization, but as a donor said to me, well, she didn't say it to me, because white people don't talk to Black people unless they talk to their handlers. So we have a kind of plantation capitalism thing here where even though I'm the CEO, as a Black queer person, many people don't talk directly to me, they'll talk to my white staff, or whoever they perceive in the ecosystem would be my handler, this overseer's handler so I get these messages from maybe my white, cis-presenting development director at the time, or I get it from my, although he's gay and Jewish, I get it from my white board president because it's like, 'Whoa, he's your handler, I won't have this conversation with you. Even though I've had eight hours with you over lunch and dinner, in 20 minutes, I'll say to him, is all the programming going to be Black and gay? That's my concern.'[66]

We repeatedly see the executive leaders trapped between pressure from the Board "above" and the workers "below." This pressure is reaffirmed by patriarchal structure and the white supremacist characteristics of individualism and a single right way[67] – all decisions have to be filtered through them, using one set of information, making one series of choices. Strong, collaborative leaders can surround themselves with great management teams who provide support and feedback. Even with these additional voices, in this model, the executive leadership is left to hold the ball when things fall apart. As we have seen through the exits of many BIPOC leaders, the onus is on them to visibly correct and carry the actions of the institution.

By avoiding giving fiscal responsibility to artistic directors, the artistic director can be the variable in an institution's structure, used to appease societal pressures and sacrificed when institutional operations go wrong. There is a limited lifespan in artistic leadership, specifically for leaders of color, and an understanding that supposed artistic differences allow an institution an out when a leader pushes too hard against the norms. Dramaturg Lauren Halvorsen refers to this rotating door as the "regional theatre game of thrones." This is a sign that artistic leaders are disposable but the financial leaders are not. As we write this, there are announcements of AD comings and goings nearly daily, including many of the BIPOC leaders whose appointments were celebrated following the Pause: Stephanie Ybarra leaving Baltimore Center Stage for a job outside of theatre; Nataki Garrett leaving OSF without a publicly announced new appointment; James Ijames's resignation from the Wilma and subsequent replacement with Lindsay Smiling; Hana Sharif moving from Repertory Theatre of St. Louis to Arena Stage and Tinashe Kajese-Bolden and Chris Moses being appointed artistic directors of Alliance Theatre. The majority of changes are in institutions employing a version of the Dual Executive Leadership model.

This isn't the only way. Shared Leadership is not the Dual Executive Leadership structure, which many thought, and some still do, was the progressive answer. Shared Leadership is having multiple leaders who, while they will certainly each bring certain strengths, share oversight over both the creative direction of the organization and also the business management. It is not having a single person be the final decision-maker; it is having multiple perspectives on issues that arise, and multiple voices envisioning the future of the organization. Sarah Clare Corporandy explained how Shared Leadership works for Detroit Public Theatre:

> And all of our brains work differently. And so the organization is getting the benefit of like many problem solvers at the table and many perspectives, even though we are three white women, roughly the same age, I understand that. But we're still very different people and we bring different perspectives and sensitivities and experiences to the decision-making process.[68]

As a relatively young and nimble organization, Detroit Public Theatre has been able to experiment with and adapt these leadership structures without feeling tied to the way it has always been done.

The Shared Leadership model alleviates the pressure on a single leader to be isolated in understanding and overseeing all aspects of the organization. And it alleviates the pressure for a single leader to be accountable to the board and the workers alike. Shared Leadership does not assume a bifurcation of art and money, building a collaborative structure from the start. It eliminates the idea that creative individuals can't be responsible with resources and sees the creativity in practical and administrative problem solving.

Having a coalition of leaders provides an invitation to community members for multiple points of contact instead of there being an individual face of the organization. The organization benefits from an inherent multiplicity of perspectives. Shared Leadership allows for a healthier ecosystem, creating breadth around work-life balance. This allows leaders to take the time and space they need as whole humans. It also creates implicit shared knowledge and therefore more preparedness for transition. All of this counters the white supremacist characteristics of perfectionism, "one right way," binary thinking, and individualism.

Centering the humanity of leaders reiterates the importance of centering the humanity of all workers. Shared leadership allows for leaders to not have all the answers, and leaders can distribute their focus, giving departments, and individual workers, more attention.

We need to disrupt the way American theatre is funded.

Money, and the power it wields, have a lot to do with the systems that continue to oppress workers. Many of the labor-related problems that are assumed to be due not having enough money actually stem from the source of the money and power structure that creates.

Nonprofit theatres, and arts organizations overall, are typically funded through a mix of individual benefactor-donors and foundation-donors, with a secondary source of income coming from ticket sales. Commercial productions are funded by producers. On the surface this is very different. But maybe it isn't as different as it seems. If few people invest in theatre for the profit, how is the producer funder model really different from the benefactor model? There are certainly differences in the legal structures of the models, but in terms of value and power and who has a say, these two models share the same DNA. While much of our data and research focuses on the nonprofit institutions, these questions apply to commercial productions and to other types of employers who hire production labor, like scene shops, rental houses, production management, and general management firms and hiring companies.

We return to the fact that a production or institution's budget is a value statement. Institutions name their values in a variety of ways: they list them on their website, record them in their production programs, post them on social media. How much are funders aware of these values? And who is responsible for ensuring that the budget breakdown and the production operations align with the organization values? Some progressive companies have made their budgets totally transparent to their audiences, but this practice is not common. It's not even commonly shared with production workers being hired full-time or seasonally, let alone for short-term projects.

In a nonprofit organization, the buck, as it were, stops with the board of directors. The board is, by one definition, "a governing body that is responsible for reviewing and approving the organization's mission and strategic direction, annual budget and key financial transactions, compensation practices and policies, and fiscal and governance policies."[69]

Principles for Good Governance and Ethical Practice

A guide for charities and foundations

From Independent Sector, which provided leadership in convening and supporting the Panel on the Nonprofit Sector and continues to support the sector in its pursuit of the highest standards of ethical practice

Charitable organizations have long embraced the need for standards of ethical practice that preserve and strengthen the public's confidence. Many such systems in fact already exist, though before the Panel on the Nonprofit Sector's 2007 Principles, none had applied to the entire range of American charitable organizations.

The pages that follow set forth a comprehensive set of principles that are an updated version of the Panel's work. Their purpose is to reinforce a common understanding of transparency, accountability, and good governance for the sector as a whole—not only to ensure ethical and trustworthy behavior, but equally important, to spotlight strong practices that contribute to the effectiveness, durability, and broad popular support for charitable organizations of all kinds.

The guide includes sections on Legal Compliance and Public Disclosure, Effective Governance, Strong Financial Oversight, and Responsible Fundraising. For the purposes of this book, the sections on Effective Governance and Strong Financial Oversight are included here.

[...]

Effective Governance

Principle 08

A charitable organization must have a governing body that is responsible for reviewing and approving the organization's mission and strategic direction, annual budget and key financial transactions, compensation practices and policies, and fiscal and governance policies.

Principle 09

The board of a charitable organization should meet regularly enough to conduct its business and fulfill its duties.

Principle 10

The board of a charitable organization should establish its own size and structure and review these periodically. The board should have enough members to allow for full deliberation and diversity of thinking on governance and other organizational matters. Except for very small organizations, this generally means that the board should have at least five members.

Principle 11

The board of a charitable organization should include members with the diverse background (including, but not limited to, ethnicity, race, and gender perspectives), experience, and organizational and financial skills necessary to advance the organization's mission.

Principle 12

A substantial majority of the board of a public charity, usually meaning at least two-thirds of its members, should be independent. Independent members should not: (1) be compensated by the organization as employees or independent contractors; (2) have their compensation determined by individuals who are compensated by the organization; (3) receive, directly or indirectly, material financial benefits from the organization except as a member of the charitable class served by the organization; or (4) be related to anyone described above (as a spouse, sibling, parent or child), or reside with any person so described.

Principle 13

The board should hire, oversee, and annually evaluate the performance of the chief executive officer of the organization. It should conduct such an evaluation prior to any change in that officer's compensation, unless there is a multi-year contract in force or the change consists solely of routine adjustments for inflation or cost of living.

Principle 14

The board of a charitable organization that has paid staff should ensure that the positions of chief staff officer, board chair, and board treasurer are held by separate individuals. Organizations without paid staff should ensure that the positions of board chair and treasurer are held by separate individuals.

Principle 15

The board should establish an effective, systematic process for educating and communicating with board members to ensure they are aware of their legal and ethical responsibilities, are knowledgeable about the programs and activities of the organization, and can carry out their oversight functions effectively.

Principle 16

Board members should evaluate their performance as a group and as individuals no less frequently than every three years, and should have clear procedures for removing board members who are unable to fulfill their responsibilities.

Principle 17

Governing boards should establish clear policies and procedures setting the length of terms and the number of consecutive terms a board member may serve.

Principle 18

The board should review organizational and governing instruments no less frequently than every five years.

Principle 19

The board should establish and review regularly the organization's mission and goals and should evaluate, no less frequently than every five years, the organization's programs, goals, and activities to be sure they advance its mission and make prudent use of its resources.

Principle 20

Board members are generally expected to serve without compensation, other than reimbursement for expenses incurred to fulfill their board-related duties. A charitable organization that provides compensation to its board members should use appropriate comparability data to determine the amount to be paid, document the decision, and provide full disclosure to anyone, upon request, of the amount and rationale for the compensation.

Strong Financial Oversight

Principle 21

A charitable organization must keep complete, current, and accurate financial records and ensure strong financial controls are in place. Its board should receive and review timely reports of the organization's financial activities and should have a qualified, independent financial expert audit or review these statements annually in a manner appropriate to the organization's size and scale of operations.

Principle 22

The board of a charitable organization must institute policies and procedures to ensure that the organization (and, if applicable, its subsidiaries) manages and invests its funds responsibly, in accordance with all legal requirements. The full board should review and approve the organization's annual budget and should monitor actual performance against the budget.

Principle 23

A charitable organization should not provide loans (or the equivalent, such as loan guarantees, purchasing or transferring ownership of a residence or office, or relieving a debt or lease obligation) to directors, officers, or trustees.

Principle 24

A charitable organization should spend a significant amount of its annual budget on programs that pursue its mission while ensuring that the organization has sufficient administrative and fundraising capacity to deliver those programs responsibly and effectively.

Principle 25

A charitable organization should establish clear, written policies for paying or reimbursing expenses incurred by anyone conducting business or traveling on behalf of the organization, including the types of expenses that can be paid for or reimbursed and the documentation required. Such policies should require that travel on behalf of the organization is to be undertaken cost-effectively.

Principle 26

A charitable organization should neither pay for nor reimburse travel expenditures for spouses, dependents or others who are accompanying someone conducting business for the organization unless they, too, are conducting such business.

Text courtesy of Independent Sector.

As is clear from these principles, the board holds great responsibility and power over the direction and operations of a charitable organization. Often board members are not theatre professionals, but are people with the social and financial resources to support an organization, and an interest in contributing to the cultural sector. Boards are often strategically composed to include members with various areas of expertise, such as marketing, law, and financial management. In the summer of 2022, the board of DC Woolly Mammoth Theatre Company reminded everyone:

> At the beginning of the nonprofit theatre field, many boards were established as groups of 'Trustees,' as distinct from the 'Directors' that govern corporate shareholder boards. While each theatre's board structure and expectations may be unique, we all have one fundamental role: to hold our theatre's mission – its principal reason for being – in trust for the communities we represent. Holding a theatre in trust this way is quite different than directing its operations. It is a stewardship that requires centering on the art and the artists and trusting their talent and expertise, even as we partner to balance a budget or provide legal and financial oversight. We commit ourselves to that 'trust' at the heart of our job title.[70]

This idea of holding the trust at the heart of the job is inspiring – but how does that show up? Ideally, the board members are holding the executive and artistic leadership accountable to the stated values and mission of the organization. But is that true? According to the State of New York Attorney General Charities Bureau:

> A primary responsibility of a nonprofit's board of directors is to ensure that the organization is accountable for its programs and finances to its contributors, members, the public and government regulators. The development of proper internal controls helps organizations ensure accountability. Accountability requires that the organization comply with all applicable laws and ethical standards; adhere to the organization's mission; create and adhere to conflict of interest, personnel, whistleblower and accounting policies; and protect the rights of members.[71]

Internal controls include "evaluating staff and programs" and "implementing personnel, conflicts of interest and whistleblower policies."[72] Internal controls should also include stewardship of the institution's mission. If the board is responsible for stewarding the mission of the organization, how does it uphold the values of the institution both internally and externally? How does the board hold, not only itself, but the executive leadership of an institution to its promises?

Linette Hwu, board member and former board chair at Woolly Mammoth, explained that in 2018 when their co-founding Artistic Director stepped down, the board was aware that in choosing the next artistic director, the mission of the organization was held by the board: "The power, the ability, the privilege that boards have to hire the leadership of the organization is huge, and the potential that the board therefore has to make change and to make a difference is huge."[73] Describing the board's role in the organization, she explained:

> I think there's that sense of stewardship in terms of the overall relationship to the institution. Obviously, there's a fiduciary relationship, or a fiduciary responsibility as well. In terms of this particular issue, what's interesting is that we are

> always trying to walk that line – maintaining our role as board members and not starting to actually cross into running the theater. That's the responsibility of the Artistic Director, the Managing Director, their teams. When it comes to the overall issue of how people get paid – all of those, let's call it HR kinds of content – we are involved, I would say, to the extent that we need to make sure that the budget that is proposed for any given fiscal year is sound and feels like it is actually focusing on the right things in terms of carrying forward the mission, but we are going to leave the nuts and bolts of managing to the budget up to the staff. Now, having said that, like you know, we have been fortunate in our leadership in that they are actually trying to move the needle in terms of how folks are getting compensated or how much they're getting compensated, and I think that our responsibility related to that is 1: to support it, for sure, and 2: to raise the money that you need to raise in order to be able to support it from a financial perspective.[74]

Obviously our interest focuses on how this value-based accountability trickles down to the production workforce. When asked how the board interacts with production leadership and with the nitty gritty of productions, budgeting, staffing, and operations, Hwu answered:

> I think that is probably considered to be getting in the weeds a little bit. We do want to know who the core leadership team are, and so they come to board meetings, the Production Manager comes to the board meetings and comes to other events that we have, but in terms of making any decisions around staffing or compensation or anything like that, we're not involved with any of that at all.[75]

How do you uphold the mission if you aren't looking at the details?

Inherent to the role of the board is examining the financial details in fulfilling their fiduciary responsibilities:

> The board of directors bears primary responsibility for ensuring that a charitable organization fulfills its obligations in accord with relevant law, its donors, staff and volunteers, clients, and the public at large. The board sets the vision and mission for an organization and establishes the broad policies and strategic direction that enable it to fulfill its charitable purpose. The board must protect the assets of the organization and provide oversight to ensure that its financial, human, and material resources are used appropriately to further its mission and to establish a level of risk tolerance appropriate for its operations. The board is also responsible for setting policies and procedures to ensure that the activities and operations of any affiliates, chapters, or branches subject to its direct or indirect control are consistent with the organization's values and mission.[76]

The governance structure of charitable organizations binds fiduciary responsibility together with the responsibility for setting and upholding the vision and mission. The board is setting and upholding organizational values, fundraising based on these values, and overseeing how the organization uses its resources. How do they know how these values are being activated? Are we assuming a hierarchical structure which relies on one or two individuals, with all of the on-the-ground production matters funneling into the leadership team and then out to the board? This is an enormous responsibility to place on a single executive leader or a pair or leaders, and creates a structure where a large portion of executive leadership's capacity goes into managing this funnel. Describing what she sees as the biggest current challenge for production labor, Nataki Garrett shares:

> We've all inherited an institutional framework that relies on a generation of people and their generosity. And it doesn't matter how big or small your theater is, it's the same at every theater. If your institutional practice is towards some sort of benefacting, then the role of the artistic or executive leader is to convince the benefactor that the work that you do is important. That has to shift.[77]

Discussing the relationship between a theatre and its donors, Anyania Muse raised the idea of "donorship as ownership," describing the mindset: "If I donate my money to a thing, I own the full narrative, the way it runs, the things that it produces, who's allowed to produce them, how often they're allowed to do it."[78] We see this mindset in nonprofit donors and commercial producers/investors alike. Especially coming out of the Pause, and the prevalence of commercial productions naming social justice driven values, these questions resonate. Commercial productions may be less tied to board governance, but there is still a flow of money and the budget is still a values statement. Are the investors aware of what labor practices their money is supporting?

The benefactor model depends on a patron with some kind of social- capital and money who agrees that the work itself has value. Garrett continues:

> The problem with that model is that the hierarchy is already in place, the thing that you do is not as important as the money that is spent to access it. And the people who make sure that everybody has access is also more important than the thing that you do, and the people who have access. And so that has to shift. As an industry, we have to shift away from them. And otherwise, you'll be in organizations in which the people who are working in the rooms and making the art are pitted against the people who are leading those organizations because the donors are not interested in the work that the people are doing, they're not interested in that work. As long as we are focused on donorship as ownership as an industry, we will continue this sort of downward spiral towards failure.[79]

Are we saying that theatre shouldn't be funded by individual donors? Or even foundations? Would a different funding model be better for the workers? Maybe. Because this one isn't working. It is vital to the future of the field that we find a way to have funding sources that recognize and value the labor that goes into making the magic onstage. Given the structure and scale of the US, this will likely rely on government support (a statement which we know opens up another book's worth of questions). We do not have the answers. We just know that change is necessary in order for the American Theatre to evolve toward an ethical model.

To reiterate, we as a field have to do this together. It doesn't work when institutions or productions try to do this on their own. It puts the institutions who are doing the work in a particularly vulnerable position when their funding is at the whim of their potentially less progressive benefactors. It's not until humans have more value than materials that these shifts can really settle into place.

Each and every one of us needs to be doing this work. As individuals, and, more importantly, in systemic ways. This is a call to disrupt the systems in which arts organizations and productions operate. We need to walk down the hallway arm-in-arm to a more sustainable future of theatremaking. We need to kill the Egregore and rebuild. And we must do it together.

NOTES

1 Michael Maag (Resident Lighting Designer, Oregon Shakespeare Festival), interview by the authors, September 2022.
2 American Theatre Editors, "The Sun Sets on Southern Rep," *American Theatre*, July 8, 2022, https://www.americantheatre.org/2022/07/08/the-sun-sets-on-southern-rep/.
3 American Theatre Editors, "New Ohio Theatre to Close This Summer," *American Theatre*, February 24, 2023, https://www.americantheatre.org/2023/02/24/new-ohio-theatre-to-close-this-summer/.
4 American Theatre Editors, "New Ohio Theatre to Close."
5 Lauren Smart, "At Dallas Theater Center, Layoffs and Cutbacks and Cancellations," *American Theatre*, April 19, 2023, https://www.americantheatre.org/2023/04/19/at-dallas-theater-center-layoffs-and-cutbacks-and-cancellations/.
6 Lindsey Wilson, "Dallas Theater Center Has Co-Pros and Familiar Favorites on Tap for 2023–24 Season," *CultureMap Dallas*, June 21, 2023, https://dallas.culturemap.com/news/arts/dallas-theater-center-has-co-pros-and-familiar-favorites-on-tap-for-2023–24-season/.
7 "Save Our Season," Oregon Shakespeare Festival, https://www.osfashland.org/support/save-our-season.
8 Lizzy Acker, "Oregon Shakespeare Festival Says It Needs $2.5 Million to Save Its Season," *The Oregonian*, April 11, 2023, https://www.oregonlive.com/entertainment/2023/04/oregon-shakespeare-festival-says-its-needs-25-million-to-save-its-season.html.
9 Jane Vaughan, "Oregon Shakespeare Festival Says It Needs $2.5 Million to Save the Theater's Future," *Oregon Public Broadcasting*, April 11, 2023, https://www.opb.org/article/2023/04/11/oregon-shakespeare-festival-fest-theater-arts-culture-pacific-northwest-actors-plays/.

10 "Westport Country Playhouse Appeals for 'Immediate' $2M," *Westport Journal*, June 20, 2023, https://westportjournal.com/arts/westport-country-playhouse-appeals-for-immediate-2m/.
11 Rob Weinert-Kendt, "Taper Cuts: L.A.'s CTG Cancels Shows at Flagship Theatre Through 2024," *American Theatre*, June 16, 2023, https://www.americantheatre.org/2023/06/16/taper-cuts-l-a-s-ctg-cancels-shows-at-flagship-theatre-through-2024/.
12 Rob Weinert-Kendt, "Oregon Shakes Restructures, Scales Back with Eye to Future," *American Theatre*, January 13, 2023, https://www.americantheatre.org/2023/01/13/oregon-shakes-restructures-scales-back-with-eye-to-future/.
13 Jesse Cameron Alick, "The Spirit of the Thing: Why the American Theater Can't Change," *Jesse Cameron Alick* (blog), April 5, 2023, https://www.jessecameronalick.com/essays/the-spirit-of-the-thing-why-the-american-theater-cant-change.
14 Alick.
15 Maag, interview.
16 adrienne maree brown, *Emergent Strategy: Shaping Change, Changing Worlds* (Chico, CA: AK Press, 2017): 104.
17 Alick.
18 Rob Jordan, "Do Plastic Straws Really Make a Difference?," *Stanford Earth Matters Magazine*, September 18, 2018, https://earth.stanford.edu/news/do-plastic-straws-really-make-difference.
19 Jordan.
20 brown, 38.
21 brown, 66.
22 Sonali Sangeeeta Balajee, "An Evolutionary Roadmap for Belonging and Co-Liberation," Othering & Belonging, August 29, 2018, http://www.otheringandbelonging.org/evolutionary-roadmap-belonging-co-liberation/.
23 Anyania Muse (Interim Chief Operating Officer, Oregon Shakespeare Festival), interview by the authors, April 2023.
24 Ineke Ceder (Advisory Board Member, Parent Artist Advocacy League) and Rachel Spencer Hewitt (Founder, Parent Artist Advocacy League), interview by the authors, September 2022.
25 Robert Barry Fleming (Executive Artistic Director, Actors Theatre of Louisville), interview by the authors, April 2023.
26 Mary Carole McCauley, "Center Stage's Latina Artistic Director Faced a Racial Reckoning, a Pandemic and a Boardroom Revolt in Tumultuous Tenure," *Baltimore Sun*, March 25, 2023, https://www.baltimoresun.com/entertainment/bs-fe-ybarra-departs-20230323-umhsfbgiwfhsppl3pkgfkqlt6a-story.html.
27 McCauley.
28 Weinert-Kendt.
29 Weinert-Kendt.
30 Edward Steinfeld and Jordana Maisel, *Universal Design: Designing Inclusive Environments* (New York: John Wiley and Sons, 2012): 28.
31 Rohan Mishra, "Universal Design: Design for Everyone," *UX Planet* (blog), October 13, 2018, https://uxplanet.org/universal-design-design-for-everyone-61ded4243658.
32 Mishra.

33 Steinfeld and Maisel, 3.
34 Nick Babich, "What Is Universal Design?," Adobe XD Ideas, July 20, 2021, https://xd.adobe.com/ideas/principles/design-systems/what-is-universal-design/.
35 Babich.
36 Babich.
37 University of Washington, "What Is the Difference Between Accessible, Usable, and Universal Design?," Disabilities, Opportunities, Internetworking, and Technology, May 24, 2022, https://www.washington.edu/doit/what-difference-between-accessible-usable-and-universal-design.
38 "5 Examples of Inclusive Design in the Workplace," Human Resources MBA, https://www.humanresourcesmba.net/lists/5-examples-of-inclusive-design-in-the-workplace/.
39 Dawn Chiang, "Tech Table: We Need a New Design," *Theatre Art Life*, February 13, 2017, https://www.theatreartlife.com/on-the-move/tech-table/.
40 Chiang.
41 Maag, interview.
42 Sarah Lozoff (Co-Founder, Production on Deck), interview by the authors, September 2022.
43 Lozoff, interview.
44 US Bureau of Labor Statistics, "Employment Projections: Education Pays," September 8, 2022, https://www.bls.gov/emp/tables/unemployment-earnings-education.htm.
45 US Bureau of Labor Statistics.
46 Katie Duncan, "Study: Americans Surprised That These High-Paying Jobs Don't Require a College Degree," *JobSage* (blog), March 8, 2023, https://www.jobsage.com/blog/top-jobs-without-degree/.
47 "Earn While You Learn," Apprentice.org, https://apprentice.org/apprenticeship/earn-while-you-learn/.
48 "Apprentice Program," Joint Industry Board of the Electrical Industry, https://www.jibei.org/education-training/apprentice-program/.
49 National Association of Colleges and Employers, "Position Statement: U.S. Internships," August 2018, https://www.naceweb.org/about-us/advocacy/position-statements/position-statement-us-internships/.
50 National Association of Colleges and Employers.
51 We See You, White American Theatre, "BIPOC Demands for White American Theatre," 11, https://static1.squarespace.com/static/5ede42fd6cb927448d9d0525/t/5f064e63f21dd43ad6ab3162/1594248809279/Tier2.pdf.
52 We See You, White American Theatre, 10.
53 "Diversity in Arts Leadership Internship," Americans for the Arts, https://www.americansforthearts.org/about-americans-for-the-arts/internships/diversity-in-arts-leadership-internship.
54 Americans for the Arts, "Diversity in Arts Leadership Internship."
55 Leah Putnam, "Here's How to Apply for SDCF's Revitalized Professional Development Program," *Playbill*, November 8, 2022, https://playbill.com/article/heres-how-to-apply-for-sdcfs-revitalized-professional-development-program.

56 Ronn Smith, "American Theatre Design Since 1945," in *The Cambridge History of American Theatre*, ed. Don B. Wilmeth and Christopher Bigsby, 1st ed. (Cambridge University Press, 2000), 522, https://doi.org/10.1017/CHOL978052166 9597.009.
57 "History of Studio School of Design," Studio School of Design, ttps://studios-choolofdesign.org/history/.
58 Christin Essin, "Coda from Working Backstage," *Theatre Design & Technology: Journal of the United States Institute for Theatre Technology*, Winter 2022, 30.
59 brown, 10.
60 "Our Services," Parent Artist Advocacy League for Performing Arts and Media, https://www.paaltheatre.com/book-online.
61 Fatima Bunafoor (Director of Talent and Equity, Pittsburgh HR/Equity Arts Cohort), interview by the authors, March 2023.
62 Bunafoor, interview.
63 Bunafoor.
64 Bunafoor.
65 Helen Shaw, "Building Trust After Inclusivity Failed: Lessons for the Theater," *Vulture*, June 10, 2023, https://www.vulture.com/2020/06/race-whiteness-black-lives-matter-lessons-for-theater.html.
66 Fleming, interview.
67 Tema Okun, "White Supremacy Culture," White Supremacy Culture, accessed April 17, 2023, https://www.whitesupremacyculture.info.
68 Sarah Clare Corporandy (Co-founder and Producing Artistic Director, Detroit Public Theatre), interview by the authors, September 2022.
69 Independent Sector, "Principles for Good Governance and Ethical Practice: A Guide for Charities and Foundations" (Washington, D.C.: Independent Sector, 2015), 21, https://independentsector.org/wp-content/uploads/2016/11/Principles2015-Web.pdf.
70 "Letter to Fellow Board Members of U.S. Theatres," https://cdn.woollymammoth.net/20221031105318/Dear-Fellow-Board-Members-of-U.S.-Theatres.pdf.
71 New York State Attorney General Charities Bureau, "Internal Controls and Financial Accountability for Not-For-Profit Boards," April 13, 2015, 1, https://ag.ny.gov/sites/default/files/publications/Charities_Internal_Controls.pdf.
72 Charities Bureau, 2.
73 Linette Hwu (Board Member, Woolly Mammoth Theatre Company), interview by the authors, March 2023.
74 Hwu, interview.
75 Hwu, interview.
76 Independent Sector, 21.
77 Garrett, interview.
78 Muse, interview.
79 Garrett, interview.

Appendix A

PRODUCTION WORKER SURVEY

Open July 1, 2022 until August 1, 2022

INTRODUCTION TEXT

We are co-authoring a book about equitable labor in theatrical production, and a key component of our research is surveying designers and technical staff. We invite you to complete this survey by July 31, and encourage you to share it with your networks as well.

Who should complete the survey?
People who have worked in or currently work in design and technical positions for professional theatre in the United States.

How much time does the survey take?
The survey typically takes 15–25 minutes to complete.

How will my responses be used?
Survey responses will be analyzed to generate qualitative and quantitative data which will be used in the book. Gathering data will allow the researchers to more effectively understand the challenges workers are

facing, identify examples of practices that are working well, and develop strategies that are targeted at the most important problems or causal factors.

What is the book about?
This book will explore equitable labor practices in theatrical production. Examining both historical precedence and current circumstances, the book will use case studies of current industry examples to document the progressive initiatives already underway in the field. The authors will investigate data collection, models for analysis, and examples from other fields which can be applied to production in American theater, specifically around gender and race equity, support for caregivers, LGBTQIAA+ representation and safety. The book will provide a series of tools and strategies for performing arts leaders to foster accessibility, representation, inclusion, belonging and sustainability.

What if I have more questions?
You can read more about the project on our website (www.productionlaborbook.com) and email us (equitablelabor@gmail.com) if you have any questions. We'd be delighted to speak with you!

Content Warning
Some of the information we are gathering may bring up harmful memories. Please care for yourself in completing the survey. Please reach out to the Entertainment Community Fund (https://entertainmentcommunity.org) for continued support if you need more resources for care.

Best,
Brídín Clements Cotton & Natalie Robin

INFORMED CONSENT

By entering the survey, you indicate that you have read the information provided at the survey introduction and agree to participate.

FORMAT

() Denotes multiple choice responses where respondents could select a single option only
[ ] Denotes multiple choice responses where respondents could select more than one option
________________________ Denotes fields where respondents could type in their answer

DEMOGRAPHICS

What state do you reside in?
[Options given include all 50 states, the District of Columbia, American Samoa; Guam; Northern Mariana Islands; Puerto Rico; and the Virgin Islands]

What city do you reside in?________________________________

What is your age group?
() Under 20
() 20 to 24
() 25 to 29
() 30 to 34
() 35 to 39
() 40 to 44
() 45 to 49
() 50 to 54
() 55 to 59
() 60 to 64
() 65 to 69
() 70 to 74
() 75 to 79
() 80+
() Prefer not to answer

How would you describe yourself? (Please use the default "Other" option to self-describe if you would prefer.)
[ ] American Indian or Alaska Native
[ ] Asian; Black or African-American
[ ] Hispanic, Latino, Latina or Latinx
[ ] Multi-racial
[ ] Native Hawaiian or Other Pacific Islander
[ ] White
[ ] Prefer Not to Answer
[ ] Other ____________________________

Pronouns ____________________________

Do you identify as (Please use the default "Other" option to self-describe if you would prefer.):
() Cis-gender
() Non-Binary
()Transgender

() Prefer Not to Answer
() Other ________________________

Where do you identify on the following spectrum? (Please use the default "Other" option to self-describe if you would prefer.)
() Male
() Non-Binary
() Female
() Prefer Not to Answer
() Other ________________________

Do you identify as part of the LGBTQIAA+ community?
() Yes
() No
() Prefer Not to Answer

What is the highest degree or level of education you have completed? (Please use the default "Other" option to self-describe if you would prefer.)
() Associate's Degree
() Bachelor's Degree
() High School Degree or Equivalent
() Less than High School
() Master's Degree
() PhD or Higher
() Some College
() Some High School
() Trade School
() Prefer Not to Answer
() Other ________________________

Primary Role(s) when you work/worked in theatrical production (Check All that Apply; Please use the default "Other" option to self-describe if you would prefer.)
[ ] Assistant Sound / Associate Sound Designer
[ ] Associate / Assistant Costume Designer
[ ] Associate / Assistant Lighting Designer
[ ] Associate / Assistant Production Manager
[ ] Associate / Assistant Projection Designer
[ ] Associate / Assistant Set Designer
[ ] Associate / Assistant Technical Director
[ ] Carpenter; Costume Designer
[ ] Costume Shop Manager
[ ] Draper; Dresser

[ ] Electrician
[ ] First Hand
[ ] Fly Person
[ ] Light Board Operator
[ ] Lighting Designer
[ ] Lighting Programmer
[ ] Lighting Supervisor
[ ] Production (Master) Electrician
[ ] Production Assistant; Production Manager
[ ] Production Stage Manager; Projection Designer
[ ] Projection Programmer
[ ] Props Artisan
[ ] Props Master / Props Head
[ ] Rigger
[ ] Scenic Artist / Scenic Painter
[ ] Scenic Charge
[ ] Set Designer
[ ] Sound Board Operator
[ ] Sound Designer
[ ] Sound Engineer / A1
[ ] Sound Engineer / A2
[ ] Stage Manager / Assistant Stage Manager
[ ] Stagehand
[ ] Stitcher
[ ] Technical Director
[ ] Wardrobe Supervisor
[ ] Other ____________________

Is your theater production work primarily as a freelancer or as a staff member?
() Freelancer
() Staff-Member
() Relatively Equal Mix
Are you a union member?
() Yes
() No

If yes, which union/local(s) are you a member of? ________________

What was your individual income in 2019 (pre-pandemic)?
() <$20,000
() $20,000–$40,000
() $40,000–$60,000
() $60,000–$80,000

() $80,000–$100,000
() $100,000–$120,000
() $120,000–$140,000
() $140,000–$160,000
() >$160,000

How much of this is from theater work?
() All
() Most
() About Half
() Some
() Very Little

What was your individual income in 2021 (during pandemic)?
() <$20,000
() $20,000–$40,000
() $40,000–$60,000
() $60,000–$80,000
() $80,000–$100,000
() $100,000–$120,000
() $120,000–$140,000
() $140,000–$160,000
() >$160,000

How much of this is from theater work?
() All
() Most
() About Half
() Some
() Very Little

Workplace Accessibility

Do you identify as neurodivergent?
() Yes
() No
() Prefer Not to Answer

For those who answered "Yes":
When you are employed in theatrical production, do you disclose your neurodivergent status?
() Yes
() No
() Sometimes

Do you receive appropriate accommodations in the theatrical production workplace(s)?
() Yes
() No
() Sometimes

If yes, to what extent do they adequately address your needs?

____

If no, are there workplace accommodations that could benefit you?

____

Do you have a clear avenue for voicing your needs?
() Yes
() No

Outside of your own personal needs and accommodations, in what ways do the theaters you've worked in facilitate an accessible working environment? ________________________________

Are there ways in which theater production workplace(s) could be more accessible for workers?

____

Do you identify as a person with a disability?
() Yes
() No
() Prefer Not to Answer

For those who answered "Yes":

When you are employed in theatrical production, do you disclose your disability status?
() Yes
() No
() Sometimes

Do you receive appropriate accommodations in the theatrical production workplace(s)?
() Yes
() No
() Sometimes

If yes, to what extent do they adequately address your needs?

____

If no, are there workplace accommodations that could benefit you?

____

Do you have a clear avenue for voicing your needs?
() Yes
() No

Outside of your own personal needs and accommodations, in what ways do the theaters you've worked in facilitate an accessible working environment? ______________________________

Are there ways your theater production workplace(s) could be more accessible for workers?

____

Caregivers

Are you a caregiver?
() Yes
() No

For those who answered "Yes":
Are you caring for:
[ ] Own Child/Children
[ ] Another Child/Children
[ ] Older Adult(s)
[ ] Disabled Adult(s)
[ ] Other ________________________

Are you a solo caregiver?
() Yes
() No
() Sometimes

If you have a co-caregiver, do they also work in theater production?
() Yes
() No

Do you have family or community support?
() Yes
() No
() Sometimes

Do you pay for caregiving?
() Yes
() No
() Sometimes

Are there instances where your theatrical production workplace has been supportive of your caregiving responsibilities? Please describe.
____

GETTING WORK

At any point in your career, have you participated in any unpaid theatrical production internships?
() Yes
() No

For those who answered "Yes":
How many unpaid internships have you participated in?
() 1
() 2
() 3
() 4
() 5+

What factors did you consider in deciding in taking/not taking an unpaid internship?
[ ] Access to the Arts/Art Making
[ ] Cost of Living
[ ] Cost of Travel
[ ] Future Work Opportunities
[ ] Professional Connections
[ ] Professional Credits
[ ] School Requirement

Did any of those internships directly affect your career trajectory in ways that you can identify?
() Yes
() No

How? ______________________________

When working in theater production, have you accepted any job(s) that paid less than minimum wage?
() Yes
() No
For those who answered "Yes":

Did any of those jobs directly affect your career trajectory in ways you can identify?
() Yes
() No

How? ___________________________________

Some of the information we are gathering may bring up harmful memories. Please care for yourself in completing the survey. Please reach out to the Entertainment Community Fund (https://entertainmentcommunity.org) for continued support if you need more resources for care.

How do you typically find out about available theatrical production jobs? (e.g. word of mouth, job postings, listserv, etc.)______________________
____

What sort of contracts are you hired under?
[ ] Union Collectively Bargained Agreement
[ ] Union Project Only Agreement
[ ] Non-Union LOA
[ ] No Contract
[ ] Other ________________________

When did you last go through a formal application process for a theatrical production position?
() Less than 6 months ago
() Between 6 to 12 months ago
() More than a year ago
() Other ________________________

How did you hear about your theatrical production current job(s) or position(s)?
[ ] Emailed Job Posting
[ ] Recommendation
[ ] Public Job Posting on Free Site
[ ] Public Job Posting on Pay-to-View Site
[ ] Word of Mouth
[ ] Other ________________________

When did you last go through a formal interview process for a theatrical production position?
() Less than 6 months ago
() Between 6 to 12 months ago
() More than a year ago
() Never
() Other ________________________

Describe the steps of the formal interview process. ___________________
____

Who do you meet with in the formal interview process?
[ ] Artistic Director
[ ] General Manager
[ ] Production Manager
[ ] Department Head
[ ] Other ________________________

At what point in the recruitment process do you typically know what a theatrical production job pays?
[ ] Before Applying
[ ] At the Interview
[ ] When you Were Offered the Job
[ ] Other ________________________

Did you have to ask?
() Yes
() No

When seeking theatrical production employment, how often do you experience each of the following?

How often do you have to fill out a formal job application?
() Never
() Rarely
() Sometimes
() Often
() Always

How often do you have a formal interview process?
() Never
() Rarely
() Sometimes

() Often
() Always

How often have you started on a project without a signed contract?
() Never
() Rarely
() Sometimes
() Often
() Always

How often have you accepted a job without knowing the pay?
() Never
() Rarely
() Sometimes
() Often
() Always

Have you seen projects or institutions make positive changes in hiring processes and practices? ________________________

Do you feel comfortable talking with your colleagues about your pay (salary or fees)?
() Yes
() No

Have you been aware of pay discrepancies between colleagues on a single production, within a season, or within an institution?
() Yes
() No

Have you spoken up about pay discrepancies?
() Yes
() No

In inequitable situations, who do you talk to?
[ ] Colleague
[ ] Department Head/Supervisor
[ ] HR Officer
[ ] Production Manager
[ ] Union Steward
[ ] Union Representative
[ ] Other ________________________

Have you felt protected/supported in having these conversations?
() Yes
() No
() Sometimes

Did the situation change?
() Yes
() No
() Sometimes

Have you seen performing arts institutions or producers make positive changes in pay equity? ______________________________

Do you feel that your identities have impacted whether or not you have gotten a theater production job?
() Yes
() No
Please explain. ______________________________

Do you feel your identities have impacted your decision to take a theater production job?
() Yes
() No
Please explain. ______________________________

ON THE JOB

Have you ever felt physically unsafe in your theatrical production workplace(s)?
() Yes
() No

Have you ever felt mentally/emotionally unsafe in your theatrical production workplace(s)?
() Yes
() No
In unsafe situations, who do you talk to?
[ ] Colleague
[ ] Department Head / Supervisor
[ ] HR Officer
[ ] Production Manager
[ ] Union Steward
[ ] Union Representative
[ ] Other __________________________

Have you felt protected/supported in these conversations?
() Yes
() No
() Sometimes

Did the situation(s) change?
() Yes
() No
() Sometimes

What changes would you like to see to increase theatrical production workplace safety? ______________________

What measures have you seen taken to increase theatrical production workplace safety? ______________________

Were these changes institutional or personal?
() Institutional
() Personal
() Both]

How were they received? ______________________

How do you define workplace safety? ______________________

Do you have clear performance development goals in your theatrical production workplace(s)?
() Yes
() No
() Sometimes
() Unsure

Do you have a clear supervisor in your theatrical production workplace(s)?
() Yes
() No
() Sometimes
() Unsure
How do you receive feedback on your work?
[ ] In-Person from Production's Director
[ ] In-Person from Staff you Supervise
[ ] In-Person from Supervisor
[ ] Performance Review Meeting with Supervisor
[ ] Post-Mortem Meeting with Production Team

[ ] Written Feedback from Production's Director
[ ] Written Feedback from Staff you Supervise
[ ] Written Feedback from Supervisor
[ ] Other ______________________

Is this feedback primarily artistic?
() Yes
() No
() Sometimes

Do you typically have a way to give feedback to your supervisor?
() Yes
() No
() Unsure

How many hours do you work in a typical work week? ______________________

Do your typical jobs use the 10 out of 12 (or 10 out of 11 and half)?
() Yes
() No

How many days off do you have in a typical work week? ______________________

Are you expected to respond to emails, calls, etc. on those days off?
() Yes
() No
() Sometimes

Is there a system in place if you need to miss work for illness or other emergencies?
() Yes
() No

Does your contract lay out a work schedule?
() Yes
() No
() Sometimes

Can you provide an example of a performing arts institution or project that had an inclusive work culture? ______________________

Can you provide an example of a performing arts institution or project that did not have an inclusive work culture? ___________________________

Do you feel that your identities have impacted how you have been treated in a theater production workplace?
() Yes
() No
Please explain. ___________________________

When working in theatrical production, how often do you experience the following:

How often have you felt affected by actions or words directed at you personally, based on your identity?
() Never
() Rarely
() Sometimes
() Often
() Always

How often have you felt affected by indirect actions or words, or other cultural aspects of a workplace-based on your identity?
() Never
() Rarely
() Sometimes
() Often
() Always

How often do you feel that you experience microaggressions in the workplace?
() Never
() Rarely
() Sometimes
() Often
() Always

Do you feel your identities have impacted your decision to leave a theater production job or the field?
() Yes
() No
Please explain. ___________________________

CONTACT INFORMATION

Though this survey is anonymous, if you would like to be contacted with follow up questions or for a potential interview, please complete the below information.

Will my name be used in the book?
No – based solely on your completion of the survey, your data would only be used anonymously. Survey respondents can choose to be anonymous or to include their contact information for potential follow-up. If a respondent chooses to include their contact information, the authors may follow up to further discuss your responses. The authors will contact any survey participant before using their name, even if you choose to share your contact information. Though we are not encrypting the data, we are not collecting personally identifiable information. We will not share any individual person's data in a way that is identifiable beyond shared anecdotes or examples shared by you in the survey.

First Name ______________________

Last Name ______________________

Email Address ______________________

Thank you!

Thank you for completing this survey. A key component of our research is the data we gather from people who have worked in the field, and we so appreciate your taking the time to share your experience.

You can find out more about the book at our website: https://productionlaborbook.com

We acknowledge that completing the survey can bring up harmful memories. Please reach out to the Entertainment Community Fund (https://entertainmentcommunity.org) for continued support if you need more resources for care.

Appendix B

PRODUCTION EMPLOYER SURVEY

Open July 11, 2022 until August 12, 2022

INTRODUCTION TEXT

We are co-authoring a book about equitable labor in theatrical production, and a key component of our research is surveying performing arts organizations. We invite you to complete this survey on behalf of your organization by August 12. Below please find more information about the survey and the book:

Who should complete the survey?

We are seeking data from professional theatre employers in the U.S. We request a single response per organization. We have tried to identify relevant contacts in your organization (management, production, communications) but please share with the appropriate members of your team as you see fit.

How will my institution's responses be used?

Survey responses will be analyzed to generate qualitative and quantitative data which will be used in the book. Gathering data will allow the researchers to more effectively understand the challenges workers are facing, identify examples of practices that are working well, and develop strategies that are targeted at the most important problems or causal factors. Individual examples from specific institutions may be cited. Though we are not encrypting the data, we are not collecting personally identifiable information. We will not share any individual person's data or information.

What is the book about?

This book will explore equitable labor practices in theatrical production. Examining both historical precedence and current circumstances, the book will use case studies of current industry examples to document the progressive initiatives already underway in the field. The authors will investigate data collection, models for analysis, and examples from other fields which can be applied to production in American theater, specifically around gender and race equity, support for caregivers, LGBTQIAA+ representation and safety. The book will provide a series of tools and strategies for performing arts leaders to foster accessibility, representation, inclusion, belonging and sustainability.

When will the book be published?

The book is expected to be published in early 2024 by Routledge, an imprint of Taylor & Francis Group.

What if I have more questions?

You can read more about the project on our website www.productionlaborbook.com or email us at equitablelabor@gmail.com. We'd be delighted to speak with you!

Best,

Brídín Clements Cotton & Natalie Robin

INFORMED CONSENT

By entering the survey, you indicate that you have read the information provided at the survey introduction and agree to participate.

FORMAT

() Denotes multiple choice responses where respondents could select a single option only

[] Denotes multiple choice responses where respondents could select more than one option

______________________________ Denotes fields where respondents could type in their answer

BASIC INFORMATION

Who is completing this survey (name(s)/job title(s))?

____

Organization/Institution? ___________________________

In what state is your institution?
(Options given include all 50 states, the District of Columbia, American Samoa; Guam; Northern Mariana Islands; Puerto Rico; and the Virgin Islands)

In what city is your institution? ___________________________

Does your institution employ unionized labor?
() Yes
() No
() Partially

Which unions are included in your institution's production work? ___________________________

EDUCATION & INTERNSHIPS

Does your institution have production internships?
() Yes
() No

For those who answered "Yes":
Are internships paid or unpaid?
() Paid
() Unpaid

If paid, how much? ___________________________

Describe the internship application and selection process. E.g. Is there a job description? Where does it get posted? What is the Interview process like? ___________________________

List the types of responsibilities or tasks of your production interns: ___________________________

What is a typical production intern work schedule? ___________________________

Does this differ by department?
() Yes
() No
() Unsure

If so, how? ____________________________

Is interning with your organization a path to potential employment at your institution?
() Yes
() No

If so, please explain. ____________________________

Who is the supervisor for production interns?

____

What structures are in place for onboarding new interns?

____

What structures are in place for evaluations and feedback throughout the internship? ____________________________

What structures are in place for evaluations and feedback at the end of the internship? ____________________________

What education opportunities are in place for your interns?

____

HIRING PRACTICES

Describe the designer application and selection process? E.g. Is there a job description? Where does it get posted? What is the Interview process like?

____

Describe the technical staff and technicians application and selection process? E.g. Is there a job description? Where does it get posted? What is the Interview process like? ____________________________

If a designer or technician is interested in working with your organization, how do they connect with you? ____________________________

Is this publicly posted?
() Yes
() No
() Other ____________________________

For every production, is there an interview process for each design position?
() Yes
() No
() Other ______________________________

Who is involved in hiring designers? ______________________________

Which staff members manage the hiring process?

____

Which staff members make the hiring decisions?

____

Is pay and type of contract listed in the job description for designers?
() Yes
() No
() Other ______________________________

Is pay and type of contract listed in the job description for technicians and technical staff?
() Yes
() No
() Other ______________________________

HR PRACTICES

What is the process for onboarding designers and technical staff

____

Who do designers report to? ______________________________

Who do technical staff report to? ______________________________

Does the institutional HR staff support production personnel?
() Yes
() No
() Other ______________________________

Do you have clear performance development goals in the workplace for designers?
() Yes
() No
() Unsure

() Other ____________________________
How do they receive feedback? ____________________________

Do you have clear performance development goals in the workplace for technical staff and technicians?

() Yes
() No
() Unsure
() Other ____________________________

How do they receive feedback? ____________________________

At the end of a project, what is the feedback and evaluation process? ____________________________

PRODUCTION OPERATIONS

Describe a typical production schedule. ____________________________

Please attach an examples [option to attach a file]

What are the typical work hours for designers? ____________________________

What are the typical work hours for assistant designers? ____________________________

What are the typical work hours for technical staff and technicians? ____________________________

At the most intense period of the process, what are the work hours for designers? ____________________________

At the most intense period of the process, what are the work hours for assistant designers? ____________________________

At the most intense period of the process, what are the work hours for technical staff and technicians? ____________________________

How many days off do designers have in a typical work week? ____________________________

How many days off do assistant designers have in a typical work week? ____________________________

How many days off do technical staff and technicians have in a typical work week? ______________________

At the most intense period of the process, how many days off do designers have? ______________________

At the most intense period of the process, how many days off do assistant designers have? ______________________

At the most intense period of the process, how many days off do technical staff and technicians have? ______________________

What if any changes have you made to your production schedules following the COVID-19 pandemic pause? ______________________

Is the institutional budget publicly available?
() Yes
() No
() Other ______________________

Are production budgets publicly available?
() Yes
() No
() Other ______________________

Are institutional budgets available to staff hired (directors, designers, etc.) to work on productions?
() Yes
() No
() Other ______________________

Are production budgets available to staff hired (directors, designers, etc.) to work on productions?
() Yes
() No
() Other ______________________

Who creates the production budget? ______________________

How much do they vary from production to production?
() Production budgets are the same for all productions.
() Production budgets are relatively similar for all productions.
() Production budgets vary somewhat depending on the production.
() Production budgets vary drastically depending on the production.

What are the main variables that impact differences in production budgets? ______________________________

SUPPORTING WORKERS

Describe your institution's support for caregivers working in production. ______________________________

Describe your institution's support for production personnel with physical and/or cognitive disabilities. ______________________________

Describe your institution's support for neurodivergent workers in production. ______________________________

How does your institution define workplace safety? ______________________________

In unsafe situations, who do workers report to? ______________________________

What measures has the institution taken to increase safety? ______________________________

How does your institution promote an inclusive work culture in production? ______________________________

Is there an established procedure for workers to report concerns in the production workplace?
() Yes
() No
() Unsure
() Other ______________________________

When there are conflicts or concerns in the production workplace, how are they handled? ______________________________

Thank you!

Thank you for completing this survey. A key component of our research is the data we gather from performing arts institutions, and we so appreciate your taking the time to share on behalf of your institution.

You can find out more about the book at our website: https://productionlaborbook.com

Appendix C

WAYNE CARINO

Data Methodology

This section summarizes the data methodologies used for the worker survey conducted in July 2022. Data methodologies and workflows described primarily focuses on the cleaning process and how the outputs produced were used for exploratory analysis. Multiple tools were utilized in order to appropriately clean and analyze the data including Microsoft Excel and Tableau.

- **Survey Period:** July 1st, 2022–August 1st, 2022
- **Number of Respondents (Records):** 1,037 Respondents
- **Step 1:** Preparing the Foundational File for Data Cleaning
- **Step 2:** Creating the Export Files
- **Step 3:** Creating the Unclean, Clean, and Groupings Files
- **Step 4:** Joining the Data

Workflow Documentation

1) Preparing the Foundational File for Data Cleaning

Description: Export files contain all the information from the raw data export in order to cross-analyze data once the data is completely cleaned and prepared for analysis. Before export files were created, a unique ID was calculated for each row from the raw data Google Forms export. This copy with the unique ID column added was used as the foundational data file for cleaning.

- **File Created:** Google Form Export + Unique ID Column
- **Reshaping Questions:** Questions within the worker survey were pivoted/reshaped in order to create a longer data format instead of a wide format the raw data was in.
- **Splitting:** The data were split (divided into multiple parts) for questions that had multiple checkboxes (respondents were able to check multiple answers). For questions that had "Other" as answer choice, some of the data values may not have split as intended. This issue was addressed in the unclean files section.
- **Reshaping Answer Split Values:** The answer split values were then reshaped again to prepare for analysis.
- **File Created:** Clean Worker Survey Analysis

2) Creating the Export Files
Description: After preparing the foundational file for data cleaning, this file is then imported into Tableau to recode a set of demographics including race/ethnicity, education, and gender. After recoding the demographic data values, this file will serve as the basis file for analyzing demographic data. A separate demographic file is created to help speed/load times in Tableau. From here, open the demographic file and create a crosstab in Tableau that mirrors the format. Filter for each reshaped question and export each file. These files will be used when joining the data.

- **Import the Clean Worker Survey Analysis in Tableau:** Create crosstabs of the original demographic values and the recoded demographic values.
- **Recode Demographic Values:** Group data values in their respective categories.
- **File Created:** Demographic Analysis – Clean Worker Survey
- **Create Export Files:** After creating the demographic file, create a crosstab in Tableau that mirrors the file's format and filter for reach reshaped question to create the export files.
- **Files Created:** Export Files (Folder)

3) Creating the Unclean, Clean, and Groupings Files
Description: Data values were recoded in order to clean the various answers represented in the "Other" answer choice. This was cleaned by creating "unclean files" that only had 1 response by unique ID after splitting the respondent's answers by reshaped question. A crosstab from Tableau is exported, then a reference worksheet is created in order to create a filter.

Ungrouped answers were placed into a "unclean file" for that particular question. All unclean files were reviewed by data value manually labeled.

- **Import Clean Worker Survey Analysis in Tableau:** Create crosstabs for each reshaped question and filter for answers split counts that equal 1. Export these crosstabs into a folder.
- **Prepare a Reference Worksheet:** Create a reference worksheet with data values form the worker survey. Use the reference worksheet and answer split counts to create a filter.
- **Creating Unclean Files:** For answer split values that are not referenced (ungrouped answers), create a new Excel workbook with these values for each reshaped question. Create a manual grouping column in each file for review. Each data value were labeled and if a new row was created, it was highlighted with the appropriate unique ID referenced. After unclean files are labeled, sort these into a clean files folder.
- **Files Created:** Clean Files (Folder)
- **Creating Groupings Files**: For unclean file, separate the reshaped question, the respondent's answers, and the manual grouping label. Save groupings files as csv to help speed/load times in Tableau.
- **Files Created:** Groupings Files (Folder)

4) Joining the Data

Description: Joins are conducted for each reshaped question in order to group the data values as reviewed. All joins uses a left join. The join clause relationship is based on the unique ID of each record/row. The output file after creating a left join is a merge file for each reshaped question. Each output file from a join will be used to analyze each respective question since they have different data formats and number of records.

- **Left Side of Join Venn Diagram:** Export Files
- **Right Side of Join Venn Diagram:** Groupings Files
- **Applied Join Clause (Relationship):** Unique ID
- **Join Type:** Left Join
- **Files Created:** Merge Files (Folder)

Acknowledgements

This project was supported by the University of the Arts Faculty and Academic Development Fund. This project was funded in part through a publication grant from NYU Abu Dhabi. In addition, our final writing retreat was possible due to professional development support from NYUAD.

We are grateful for the resources and case studies from the following individuals, collectives, and organizations: Twi McCallum's open letter to the Theatre Community as published in BroadwayWorld, North Carolina Theatre Conference with the "Making Theatre Hiring More Equitable, Diverse and Inclusive" guide, NO MORE 10 Out Of 12's Working Group with "Why no more 10 out of 12's?", the Parent Artist Advocacy League for Performing Arts + Media (PAAL) with the "New Standard of Care for Caregivers", Behind the Scenes Foundation's Mental Health Initiative with "Put Together Your Toolbox Talk", the universal design principles from NC State University's Center for Universal Design, the apprenticeship information from The Electrical Industry of IBEW Local Union No. 3, and Independent Sector with "Principles for Good Governance and Ethical Practice".

This project is the result of tremendous generosity from many, many people. Thank you,

Amy Holzapfel and Fadi Skeiker, for your early guidance. Emily Rea, for your time and confidence.

Meg Friedman and David J. McGraw, for going out of your way to compile your data for this use. Porsche McGovern, for setting an example of how powerful the numbers can be, and for sharing your learnings on the how of it.

Wayne Carino, for demystifying the data. Delaney Teehan, for strengthening the research. Christie Debelius, for caring for the details. Noah Mease, for your energizing illustrations. Carmen Morgan, for your powerful words.

Aedín Clements, Will Cotton, Allison Krumsiek, Carolyn Mraz, for your thoughtful feedback as the very first ones to read any part of this text. Sherrice Mojgani, Kathleen Mulligan, Cherie B. Tay, Joshua Webb, and Delaney (again), for your generosity and wisdom as the first to read the entire text.

The 21 individuals who took the time to speak with us; for sharing your thoughts, your questions, your experiences, your joys, your traumas, your fears, and your hopes.

The 23 institutions who provided insight into your workplace cultures; for your transparency in sharing this information, and for being a part of this movement.

The 1,037 current and former production workers who shared your stories with us; thank you. For clicking through every single section of that incredibly long form. For your frankness, your vulnerability, your humor, and for your work.

And to everyone who has worked in production within and in spite of these broken systems, everyone who has and will work to change them, and everyone who comes after us to make it better.

FROM BRÍDÍN

So many more people than I can list have shaped me and this work. I am overflowing with gratitude.

Thank you, to my family, for your unwavering trust in me and in this project, and for instilling in me a deep belief in social justice.

Thank you, to my Kalamazoo community, for helping me discover my place as a theatremaker and as an activist, and for nurturing my love of books.

Thank you, to my NYU Tisch community, for supporting me through so many things, and for empowering me to develop my own voice. I am grateful to have such a badass team of mentors in my corner.

I am fortunate to now call one of those mentors my co-author. Thank you, Natalie, for embarking on this journey together, for finding the words for it all, and for showing up with kindness, patience, and humor every day of this process.

To the ones who keep me going: thank you. This has been a year of risktaking, made possible by the care and adaptability of my remarkable crew of friends. Thank you for sharing, for listening, for supporting this project directly and indirectly, and for being who you are, each of you. I am because we are.

Lastly, to my two constants. My mother and confidante, Aedín. And my love, Will. For your endless support… Thank you both for never saying no to talking about this project; for asking thoughtful questions; for giving critical feedback; for taking care of me; for challenging me; and for encouraging me, always.

FROM NATALIE

It would be impossible to thank everyone who supports me and my work or the work of this book.

Thank you to all of my many, many colleagues, friends, mentors and students who work in production and have taught me more than I can say.

Thank you to the membership of USA 829 for putting their faith in me as a leader. And to the members of governance and union staff who I am so lucky to serve with.

Thank you to Brí for inviting me to go on this journey, for working through the hard questions and the hard collaborations and for inspiring me every day with your dedication, passion and sense of humor – and your true love of doughnuts.

Thank you to Carl Mulert who has supported me from day one and who took a giant risk hiring me as a full time organizer.

Thank you to Lenore Doxsee whose daily impact on my life, even after her passing, is immeasurable.

Thank you to Susan, Carolyn, Maggie-Kate, Sandy, Tim, Sarah, Allison, Rose, Zach, Rebecca, and everyone who holds me together on all of the days I can't do it alone.

Thank you to my mom who has supported me in every insane idea from the day I called to tell her I wasn't going to be a doctor to the day I told her I was quitting my job in academia to work in Labor and every day before, after and in-between. And to my dad who did the same and whose memory is, in fact, both a blessing and a revolution.

Bibliography

Abe, Emika, Connie G. Deckard, Kelvin Dinkins, Jr., Stephanie Rolland, and Sarah Williams. "LORT Equitable Recruitment and Hiring Guide." New York, NY: League of Resident Theatres, 2017. https://lort.org/assets/documents/LORT-EQUITABLE-RECRUITMENT-AND-HIRING-GUIDE_2017.pdf.

Actors' Equity Association. "Agreement and Rules Governing Employment in Resident Theatres." New York, NY: Actors' Equity Association, 2017.

Actors Fund. "Survey of Entertainment Professionals Helped by The Actors Fund." New York, NY: The Actors Fund, March 2021. https://drive.google.com/file/d/1LlCjCTsl7jUFxoDYok59YDRa-EH7plHx/view.

ADP. "Pay Equity." https://www.adp.com/resources/articles-and-insights/articles/p/pay-equity.aspx.

AFL-CIO. "Our Labor History Timeline." https://aflcio.org/about-us/history.

AFL-CIO. "Triangle Shirtwaist Fire." https://aflcio.org/about/history/labor-history-events/triangle-shirtwaist-fire.

"Agreement By and Between the Off-Broadway League and United Scenic Artists, Local USA 829, IATSE," April 22, 2021. https://static1.squarespace.com/static/60be748b0b55be0c7e119dab/t/62bdb8fac461613318df8da1/1656600826797/USAOBLAgreement+21-25+FE-compressed.pdf.

Alcorn, Narda E., and Lisa Porter. "We Commit to Anti-Racist Stage Management Education." *HowlRound Theatre Commons*, July 28, 2020. https://howlround.com/we-commit-anti-racist-stage-management-education.

Alexander, Philip Andrew. "Staging Business: A History of the United Scenic Artists, 1895-1995"." PhD diss., City University of New York, 1999.

Alick, Jesse Cameron. "Emerging from the Cave: Reimagining Our Future in Theater and Live Performance." Park City, UT: Sundance Institute, August 2021. https://drive.google.com/file/d/1AGGaIDFdh_pTT92RewhSLOfZWEYhSHoo/view.

Alick, Jesse Cameron. "The Spirit of the Thing: Why the American Theater Can't Change." *Jesse Cameron Alick* (blog), April 5, 2023. https://www.jessecameronalick.com/essays/the-spirit-of-the-thing-why-the-american-theater-cant-change.

Altman, Alex. "Why the Killing of George Floyd Sparked an American Uprising." *Time*, June 4, 2020. https://time.com/5847967/george-floyd-protests-trump/.

American Academy of Arts and Sciences. "The Arts and Public Education." Art for Life's Sake: The Case for Arts Education, 2021. https://www.amacad.org/publication/case-for-arts-education/section/2.

American Theatre Editors. "New Ohio Theatre to Close This Summer." *American Theatre*, February 24, 2023. https://www.americantheatre.org/2023/02/24/new-ohio-theatre-to-close-this-summer/.

American Theatre Editors. "The Sun Sets on Southern Rep." *American Theatre*, July 8, 2022. https://www.americantheatre.org/2022/07/08/the-sun-sets-on-southern-rep/.

American Theatre Wing. "Springboard to Design." https://americantheatrewing.org/program/springboard-to-design/.

Americans for the Arts. "Diversity in Arts Leadership Internship." https://www.americansforthearts.org/about-americans-for-the-arts/internships/diversity-in-arts-leadership-internship.

Apprentice.org. "Earn While You Learn." https://apprentice.org/apprenticeship/earn-while-you-learn/.

Arts, Crafts, and Theater Safety. "What Is ACTS?" https://www.artscraftstheatersafety.org/aboutacts.html.

Associated Press. "3 of the Biggest Broadway Shows Reopen with COVID Rules." *NPR*, September 14, 2021. https://www.npr.org/2021/09/14/1037194157/3-big-broadway-shows-reopen-with-covid-rules.

Association of Art Museum Directors. "Association of Art Museum Directors Passes Resolution Urging Art Museums to Provide Paid Internships," June 20, 2019. https://aamd.org/for-the-media/press-release/association-of-art-museum-directors-passes-resolution-urging-art-museums.

Audra McDonald. "Announcing Black Theatre United." https://audramcdonald.com/announcing-black-theatre-united/.

Axelrod Performing Arts Center. "Hiring: Master Electrician." Playbill. https://web.archive.org/web/20220927194713/https://playbill.com/job/hiring-master-electrician/752f376f-84ee-4679-b6a0-81fa27dcb814.

Babich, Nick. "What Is Universal Design?" Adobe XD Ideas, July 20, 2021. https://xd.adobe.com/ideas/principles/design-systems/what-is-universal-design/.

Bader, Jenny Lyn. "A Brief History of the Gender Parity Movement in Theatre." *Women in Theatre Journal Online*, March 18, 2017. https://witonline.org/2017/03/18/on-the-gender-parity-movement-jenny-lyn-bader/.

Balajee, Sonali Sangeeeta. "An Evolutionary Roadmap for Belonging and Co-Liberation." Othering&Belonging, August 29, 2018. http://www.otheringandbelonging.org/evolutionary-roadmap-belonging-co-liberation/.

Bateman, Nicole, and Martha Ross. "The Pandemic Hurt Low-Wage Workers the Most--and So Far, the Recovery Has Helped Them the Least." Brookings Metro's COVID-19 Analysis. Washington, D.C.: Brookings Institute, July 28, 2021. https://www.brookings.edu/research/the-pandemic-hurt-low-wage-workers-the-most-and-so-far-the-recovery-has-helped-them-the-least/.

Behind the Scenes. "BTS Home." https://wp.behindthescenescharity.org.

Bellinger, Bear. "Production on Deck: Eliminating Excuses." *PLSN: Production Lights and Staging News*, February 4, 2022. https://plsn.com/articles/stage-directions-articles/production-on-deck-eliminating-excuses-2.

Berkeley People and Culture. "Performance Management - Definition." In *Guide to Managing Human Resources*. Berkeley, CA: University of California Berkeley. https://hr.berkeley.edu/hr-network/central-guide-managing-hr/managing-hr/managing-successfully/performance-management/concepts.

Berkshire Art Center. "Berkshire/Columbia Counties Arts Organizations Launch Regional Pay Equity Initiative." November 14, 2022. https://berkshireartcenter.org/news/equitysurvey2022.

Black Theatre Coalition. "BTC Application Portal." https://btc.smapply.io/.

Black Theatre Coalition. "Home." https://blacktheatrecoalition.org.

Black Theatre Coalition. "Who We Are." https://blacktheatrecoalition.org/who-we-are/.

Black Theatre United. "A New Deal for Broadway: Equity, Diversity, Inclusion, Accessibility & Belonging in the Theatrical Industry," 2021. http://www.blacktheatreunited.com/wp-content/uploads/2022/05/BTU-New-Deal-For-Broadway.pdf.

Black Theatre United. "Timeline." https://www.blacktheatreunited.com/portfolio/timeline/.

Black Theatre United. "Who We Are." https://www.blacktheatreunited.com/portfolio/who-we-are/.

Blumberg, Sophie, Jonathan Secor, and Ben Johnson. "Perspectives on Safety and Sustainability for Venues and Cultural Spaces." *HowlRound Theatre Commons*, October 5, 2021. https://howlround.com/perspectives-safety-and-sustainability-venues-and-cultural-spaces.

Bolli, Thomas, Katherine Caves, and Maria Esther Oswald-Egg. "Valuable Experience: How University Internships Affect Graduates' Income." *Research in Higher Education* 62, no. 8 (December 2021): 1198–1247. https://doi.org/10.1007/s11162-021-09637-9.

brown, adrienne maree. *Emergent Strategy: Shaping Change, Changing Worlds*. Chico, CA: AK Press, 2017. http://ebookcentral.proquest.com/lib/nyulibrary-ebooks/detail.action?docID=4548573.

Brown, Lorraine. "A Story Yet to Be Told: The Federal Theatre Research Project." *The Black Scholar* 10, no. 10 (July 1979): 70–78. https://doi.org/10.1080/00064246.1979.11412728.

Brownlow-Calkin, Rosie. "The Theatre Industry's Internship Problem." *American Theatre*, September 10, 2021. https://www.americantheatre.org/2021/09/10/the-theatre-industrys-internship-problem/.

Brownlow-Calkin, Rosie. "To Be or Not to Be: Theatres Brace for Another Season of Uncertainty." *American Theatre*, October 26, 2020. https://www.americantheatre.org/2020/10/26/to-be-or-not-to-be-theatres-brace-for-another-season-of-uncertainty/.

Buckley, Cara. "Sued Over Pay, Condé Nast Ends Internship Program." *New York Times*, October 23, 2013. https://www.nytimes.com/2013/10/24/business/media/sued-over-pay-conde-nast-ends-internship-program.html.

Bunafoor, Fatima. Interview by authors. March 2023.

California State University, Fullerton. "Cost of Attendance." https://www.fullerton.edu/financialaid/ugrd/coa.php.

Carlson, Jen. "A Guide to New York City's Reopening." *Gothamist*, June 8, 2020. https://gothamist.com/news/guide-new-york-city-reopening-phases.

Carpi, Raffaele, John Douglas, and Frédéric Gascon. "Performance Management: Why Keeping Score Is So Important, and So Hard." McKinsey and Company, October 4, 2017. https://www.mckinsey.com/capabilities/operations/our-insights/performance-management-why-keeping-score-is-so-important-and-so-hard.

Ceder, Ineke, and Rachel Spencer Hewitt. Interview by authors. September 2022.

Challenging White Supremacy Workshop. "White Supremacy." https://www.cwsworkshop.org/pdfs/WIWS/Defn_White_Supremacy.PDF.

Chartered Institute of Personnel and Development. "Performance Management: An Introduction." August 17, 2022. https://www.cipd.org/uk/knowledge/factsheets/performance-factsheet/#gref.

Chiang, Dawn. "Tech Table: We Need a New Design." *Theatre Art Life*, February 13, 2017. https://www.theatreartlife.com/on-the-move/tech-table/.

Chowdhury, Sabrin. "How Effective Goal-Setting Motivates Employees." McKinsey and Company. People and Organization, December 27, 2017. https://www.mckinsey.com/capabilities/people-and-organizational-performance/our-insights/the-organization-blog/how-effective-goal-setting-motivates-employees.

Chukwujama, Chuma. "A Guide to the HR Lifecycle." *LinkedIn*, November 30, 2018. https://www.linkedin.com/pulse/guide-hr-lifecycle-chuma-chukwujama/.

Clean Clothes Campaign. "Gender: Women Workers Mistreated." https://cleanclothes.org/issues/gender.

Clement, Olivia. "300 BIPOC Theatre Artists Call for Reckoning in the White American Theatre." *Playbill*, June 9, 2020. https://www.playbill.com/article/300-bipoc-theatre-artists-call-for-reckoning-in-the-white-american-theatre.

Cody Renard Richard. "The Cody Renard Richard Scholarship Program." https://www.codyrenard.com/scholarship.

Cohen, Randy. "The American Public Says YES to Arts Education." *Artsblog, Americans for the Arts* (blog), March 5, 2016. https://blog.americansforthearts.org/2019/05/15/the-american-public-says-yes-to-arts-education.

Coleman, Nancy. "'Hadestown' Director Rachel Chavkin: Diversity 'Is Not a Pipeline Issue.'" *New York Times*, June 9, 2019. https://www.nytimes.com/2019/06/09/theater/hadestown-rachel-chavkin-tony-awards.html.

College Factual. "2023 Drama & Theatre Arts Degree Guide." https://www.collegefactual.com/majors/visual-and-performing-arts/drama-and-theater-arts/.

Commission for Women. "Pay Equity." Augusta, ME: Commission for Women, 1980. https://search.alexanderstreet.com/preview/work/bibliographic_entity%7Cbibliographic_details%7C2520364.

Conley, Danee. "Progress During an Atypical Year: Hiring Bias and Wage Gaps in Theatre in 2021." New York, NY: Actors' Equity Association, 2021. https://cdn.actorsequity.org/docs/HiringBiasWageGaps2021.pdf.

Cooper, David, Sebastian Martinez Hickey, and Ben Zipperer. "The Value of the Federal Minimum Wage Is at Its Lowest Point in 66 Years." Economic Policy Institute. *Working Economics* (blog), July 14, 2022. https://www.epi.org/blog/the-value-of-the-federal-minimum-wage-is-at-its-lowest-point-in-66-years/.

Corporandy, Sarah Clare. Interview by authors. September 2022.

Court, Jessa-Raye. Interview by authors. September 2022.

COVID-19 RSFLG Data and Assessment Working Group, and Argonne National Laboratory. "Analysis: COVID-19's Impacts on Arts and Culture." COVID-19 Weekly Outlook, January 4, 2021. https://www.arts.gov/sites/default/files/COVID-Outlook-Week-of-1.4.2021-revised.pdf.

Cox, Daniel, Juhem Navarro-Rivera, and Robert P. Jones. "Race, Religion, and Political Affiliation of America's Social Networks." Washington, D.C.: Public Religion Research Institute, August 3, 2016. https://www.prri.org/research/poll-race-religion-politics-americans-social-networks/.

Cox, Josie. "The US Push for Pay Transparency." *BBC*, September 29, 2022. https://www.bbc.com/worklife/article/20220929-the-us-push-for-pay-transparency.

Crenshaw, Kimberle. "Demarginalizing the Intersection of Race and Sex: A Black Feminist Critique of Antidiscrimination Doctrine, Feminist Theory, and Antiracist Politics." In *Living with Contradictions*, edited by Alison M. Jaggar, 1st ed., 39–52. Routledge, 2018. https://doi.org/10.4324/9780429499142-5.

Daly, Mary C., Shelby R. Buckman, and Lily M. Seitelman. "The Unequal Impact of COVID-19: Why Education Matters." *FRBSF Economic Letter*, June 28, 2020. https://www.frbsf.org/wp-content/uploads/sites/4/el2020-17.pdf.

Datablog. "Women in Theatre: How the '2:1 Problem' Breaks Down." The Guardian. https://www.theguardian.com/news/datablog/2012/dec/10/women-in-theatre-research-full-results.

Data USA. "Technical Theatre Design and Technology." https://datausa.io/profile/cip/technical-theatre-design-technology.

Delaware Theatre Company. "Safety Manual," 2020. https://docs.google.com/document/d/1rC20649OrX4rEDblTlb5EzuR7exwCRHuhYSRDncRGCg/edit?usp=sharing.

Design Action. "About Us." https://www.design-action.com/about-us.

Dew, Sarah. "An Open Letter to the 'Launchpad of the American Theater.'" *Sarah Dew* (blog), July 2, 2021. https://www.sarahdew.com/post/dear-launchpad-for-american-theatre.

Diane, Ciara. "How Do You Pay Your Dues When You Can't Pay Your Bills?" *American Theatre*, May 1, 2020. https://www.americantheatre.org/2020/05/01/how-do-you-pay-your-dues-when-you-can-barely-pay-your-bills/.

Dilena, Natasha. "Onboarding vs. Orientation—Is There Really a Difference?" Factorial HR, June 1, 2022. https://factorialhr.com/blog/onboarding-vs-orientation/?utm_source=Sailthru&utm_medium=email&utm_campaign=IHIH%2010/24/22&utm_term=I%20Hate%20It%20Herehttps://factorialhr.com/blog/onboarding-vs-orientation/?utm_source=Sailthru&utm_medium=email&utm_campaign=IHIH%2010/24/22&utm_term=I%20Hate%20It%20Here.

Duncan, Katie. "Study: Americans Surprised That These High-Paying Jobs Don't Require a College Degree." *JobSage* (blog), March 8, 2023. https://www.jobsage.com/blog/top-jobs-without-degree/.

Economic Policy Institute. "Family Budget Calculator." https://www.epi.org/resources/budget/.

Eddy, Michael S. "Industry Advocates: Costume Industry Coalition." *Stage Directions*, June 2021.

Edmondson, Amy C. "Psychological Safety." Amy C. Edmondson. https://amycedmondson.com/psychological-safety/.

Edmondson, Amy C., and Per Hugander. "4 Steps to Boost Psychological Safety at Your Workplace." *Harvard Business Review*, June 22, 2021. https://hbr.org/2021/06/4-steps-to-boost-psychological-safety-at-your-workplace.

Elting, Liz. "The She-Cession by the Numbers." *Forbes*, February 12, 2022. https://www.forbes.com/sites/lizelting/2022/02/12/the-she-cession-by-the-numbers/?sh=6c0cf6510530.

Entertainment Community Fund. "Stay Healthy and Insured." https://entertainmentcommunity.org/services-and-programs/healthcare-and-health-insurance.

Eotcsummer21. "A Call In To the Eugene O'Neill Theater Center." *Medium*, July 21, 2021. https://medium.com/@eotcsummer21/a-call-in-to-the-eugene-oneill-theater-center-4cf5c42ea933.

Equity Through Design Mentorship. "ETDM Mission." http://www.etdmentorship.org/about.

Essin, Christin. "Coda from Working Backstage." *Theatre Design & Technology: Journal of the United States Institute for Theatre Technology*, Winter 2022.

Essin, Christin. *Working Backstage: A Cultural History and Ethnography of Technical Theater Labor.* Ann Arbor, MI: University of Michigan Press, 2021.

Event Safety Alliance. "Home." https://www.eventsafetyalliance.org/.

Event Safety Alliance. "Who We Are." https://www.eventsafetyalliance.org/ourmission.

Fair Wage On Stage. "Myths That Keep Actors and Stage Managers Exploited and Broke." September 3, 2017. https://fairwageonstage.org/myths-keep-actors-stage-managers-exploited-broke/.

Filtness, A.J., and A. Naweed. "Causes, Consequences and Countermeasures to Driver Fatigue in the Rail Industry: The Train Driver Perspective." *Applied Ergonomics* 60 (April 2017): 12–21. https://doi.org/10.1016/j.apergo.2016.10.009.

Fischer, Sarah. "Exclusive: LinkedIn Aims to Close 'Network Gap.'" *Axios*, September 26, 2019. https://www.axios.com/2019/09/26/linkedin-inequality-network-gap-job-opportunities.

Fleming, Robert Barry. Interview by authors. April 2023.

Flores, Miguel, R. Christopher Maxwell, John Meredith, Alexander Murphy, Quinn O'Connor, Phyllis Smith, and Chris Waters. "Hold Please: Addressing Urgency and Other White Supremacist Standards in Stage Management." *HowlRound Theatre Commons*, October 15, 2020. https://howlround.com/hold-please.

Florida, Richard, and Michael Seman. "Lost Art: Measuring COVID-19's Devastating Impact on America's Creative Economy." Washington, D.C.: Brookings Institute, August 2020. https://www.brookings.edu/wp-content/uploads/2020/08/20200810_Brookingsmetro_Covid19-and-creative-economy_Final.pdf.

Follows, Stephen. "What Percentage of a Film Crew Is Female?" *Stephen Follows: Film Data and Education* (blog), July 22, 2014. https://stephenfollows.com/gender-of-film-crews/.

Frederick, Rachel. "An Interview with Amber Whatley, Lighting Designer." *Et Cetera...: A Blog of Bright Ideas from ETC* (blog), January 27, 2022. https://blog.etcconnect.com/2022/01/amber-whatley.

Frenette, Alexandre. "The Intern Economy: Laboring to Learn in the Music Industry." PhD diss., City University of New York, 2014. https://academicworks.cuny.edu/cgi/viewcontent.cgi?referer=&httpsredir=1&article=1038&context=gc_etds.

Frenette, Alexandre, Gillian Gualtieri, and Megan Robinson. "Growing Divides: Historical and Emerging Inequalities in Arts Internships." SNAAP Special Report. Providence, RI: Strategic National Arts Alumni Project, Spring 2021. https://snaaparts.org/uploads/downloads/SNAAP-Special-Report-Inequalities-210301_2021-11-09-220850_gmjl.pdf.

Friedman, Meg, and David McGraw. "Return to the Stage: A Performing Arts Workforce Study." Return to the Stage. https://www.returntothestage.com/.

Frye, Jocelyn. "On the Frontlines at Work and at Home: The Disproportionate Effects of the Coronavirus Pandemic on Women of Color." Washington, D.C.: Center for American Progress, April 23, 2020. https://www.americanprogress.org/article/frontlines-work-home/.

Garcia, Emma, and Elaine Weiss. "Education Inequalities at the School Starting Gate: Gaps, Trends, and Strategies to Address Them." Washington, D.C.: Economic Policy Institute, September 27, 2017. https://www.epi.org/publication/education-inequalities-at-the-school-starting-gate/.

Garrett, Nataki. Interview by authors, April 2023.

Garrett, Nataki. "The Threat of An Inclusive American Theatre." *The Root*, October 28, 2022. https://www.theroot.com/the-threat-of-an-inclusive-american-theatre-1849715600.

Garrity, Caitlyn. "Building a Better Workplace: Women+ Increasingly Abandon Technical Theatre over Lack of Parity and Equity." *Theatre Design & Technology: Journal of the United States Institute for Theatre Technology*, Summer 2019.

Gelt, Jessica. "The Spreadsheet That Shook the Theater World: Marie Cisco's 'Not Speaking Out' List." *Los Angeles Times*, June 9, 2020. https://www.latimes.com/entertainment-arts/story/2020-06-09/theaters-not-speaking-out-list-george-floyd-protests-black-lives-matter.

Gibbs, Alarie A. "The Perception of Nonprofit Arts and Culture Leaders Regarding Their Role in K-12 Arts Education." PhD diss., University of North Florida, 2018.

Gieras, Angela. Interview by authors. April 2023.

Goldin, Claudia. "Understanding the Economic Impact of COVID-19 on Women." Cambridge, MA: National Bureau of Economic Research, April 2022. https://doi.org/10.3386/w29974.

Gray, Ilasiea. "Why Are There No Great Kids of Color in the Performing Arts." *Stage Directions*, May 2021.

Green, Jesse. "When Paying Dues Doesn't Pay the Rent, How Does the Theater Survive?" *New York Times*, July 6, 2022. https://www.nytimes.com/2022/07/06/theater/pay-equity-salaries.html.

Gutierrez, Karla. "The Importance of Training at Each Stage of the Employee Lifecycle." *SHIFT ELearning* (blog). https://www.shiftelearning.com/blog/training-in-each-stage-of-the-employee-lifecycle.

Halvorsen, Lauren. "About." Substack. Nothing for the Group. https://nothingforthegroup.substack.com/about.

Halvorsen, Lauren. "The Week of May 2–6, 2022." Substack. Nothing for the Group, May 6, 2022. https://nothingforthegroup.substack.com/p/the-week-of-may-2-6-2022.

Halvorsen, Lauren. "The Week of November 5–11, 2022." Substack. Nothing for the Group, November 11, 2022. https://nothingforthegroup.substack.com/p/the-week-of-november-5-11-2022?utm_source=substack&utm_medium=email.

Halvorsen, Lauren. "The Week of October 1–7, 2022." Substack. Nothing for the Group, October 7, 2022. https://nothingforthegroup.substack.com/p/the-week-of-october-1-7-2022?utm_source=email.

Harper, Jon, and Lauren Parrish. Interview by authors. September 2022.

Harrison, Alan. "Nonprofit Arts Boards—Pay Equity Starts with YOUR Nonprofit." *Scene Change* (blog), July 19, 2022. https://medium.com/nonprofits-arts-politics-leadership/nonprofit-arts-boards-pay-equity-starts-with-your-nonprofit-4598441e9a3f.

Hartnett, D. Joseph. Interview by authors. October 2022.

Henry, Sean Patrick. "Broadway by the Numbers 2019." ProductionPro, April 9, 2019. https://production.pro/broadway-by-the-numbers.

Hertvick, Nicole. "Under a Cloud: Artists Describe Toxic Work Conditions at Spooky Action Theater." DC Theater Arts, May 20, 2022. https://dctheaterarts.org/2022/05/20/under-a-cloud-artists-describe-toxic-work-conditions-at-spooky-action-theater/.

Herway, Jake. "How to Create a Culture of Psychological Safety." *Gallup*, December 7, 2017. https://www.gallup.com/workplace/236198/create-culture-psychological-safety.aspx.

Hetrick, Adam. "Women Playwrights, Citing Inequitable Production Opportunities, Hold Meeting Oct. 27." *Playbill*, October 27, 2008. https://playbill.com/article/women-playwrights-citing-inequitable-production-opportunities-hold-meeting-oct-27-com-154666.

Hiltner, Elsa. "A Call for Equal Support in Theatrical Design." *HowlRound Theatre Commons*, November 23, 2016. https://howlround.com/call-equal-support-theatrical-design.

Hiltner, Elsa. Interview by authors. September 2022.

Hiltner, Elsa. "Inequity by Design." *HowlRound Theatre Commons*, July 13, 2020. https://howlround.com/inequity-design.

Hollands, Aisha. "Framework for Fair and Just Hiring Processes." *School Business Affairs*, January 2020.

Hoo, Fawnia Soo. "The Real Reason Costume Designers Are Paid Less than Their Peers." *Fashionista*, May 5, 2022. https://fashionista.com/2022/05/costume-designers-pay-equity-wage-gap.

Human Resources MBA. "5 Examples of Inclusive Design in the Workplace." Accessed May 17, 2023. https://www.humanresourcesmba.net/lists/5-examples-of-inclusive-design-in-the-workplace.

Hwu, Linette S. Interview by authors. March 2023.

ia_costumes (@iatse_costumes). "While Pay Equity Is on Everybody's Lips, Here Are the Statistics Sent to Us Regarding Local 1 (NYC Broadway Stage Crew) and Local 764 (NYC Broadway Wardrobe)." Photo. *Instagram*, March 30, 2022. https://www.instagram.com/p/Cbv_GCJufmL/?igshid=YmMyMTA2M2Y%3D.

IATSE. "Apollo Theater Stagehands Join IATSE." https://www.legacy.iatse.net/history/apollo-theater-stagehands-join-iatse.

IATSE. "IATSE Women's Committee." https://www.legacy.iatse.net/history/iatse-womens-committee.

IATSE. "Performing Arts and Motion Picture Hazard Information." Occupational Safety and Health Administration, August 2018. https://www.osha.gov/sites/default/files/IATSE_2018.pdf.

IATSE. "Together We Rise: 69th Quadrennial Convention Resolutions, Book 1," 2021. https://www.iatseconvention.com/Doc-Page/FileId/3193/Extension/pdf?FileName=Resolutions+Book+1.

IATSE. IATSE Entertainment and Exhibition Industries Training Trust Fund. "Individual Courses: LinkedIn Learning Subscription." https://www.iatsetrainingtrust.org/lil.

IATSE. "Providing Training Opportunities for the IATSE Workforce." https://www.iatsetrainingtrust.org/about.

IATSE Local 4 (@iatse_local4). "Today @iatse_local4 Celebrates #internationalwomansday by Celebrating Our Very First Sister and Lead #electrician over @sesamestreet Sister Karen

Sunderlin." Photo. *Instagram*, March 8, 2023. https://www.instagram.com/iatse_local4/?hl=en.

IATSE Local 524. "IATSE Training Trust Fund." https://www.iatse524.com/ttf.

IATSE Local USA 829. "The Case for Costume Department Coordinators: An Equitable Path for United Scenic Artists, Local USA 829 Costume Coordinators." New York, NY: IATSE Local USA 829, December 2022. https://mcusercontent.com/cd56c12d8cc5b412b582b737f/files/44d02bd0-a237-b7bd-566a-903daddda37f/CDC_Pamphlet_12_22.pdf?fbclid=PAAaZHl7WD39UnfjgRjHuvJAbFJuERQh_BmqNonrrnXtLeMcOooLI_DkgYgS4.

IATSE Local USA 829. "History." https://www.usa829.org/About-Our-Union/History.

IATSE Local USA 829. "History of the United Scenic Artists, Local USA 829, IATSE." *Vimeo*, February 24, 2023. https://vimeo.com/802026723?share=copy.

IATSE Local USA 829. "We Will Do Better: United Scenic Artists, Local USA 829, IATSE, Releases Membership Demographic Data," September 8, 2022. https://www.usa829.org/News-Detail/ArticleID/1148.

Imagination Stage. "About Us." https://imaginationstage.org/about/.

"In Memoriam: Tayneshia Jefferson." *Sightlines: The Monthly Newsletter for USITT Members*, September 2013. http://sightlines.usitt.org/archive/2013/09/TayneshiaJefferson.asp.

Independent Sector. "Principles for Good Governance and Ethical Practice: A Guide for Charities and Foundations." Washington, D.C.: Independent Sector, 2015. https://independentsector.org/wp-content/uploads/2016/11/Principles2015-Web.pdf.

International Centre for Women Playwrights. "Women Playwrights Organize in NYC." https://www.womenplaywrights.org/jordan.

Jackson, Susan E., Randall S. Schuler, and Steve Werner. "Conducting Performance Management." In *Managing Human Resources*, 10th ed. Mason, OH: Cengage, 2009.

Jayaraman, Saru. Interview by authors. September 2022.

Jefferson, Tayneshia, and David S. Stewart. "Diversity in the Booth: What It's Like Being a Minority in Technical Theatre." *Stage Directions*, January 2012.

Joint Industry Board of the Electrical Industry. "Apprentice Program." https://www.jibei.org/education-training/apprentice-program/.

Jonas, Susan, and Suzanne Bennett. "Report on the Status of Women: A Limited Engagement?" Berkeley, CA: Women Arts, January 2022. https://www.womenarts.org/nysca-report-2002/.

Jordan, Rob. "Do Plastic Straws Really Make a Difference?" *Stanford Earth Matters Magazine*, September 18, 2018. https://earth.stanford.edu/news/do-plastic-straws-really-make-difference.

Joseph & Norinsberg LLC: Fighting for Employee Justice. "Unpaid NBC Interns Settle Lawsuit for Over $6 Million," November 10, 2014. https://employeejustice.com/unpaid-nbc-workers-settle-lawsuit-for-over-6-million/.

Kao, Joanna. "'Waitress' Is Making Broadway History with Its All-Female Creative Team." FiveThirtyEight, March 25, 2016. https://fivethirtyeight.com/features/waitress-is-making-broadway-history-with-its-all-female-creative-team/#:~:text=The%20creative%20team%20for%20the, charge%20of%20a%20Broadway%20show.

Kaplan, Juliana. "AOC Joins Cárdenas and Other Top Lawmakers in Calling on Biden's Labor Department to Revolutionize Oversight of Unpaid Internships." *Business Insider*, September 28, 2021. https://www.businessinsider.com/lawmakers-call-on-department-of-labor-to-track-unpaid-internships-2021-9.

Kaufman, Wendy. "A Successful Job Search: It's All About Networking." *NPR*, February 3, 2011. https://www.npr.org/2011/02/08/133474431/a-successful-job-search-its-all-about-networking.

Kibben, Kat. "Developing an LGBTQ-Friendly Hiring Process." *ERE Media* (blog), July 26, 2022. https://www.ere.net/developing-an-lgbtq-friendly-hiring-process/.

Kibben, Katrina. "Job Postings That Work (And Some That Don't)." *Writing Advice for Recruiting* (blog), April 20, 2021. https://katrinakibben.com/2021/04/20/job-postings-that-work/.

Kizer, Matt. "The Ten Out of Twelve: It's a Lie." *Matt Kizer: Scenic and Lighting Design* (blog), April 16, 2021. https://scenicandlighting.com/article/the-ten-out-of-twelve-its-a-lie/.

Lada, Jennifer, and Stephanie M. Merabet. "Seeing Through the Pay Transparency Law." Holland and Knight, October 19, 2022. https://www.hklaw.com/en/insights/publications/2022/10/seeing-through-the-pay-transparency-law#:~:text=NYC%20Local%20Law%2032%2C%20known, on%20Nov.%201%2C%202022.

Lake, Beth. Interview by authors. September 2022.

Landers, Pat. Interview by authors. November 2022.

League of Resident Theatres. "Resources for Racial Diversity, Equity and Inclusion." League of Resident Theatres. https://lort.org/edi-resources.

Lee, Ashley. "In-Person Theater Is Back. A Lost Generation of Artists Chose Not to Return With It." *Los Angeles Times*, March 24, 2022. https://www.latimes.com/entertainment-arts/story/2022-03-24/pandemic-artists-theater-lost-generation.

Lee, Ashley. "Inside the Battle to Change a Prestigious Theater Festival's 'Broken' Culture." *Los Angeles Times*, September 25, 2021. https://www.latimes.com/entertainment-arts/story/2021-09-25/williamstown-theatre-festival-workplace-safety-culture.

Lee, Ashley. "Williamstown Festival Crew Walks Off the Job. It's a Cautionary Tale for Outdoor Theater." *Los Angeles Times*, July 20, 2021. https://www.latimes.com/entertainment-arts/story/2021-07-20/williamstown-theatre-festival-sound-crew-walks-out.

"Letter to Fellow Board Members of U.S. Theatres." https://cdn.woollymammoth.net/20221031105318/Dear-Fellow-Board-Members-of-U.S.-Theatres.pdf.

Lift the Curtain. "Internship Criteria Standards." https://drive.google.com/file/d/1plJgSW_6r_jU3ofT2WzZKGOMEyt3Ft4q/view.

Lift the Curtain. "Our Mission." https://www.liftthecurtain.co/our-mission.

Lift the Curtain. "Resources." https://www.liftthecurtain.co/resources.

Lithgow, John A., Deborah F. Rutter, and Natasha D. Trethewey. "The Case for Arts Education Is Strong. Our Commitment Should Be, Too." American Academy of Arts and Sciences, November 4, 2021. https://www.amacad.org/news/strong-case-arts-education-commitment.

Live Design. "Studio School of Design Announces Inaugural Classes for June 2021," April 21, 2021. https://www.livedesignonline.com/business-people-news/studio-school-design-announces-inaugural-classes-for-june-2021.

Long, Heather, Andrew Van Dam, Alyssa Flowers, and Leslie Shapiro. "The Covid-19 Recession Is the Most Unequal in Modern U.S. History." *Washington Post*, September 30, 2020. https://www.washingtonpost.com/graphics/2020/business/coronavirus-recession-equality/.

Lozoff, Sarah. Interview by authors. September 2022.

Maag, Michael. Interview by authors. September 2022.

Maag, Michael, and Annie Wiegand. "Illuminating the Careers of Disabled Lighting Designers." *HowlRound Theatre Commons*, February 25, 2021. https://howlround.com/illuminating-careers-disabled-lighting-designers.

MAESTRA. "About." https://maestramusic.org/about/.

Mandell, Jonathan. "Theater and Black Lives Matter. Reopening Fears and Plans. Project Pride." New York Theater, June 1, 2020. https://newyorktheater.me/2020/06/01/theater-and-black-lives-matter-reopening-fears-and-plans/.

Marks, Kate. *HR for Creative Companies*. Newcastle upon Tyne, UK: RIBA Publishing, 2016.

McCauley, Mary Carole. "Center Stage's Latina Artistic Director Faced a Racial Reckoning, a Pandemic and a Boardroom Revolt in Tumultuous Tenure." *Baltimore Sun*, March 25, 2023. https://www.baltimoresun.com/entertainment/bs-fe-ybarra-departs-20230323-umhsfbgiwfhsppl3pkgfkqlt6a-story.html.

McGovern, Porsche. "Who Designs and Directs in LORT Theatres by Pronoun." *HowlRound Theatre Commons*, December 22, 2020. https://howlround.com/who-designs-and-directs-lort-theatres-pronoun-2020.

McGraw, David J. "2021 Stage Manager Survey," January 2022. https://www.stagemanagersurvey.com/uploads/6/4/6/6/6466686/2021_smsurvey.pdf.

McGraw, David and Meg Friedman. "Return to the Stage January 2021 Survey." Return to the Stage, February 2021. https://www.returntothestage.com/uploads/6/4/6/6/6466686/return_to_the_stage_february_2021.pdf.

McKinsey & Company. "Is It Safe?" McKinsey Quarterly. https://www.mckinsey.com/featured-insights/leadership/five-fifty-is-it-safe.

McPhee, Ryan. "Broadway Will Officially Remain Closed through 2020." *Playbill*, June 29, 2020. https://playbill.com/article/broadway-will-officially-remain-closed-through-2020.

Mishra, Rohan. "Universal Design: Design for Everyone." *UX Planet* (blog), October 13, 2018. https://uxplanet.org/universal-design-design-for-everyone-61ded4243658.

Mohlman, Danielle. "Why You Need an HR Department." *American Theatre*, January 2, 2019. https://www.americantheatre.org/2019/01/02/why-you-need-an-hr-department/.

Morash, Karen. "Acting Unpleasantly: Why Harassment Is so Common in the Theatre." *The Conversation*, November 16, 2017. https://theconversation.com/acting-unpleasantly-why-harassment-is-so-common-in-the-theatre-87374.

Morton, Jacqui. "Putting a Stop to Harassment and Abuse in the Theatre Industry." *Abuse Survivors Blog, Emmott Snell Solicitors* (blog). https://www.emmottsnell.co.uk/blog/putting-a-stop-to-harassment-and-abuse-in-the-theatre-industry.

Moser, Stephanie. "A Calculation of the Living Wage." Living Wage Calculator, May 19, 2022. https://livingwage.mit.edu/articles/99-a-calculation-of-the-living-wage.

Muse, Anyania. Interview by authors. April 2023.

Nagarajan, Mala. "How Do We Quantify a Living Wage?" Vega Mala Consulting, February 6, 2023. https://www.vegamala.com/how-do-we-quantify-a-thriving-wage.

National Association of Colleges and Employers. "Equity." Accessed September 9, 2022. https://www.naceweb.org/about-us/equity-definition/.

National Association of Colleges and Employers. "Position Statement: U.S. Internships," August 2018.https://www.naceweb.org/about-us/advocacy/position-statements/position-statement-us-internships/.

Nelson, Mallory Kay. "Inclusion of the Disabled Theatre Artist." Master's thesis, Carnegie Mellon University, 2010. https://mallorykaynelson.files.wordpress.com/2019/03/inclusion_of_the_disabled_theatre_artist-nelson.pdf.

New York State Attorney General Charities Bureau. "Internal Controls and Financial Accountability for Not-For-Profit Boards," April 13, 2015. https://ag.ny.gov/sites/default/files/publications/Charities_Internal_Controls.pdf.

New School News. "Teaching to Transgress: Bell Hooks Returns to The New School," October 7, 2014. https://blogs.newschool.edu/news/2014/10/bellhooksteachingtotransgress/.

New York University. "Cost of Attendance." https://www.nyu.edu/admissions/financial-aid-and-scholarships/applying-and-planning-for-undergraduate-aid/tuition-and-other-costs/cost-of-attendance.html.

New York University Tisch School of the Arts. "Tisch Drama Announces Lenore Doxsee Scholarship." October 30, 2020. https://tisch.nyu.edu/drama/news/tisch-drama-launches-lenore-doxsee-scholarship.

Newton, Pamela. "The Broadway Season Was Diverse Offstage Too, Not That You'd Notice." *American Theatre*, June 7, 2016. https://www.americantheatre.org/2016/06/07/the-broadway-season-was-diverse-offstage-too-not-that-youd-notice/.

Nidweski, Victoria. "Through the Stage Door, a Spotlight on 'Backstage' Work: Women Designers and Stagehands in Theatrical Production." Master's thesis, Sarah Lawrence College, 2021. https://digitalcommons.slc.edu/womenshistory_etd/57.

North Carolina Theatre Conference. "Making Theatre Hiring More Equitable, Diverse and Inclusive: A Guide from the North Carolina Theatre Conference." https://www.nctc.org/wp-content/uploads/2021/02/NCTC-Hiring-Guide-V5-links.pdf.

Nottage, Lynn. "Women Are Missing from Tonys and Broadway." *New York Times*, June 6, 2014. https://www.nytimes.com/roomfordebate/2014/06/06/can-tony-award-voting-be-improved/women-are-missing-from-tonys-and-broadway.

Occupational Safety and Health Administration. "USITT-IATSE Alliance Agreement," United States Department of Labor, July 16, 2013. https://www.osha.gov/alliances/national/usitt_iatse_alliance-agreement_20130716.

Occupational Safety and Health Administration. "Workers' Rights." Washington, D.C.: United States Department of Labor, 2019.

Off-Broadway Assistant Designer Advisory Group (electronic mailing list). "Asst Coverage Enters 2nd Season & Rate Increase WIN at Public Theater," August 26, 2022.

Okun, Tema. "White Supremacy Culture." White Supremacy Culture. Accessed April 17, 2023. https://www.whitesupremacyculture.info.

Olson, Allana. "Wage Theft and What You Can Do About It." *Technicians for Change* (blog), January 2022. https://techniciansforchange.org/2022/01/05/wage-theft/.

On Our Team. "About Us." Accessed April 25, 2023. https://www.onourteam.org/about.

On Our Team. "The Pay Equity Standards." On Our Team. https://www.onourteam.org/pay-equity-standards.

Open Stage Project. "Home." https://www.openstageproject.org/.

Open Stage Project. "Program Overview." Open Stage Project. https://www.openstageproject.org/program.

Oregon Shakespeare Festival. "Save Our Season." https://www.osfashland.org/support/save-our-season.

Oregon Shakespeare Festival. "Scenic Artist II: Job Details." Oregon Shakespeare Festival, September 2, 2022. https://recruiting2.ultipro.com/ORE1002OREG/JobBoard/705d9861-cd29-4b49-8d5c-6b35177a1435/OpportunityDetail?opportunityId=17269599-b214-4e00-be09-fa11d43c6064.

Parents and Carers in Performing Arts. "Backstage Workforce Report." April 23, 2020. https://pipacampaign.org/research/backstage-workforce-report?referrer=/research.

Parents and Carers in Performing Arts. "PiPA Backstage Workforce Report." Sheffield, UK: Parents and Carers in Performing Arts, February 2020. https://pipacampaign.org/uploads/ckeditor/PiPA_backstage_workforce_survey_Feb2020_v11.pdf.

Parent Artist Advocacy League for Performing Arts and Media. "About Us." https://www.paaltheatre.com/about-us.

Parent Artist Advocacy League for Performing Arts and Media. "Our Services." https://www.paaltheatre.com/book-online.

Parent Artist Advocacy League for Performing Arts and Media. "The New Standard of Care." Accessed April 26, 2023. https://www.paaltheatre.com/new-standard-of-care.

Parent Artist Advocacy League for Performing Arts and Media. "Using Five-Day Rehearsal-Week Contracts, Negotiation, and Execution." https://www.paaltheatre.com/post/five-day-rehearsal-week.

Paulson, Michael. "Broadway Power Brokers Pledge Diversity Changes as Theaters Reopen." *New York Times*, August 23, 2021. https://www.nytimes.com/2021/08/23/theater/broadway-diversity-pledge-reopening.html?action=click&module=RelatedLinks&pgtype=Article.

Pedulla, David S., and Devah Pager. "Race and Networks in the Job Search Process." *American Sociological Review* 84, no. 6 (December 2019): 983–1012. https://doi.org/10.1177/0003122419883255.

Perkins, Kathy Anne. "Black Backstage Workers, 1900-1969." *Black American Literature Forum* 16, no. 4 (1982): 160. https://doi.org/10.2307/2904226.

Pliska, Jessica. "How Our White Networks Exclude Young People of Color from Career Access and Opportunity." *Forbes*, March 31, 2021. https://www.forbes.com/sites/jessicapliska/2021/03/31/how-our-white-networks-exclude-young-people-of-color-from-career-access-and-opportunity/?sh=68308ebd2cdd.

Preston, Camille. "Promoting Employee Happiness Benefits Everyone." *Forbes*, December 13, 2017.https://www.forbes.com/sites/forbescoachescouncil/2017/12/13/promoting-employee-happiness-benefits-everyone/?sh=4fb6f1ea581a.

Production on Deck. "Consulting." https://www.productionondeck.com/about.

Propublica. "The Santa Fe Opera." Nonprofit Explorer. Accessed April 26, 2023. https://projects.propublica.org/nonprofits/organizations/850131810.

Putnam, Leah. "Here's How to Apply for SDCF's Revitalized Professional Development Program." *Playbill*, November 8, 2022. https://playbill.com/article/heres-how-to-apply-for-sdcfs-revitalized-professional-development-program.

Ralston, Nicole Caridad. "White Supremacy & Anti-Blackness: A Covert & Overt Beast." Beloved Community, May29,2020. https://www.wearebeloved.org/blog/2020/5/29/white-supremacy-amp-anti-blackness-a-covert-amp-overt-beast.

Richardett, Tanner A. "No More 10/12s: Considerations for a More Equitable Theatre Rehearsal Structure in Philadelphia." Master's thesis, Drexel University, 2021. https://drive.google.com/file/d/1CoYdONhCUwzE6DSSfXlmtHkH1p507Zem/view.

RISE Theatre. "RISE." https://www.risetheatre.org.

Riviera, Lauren A. "Homosocial Reproduction." In *Sociology of Work: An Encyclopedia*, edited by Vicki Smith, 376. Thousand Oaks, CA: SAGE Publication, 2013.

Robinson, Bryan. "10 Red Flags That Psychological Safety Is Lacking in Your Workplace." *Forbes*, June 13, 2021. https://www.forbes.com/sites/bryanrobinson/2021/06/13/10-red-flags-that-psychological-safety-is-lacking-in-your-workplace/?sh=5a1cf8c310c1&utm_source=Sailthru&utm_medium=email&utm_campaign=IHIH%2011/21/22&utm_term=I%20Hate%20It%20Here.

Rossol, Monona. "Data Sheet: OSHA Rules and Scenic Arts." Local USA 829, 2010. https://www.usa829.org/LinkClick.aspx?fileticket=M6xZptQuLvs%3D&portalid=0.

Schmidt, Lydia Milman. "2019 Report—Lost Voices." *PICT: Parents in Chicago Theatre* (blog), July 21, 2019. https://parentsinchicagotheatre.wordpress.com/2019/07/21/2018-research-in-chicago-theatre-lost-voices/.

Schmidt, Lydia Milman. "Barriers to Work for Parents in Chicago Theatre—Survey Results." *PICT: Parents in Chicago Theatre* (blog), April 6, 2017. https://parentsinchicagotheatre.wordpress.com/2017/04/06/first-blog-post/.

Schwartz, Robert M. *The Legal Rights of Union Stewards*. 6th ed. Detroit, MI: Work Rights Press, 2017.

Seymour, Lee. "'We're Not Going Back': Inside Broadway's Racial Reckoning." *Forbes*, April 28, 2021.https://www.forbes.com/sites/leeseymour/2021/04/28/were-not-going-back-inside-broadways-racial-reckoning/?sh=7f997e11a60c.

Shaw, Helen. "Building Trust After Inclusivity Failed: Lessons for the Theater." *Vulture*, June 10, 2023. https://www.vulture.com/2020/06/race-whiteness-black-lives-matter-lessons-for-theater.html.

Siegel, Tatiana. "Everyone Just Knows He's an Absolute Monster: Scott Rudin's Ex-Staffers Speak Out on Abusive Behavior." *Hollywood Reporter*, April 7, 2021. https://www.hollywoodreporter.com/movies/movie-news/everyone-just-knows-hes-an-absolute-monster-scott-rudins-ex-staffers-speak-out-on-abusive-behavior-4161883/.

Smart, Lauren. "At Dallas Theater Center, Layoffs and Cutbacks and Cancellations." *American Theatre*, April 19, 2023. https://www.americantheatre.org/2023/04/19/at-dallas-theater-center-layoffs-and-cutbacks-and-cancellations/.

Smith, Ronn. "American Theatre Design Since 1945." In *The Cambridge History of American Theatre*, edited by Don B. Wilmeth and Christopher Bigsby, 1st ed., 514–33. Cambridge University Press, 2000. https://doi.org/10.1017/CHOL9780521669597.009.

Solá-Santiago, Frances. "Costume Designers Are Stars on Social Media. So Why Aren't They Being Paid That Way?" *Refinery 29*, September 17, 2021. https://www.refinery29.com/en-us/2021/09/10676505/costume-designers-pay-inequality-social-media.

SpriggHR. "6 Stages of the Employee Lifecycle." SpriggHR, August 13, 2020. https://sprigghr.com/blog/360-degree-continuous-feedback/the-6-stages-of-the-employee-life-cycle/.

Steinfeld, Edward, and Jordana Maisel. *Universal Design: Designing Inclusive Environments.* New York: John Wiley and Sons, 2012.

Steinmetz, Katy. "She Coined the Term 'Intersectionality' Over 30 Years Ago. Here's What It Means to Her Today"." *Time*, February 20, 2020. https://time.com/5786710/kimberle-crenshaw-intersectionality/.

Steketee, Martha Wade, and Judith Binus. "Women Count VI: Women and Non-Binary Hires Off-Broadway 2019/20." Women Count Report Series. New York, NY: League of Professional Theatre Women, May 2022. https://msteketee.files.wordpress.com/2022/05/wc-vi-report-may-2022-1.pdf.

Steketee, Martha Wade, and Judith Binus. "Women Count Women Hired Off-Broadway." League of Professional Theatre Women. https://archive.theatrewomen.org/women-count/.

Stewart, David ("dStew"). Interview by authors. September 2022.

Stewell, Don. "Unionization of the Stage Designer - Male and Female." *Theatre Design & Technology: Journal of the United States Institute for Theatre Technology*, no. 38 (October 1974): 6–9, 36–37.

Strategic National Arts Alumni Project. "Study: Arts Internships Are Important, but Some Are Better than Others," June 18, 2015. https://snaaparts.org/uploads/downloads/Media-Releases/SNAAP-Release-Special-Report-2015.pdf.

Stolzoff, Simone. "Please Don't Call My Job a Calling." *New York Times*, June 5, 2023. https://www.nytimes.com/2023/06/05/opinion/employment-exploitation-unions.html?searchResultPosition=4.

Studio School of Design. "History of Studio School of Design." https://studioschoolofdesign.org/history/.

Studio School of Design. "Mission." https://studioschoolofdesign.org/mission/.

Taylor, Brian and Al Duncan. "Stage Workers Strike For Benefits At Theater In Harlem." *The Militant*, September 14, 1998, vol. 62, no. 32. https://themilitant.com/1998/6232/6232_16.html.

The 1/52 Project. "Home." https://www.oneeveryfiftytwo.org/.

The White House. "Biden-Harris Administration Announces the First Session of the White House Internship Program, Administration Will Pay Interns for the First Time in History." June 2, 2022. https://www.whitehouse.gov/briefing-room/statements-releases/2022/06/02/biden-harris-administration-announces-the-first-session-of-the-white-house-internship-program-administration-will-pay-interns-for-the-first-time-in-history/.

The White House. "Executive Order on Diversity, Equity, Inclusion, and Accessibility in the Federal Workforce." June 25, 2021. https://www.whitehouse.gov/briefing-room/presidential-actions/2021/06/25/executive-order-on-diversity-equity-inclusion-and-accessibility-in-the-federal-workforce/.

The WTF, Williamstown?! Collective. "The WTF, Williamstown?! Collective to Mandy Greenfield, Laura Savia, Jeffrey Johnson, Joe Finnegan, Annie Pell, Brad Svrluga, and Donald B. Elitzer; as Well as the Rest of the Staff and Board of Trustees of Williamstown Theatre Festival." https://ca-times.brightspotcdn.com/06/37/5851edc0482387ff1b2fee01b155/updated-williamstown-theatre-festival-letter.pdf.

Theatre Communications Group. "The Willa Kim Costume Design Scholarship." https://circle.tcg.org/resources/grant-professional-development-programs/willa-kim-costume-design-scholarship/willa-kim-costume-design-scholarship-description?ssopc=1.

Theatre for Young Audiences. "State of the Field Research Report." Logan, UT: Utah State University, 2019. https://www.tyausa.org/wp-content/uploads/2019/11/TYA-State-of-the-Field-Report-2019.pdf.

Thomas, Stephanie R. *Compensating Your Employees Fairly: A Guide to Internal Pay Equity.* New York, NY: Apress, 2013.

Thompson, Nicholas. "Wired25: The New Networks with Jeff Weiner." *LinkedIn*, November 9, 2019. https://www.linkedin.com/pulse/wired25-2019-new-networks-jeff-weiner-nicholas-thompson/?src=aff-lilpar&veh=aff_src.aff-lilpar_c.partners_pkw.10078_plc.Skimbit%20Ltd._pcrid.449670_learning&trk=aff_src.aff-lilpar_c.partners_pkw.10078_plc.Skimbit%20Ltd._pcrid.449670_learning&clickid=U1fyToxXAxyJRxSoEkzjZTwgUknQwl3NLUoMR40&irgwc=1.

Time's Up. "Gender and Racial Inequity During Crisis: The Pay Gap." https://timesupfoundation.org/work/times-up-pay-up/gender-and-racial-inequity-during-crisis-the-pay-gap.

Tommy, Liesel. "Hey American Theaters! Please Post Your Statement of Solidarity with the Black Lives Matter Struggle." *Facebook*, May 31, 2020. https://www.facebook.com/liesl.tommy/posts/10157195311500887.

Tran, Diep. "What the Save Our Stages Act Means for You." *Backstage*, March 13, 2021. https://www.backstage.com/magazine/article/save-our-stages-act-actors-performing-artists-72354/.

Trusaic. "Pay Equity 101." https://trusaic.com/pay-equity-complete-overview/.

United States Institute for Theatre Technology. "Entertainment Design and Technology Workforce Demographics Study Results." September 2021. https://www.usitt.org/sites/default/files/2021-09/USITT%20WDS%20Final%200921.pdf.

United States Institute for Theatre Technology. "Gateway Program." https://www.usitt.org/gateway.

United States Institute for Theatre Technology. "Recipients of the Inaugural Collier Robert Woods, Jr. Scholarship Announced by USITT." August 2, 2021. https://www.usitt.org/inaugural-collier-woods-scholarship-recipients-announced.

University of Washington. "What Is the Difference Between Accessible, Usable, and Universal Design?" Disabilities, Opportunities, Internetworking, and Technology, May 24, 2022. https://www.washington.edu/doit/what-difference-between-accessible-usable-and-universal-design.

U.S. Bureau of Labor Statistics. "Employment Projections: Education Pays," September 8, 2022. https://www.bls.gov/emp/tables/unemployment-earnings-education.htm.

U.S. Department of Labor. "The Union Advantage." https://www.dol.gov/general/workcenter/union-advantage.

U.S. Department of Labor. "Wages and Hours Worked: Minimum Wage and Overtime Pay." Employment Law Guide, December 2019. https://webapps.dol.gov/elaws/elg/minwage.htm.

U.S. Department of Labor Wage and Hour Division. "Fact Sheet #71: Internship Programs Under the Fair Labor Standards Act," January 2018. https://www.dol.gov/agencies/whd/fact-sheets/71-flsa-internships.

Vaughan, Jane. "Oregon Shakespeare Festival Says It Needs $2.5 Million to Save the Theater's Future." *Oregon Public Broadcasting*, April 11, 2023. https://www.opb.org/article/2023/04/11/oregon-shakespeare-festival-fest-theater-arts-culture-pacific-northwest-actors-plays/.

Walby, Sylvia. "Theorising Patriarchy." *Sociology* 23, no. 2 (May 1989): 213–34. https://doi.org/10.1177/0038038589023002004.

Walnut Street Theatre. "Professional Apprentice Program." https://www.walnutstreettheatre.org/about/apprenticeships.php.

We See You, White American Theatre. "About." https://www.weseeyouwat.com/about.

We See You, White American Theatre. "BIPOC Demands for White American Theatre." https://static1.squarespace.com/static/5ede42fd6cb927448d9d0525/t/5f064e63f21dd43ad6ab3162/1594248809279/Tier2.pdf.

We See You, White American Theatre. "Principles for Building Anti-Racist Theatre Systems." https://www.weseeyouwat.com/statement.

Weinert-Kendt, Rob. "Oregon Shakes Restructures, Scales Back with Eye to Future." *American Theatre*, January 13, 2023. https://www.americantheatre.org/2023/01/13/oregon-shakes-restructures-scales-back-with-eye-to-future/.

Weinert-Kendt, Rob. "Taper Cuts: L.A.'s CTG Cancels Shows at Flagship Theatre Through 2024." *American Theatre*, June 16, 2023. https://www.americantheatre.org/2023/06/16/taper-cuts-l-a-s-ctg-cancels-shows-at-flagship-theatre-through-2024/.

Westport Journal. "Westport Country Playhouse Appeals for 'Immediate' $2M." June 20, 2023. https://westportjournal.com/arts/westport-country-playhouse-appeals-for-immediate-2m/.

"What Is Human Resource Management?" In *Human Resource Management*, 1 ed. University of Minnesota Libraries Publishing, 2011. https://doi.org/10.24926/8668.0801.

Whatley, Amber. "Black Out Lighting Design and Technology Workshop for Black Youth." Amber Whatley. https://www.awhatleylighting.com/blackout-workshop.

Whatley, Amber, Sherrice Mojgani, and Calvin Anderson. "Not a Pipeline Problem, A Problem with the Pipeline." *HowlRound Theatre Commons*, September 1, 2021. https://howlround.com/not-pipeline-problem-problem-pipeline.

White, Abbey. "Broadway's Return Is Triumphant, but Uncertainty Looms: 'Humans Have to Be as Important as the Show.'" *The Hollywood Reporter*, November 22, 2021. https://www.hollywoodreporter.com/lifestyle/arts/broadway-reopening-pandemic-new-york-city-1235046751/.

Wild, Stephi. "Twi McCallum Shares an Open Letter to the Theatre Community on Hiring Black Designers and Creatives." *Broadway World*, June 8, 2020. https://www.broadwayworld.com/article/Twi-McCallum-Shares-an-Open-Letter-to-the-Theatre-Community-on-Hiring-Black-Designers-and-Creatives-20200608.

Wilson, Lindsey. "Dallas Theater Center Has Co-Pros and Familiar Favorites on Tap for 2023-24 Season." *CultureMap Dallas*, June 21, 2023. https://dallas.culturemap.com/news/arts/dallas-theater-center-has-co-pros-and-familiar-favorites-on-tap-for-2023-24-season/.

Wingspace Theatrical Design. "Wingspace Mentorship Program." https://wingspace.com/mentorship.

Witters, Dan. "50% in U.S. Fear Bankruptcy Due to Major Health Event." *Gallup*, September 1, 2020. https://news.gallup.com/poll/317948/fear-bankruptcy-due-major-health-event.aspx.

WS Virtual Salon 29 Pay Equity. YouTube video, 2022. https://www.youtube.com/watch?v=jTaNBzc1AAE.

Wyckoff, Anna. "Pay Equity – We Can Do It." Costume Designers Guild, February 10, 2020. https://www.costumedesignersguild.com/press_news/pay-equity-we-can-do-it/.

Ybarra, Stephanie. Interview by authors. September 2022.

Youssef, Hebba. "Employees Don't Feel Psychologically Safe at Work and It Stifles Innovation." Workweek, November 21, 2022. https://workweek.com/2022/11/21/employees-dont-feel-psychologically-safe-at-work-and-it-stifles-innovation/.

Zakaria, Sabarudin, and Wan Fadzilah Wan Yusoff. "Transforming Human Resources into Human Capital." *Information Management and Business Review* 2, no. 2 (February 15, 2011): 48–54. https://doi.org/10.22610/imbr.v2i2.882.

Zippia. "20 Essential Employee Feedback Statistics [2022]," June 29, 2022. https://www.zippia.com/advice/employee-feedback-statistics/.

Index

Note: *Italic* page numbers refer to figures.

Printed in the United States
by Baker & Taylor Publisher Services